XENOPHON'S *ANABASIS:* A SOCRATIC HISTORY

For my dad

XENOPHON'S *ANABASIS*: A SOCRATIC HISTORY

SHANE BRENNAN

EDINBURGH
University Press

Edinburgh University Press is one of the leading university presses in the UK. We publish academic books and journals in our selected subject areas across the humanities and social sciences, combining cutting-edge scholarship with high editorial and production values to produce academic works of lasting importance. For more information visit our website: edinburghuniversitypress.com

© Shane Brennan 2022, 2024

Edinburgh University Press Ltd
The Tun – Holyrood Road
12(2f) Jackson's Entry
Edinburgh EH8 8PJ

First published in hardback by Edinburgh University Press 2022

Typeset in 11/13 Minion Pro by
IDSUK (DataConnection) Ltd,
Croydon, CR0 4YY

A CIP record for this book is available from the British Library

ISBN 978 1 4744 8988 1 (hardback)
ISBN 978 1 4744 8989 8 (paperback)
ISBN 978 1 4744 8990 4 (webready PDF)
ISBN 978 1 4744 8991 1 (epub)

The right of Shane Brennan to be identified as the author of this work has been asserted in accordance with the Copyright, Designs and Patents Act 1988, and the Copyright and Related Rights Regulations 2003 (SI No. 2498).

Contents

List of Illustrations	vii
Preface	viii
Acknowledgements	xi
Notes	xiii

	Introduction: The Philosopher Armed	1
1	Xenophon the Athenian	10
	Biography	10
	Factors Influencing Xenophon's Life and Writings	26
2	*Anabasis* in Historiographical and Literary Context	47
	Listeners and Readers	48
	What Is It?	51
	The Exemplary Author	62
	The Apologetic Author	72
3	Xenophon *Didaskalos*: Leaders and Leadership in *Anabasis*	82
	The Leadership Theme	84
	Cyrus the Younger	94
	The Spartans: Klearchos and Cheirisophos	102
	Xenophon the Athenian	113
4	Xenophon's Self-Defence	136
	Charges Made against 'Xenophon'	138
	Criticisms of Xenophon from External Audiences	150
	Xenophon in Spartan Service: The Exile Question Again	180
5	Socrates in *Anabasis*	185
	The Philosopher and His Circle	188
	The Framing of Xenophon in Anabasis: *The Philosopher Armed*	205
	The Socratic Commander Again	220

CONTENTS

Conclusions: The Philosopher Unarmed   245

Appendices
A   Xenophon's Life and Times   258
B   Xenophon's Writings   260

Bibliography   262
Index   281

Illustrations

Figures

I.1	Temple of Artemis, Sardis. The beginning of Cyrus's expedition (Author)	2
I.2	View back to Muş Plain, eastern Anatolia (Author)	8
1.1	Socrates, a Visionary Head. William Blake, c. 1820. Yale Center for British Art, Paul Mellon Collection	27
3.1	Euphrates River, western Anbar, Iraq (Author)	86
3.2	Detail from Persepolis bas-relief showing *proskunesis*. National Museum of Iran (Author)	97
3.3	Snowbound village in eastern Anatolia (Author)	110
3.4	Fourth-century BC Boiotian helmet recovered from Centrites River in the mid-nineteenth century. Gts-tg, CC BY-SA 4.0, Ashmolean Museum	116
5.1	View towards the sea from spur of Polut Dağı in the Black Sea Mountains (Author)	243

Maps

Route of the Ten Thousand	xv

Preface

This book explores Xenophon's *Anabasis* as a work in its own right and as one that forms an integral part of the author's *oeuvre*. Drawing primarily on historiographical and literary perspectives, it examines the dynamics of *Anabasis* in relation to its treatment of leadership and apologia. A central argument is that these key Xenophontic elements are driven in an important way by the influence of Socrates. The extent of this influence gives rise to the book's subtitle, 'A Socratic History', which I explain as a narrative rooted in a historical event or period and in which the author embeds a reflection of the philosopher and his values.

The study is part of a burgeoning scholarly interest in Xenophon that has its origins in the 1960s with the contributions of Hartmut Erbse, 'Xenophon's *Anabasis*' (1966), William Henry, *Greek Historical Writing* (1966) and Hans Breitenbach (in *Real-Encyclopädie*, 1967). The seminal work of William Higgins, *Xenophon the Athenian* (1977), a decade later was a further important stimulus. Reflecting on the dramatic decline in Xenophon's reputation in modern times, Erbse identified the eminent nineteenth-century historian, Barthold Niebuhr, as instrumental in setting aside the high reputation he had enjoyed for most of the preceding two millennia.[1] Already before the emergence of new, unfavourable comparable historical evidence (*Hellenika Oxyrhynchos*), Niebuhr took aim at *Hellenika*, descending into a rant about the degenerate character of its author.[2] Paul Cartledge points as well to George Grote, a disciple of Niebuhr. In his multi-volume *History of Greece* Grote wrote:

---

1 Erbse 2010 (= 1966): 500.
2 Niebuhr's 'Über Xenophons Hellenika' was published in 1827 (reprinted the following year with a postscript). On the article and its impact, see further Tuplin (a 'brief and rather acrimonious essay') 1993: 13, Kelly 1996: 157–8.

to pass from Thucydides to the *Hellenika* of Xenophon is a descent truly mournful: and yet, when we look at Grecian history as a whole, we have great reason to rejoice that even so inferior a work as the latter has reached us.³

The decline of the nineteenth century continued well into the twentieth. The discovery in the 1900s at Oxyrhynchos in Egypt of papyri covering the same field as *Hellenika* seriously undermined Xenophon's standing as a historian. Comparison revealed bias, omissions and inaccuracies. Meanwhile in the philosophy arena his capacity for thinking came under growing scrutiny. From Burnet's *Greek Philosophy* in 1914 authorities continued to highlight faults in his writings and person. In his *History of Western Philosophy* (1946) Bertrand Russell described him as a man 'not very liberally endowed with brains, and on the whole conventional in his outlook', while Guthrie, *Socrates* (1971), discerned 'little sign of any capacity for profound philosophical thought'. Sandbach in *The Cambridge History of Classical Literature* (1985) opined that 'unlike Plato, Xenophon was unable to paint a portrait that could explain the fascination which [Socrates] had undoubtedly exerted', with the conclusion that he was 'a superficial thinker'. In his monumental *Agesilaos* (1987), Paul Cartledge summed up his judgement of the man as a thinker: 'All that can and should, I think, be salvaged from the case for Xenophon the thinker is a handful of banal moral platitudes which sort only too well with the kind of plain man's guide to Socratic thinking that he provides in the *Memorabilia*.'⁴

It is hardly surprising given the high standing of these scholars that their views have strongly influenced academic readings and played a role in shaping the popular perception of Xenophon. For generations, mention of the author summoned a grainy image of a blunderbuss-bearing country squire out of touch with democratic culture. However, on the back of Henry, Erbse, Breitenbach and Higgins, this trend ground to a halt and in more recent years has reversed. The establishment of a conference series on Xenophon at Liverpool (held in 1999, 2009 and, virtually, 2021) is testimony to this, as is the appearance of major volumes such as *The Landmark Xenophon's Hellenika* (2009) and *Anabasis* (2021), *The Cambridge Companion to Xenophon* (2017) and *Xenophon's Anabasis and Its Reception* (in press).

An aim of this book is to move towards an integrated reading of *Anabasis* that does not consciously close off any one interpretative approach. While across a range of scholarship negativity has come to be replaced

---

3 Grote 1850: 155. Cartledge reference to Grote: 1987: 62.
4 Russell 1946: 102, Guthrie 1971: 15, Sandbach 1985: 478, 480, Cartledge 1987: 64.

with a more appreciative and balanced assessment of Xenophon's intellectual abilities and achievements, it is still the case that the author is often viewed predominantly through a single disciplinary lens. For example, in his monograph on *Anabasis* Eric Buzzetti interprets his subject as an introduction to philosophy, while Benjamin McCloskey, in his article 'Xenophon the Philosopher', argued that the entire corpus should be primarily approached as philosophy and not historiography.[5] Remarking on this trend at the opening of a conference on *Anabasis* in Crete in 2018, Melina Tamiolaki identified negative tension between philosophers and historians as a striking feature of the Xenophontic landscape; in his introduction to a recent volume on Xenophon and Sparta, the late Anton Powell sounded a similar note, in this case highlighting the divergence in the field between historical and literary approaches.[6] One notable branch of scholarship, many of whose adherents adopt a Straussian approach towards Xenophon, sees almost every contradiction and anomaly as consciously contrived and a mark of the author's cleverness. While recognising and enjoying the insights produced by this way of reading, I do not think Xenophon was always clever, and suspect that at numerous junctures, especially on matters of self-defence, he exposes himself where he did not intend to do so. Rather than looking for an ingenious explanation for individual slips I consider we should recognize them as such and learn from what they tell us.

Healthy interest in *Anabasis* allows it a fair claim to be at the forefront of Xenophon's modern revival. Its popularity in the Western world can be measured by the fact that there are six English-language translations in print, numerous literary platforms which reference the book and dozens of travel- and history-based sites where the story features as part of narrative sweeps of the ancient Near East. On the research side, since the turn of the millennium there have been monographs on the subject by Lee (2007), Flower (2012) and Buzzetti (2014), together with a substantial number of book chapters and journal articles, and also the conference in Crete mentioned above. The impact of *Anabasis* is notable as well in wider cultural circles, with the story being recast in fictional terms on both the page and screen. Nor is it just in the Western world that the story of the Ten Thousand is popular. In Turkey, where much of the narrative plays out, four translations are available, and in Iran, whose extraordinarily rich history is interwoven into the text, the book is readily accessible. By dint of the story crossing over and resonating with different cultural histories, its prominence seems secure for some time to come.

---

5 Buzzetti 2014: 2, 296, McCloskey 2017: 606.
6 Tamiolaki 2018, Powell and Richer 2020: ix.

Acknowledgements

Reflecting on his long relationship with Xenophon's *Memorabilia*, Louis-André Dorion wrote, 'the more I liked this text, the better I understood it, and vice versa, so that I am now persuaded that it is impossible, if one has not taken a strong liking to a text, to come to a profound understanding of it'.[7] I am deeply grateful to all those colleagues with a strong liking for Xenophon's *Anabasis* who have shared their thoughts and ideas on the subject with me over the years I have engaged with the text. I hasten to say before naming any of them that all errors and misunderstandings in this book are my own.

First and foremost is David Thomas, whom I worked with for a decade on producing *The Landmark Xenophon's Anabasis*. Despite the demands of that project, he was extremely generous with his time as regards this monograph, providing thoughtful analyses and criticisms on more than one draft. I am grateful as well to the contributors to the Landmark volume, whose appendices provided me with a breadth and depth of perspective on the subject during the monograph's developmental stage. Many were generous in taking time to listen to half-formed ideas and to respond to questions, notably Christopher Tuplin, Tom Martin, John Lee and Robin Waterfield. When this work was in its very earliest stages, as a doctoral thesis at the University of Exeter, I profited much from the experience of Stephen Mitchell and Christopher Gill, and especially from the encouragement of Daniel Ogden. Thanks also to Christine Allison, Giorgos Andrikopoulos, Anna Blurtsyan, Jill Child, Anna Collar, Kyle Erickson,

---

[7] In its fuller context: 'when I began to translate the *Memorabilia*, I shared most of the common prejudices going around about Xenophon, and in particular, the one according to which his mediocre mind could never have understood the subtleties of the philosophical positions defended by Socrates. By dint of reading Xenophon, I happily came to change my opinion, and I developed a real fondness for the text of the *Memorabilia*. To my great surprise, I realised that the more I liked this text, . . .' (Dorion 2018a: 66–7).

Marc Herzog, Claude and Lindsay Kananack, Steven Kennedy, Natasha Lushetich, John Marr, Matthew and Michelle Smith and Clémence Scalbert-Yücel. In periods before and after Exeter, I would like to record my gratitude to friends, colleagues and teachers at NUI Galway and then Mardin Artuklu University in Turkey, in particular Brian Arkins, Michael Clarke, Edward Herring, John Madden (NUIG), Rysbek and Elvira Alimov, Ibrahim Bor, Cengiz Çakmak, Hıdır Çakmak, Bülent Diken, Lokman Ece, Ömer Oruç, Hatip Özer, Ülker and Zeynep Sayın, Mark Soileau and Habip Türker (MAÜ).

In more recent time my thanks to David Schmidt and Sabrina Joseph at the American University in Dubai for arranging research release time and for helping in other practical ways. Thanks as well to Elizabeth and Chrisa at the AUD Library for managing to meet practically every request for research material. I am grateful to the very accommodating editorial staff at Edinburgh University Press, and especially to Carol Macdonald for her patience. The detailed comments of the publisher's anonymous readers have greatly improved the text, as has the careful copy-editing of Jane Burkowski. I would like to acknowledge Bob Strassler, chief editor of the Landmark Ancient History series, and David Thomas, translator of the *Anabasis* volume, for allowing me to quote extensively from the *Anabasis* translation. Finally, my family in Ireland has been tremendously supportive, especially my sister Anna Marie. I dedicate the book to my father, a role model whom Xenophon, I think, would have approved.

Notes

Translations

For *Anabasis* I use the Landmark Ancient History edition. The translation, on which I supported David Thomas, is based on an implied text. The published Greek one to which it is closest is John Dillery's in the Loeb but it also draws on manuscript readings and conjectures reported in other editions, as well as a few conjectures of the translator's own. A list of Greek editions is provided in the bibliography, and a table of 'Variations from the Loeb Text' can be found in the Landmark volume. Translations from other ancient works are usually from either the Landmark or Loeb series: a list is given at the end of the bibliography. Although a number of Marchant's translations of Xenophon for the Loeb have been revised to bring them in line with contemporary style, as this is an ongoing process I have chosen to use the originals and trust that readers will appreciate the translations as products of their time. I have sought to conform spellings in these to those used in this book. Where I have used my own translations, this is initialled (SB).

Spelling

Greek names are transliterated, except where their Latinate or Anglicised forms have a marked currency. The many peculiarities and inconsistencies are down to me. Possessives with Greek names of more than one syllable are marked by an apostrophe alone when they end with 's': for example, Socrates' teaching, Pericles' speech. Cyrus takes possessive 's'.

Dates

All dates are BC unless otherwise stated.

Abbreviations

In the text I use the full names of ancient works but in the footnotes usually abbreviated ones. A list of Xenophon's writings and the shortened titles I use for them is given in Appendix B. All other ancient works are abbreviated according to the conventions in the *Oxford Classical Dictionary* (4th ed., 2012). I list below modern works that are cited in short form in the monograph:

Erbse	Erbse, H. 2010. 'Xenophon's *Anabasis*'. Pages 476–501 in *Xenophon*. Edited by V. Gray. Oxford. Translated from 1966 German original in *Gymnasium* 73: 485–505.
Jacoby	Jacoby, F., ed. 1923–58. *Die Fragmente der griechischen Historiker*. 15 vols. Berlin and Leiden.
Higgins	Higgins, W. 1977. *Xenophon the Athenian: The Problem of the Individual and the Society of the Polis*. Albany, NY.
H-R	Huitink, L., and T. Rood, eds., comm. 2019. *Xenophon Anabasis Book III*. Cambridge.
LXA	Brennan, S., and D. Thomas, eds. 2021. *The Landmark Xenophon's Anabasis*. Translated by D. Thomas. New York.
T-H	Tuplin, C., and F. Hobden. 2012. 'Introduction'. Pages 1–41 in *Xenophon: Ethical Principles and Historical Enquiry*. Edited by F. Hobden and C. Tuplin. Leiden.

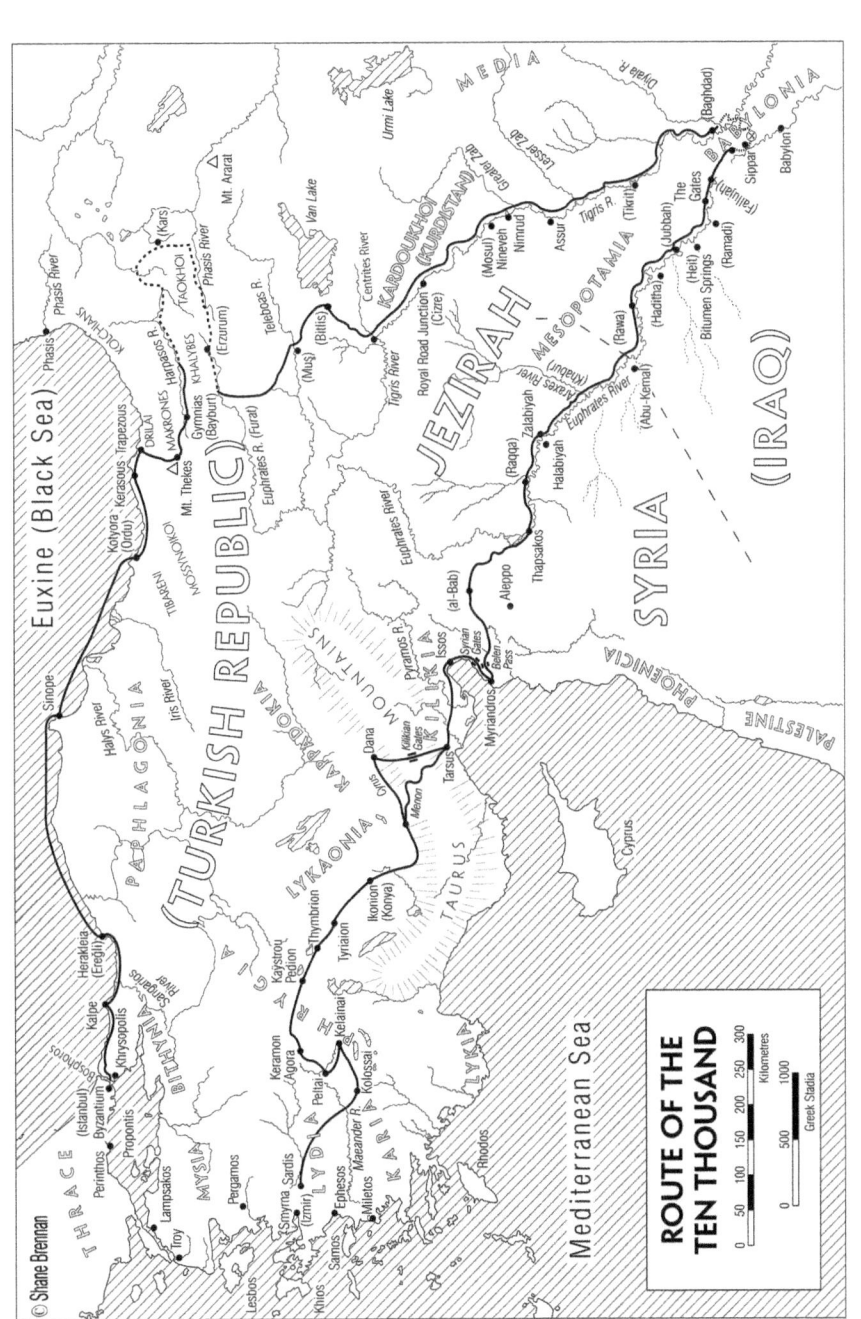

Route of the Ten Thousand

Introduction
The Philosopher Armed

In May 401 the Persian prince, Cyrus the Younger, set out from his satrapy in western Anatolia to pacify a tribe of the interior. His army comprised levies drawn from the areas under his command and some 12,000 Greek mercenaries.[1] However, unknown to all but a few of these men, his real destination was Babylonia, his true aim, to seize the royal throne from his older brother. Although he managed to lead the force into the heart of Mesopotamia, Cyrus was killed in the ensuing battle with King Artaxerxes, who went on to reign for forty years more. With Cyrus dead, the Persians had no serious incentive to destroy his Greek mercenaries and instead led them northward out of Mesopotamia. After seizing their generals in a ruse at the Zapatas River, they funnelled the men into the highlands of the Kardouchoi, a fiercely independent people once said to have destroyed a large contingent sent by the King to pacify them. The satrap Tissaphernes, who had orchestrated the removal of the Greeks from Babylonia, must have been confident as he rode west to take over Cyrus's dominion that he would not see or hear of them again as a unit. Yet they managed to fight through the territory of the Kardouchoi and, eventually, to make their way to the Black Sea.[2] Within two years, those who had survived the retreat

---

1 Cyrus governed several important territories including Lydia and Greater Phrygia. Figure I.1 shows the Artemis temple at Sardis, his satrapal capital. For the size and make-up of the Greek force at different junctures of the expedition, see Thomas 2021b. None of the contemporary sources use the popular term for the army, the 'Ten Thousand' (*murioi*). Xenophon himself refers to the mercenaries in *Hellenika* simply as 'the men who had fought with Cyrus' (3.2.7). The readiest explanation for the term is that it was employed by later writers as a suitably round number. Its first appearance comes around 300 years after the event: see Arrian, *Anabasis Alexandrou* 1.12.3, 2.7.8, 4.11.9 and Plutarch, *Antony* 45.6. H-R (4) suggest the term could have been partly inspired by *An.* 3.2.31, 5.7.9, 6.4.3. See further Bonner 1910.
2 Figure I.2, at the end of the Introduction, shows a view back towards the distant Muş Plain, through which the army passed on its journey north to the Black Sea. See Figure 5.1, at the end of Chapter 5, for a view of the sea near the end of this phase (*katabasis*) of the retreat.

Figure I.1 Temple of Artemis, Sardis. The beginning of Cyrus's expedition. (Author)

were on the offensive against Tissaphernes as part of a Spartan-led force in Asia Minor.[3]

One of the Greeks on the march, Xenophon of Athens, later wrote an account of Cyrus's expedition and its aftermath. Offering an eyewitness version of events, it succeeds in conveying a palpable sense of the trials endured by the army as it fought its way home from the heart of Persian territory. Yet the work is at once more than and not quite a personal history of the expedition and retreat. Xenophon, who becomes the key protagonist in the story, refers to himself in the third person, and this 'Xenophon' appears more like an exemplar than a historical figure. Moreover, the intense focus on Xenophon's character throughout Books 3–7 is at the expense of a more balanced view of events. A flashforward in Book 5 gives us further cause to wonder about the book's purpose and its peculiar, unprecedented character. In the prolepsis Xenophon talks about his later life at Skillous in the Peloponnese, where he lived for many years following his return to Greece

---

3 See Map for the army's route. A more detailed one, together with a suite of maps covering sections of the route, can be found in *The Landmark Xenophon's Anabasis*. The Introduction (Brennan 2021a) to that volume discusses a number of the main ideas developed in this monograph.

in 394. The language and nostalgic tone of the episode suggest that *Anabasis* was completed after he had left his estate, so probably at some time in the early 360s – more than thirty years after the end of the expedition. Why did Xenophon decide to write his account then, after such a gap? While we may never be able to answer this question with any certainty, by taking account of the author's personal circumstances and the content of his other writings, further layers of meaning are revealed in the text. Taking an overview of his writings, we see that in fact they are closely bound by a number of outstanding themes and concerns, among them historiography and memorialisation, leadership, panhellenism, apologia, Sparta and Socrates.

While the weight of these elements varies according to the aims and nature of each work, I believe that Xenophon's major preoccupation in his writing was Socrates. The main argument of this study is that *Anabasis* was written principally to reflect and promote the author's image of Socrates. Had the main object been to write the (hi)story of the expedition, and bearing in mind at least one of his works is dated to the 390s, then it would surely have been written earlier. Xenophon's method in *Anabasis* is not fundamentally different to that used in the more conventional Socratic works. He implicitly defends Socrates against the charges which resulted in his death in 399, while his own character in the story is in ways a stand-in for Socrates; for instance, he perpetuates the philosopher's values through his words and actions and takes a conspicuously analytical approach to problem-solving. While the connection between the thinker and his pupil is not established until Book 3, the story's understated philosophical aspect does not depend on this alone: right at the outset, long before we meet Xenophon or Socrates in person, the account is set up in philosophical terms by way of the Persian prince whose ambition – the cause of all of the events to follow – and sense of rectitude drive him to fight for the kingship.[4] We might see the relationship between Socrates and his pupil as nested within this broader consideration of the nature of power and justice. Together with many of his other works, and in particular those involving the philosopher, *Anabasis* is indicative of Xenophon's

---

4 The succinct prologue to the story (1.1.1–5) contains several key terms that register the themes of moral and political philosophy, among them, obedience to one's father and to the ruler, loyalty and betrayal, injustice and ambition. In the field of comparative literature we see how the openings to stories regularly serve a framing function for the key themes to follow. For example, Enass Khansa shows that in *The Thousand and One Nights (Alf Laylah wa-Laylah)* the opening story, as well as the two immediately following ones, 'engage in a cohesive debate about the coincidence of successful interpretation and just rulership. In doing so, the stories broach a question of ethics frequently encountered in advice literature' (2020). Rood (2017: 274) examines the opening, pointing out similarities to *Kyroupaideia* and *Hellenika* and drawing a parallel to the *Iliad*'s proem, but does not discuss any philosophical dimension.

interaction with what might be referred to as the contemporary 'Socrates literary-philosophical industry'. I use this term in the monograph to refer to the activity of followers of Socrates seeking through writing to defend and promote the teacher. There were many of them. We get indications of this in Xenophon's own writings – Johnson points to *Apologia* 1.1 and *Memorabilia* 1.4.1, 4.3.1–2[5] – and scholars suggest there may have been hundreds of authors of Socratic *logoi* in the decades after the philosopher's death (see Chapter 1 n.41).

Within this frame I see the predominant elements in *Anabasis* as military leadership and apologia. Leadership and the problem of how to rule recur across the *oeuvre*, and it should not be a surprise that *Anabasis*, the story of an army on campaign, treats the subject in detail. By way of Prince Cyrus, the Spartan commanders Klearchos and Cheirisophos, and finally Xenophon's character, we learn about different styles of leadership and their effectiveness. The problem of how to rule in Xenophon's writings is often but not always linked to Socrates' activities in Athens. *Kyroupaideia* and *Anabasis* are examples of exceptions, yet while in both we are in a different geographical and literary space, we are still in a Socratic environment. In the case of *Anabasis* this is realised through Xenophon's representing of his character as a Socratic figure; so not just by dint of his being a student of the philosopher but because to some extent he is actually doing the same sorts of things. Nonetheless, the Socratic story of 'Xenophon' is a different one from that of Socrates, and its presentation is necessarily unlike that in Xenophon's conventional philosophy works. Both categories instruct by presenting exemplary material, but that is the limit of the similarity.

That *Anabasis* has a strong apologetic flavour is a traditional view. Since antiquity it has been recognised that the author was interested in portraying himself in glowing light. One of the oldest modern explanations for the book is that it is a response to another account that did not do Xenophon justice. Tarn wrote in the first edition of the *Cambridge Ancient History*: 'Sophaenetus wrote the first story of the expedition, and Xenophon probably wrote his own account, the *Anabasis*, largely because he thought Sophaenetus had overlooked his merits.'[6] I reject this view and show that the persistence of the idea (albeit a much less popular one today) has tended to obscure the presence of other apologetic strands in the text not all of which relate solely to the author (the Ten Thousand, the *hippeis*). On Xenophon and his character, there are a number of lengthy speeches answering specific charges – of deceiving the soldiers, *hubris*,

---

5 Johnson 2021: 7–8.
6 Tarn 1927: 5. See also Dürrbach 1893: 371–2. This Sophainetos is identified with the oldest of the Greek generals on the march: 6.5.13.

corruption – and there is a concerted attempt to address matters related to his involvement in the expedition: service as a mercenary, service with Cyrus the Younger, campaigning against the Persian King and close association with Sparta. These issues, as we learn from a revelation late on in the text, are set against the background of the young philosopher's exile from Athens, and I argue that this very public stain on his character was a driver of his personal apologia. Highlighting the collaborative nature of the text's thematic elements, I also show how some of these matters fit into the Socratic aspect of the work.

Anabasis as a defence of Socrates may be thought a novel claim, although in light of Xenophon's relationship with him and the fact that several of his other writings defend and promote the philosopher it cannot be regarded as an extraordinary one.[7] It may be the case generally that defence against the historic charges, whether these are made explicit or are implied, was a literary peg, intended to facilitate presentation of the author's own image of Socrates rather than constituting engagement with an episode that had played out some four decades before. That said, with our knowledge that the trial remained contentious at the time of writing, we cannot rule out the live reading. Accordingly, in the monograph I take account of both types of Socratic apologia but consider promotion of Socrates – as a paradigm of wisdom and moral excellence – as the more pressing in the author's mind. I presume this was also the case for many of the other Socratics, who sought to present their own versions of Socrates as a model of virtue to be imitated in the interests of the public good.

A cornerstone of the argument is the manner and timing of Xenophon's formal introduction into the story. The setting could not be more dramatic. At the start of Book 3 we find the army in disarray, shorn of its key commanders and surrounded by the enemy in northern Mesopotamia:

> [3] With these thoughts in their minds and with heavy hearts, few of them touched their meal for the evening and few kindled fires. Many did not come into the camp that night, each individual instead trying to take his rest where he happened to be. But they were unable to sleep because of their distress and longing for their native lands and their parents, wives, and children, whom they thought they would never see again. It was in this state of mind that they all tried to take their rest. [4] In the army there was a certain Xenophon, an Athenian. He did not accompany the army as a general, nor as a captain, nor as an ordinary soldier. (3.1.3–4)

---

7 *Anabasis* as a Socratic defence: see Brennan 2011. Flower 2012: 120, Humble 2018: 591 and H-R 22 all touch on the idea. McCloskey (2021) takes the opposite view to my monograph thesis. 'The *Anabasis*' Xenophon', he concludes, 'is a Socratic failure'.

In his subsequent explanation of how he came to join the expedition, Xenophon recalls how he sought the advice of Socrates and, taking this (though not, as it turns out, faithfully), went to Delphi to consult Apollo about the journey (3.1.5–6). Behind the summary account of how Socrates directed him to Delphi, and especially in the encounter between the men after the visit (3.1.7), we envisage fuller dialogues such as those reported in *Memorabilia*. The involvement of Socrates in the story at the point of Xenophon's emergence as a leader on the historical stage brings to the fore of the reader's mind the relationship between the two and sets up an expectation of how Xenophon will meet the daunting challenge that lies ahead. The fact that the young philosopher is adrift from his teacher, thousands of kilometres away in Athens, adds another layer of tension to the story. From the moment he stands up to address the army at dawn on the banks of the Zapatas River, Xenophon acts as a pupil of Socrates should have done on finding himself in such dire straits. His actions, counsel and moral bearing throughout the course of the retreat are both a testimony to the value of his teacher's training and an implicit rebuttal of the charges of corrupting the youth and impiety levelled against Socrates in 399.

* * *

The book is structured around five chapters. The first begins with a short biography of Xenophon before going on to look at major influences in his life: Socrates, war and civil war at Athens, and the decree banishing him from the city. The exile decree features uniquely in *Anabasis*, Xenophon's most autobiographical work, which I examine in Chapter 2 (I should say when I use the term 'autobiographical' in relation to *Anabasis*, I mean that it has an autobiographical character, not that it is necessarily a source for faithful detail on the life of the author: which is not to say that the genre has ever been limited to the verifiable facts of a life history). In the chapter I look at historiographical and literary aspects of *Anabasis*, highlighting the richness of the text and addressing questions surrounding its writing. In particular, I bring out the extent to which exemplars shape the narrative and point to the presence of, and the strategies used to support, 'literary apologia', a concept which I argue Xenophon adopts in the work. With its historical aspect in mind and considering Xenophon's broader mission to promote his image of Socrates, I propose as a new description for *Anabasis* 'Socratic history', where the adjective denotes both the neutral sense, pertaining to Socrates, and a particular set of qualities.

Turning to the first of the two principal thematic strands in the work, Chapter 3 demonstrates how Xenophon uses the story of the campaign to engage in didaxis on military leadership. I show that in addition to a range of instructional episodes, he presents three different styles and leads his reader to conclude that the one which his own character represents is the optimal. As becomes clear in the following chapters, this outcome complements the author's apologetic agenda. Xenophon's success and the manner in which it is achieved counters charges against himself and at the same time promotes the value of the Socratic education. However, it could as well be that Xenophon furnishes an apologetic context in order to facilitate and illustrate his leadership lessons. Of an episode where he defends himself against having struck a soldier in a prior phase of the march (5.8), Rood writes: 'Xenophon's defence of his earlier conduct ensures that the positive qualities of his leadership (his maintenance of discipline and morale, for instance) are not left to be inferred from the narrative, but presented as such in a speech, and acknowledged by his internal audience.'[8] I take the opportunity to note that reuse of episodes such as this one as part of different arguments in the monograph is one of its features; I hope that rather than a sense of repetition this approach functions to bring into further relief the multifaceted character of *Anabasis*.

The fourth chapter looks in detail at Xenophon's personal defence. It is organised around two main parts, the first of which examines accusations made against the character Xenophon on the retreat and his responses to these, while the second considers criticisms of the author by external audiences and the stratagems he uses to combat these. I suggest that some of the accusations, just like some of the episodes that underlie the lessons on leadership, were included above others as they fit more closely to the author's agenda. Whereas the accusations considered in the first part originate from episodes recounted in the story and are formally intended for the internal audience, the matters on which Xenophon constructs a defence discussed in the second part stem from the fact of his participation on the march and speak to the external audience. One is his mercenary status, compromising for a member of the elite class, another his association with Sparta, which placed his loyalty to Athens under the spotlight. The analysis of the chapter brings out the extent to which personal apologia impacts on the text.

In the last chapter, offering a limited engagement with Xenophontic philosophy, I seek to show how the figure of Socrates pervades *Anabasis*. His introduction into the narrative in a flashback that forms part of the introduction of Xenophon's character to the story links the pair in a special way and serves to remind the reader of their close relationship at home; that might be especially important for Xenophon if, as I argue, he is interacting with the Socrates literary-philosophical industry of the 370–360s and wished to emphasise the fact that he has a primary claim for knowledge of

---

8 Rood 2006: 56.

Figure I.2 View back to Muş Plain, eastern Anatolia. (Author)

INTRODUCTION: THE PHILOSOPHER ARMED

Socrates. The meeting between the men further sets up an expectation about how Xenophon, the young pupil who joined Cyrus, will deal with the challenges that lie ahead. The significant degree to which his fate – and indeed that of the army as a whole – depends on the relationship is underlined by the dire circumstances in which the flashback is inset. Now adrift in Asia, and without possibility of further first-hand guidance from his teacher, Xenophon faces the ultimate test of his learning. As we see in the course of the search for Socrates beyond 3.1.5-7, his character in the story duly exemplifies key (Xenophontic) Socratic virtues and teachings in the way he carries out his responsibilities as a leader.

CHAPTER 1

Xenophon the Athenian

And yet, for all his confident intellectual awareness, there is in Xenophon a profound feeling of human inadequacy and a sense, never forgotten, that permanence and perfection always elude.

William Higgins, *Xenophon the Athenian*[1]

Xenophon was the son of Gryllos, an Athenian who owned land in Erchia in the east of Attica. The year of his birth is not known, nor is there reliable information on when, or where, he died. For the more than seventy years that he may have lived there are few solid biographical details, and most of these derive from his own works. Yet if the facts of his own life are sparsely documented, knowledge of Classical Athenian life is comparatively rich, and by drawing on the political and social history of the city in the late fifth century we can garner a sense of the world in which he grew up and which defined who he was and became. Following a short biography, I examine three factors from the earlier years which I suggest were major influences on his life and underpin the strong apologetic *Tendenz* in his writings.[2] The content and analysis of this chapter and the following one on *Anabasis* furnish background for the arguments in the rest of the monograph.

Biography

Sources

Xenophon was the author of fourteen complete works, a number of which supply detail about his life.[3] In some cases the detail seems clearly

---

1 Higgins 142.
2 For introductions to Xenophon and *Anabasis*, see Cawkwell 1972, Dillery 1998, Rood 2005, Buzzetti 2008; my treatment in this chapter expands on Brennan 2021a. The standard biography is Anderson 1974, with more recent treatments by Badian 2004, Thomas 2009 and Lee 2017. Higgins, quoted above, provides a more unorthodox study. See Appendix A for a timeline of events during Xenophon's life.
3 An *Athenaion Politeia* was also attributed to him in antiquity; however, the work, though it is alleged to express his sentiments, is by dint of its early dating almost

autobiographical, while in others reasonable arguments can be made that he is referring to personal experience. The most prominent of these is *Anabasis*, his account of Cyrus the Younger's march upcountry in 401 and the subsequent retreat of his Greek mercenaries. The story provides us with a timeline for the author's movements in the period of the march and, by way of a flashforward, a window into his later life in the Peloponnese. However, there is a need for care in interpreting what he tells us about himself in his works, especially in the case of *Anabasis*. While many regard it as the most important source for his life, I argue in this study that the Xenophon we see in the text is an exemplary figure, a young Athenian and pupil of Socrates who applies the lessons of his teacher to the extreme situation in which he has found himself.[4] As remarked in the Introduction, this is not to deny the work has an autobiographical character, and detail concerning 'Xenophon' need not in principle be inconsistent with Xenophon's life.

Elaborating on this, what I believe we have in *Anabasis* in terms of writing about the self is an author who has constructed an ideal type and playfully created an ambiguity about whether that model mirrors himself on the retreat. In this sense the generic affiliation might be said to be closer to fictional biography, the subject being a Socratic commander (that he is a model one is evident from his performance on the retreat). A further nod in this direction is Xenophon's apparent attribution of authorship to another, a signal, as I argue later, that the work is not to be taken autobiographically (at *Hellenika* 3.1.2, Xenophon writes that the story of Cyrus's

---

certainly not his. Most commentators believe it was written before 411, probably during the Archidamian War (431–421). On the association, MacDowell's (2009: 8–9) explanations for works that may have been wrongly attributed to Demosthenes are attractive: 'A papyrus roll would not necessarily bear the writer's name. Demosthenes may have been given a copy of someone else's speech which, when found among his possessions after his death, was assumed to be his own. Or a bookseller may have thought he could get a higher price for a copy of a speech if he attached Demosthenes' name to it.' For a treatment of issues surrounding the text, see Marr and Rhodes 2008. See Appendix B for a list of Xenophon's writings.

4 Among those who see autobiography as a distinct feature of the work are Momigliano 1993: 57–8, Stadter 2007: 529 and Humble 2011: 16. Others are more circumspect. Dan warns it 'is not an autobiography *stricto sensu*' (2014: 166), while Most (1989: 123) writes that 'the distance between such a text and authentic autobiography is measured not only by his having written it in the third person, but above all by his having published it pseudonymously'. So Tuplin (2003: 154): 'the text is not technically autobiographical at all – not just because it is cast in the third person but because it appears to have been disseminated under the name of Themistogenes of Syracuse'. McCloskey (2017) emphasises that an anonymous narrator 'may be the author speaking *sua voce*, but this cannot be assumed' (606–7). For a broader context on the subject, see Most 1989 (especially 120–7), Momigliano 1993: 46–57, Reichel 2007, Ní-Mheallaigh 2010, Marasco 2011, Hägg 2012.

campaign was told by one Themistogenes of Syracuse, a figure otherwise unknown except for a short entry in the tenth-century AD *Souda*).[5]

The question of the role and actions of the historical Xenophon on the retreat is a separate one, and one sharpened by his near absence in the only other intact account of the expedition that has come down to us.[6] While I believe that the episodes in which his character features are based on real events and that the detail is by and large true, on the other hand I am minded to think that not every important event relating to Xenophon is mentioned. And these might be ones that would be in tension with the given narrative. I add my view that Xenophon will not have been put out by the risk that some readers might miss the subtlety of his presentation and take the exemplary performance as being his own. But in saying that, as mentioned, I think that *Hellenika* 3.1.2 may have been a corrective posted after it became apparent to him that there was too much of a tendency among readers to equate character and author.

The only surviving biography of Xenophon from antiquity is Diogenes Laertios' in the third century AD (*Lives of the Philosophers* 2.48–59). He seems to have derived his material from a variety of sources, although not all of these are regarded as reliable, and nor is Diogenes himself.[7] Noreen Humble argues that he makes use of 'recognisable biographical *topoi* which often contain patently false information',[8] and there is a view that he adapted passages in the *oeuvre* for his own work. John Kinloch Anderson, the modern biographer of Xenophon, marked the report

---

5   The *communis opinio* going back to Plutarch is that Themistogenes is a pseudonym and that by using one – by having someone else tell the story – Xenophon sought to establish greater credibility for his portrayal on the retreat (*De glor. Ath.* 345e). In this scenario the work of course is still autobiography. I put forward a different idea in Chapter 4 where I discuss Themistogenes.

6   In the Diodoros/Ephoros version of the march, Xenophon is only referred to once, this in Thrace at the end of the journey (14.37.1–4). But this account may well be based on Xenophon's: for discussion, see Chapter 4 pp. 151–6.

7   Diogenes names ten sources in the biography and alludes to several others. Of the writers he uses, one in particular, Dinarchos, deserves notice for being a source that may not ultimately derive from Xenophon himself. Dinarchos wrote a speech for a freedman against (probably) the grandson of Xenophon, and in this, as was the custom in Attic oratory, it is believed a potted history of the family was provided. Diogenes (2.52) refers to his mentioning of Xenophon's sons – Gryllos and Diodoros, known as the Dioskouroi – and cites him as his source for the tradition that the Spartans provided Xenophon with a house and land. Lipka (2002: 3) thinks that Dinarchos might have been personally acquainted with our author.

8   Humble 2002: 69. Basic detail is also wrong. Badian (2004: 34), highlighting weakness in his method, points to the incorrect date (360/59) which Diogenes gives for Xenophon's death (*Por.* was written after this point, as was *Hell.* 6.4.33–7: see further the discussion on the chronology of Xenophon's writings in this chapter).

of Xenophon's first encounter with Socrates (*Lives* 2.48) as a possible instance: the pair meet in an alleyway, and Socrates tests the young man's knowledge, inspiring him to become a follower. Anderson suggests that this scene may have come from *Memorabilia* 4.4.5, where Hippias, who had not been in Athens for a considerable time, finds the teacher probing for the origins of virtue and justice.[9]

Athens

Family

It is from Diogenes (2.48) that we learn Xenophon's father's name was Gryllos and that he belonged to the deme of Erchia.[10] Xenophon provides no information about his parents, though in light of Athenian practice the fact that he named one of his sons Gryllos supports what Diogenes says about his father's name.[11] From Xenophon's writings, notably *Peri Hippikes*, *Hipparchikos* and *Anabasis*, we can infer that he was an experienced horseman and something of an authority on equine matters; if, as seems probable, he served in the Athenian cavalry, then given the costs involved it would almost certainly follow that his family owned an estate. A mount at Athens in the fourth century would have cost a minimum of 100 drachmas, with most paying in the order of 500. 'The minimum', Spence writes in his study, 'was equivalent to ten months' wages for a skilled craftsman (or over two years' fairly generous wheat ration for an adult male) while the average would have bought nearly twenty months' wheat supply for a family of six.'[12] Running costs were similarly high. In addition to the need to have slaves to groom and exercise them, if they were to be in good condition the horses needed a diet that included grain, a produce never in ready supply in Attica. As Spence concludes,

---

9 Anderson 1974: 9. Another possible origin for the Diogenes passage could be *Oik*. 2.16, where Socrates declares his interest in 'finding out who are the greatest masters of various sciences to be found in Athens'. But it may also emanate from the mind, if not the records, of Diogenes himself; see for instance his biography of Zeno, whose initiation to philosophy is described in very similar terms (7.1.2–3).

10 For Erchia, see Vanderpool 1965. The international airport at Spata may now cover the family's ancestral lands. Depending on one's view about whether Ischomachos in *Oikonomikos* is a version of Xenophon, the former's statement at 20.22–4 could suggest that Xenophon's father was an agricultural property developer.

11 The norm in Classical Athens was for parents to name a son after the grandfather (see Plato, *Lach*. 179a), with the father's name used as a patronymic in the genitive (Golden 2015: 21–2). As remarked in note 7, the defendant in Dinarchos' speech, *Against Xenophon*, is thought to be the author's grandson, though this is far from certain.

12 Spence 1993: 183. Evidence from the late fifth century shows that, at the high end, sums of more than 1,000 drachmas were paid. See *An*. 7.8.6, Aristophanes, *Nub*. 21–3, 1224–5.

'membership of the equestrian milieu was an expensive pastime which few citizens could afford'.[13]

There is other evidence too pointing to privileged status. In *Anabasis* (3.1.4) Xenophon informs us that he was a longstanding 'guest-friend' of Proxenos of Boiotia. Guest-friendship was an elite institution, and at the least the relationship suggests his family was well connected.[14] Then the leisure to pursue writing would be another indicator of privilege.[15]

Age

The content of Xenophon's writings complicates somewhat attempts to estimate when he was born, though in circling the early 420s, in my view, we will not be far out. In *Anabasis*, after the Persians have seized a number of Greek commanders on the banks of the Zapatas River, Xenophon awakens from a fitful dream and poses himself a series of questions about his fate and that of the army: 'Why am I lying down? ... From what city am I expecting the general to come to take action here? What age am I waiting to reach?' (3.1.13–14). When he subsequently addresses the captains of Proxenos, he tells them that if they make him leader, he will not make his age 'an excuse for refusing it' (3.1.25). And then, when in a leadership position, he suggests an order of march whereby the younger generals, Timasion and himself, take the rear (3.2.37). Clearly, as represented, he is a young man; but we can probably be a little more precise for the historical actor anyway. Greek states frequently laid down minimum ages for various offices, and at Athens, for a *strategos* or other high-ranking military official, it is thought to have been thirty, so it seems reasonable to put Xenophon under that age at this time.[16]

---

13 Spence 1993: 272. On horse ownership as a sign of wealth, see Xenophon, *PH* 2.1, Thucydides 6.15, Isokrates 16.33, Lysias 24.11–12, Aristotle, *Pol.* 1289b. Lee (2017: 19) does not think that Xenophon's family was from the wealthiest stratum of Athenian society. Farrell 2012 challenges the assumptions that underlie the widely held view that Xenophon was a *hippeus*.

14 Badian (2004: 39–40) speculates reasonably that the relationship was an inherited one. On Xenophon and guest-friendship, see further Chapter 4 pp. 167–8.

15 Gray (2010: 10), envisaging Xenophon maintained in 'Socratic idleness' by his family, comments that it 'would be exceptional to find any writer of humble origins in the ancient world'. Xenophon published most of his work late in life, though he probably wrote for several decades. Once he left Athens in 401, he supported himself, principally through wages and patronage from Sparta, and there was spear-won booty from the expedition with Cyrus.

16 Minimum ages: Aristotle, *Ath. Pol.* 4.3; Rhodes (1981: 510) thinks it possible that men under thirty could have held military office. Xenophon born in the early 420s (under thirty): Breitenbach 1967: 1571, Cawkwell 1972: 143 n.2, Anderson 1974: 9–10, Krentz 1989: 1, Lee 2007: 4.

A less-cited passage in the discussion is 7.3.46, where Xenophon's character summons troops up to the age of thirty and himself joins these. There is no reason the historical figure must have been in the same age bracket, but if he were clearly outside of it his action would have risked showing other, older leaders in a poor light (for another link to the under-thirties, see 6.4.25).

Still in Thrace, but taking a different view on the subject, John Dillery argues that 7.2.38 furnishes evidence for an older Xenophon: 'For Seuthes to imagine that Xenophon had a daughter of roughly marriageable age (which, of course, could be as early as twelve or thirteen), he could not have been quite as young as 3.1.25 implies'.[17] It bears remarking that this would resonate with *Symposion* 1.1, where Xenophon – but it could be that the narrator is not Xenophon – is present at a drinking party whose dramatic date is 422. Further support for an older age could come from Diogenes, who writes in his biography (2.55) that Xenophon 'flourished in the fourth year of the ninety-fourth Olympiad [401/0], and he took part in the expedition of Cyrus in the archonship of Xenainetos in the year before the death of Socrates'. References to the high point of a subject's life often imply the fortieth year (the second-century chronographer Apollodoros uses such a scheme); however, in this case, on account of the next clause stating that Xenophon marched with Cyrus, there is an argument that it is his most famous exploit which is being referred to as his *acme*.[18]

Staying with Diogenes, another hint that Xenophon was older surfaces at the conclusion, where the biographer writes (2.59): 'In other authorities I find the statement that he [Xenophon] flourished, along with the other Socratics, in the eighty-ninth Olympiad [424–421].' The origin of this is probably the story passed down through Strabo (9.2.7), repeated by Diogenes in his *Socrates* (2.22), of how the philosopher saved Xenophon's life at the Battle of Delion in 424. Yet placing Xenophon's birth in the 460s would put him into his 100s when he wrote his final work, and would have him over sixty on the march, surely an extremely unlikely scenario. Badian, who dismisses the idea, thinks Diogenes did too by virtue of his placement of the information at the end of the biography, almost as a 'footnote'.[19] Nonetheless, there are reasons why this possibility cannot be completely discounted. One is the claim by Lucian that Xenophon was over ninety

---

17 Dillery 1998: 4. But Seuthes (a Thracian dynast) might be imagining a future scenario – καὶ εἴ τις σοὶ ἔστι θυγάτηρ – rather than a present one: see 7.6.34.
18 The case of the sculptor Praxiteles may provide a parallel. While he is said to have flourished in the 103rd Olympiad, 368–365, and this may have him at forty during this period, it is thought equally likely it refers to the creation of his most famous work, the Aphrodite of Knidos.
19 Badian 2004: 36.

when he died (*Makrobioi* 21) and alongside this the fact that Isokrates, a contemporary of Xenophon's, lived to be almost 100 and was writing into his nineties (*Panathenaikos* 270). Another relevant detail is the statement in *Anabasis* that Klearchos was fifty on the march (2.6.15), and he was not the oldest general. As to the internal evidence (3.1.14, 3.1.25, 3.2.37), I argue in this study that Xenophon in *Anabasis* is an exemplary figure and that a part of his persona is the youth he emphasises in the work.

Early Years

If we place Xenophon's birth in the early 420s, which I think is about right, then it was into rough times that he was born. With the outbreak of the Peloponnesian War in 431, Sparta subjected Attica to annual raids, the aim of which was to disrupt the supply of food into Athens. As landowners, Xenophon's family would have suffered directly, and what wealth they had stored (in whatever form) must have depleted as one prospective harvest after another was destroyed.[20] Attendant on this disruption would have been periodic dislocation, the *oikos* moving into the city at least for the duration of the raiding season. Because of the war, some consider that Xenophon grew up in Athens, though the intimate knowledge of the countryside which he shows in several of his works would seem to point to a substantial experience of rural life. Moreover, from 425, following the capture of a large contingent of Spartans at Sphakteria, the countryside was relatively safe from attack.

Privileged Athenians educated their sons in private schools, where they developed their skills in reading and writing, arithmetic, poetry, music and physical education.[21] In a world where war was more common than peace, body training especially was beneficial for both individual and *polis*. Pursuits taught to the boys in the *gymnasion* included running, the long jump, discus, javelin, boxing and wrestling. There is reason to believe that Xenophon acquitted himself well in this sphere, for in his writing he represents himself as hardy (for example, in freezing winter conditions, rising at dawn without his cloak to chop wood, 4.4.12) and fit (racing up a hillside fully accoutred,

---

20   Gryllos may have had a stake in the silver mines at Laureion, but as Xenophon himself implies in *Poroi* (4.25), income from this resource dwindled following the Spartan seizure of Dekeleia (in 413: Dekeleia was situated in the north of Attica and was visible from the city). Still, affairs could have picked up after the war, and at any rate, as his departure from Athens in 401 with at least one horse, a shield-bearer and surplus armour shows, the family was not impoverished.

21   For a picture of the ancient classroom, see Plato, *Prt.* 325e–326a. On education in the ancient world, see B. Strauss 1993, Pernot 2008. In discussing Socrates' education at Athens, Ober (2011: 161) makes a distinction between a basic primary education (reading and writing) and a 'more advanced cultural education offered by private tutors'.

3.4.47–9). In several works he stresses the importance of physical fitness for warfare (*Kynegetikos* 13.11, *Kyroupaideia* 8.1.34, *Memorabilia* 3.12.4–5, *Lakedaimonion Politeia* 12.5–6) and of the need to take care of one's health (*Memorabilia* 4.7.9).

The question of Xenophon's knowledge of foreign languages is one that does not, I think, come up often. Yet, given that he spent seven years or more in Asia, curiosity on this score seems warranted. In keeping with his Socratic education, we should probably expect there to be in principle effort to learn another tongue where that might impinge on good management and tactful dealing. In *Anabasis*, the work which tracks Xenophon's early time in Asia, we hear on a few occasions of translators (1.2.17, 1.8.12, 4.8.4), who include Greek speakers, but there is no direct evidence for Xenophon knowing a foreign language. The closest we really get is his use in the narrative of Persian technical terms.[22]

An important part of Xenophon's education was learning how to hunt and ride. 'The first pursuit, therefore, that a young man just out of his boyhood should take up is hunting, and afterwards he should go on to the other branches of education, provided he has means' (*Kynegetikos* 2.1). Xenophon is effusive in his praise for hunting (*Kynegetikos* 12.1) and was clearly an enthusiastic horseman as well. He gives a full account of the training of men and horses in his works, writing of riding in *Hipparchikos*, his treatise on cavalry command, that 'no action of man bears a closer resemblance to flying' (8.6, and see also 1.11, τὰ ἐν ἱππικῇ λαμπρά, 'the brilliancy of horsemanship'). Indeed, a theme running through his *Anabasis* is the benefit of cavalry.[23] Xenophon both spells this out (2.4.6, 7.6.29) and shows through numerous examples how an army gains an edge with riders (3.4.4, 6.3.14, 6.3.19, 6.5.28), and conversely how it can be seriously disadvantaged without them (3.3.7–10). His effectiveness throughout the retreat on horseback also nicely complements *Hipparchikos*, providing real examples of the value of cavalry in military operations.

It is worth remarking finally that education, from the physical arena to music and festivals where individuals were judged on their skill and presentation, was inherently competitive. The agonistic culture promoted the ideal of excellence and underlined the importance of *nike* (victory) to the *polis*. With its high achievement across many fields, Athens embodied this phenomenon, and I argue in Chapter 3 that Xenophon plays on his

---

22 Due (1989: 141) maintains he is the first Greek author to do so correctly. On the question of his knowledge of Near Eastern languages, see ibid. p. 141 with references, and Wylie 1992: 132. For the avoidance of doubt, in the episode prior to the battle with the King where Xenophon approaches Cyrus and speaks with him (1.8.15–17), I assume that the interpreter mentioned just prior to this (1.8.12) is active.
23 This is also a theme in *Hellenika*: see Thomas 2009: xlvi.

Athenian background in winning support for his leadership on the retreat of the Ten Thousand.

The Peloponnese

I look at the circumstances of Xenophon's departure from Athens and his exile from the city later in the chapter; here I sketch events from the end of the retreat of the Ten Thousand in 399 to his settlement in the Peloponnese and his leaving of his home there following the defeat of Sparta at Leuktra in 371. The intermediate years, 401–399, are the most illuminated of Xenophon's life, as we have details in his *Anabasis* of Cyrus's campaign and its aftermath. Notwithstanding uncertainty over how accurately the story of the character reflects that of the historical figure, we get to follow Xenophon's path through Anatolia, Mesopotamia and Thrace, garnering as we do a taste of his experiences on the long march.

While he tells us near the end of *Anabasis* that he intended to return to Athens, instead he went on to join the Spartan campaign against Persia in Asia Minor. Overshadowed by the account of the expedition and with only limited detail about the period in *Hellenika*, this much longer stint in Asia (399–394) is often passed over in surveys of Xenophon's life. Yet it must have been a time in which he grew both his first-hand knowledge of the empire and his learning about the cultures and history of the region. As Tuplin remarks, 'no surviving classical author is *known* to have seen so much of [Anatolia], and the time he spent there is measured in years, not months'.[24] Of relevance in terms of the construction of the *Anabasis* march framework is that Xenophon could have used this, for the most part comparatively more stable, time to gather detail for his later account.

In 394 Xenophon returned to Greece with Agesilaos.[25] His recording of the march home (*Hellenika* 4.3, *Agesilaos* 2.1–5) bookends the period in Asia which began with the conclusion of *Anabasis*. Xenophon indicates in *Hellenika* (3.4.20, 4.3.15) that the Cyreans were on the Spartan side at Koroneia, though whether he fought himself is a matter of dispute. After the battle he went to Sparta with the king (Plutarch, *Agesilaos* 19–20) and for his services, and presumably in light of his exile from Athens, he was awarded an estate near Olympia.[26] There is some debate about whether he

---

24 Tuplin 2007: 7. It is quite possible that Xenophon campaigned in Ionia during the Peloponnesian War: see pp. 32–3 on *Hell.* 1.2.5.
25 Humble (2002: 78) unearths the view of Grote in the nineteenth century that he went back after the death of Socrates, and then returned to Asia Minor to continue his service with Sparta, but except for Buzzetti (2014: 192 n.33) this scenario has no modern support.
26 For the estate, see *An.* 5.3.7, Diogenes 2.51–2, Pausanias 5.6.5. Tuplin (2004: 255–7) discusses its probable location. Cartledge (1987: 60, after Swaddling 1980) and Lendle (1995: 316) respectively show the site on sketches of the north-west Peloponnese. See also Talbert 2000: map 58.

went to live there at once or continued to campaign with Agesilaos, but the two possibilities need not be mutually exclusive.[27]

By his own account, given as a flashforward in *Anabasis* (5.3.7–13), Xenophon's time at Skillous was idyllic. Out of his share of the money from booty taken on the retreat and earmarked for the gods, he built a temple to Artemis, a scaled copy of the one at Ephesos, and he organised an annual festival in her honour. Together with his sons he hunted wild animals and cultivated fruit trees, and we can suppose that he was able regularly to attend the games at nearby Olympia. Given, as I argue, that *Anabasis* is to a notable extent a paradigmatic text, it is tempting to see the picture painted as an ideal representation, a sort of *paradeisos* on earth, and in the next chapter I suggest that the portrayal of Skillous is intended to be a moral exemplar. Xenophon's fortune in receiving this bounty confirms him as just and at the same time holds out such a prospect for others who would follow a virtuous path (see 3.1.43).[28]

In reality, of course, daily life at Skillous would have involved much toil. Making a success of the land will have required labour and attention from the landowner: we might suppose that the material for *Oikonomikos*, Xenophon's essay on estate management, is based in some part on his experience here.[29] It was at Skillous too that Xenophon sat down to begin in earnest his literary project. Even though he finished or published many of his writings in the post-Skillous years, work on them, and underlying that the process of their development, surely began on the estate. It is worth noting that his proximity to Olympia, site of the most important Greek cultural festival, connected him to currents of thought in the Greek world.[30]

27 Anderson (1974: 165) considers that by about 393 Xenophon was in Skillous with his wife but continued in Spartan service. Similarly, Wood (1964: 36–7), who says that he was honoured with the estate after Koroneia, thinks he was engaged in military missions for Sparta for six or seven years following the battle. Lee (2005: 44) believes that he was granted the estate in 387. Arguments for Xenophon continuing in active service, like those deployed to support his participation in earlier wars, tend to be based on the detail of his descriptions, here of campaigns in the Corinthian War: see *Hell.* 4.5–6.
28 The copying of the Artemis temple, which must have been on a much smaller scale, may reflect Xenophon's instinct for modelling. Ephesos was his disembarkation point in 401 (6.1.23), and he was there prior to leaving for Greece with Agesilaos in 394 (5.3.6). It is quite likely that he visited the temple on other occasions during the lengthy period of his stay in Asia. Humble (2006: 43) considers the Skillous passage 'one of the few solid autobiographical details we have about Xenophon outside the time frame of the *Anabasis*'. Regardless of debate about the faithfulness of the representation, I am unaware of any who doubt that Xenophon lived at Skillous: see Diogenes 2.52, Plutarch, *De exil.* 10, 14, Pausanias 5.6.5.
29 See Pomeroy 1994: 5, Macleod 2008: 14. Some believe that Ischomachos in the philosophical text is Xenophon himself (see Wood 1964: 65).
30 He could have attended up to half a dozen Olympic Games. On the festival, see Casson 1974: 77–9. Pomeroy, who thinks that Xenophon had his own collection of books, cites Delebecque's opinion that he had a library at Skillous (1994: 16).

One such worth remarking on in the context of *Anabasis* is panhellenism, a doctrine which agitated for a unified Greek campaign against Persia. This was in vogue for much of the early and mid-fourth century, and some have argued that *Anabasis*, being the account of a military march by Greeks into and out of the Persian Empire, was an obvious canvass on which to promote the ideology. But it seems that, though he certainly engaged with it, Xenophon was not a straightforward advocate of the doctrine; it may even be that *Anabasis* constitutes a negative paradigm for panhellenism. Descriptions of the empire's intractability (1.7.6) and the resources available to the King (3.1.19) on the one hand, and the existential danger that success might pose to Greek identity on the other (3.2.25), suggest a circumspection that fits well with the thoughtful composition of the text.[31]

The Battle of Leuktra in 371 ended Spartan hegemony in Greece and obliged Xenophon to leave Skillous.[32] While in *Anabasis* he speaks of or hints at returning home on a number of occasions (3.2.26, 7.1.4, 7.1.38, 7.6.11, 7.6.33, 7.7.57), and prior to leaving Athens he indicates his intention to return (3.1.6), there is no hard evidence that he ever did so. Diogenes Laertios says that after leaving Skillous he ultimately travelled to Corinth and that he died there at an advanced age (2.53, 56).[33] However, he also writes that the decree of exile was rescinded (2.59; this cannot have been later than 362, when Xenophon's sons were fighting for Athens in the Mantineian War), and on this basis, and in light of the Atheno-centric character of *Poroi* and *Hipparchikos*, both among Xenophon's later works, it has been argued that he did return to his home city.[34] Additional support

---

31 On panhellenism and *Anabasis*, see Erbse 478–9, Dillery 1995: 59–63 (p. 62 for the threat settlement would pose to Greekness), Luce 1997: 72, Cawkwell 2004: 64–7, Rood 2004a, Flower 2012: 170–88 (p. 201 for bibliography; Flower 2000 for useful context), Waterfield 2011: 130–1, Gray 2021. I examine the subject further in Chapter 2 pp. 64–8.

32 See Diogenes 2.53. Pausanias, however, says that having tried Xenophon for receiving land from the Spartans the Eleans pardoned him, and he remained on the estate for the rest of his life (5.6.6). This view has few followers, though Badian (2004: 38) has suggested that Xenophon might later have been given the chance to return to his estate and that he would 'certainly have accepted such an offer if it was made'. Xenophon does not refer to himself leaving his estate or to the circumstances of his later life. In any event it is possible he remained there until 370, as the Spartans did not lose control of the Peloponnese at once (*Hell*. 6.5.1–3).

33 Some cite passages in *Hellenika*, notably 7.1.18–19, as evidence that Xenophon was present in Corinth in the 360s (see Anderson 1986: 37, Cartledge 1987: 61), although others counter that the same work shows it was unlikely he was there (Higgins 128).

34 See Delebecque 1957: 334–41, Wood 1964: 37, Higgins 128, Jansen 2007: 35–50, Macleod 2008: 11, Thomas 2009: xx, LaForse 2013: 30 n.12. *Contra* Breitenbach (1967: 2501), who considers it inconceivable that Xenophon ever returned to Athens. Anderson ploughs a middle way, suggesting that our author remained at Corinth but was an occasional visitor to Athens. This is not implausible, though as a high-profile author of Socratic works it cannot be right that Xenophon failed 'to make an impression on Athenian intellectual life' (Anderson 1986: 36). See also Whitehead 2019: 12–15.

for this opinion is said to be furnished by the outpouring of eulogies for his son after his death at Mantineia in 362, this marking 'a strong link with Athens at this time'.[35] Nevertheless, people could perfectly well have written praises for Xenophon's sons even if he himself had been absent from the city though no longer an exile. Nor is it necessarily true that he would have wanted to return home when the decree of banishment was lifted. The desire to return recorded in *Anabasis* predates the exile event. Moreover, I suggest that this wish for *nostos* could have been inscribed by the author on foot of his personal agenda at the time of writing. The expression paints him clearly as a patriotic figure in 399 and underscores the personal loss he has experienced over the intervening decades.

On the literary side, Flower draws attention to the dream which Xenophon's character has in the night following the seizure of the Greek generals near the Zapatas River (3.1.11): in it he sees his father's house go ablaze after it has been hit by a lightning bolt, arguably an indication that he will never see his home again.[36] Regarding *Poroi* and *Hipparchikos*, I suggest in the following section that they originate in solicitation and are not in the first instance offerings to his countrymen.

The last (uncontested) dateable event in Xenophon's works is the Phokian occupation of Delphi in late 356, referred to at *Poroi* 5.9. It is widely believed that he died not long after this. Assuming that he was born around the start of the Peloponnesian War, he would have been in his seventies.

Writings

To conclude this survey of Xenophon's life I touch on its outstanding legacy, fourteen books. Gray remarks: '[Xenophon] was so highly regarded that all of his writings were preserved, and one (*Respublica Atheniensium*) credited to him as an extra'.[37] Covering a range of subjects, from farming and hunting to history and philosophy, arguably no other ancient collection apart from Cicero's is comparable in terms of diversity. For all its variety, though, the presence of certain themes and concerns underpin the corpus, which may even be said to be the product of a single literary project. It would nevertheless probably be more accurate to say this of the major writings, and to regard some of the minor ones as ad hoc. I think, for example, that as just

---

35 Eulogies: see Diogenes 2.55; Pausanias (1.3.4) mentions a painting of the Mantineia battle by Euphranor at the Agora in Athens which featured Gryllos. Strong link: Humble 2002: 84.
36 Flower 2012: 126–7. Cf. H-R 80–1: 'The dream's ambiguity might suggest an anticipation of Xenophon's exile... but the house is lit up rather than explicitly destroyed by fire. For light in darkness as a mark of salvation, see *Cyr.* 4.2.15 (portent); John 1:5.'
37 Gray 2010: 1. On *Ath. Pol.*, see note 3 above; for summary detail of Xenophon's writings, see Appendix B.

mentioned, *Poroi* and *Hipparchikos* originate in requests to Xenophon in his later years to share his expertise and experience on these subjects.

In this section I seek to add to the context for the production of Xenophon's writings through an examination of their chronology. The task of establishing one has proved to be difficult, as the internal evidence and limited biographical information rarely allow for solid assertions on the date of authorship of individual works to be made.[38] The desire to date individual books stems from the potential benefit of being able to situate them in a personal and historical setting. A precise dating, or even a window of time in which it is likely that a work was composed, enables us to appreciate better the circumstances of authorship and the particular motivation(s) which the author may have had. Most scholars today are of the view that Xenophon composed his main works late in life, even if they disagree fiercely on the relative chronology. Some assert that he wrote most of them after Skillous, although it is counterintuitive not to see him taking advantage of conditions on his estate to write.[39] At the least, as suggested in the previous section, the development of subjects in terms of the author's thinking and experiences must have been advanced there during his lengthy residence. Pomeroy believes that Xenophon completed a draft of *Oikonomikos* at Skillous, and I would think the same likely for other major works.[40]

With the interrelated nature of the corpus in mind, we can conceive of groups of writings that emanated, as it were, from the same moment or source of interest. One would then complement and build on the other, completing, or reinforcing in a different way, the underlying idea(s). Such an approach would impact on the chronology problem by serving to dissolve the notional boundaries around different works. For example, the relative dating of *Memorabilia* and *Oikonomikos*, both inspired by Socrates, would not be pressing, since in whichever order they were written or circulated, Xenophon had both in mind as he wrote each of them and expected that shortly his readers would also look at them together.

Without question the main source of inspiration for Xenophon's writings was Socrates. Conceivably this fact could extend the chronology window back to the philosopher's living days, but we do not see the

---

38 For chronology considerations, see Delebecque 1957, Higgins 1977, Krentz 1989, Flower 2012. Studies which consider the dating of particular works include: Dürrbach 1893, Körte 1922, Høeg 1950 – *Anabasis*; Stokes 2012, Johnson 2021 – *Apologia*, *Memorabilia*; Krentz 1989 – *Hellenika*; Aalders 1953 – *Hiero*; Thomas 2018 – *Kynegetikos*; Gera 1993 – *Kyroupaideia*; Bandini and Dorion 2000 – *Memorabilia*; Pomeroy 1994 – *Oikonomikos*; Jansen 2007 – *Poroi*; Huss 1999 – *Symposion*; Marr and Rhodes 2008 – *Athenaion Politeia*.
39 Huss (1999: 402–3), championing the earlier view of Schwarz (1889), claims that 'Xenophon's datable writings were indeed composed or completed after 371'.
40 Pomeroy 1994: 7.

emergence of large-scale Socratic literary activity until some time after his death: the 370s and 360s, for instance, encompass much of the later writing activity of Plato and Antisthenes.[41] As a principal purpose of Xenophon's Socratica in my view was to depict a fuller picture of the philosopher, assigning the bulk of his Socratic output to this period seems appropriate.

The first of Xenophon's Socratic offerings looks to be *Apologia*, which dates possibly to some time in the late 370s but could belong to the 390s and, if so, would be a concrete marker of early influence.[42] The first book of *Memorabilia* might belong to the 370s, although some think that references in the third book (3.5.25–7) place that after the Spartan defeat at Leuktra in 371;[43] that could be some time after, and a full version might not have been in circulation until well into the 360s. Of the two other works in the formal cycle, *Oikonomikos* is one naturally associated with Xenophon's time at Skillous but probably should still in its final form postdate *Memorabilia*, as the opening of the former does not name Socrates. The reader is therefore expected to know that he is the person being referred to, this being confirmed at *Oikonomikos* 1.3, something difficult to credit unless the author has already established himself as the writer of Socratic works. The *Symposion* might also be assigned to the mid-360s, though there are arguments for at least a first version as early as the 380s.

---

41 There may have been hundreds of dialogues centring on Socrates written in the decades following his death. See further Rossetti 2011, Rowe and Boys-Stones 2013. For background to the fourth-century intellectual climate and the influence of Socrates, see the opening chapter of Pownall 2004. Christ argues that Xenophon viewed himself as an active participant in Athens' literary culture, pointing for example to his documented rivalry with Plato, his continuation of Thucydides and his attack on contemporary sophists in *Kynegetikos* (2020: 4–5). The fourth century, he remarks, 'witnessed a surge in the production and presumably also in the reading of prose works in Athens, including philosophical, oratorical, and historical texts' (ibid. p. 6, with references to book culture n.15). In the next part of this chapter, I look at Xenophon's relationship with Socrates.

42 Tuplin (2012) describes it as a 'brief (perhaps very early) work'. In a study of the relative chronology of several related works, Stokes (2012) places *Apologia* before *Memorabilia*, and before Polykrates' (lost) *Accusation of Socrates*, which is usually dated to the late 390s. Johnson (2021: 120–1) questions the validity of the exercise on the grounds that *Apologia* and *Memorabilia* have different goals. More generally, he contends that Xenophon's Socratic works 'lack any clear chronological markers' (ibid. p. 16).

43 See for example Anderson 1974: 175 n.1, Bandini and Dorion 2000: ccxl–cclii. Johnson (2021: 25 n.40) disputes this and sees no reason to assume the passage was written after 371; see also Johnson 2018: 484 n.3, noting the presence of anachronisms in the Socratic writings. As remarked above, I do not believe there is a hard border between these works: see also Denyer (2019: 126), who thinks that the use of a connective particle in the opening of *Apologia* may mark it as an instalment of *Memorabilia*, and Rood (2017: 266), who suggests *Oikonomikos* could be a continuation of *Memorabilia*.

Several of the author's other big works bear the influence of Socrates, albeit in less direct fashion. The most prominent of these is usually said to be *Kyroupaideia*, which from 8.8.3–4 we can suppose was written after the Satraps' Revolt of 361. Assuming the Socratic presence, one inference might be that the work represents a development in literary thought, with a universally recognisable historical figure becoming the basis for discourses on ethics and political philosophy. In the next chapter I argue that another of the major works, *Hellenika*, bears marks of a 'Socratic history', which would place us broadly in the 370s–360s. However, it looks to have been composed in two separate parts, with the first (1–2.3.10) probably dating to the 380s and the second (2.3.11–7.5.27) to as late as the 350s. Having in mind the connection to Thucydides at the beginning, and the personalised nature of the ending, I think that Xenophon regarded this as a book he was obliged to undertake as a historian, though this did not deter him from admitting Socratic influence.[44]

Turning to the seven 'minor writings', I suggested that we may want to regard some of these as ad hoc, a result (say) of requests to Xenophon by peers to share his knowledge and learning. Athenians and Spartans, who he was intricately connected with on various levels, are both equally reflected in the *opuscula*. Doubtless such approaches, were they made, would have resonated with the author's Socratic inclination to benefit others. While this context would not necessarily incline us to see such works as dating to the later phase of his life, the implication that Xenophon was knowledgeable and experienced does support this view. The fact that smaller groupings within the seven cohere around common Xenophontic subjects further encourages us to see a 'late' imprint.

Taking account of historical detail for their chronology, the *Poroi* reference to the Phokian occupation of Delphi (5.9) indicates an authorship date in the mid-350s. *Hipparchikos*, also marked by an Athenian interest, is usually assigned to the post-Leuktra period (after 371) and improved Atheno-Spartan relations; it predates, probably not by much, its companion piece, *Peri Hippikes*. *Hiero* most likely comes after 360, while *Agesilaos* postdates the Spartan king's death in the same year. Studies next move us back several decades. *Kynegetikos* tends to be placed in the 390s, and

---

44 Rood (2004b: 341) observes that Xenophon evokes 'his own beginning at his end (the initial "after this", μετὰ δὲ ταῦτα, is picked up by the closing "after this", τάδε μετὰταῦτα)'. Higgins (169), rightly in my view, dismisses a belief that Xenophon was employed by Thucydides as a secretary in the last years of the fifth century and that he wrote the first two books of *Hellenika* in this period. See further Rahn 1971, who investigates differences between the two parts, surmising from his conclusions that it was 'unlikely that Xenophon wrote the first section at the end of his life' (502 n.13). For a unitarian view, see Henry 1966, Higgins 1977, Gray 1991, Pownall 2004. On the dating, see Cawkwell 1979: 17–33, Cartledge 1987: 65–6, Thomas 2009: xxxiv.

may be the earliest of all Xenophon's works, though conceivably a part of *Hellenika* and even the *Lakedaimonion Politeia* predate it. The latter is the most discussed of the minor writings in terms of dating: possibilities mooted include the late 390s, 378–377, the 360s and early 350s.

Looking finally at *Anabasis*, as Paul Cartledge points out, 6.6.9 ('at that time the Lacedaemonians ruled all the Greeks') shows that Sparta was no longer the leading power in Aegean Greece when Xenophon was writing (this part of) the book. 'Scholars', he writes, 'differ considerably over when exactly that was. One strong possibility is that it was sometime soon after Sparta's disastrous defeat at the Battle of Leuktra, in 371.'[45] A date after the defeat harmonises as well with the nostalgic tone of 5.3.7–13,[46] which indicates that Xenophon had left Skillous when he was writing. It seems at least plausible, though, to regard it as being a work in progress at the time of departure: its thematic richness, complex narratorial structure and abundance of travel and geographic detail point to a work that would not have been finished within a short time span. Perhaps the upheaval proved to be the spur Xenophon needed to collate and publish several works in progress. On the thematic element, the apparent referencing of *Memorabilia* 3 in the treatment of leadership, a major interest in *Anabasis*, may reveal a chronological clue as to the relative dating of these works, but it also brings into relief the earlier theory of a common conception for some works with the theme of leadership underlying these two to a notable degree.[47] I look at instances of intertextuality between them in Chapter 3.

The picture which emerges overall is of a body of work shaped by the author's extensive life experiences, in particular his association with Socrates. While this influence played into his earliest writings, it is most prominent in their main phase of production, dateable to a period either side of the author's residence at Skillous. I emphasised the fact that this was a time in which other Socratics were publishing as well, and so we should see the phase as reflecting Xenophon's participation in a wider Socrates literary-philosophical industry wherein writers sought to promote their own versions of the great man's life and teaching.

---

45 Cartledge 2021: 281. See also Dürrbach 1893: 368, Körte 1922: 16–17, Dan 2014: 168.
46 Cf. H-R 17 n.60.
47 With most writers, I consider that *Anabasis* was written as a unit, albeit its composition could well have extended over a considerable period. Anderson (1974: 83) suggests that there were two editions of the work, the one attributed to Themistogenes of Syracuse in *Hellenika* covering the same ground as 'our Anabasis I–IV'; Tsagalis (2009: 453–4) posits something similar, with a later work by Xenophon expanding and improving on the earlier one. Themistogenes and the *Hellenika* passage are discussed in detail in Chapter 4 pp. 156–9.

Factors Influencing Xenophon's Life and Writings

It is a slippery exercise, trying to identify life-changing experiences and landmarks in a subject's life, the more so when so little of it is known for certain. With that caveat in mind, the first of three factors I discuss in this part is, not surprisingly from the chronology discussion, the figure of Socrates. The philosopher may be said to be the most widely acknowledged but, paradoxically, underrated influence on Xenophon's life. I explain this by the received tradition of a Socratic cycle which forms just a component of Xenophon's overall output (four works of the fourteen), and by the fact that it is generally thought of today as inferior to Plato's, with the implication that Xenophon did not understand Socrates well and was not therefore as touched by the contact as his compatriot. In this study I argue that the philosopher's influence is pervasive and can be traced through all of Xenophon's works, not least his *Anabasis*.[48]

The second factor identified, the Peloponnesian War and internal strife at Athens, tends to be packaged as part of Xenophon's early political experience, yet it is worth exploring to see what elements of it might be directly traceable in his later writings. One discernible link is an abiding interest in order and leadership, an understandable response to the disorder and danger of the times in which he grew up.

The third is the decree of exile which was passed against him in 399 or later. I argue this may have been a consequence of the trouble at Athens, and to bring this into relief I look at the circumstances of his departure from the city in 401. While I have not explicitly discussed Sparta in this part, that important influence is examined in Chapter 4. I note the importance of Agesilaos in the author's life, but focus the study on those figures featuring in *Anabasis*.

Socrates

From his early years Xenophon appears to have pursued an interest in higher thought. He attended occasions when Socrates spoke at Athens, and he may even have listened to sophist lectures given by Prodikos in Boiotia (see below). Whether his interest in philosophy was inspired by Socrates, as Diogenes Laertios relates (2.48), or itself brought him into contact with

---

48 See also Brennan 2011: 246, Humble 2018: 591. Arguing that the influence of Socrates pervades Xenophon's works is not novel (see e.g. Due 1989: 145), but not the *communis opinio* either. A recent study (*Xenophon's Socratic Works*) focuses on the traditional cycle of four (Johnson 2021).

Figure 1.1 Socrates, a Visionary Head. William Blake, c.1820. Yale Center for British Art, Paul Mellon Collection.

Socrates, is a question that can hardly be definitively answered. Hard too to answer is what exactly his philosophical interests were, though we are safe enough to name ethics and the problem of how to rule as prominent among these. Socrates discourses on both at length in Xenophon's writings, and the author himself engages with them in those works where the philosopher is not apparently a central subject. Turning this around, and keeping in mind that Plato paints a somewhat different picture of him, what may be hardest of all to know is what Socrates himself thought/taught. I look at this much written-about problem in Chapter 5.[49]

While Xenophon appears only once in *Memorabilia* (1.3.8–13) engaged in conversation with Socrates, elsewhere in this work we understand that he was often in attendance at talks ('For I myself never heard Socrates indulge in the practice...' [of making the worse appear the better argument], 1.2.31, and see 1.4.2, 1.6.14, 2.4.1, 2.5.1, 4.3.2). In the opening of *Oikonomikos* (1.1) he claims to have been present at the events about to be related, even though he could not have been on hand when Socrates referred to the death of Cyrus the Younger (4.18): Cyrus died in 401, and Socrates was executed in spring 399, at which time Xenophon had not returned to Greece from the campaign against the King. If the view that he was born in the early 420s is right, it is similarly unrealistic that he attended the evening with Socrates recorded in *Symposion*, dramatic date 422,[50] or that Socrates saved his life at Delion in 424 (Diogenes 2.22). Taking a minimalist perspective on the relationship, we might conclude that either Xenophon's details are in some sense fictional or that he derived his knowledge in the main from others in the Socratic circle. Both may be true, but the *Oikonomikos* and *Symposion* peculiarities need not undermine the integrity of the texts, which are not after all intended to be primarily historical. In each case the problem is resolved if, as McCloskey argues we should, we drop the assumption that the narrator and author are one and the same.[51]

The most compelling piece of evidence pertaining to the relationship between the men comes from *Anabasis*, a work with a distinct if complex historical aspect. Recalling how he came to leave Athens, Xenophon recounts that he consulted Socrates about whether he should accept an invitation to join Cyrus the Younger in Asia:

> Socrates was apprehensive that becoming a friend of Cyrus' would be something blameworthy in the eyes of the city of Athens, because Cyrus was reputed to have assisted the Lakedaimonians whole-heartedly in their war against Athens, and he counselled Xenophon to go to Delphi and take the advice of the god about the journey. (3.1.5)

---

49 The Socratic Question, the search for the historical Socrates, may be better understood as a nexus of questions revolving around each of the authors of Socratica. Taking the case of Xenophon: is the figure of Socrates a vehicle for his own ideas? Did he rely on the writings of other Socratics when producing his own? Did he intend to represent the 'real' Socrates or give us some other picture, a correction to Plato's, or even some negative fictional paradigm? See Figure 1.1 for an image of the philosopher.
50 Gray (2011b: 11) thinks he might have been at the drinking party as a *meirakion*.
51 McCloskey 2017. Also on the literary side, we can note that Xenophon is fond of anachronism, sometimes for example associating Socrates with events that took place after his death (e.g. *Mem*. 3.5.25, 27). Johnson (2021: 58 n.18) remarks that the Socratic *logoi* was a genre 'known to welcome anachronism'.

In *Memorabilia* (1.1.6) Xenophon writes that this was how Socrates dealt with intimate friends (πρὸς τοὺς ἐπιτηδείους), so there is an implication that he himself was one of these. Famously, Xenophon disregarded the advice he was given and instead asked to which of the gods he should sacrifice to ensure the success of the journey he had in mind (3.1.6).[52] Socrates' response – annoyance and then acceptance (3.1.7) – indicates an avuncular relationship between the men, an impression underlined in the one meeting between them recorded in *Memorabilia* (1.3.8–13) and reflected in the later account given by Diogenes of their very first meeting (2.48).

To complicate this reading and leave open the question of Xenophon's proximity to Socrates, I suggest later in the chapter that the encounter in *Anabasis* may not in fact be historical; we might instead have an adaptation from some meeting or, less likely in my view, a fictional episode invented for the purposes of the story. Be that as it may, from the broader evidence a real link between the two men seems very probable. Given a tangible connection, it is worth reflecting that the author must have considered the negative ways in which his involvement of Socrates in the narrative could have played out with his audience, to include his fellow Socratics. Even at such a long remove in time from the event, he must have been wary of drawing Socrates too deeply into the story – one of a young Athenian joining mercenaries engaged in a morally suspect enterprise. That may be one reason for his minimalist approach with regards to the role of Socrates in a narrative that I argue is in a real sense about him.

It is worth underlining that in antiquity Xenophon was known mainly, if not exclusively, as a philosopher (Lucian, *De historia conscribenda* 39, refers to his high standing as a historian). Notably, Diogenes places him immediately after Socrates in his catalogue of philosophers, a fact which Dorion sees as 'a resounding confirmation of his recognition of Xenophon's status as a Socratic'.[53] Yet the degree to which he was a participant in Socrates' circle, and by extension his ability as a thinker, has been much debated by moderns, albeit it is fair to say that this subject has become less topical as interest in the author has grown. In the past century portraits of Xenophon as a philosopher were often negative, often by explicit contrast with Plato. Bertrand Russell's view of a man 'not very liberally endowed with brains,

---

52 Flower points out that the question Xenophon asked was not an unusual formulation for oracular consultations, but nonetheless that he had put it 'in such a way as to almost guarantee the response that he wanted by restricting the range of possible answers that the god could give' (2012: 123).

53 Dorion 2017: 45. For Xenophon as a philosopher and key Socratic, see Dorion 2006; in a later contribution (2017) he explores the place of Xenophon in the philosophical tradition. See Kaldellis (2015: 23–5) for a discussion of the late Roman author Eunapios' tribute to Xenophon at the outset of his *Lives of Philosophers and Sophists*. Tuplin (1993: 28 n.56) supplies an exhaustive list of the antique references to Xenophon as a philosopher.

and on the whole conventional in his outlook' is not untypical.[54] Vlastos found it almost inconceivable that Xenophon could have been part of the Socratic circle, though he sees fit to respond to Russell's claim of a stupid Xenophon.[55] Others are even more damning, with Brickhouse and Smith, who consider that 'Xenophon was *not* a philosopher', one of the milder examples of some quite adverse opinions about the author as a thinker.[56]

The defenders of Xenophon's status as a philosopher have been similarly prone to exaggerated statement. Leo Strauss, for instance, argued fervently that Xenophon is the primary source for our knowledge of Socrates. That he should not be considered so, he writes, is the result of 'a powerful prejudice which emerged in the course of the nineteenth century and is today firmly established. According to that prejudice Xenophon is so simple-minded and narrow-minded or philistine that he cannot have grasped the core or depth of Socrates' thought.'[57] He does not elaborate on the source of this prejudice, but it is reasonable to assume that he has in mind followers of Plato, the

---

54 Russell 1946: 102. He goes on: 'There has been a tendency to think that everything Xenophon says must be true, because he had not the wits to think of anything untrue. This is a very invalid line of argument. A stupid man's report of what a clever man says is never accurate, because he unconsciously translates what he hears into something that he can understand. I would rather be reported by my bitterest enemies among philosophers than by a friend innocent of philosophy. We cannot therefore accept what Xenophon says if it either involves any difficult point in philosophy or is part of an argument to prove that Socrates was unjustly condemned' (102–3).
55 'But Xenophon is anything but a stupid man. His *Cyropaedia* is as intelligent a venture in belletrist didactic fiction as has come down to us from classical antiquity. Both in that work and copiously elsewhere Xenophon displays shrewd judgment of the world and of men. If I had been one of those ten thousand Greeks, left leaderless in the wilds of Anatolia, casting about for a commander we could trust to lead us safely back to civilization, I doubt if I could have hit on anyone better than Xenophon for the purpose; my vote would certainly have gone to him over Russell' (Vlastos 1991: 101–2; 99, 103 for Xenophon not part of Socrates' circle).
56 Brickhouse and Smith 2000: 38. They go on to conclude that, at best, 'we would have to say that Xenophon's attempt to reveal the character and activities of the historical Socrates is distorted and incomplete' (42). Grant writes (1989: 203): 'Xenophon was very proud to have known Socrates, although, since his philosophical capabilities fell short of his pretensions, he must have been one of the great man's more or less uncomprehending, intermittent hangers-on, rather than a serious student. What he later had to say about his hero, therefore, is just a rag-bag of second-hand hearsay and reading and invention.' Nails (1995: 20): 'The way I employ Xenophon's texts is as a sort of layman's appendix to Plato. Xenophon shows not the slightest inclination or talent for philosophy in anything that he writes.' Kahn (1996: 30) sees Xenophon as being 'rather like a sponge, soaking up ideas, themes, and even phrases from Antisthenes, Aeschines, and Plato'.
57 Strauss 1970: 83. Strauss's close reading approach and his conception of an ironic Xenophon continue to influence literary and political science scholars especially, for example Nadon 2001, Ambler 2008, Buzzetti 2014, Pangle 2018 and 2020, Sebell 2021. Hobden (2020: 36–9) offers a concise critique of the Straussian view.

Socratic *par excellence* for many modern philosophers. For this group, the Socrates of Xenophon, concerned primarily with ethics and practical living, is much less appealing than the figure we see in Plato deliberating on the nature of the soul.[58]

The emphasis on virtue in Xenophon's works surely, though, reflects important aspects of Socrates' life and teaching, albeit it is true that these elements – self-discipline, self-sufficiency, endurance, piety, obedience, courage – were common in wider Greek culture and would have featured in Xenophon's early education. Xenophon's version of Socrates, which I consider is meant to be a complement and at some points a corrective to Plato's and others', is undeniably marked by a decided interest in learning how to become beneficial to friends and country alike. To this Socrates' way of thought, practical endeavour is the true path to virtue. 'For the beautiful and good man,' he says in *Oikonomikos*, 'the best labour and field of study is farming' (SB) (ἐδοκιμάσαμεν δὲ ἀνδρὶ καλῷ τε κἀγαθῷ ἐργασίαν εἶναι καὶ ἐπιστήμην κρατίστην γεωργίαν, 6.8).[59]

I make a couple of final observations. In *Anabasis* Xenophon's failure to follow the advice of Socrates on the matter of the expedition marks him

---

58 Dorion articulates this prejudice better (2017: 55–6): 'It would appear that it is rooted in the idea of philosophy as an essentially critical and/or speculative activity. Since Xenophon's Socratic works have little to do with critical or speculative philosophy, those who accept this hyper-modern view of philosophy draw the conclusion – as if it were self-evident – that these writings are of no philosophical value. But what if it were more legitimate to see philosophy as the ancients did – as *a way of living one's life*? How then could Xenophon – whose Socrates strives to make human action and speech consistent with one another in order to help other men improve their lives – be denied the title of philosopher?' See also Johnson 2021: 1–2. For an overview of the longstanding debate as to which of Xenophon or Plato, if either, paints the more realistic picture of Socrates, see Pomeroy 1994: 22–6. I find appealing her view that the length of Socrates' life and his range of interests make it permissible for the portraits of both men to have a claim of historicity. See further Kahn 1996, Waterfield 2004, Dorion 2006, Macleod 2008, Johnson 2018. In an article exploring Socrates in Hellenistic philosophy, Long shows that the Xenophontic interpretation of a predominantly ethical figure was widely taken as the norm. 'By the end of the Hellenistic period it is a commonplace that Plato attributed to Socrates interests and theories which were entirely Plato's own (cf. Cicero, *Rep.* 1.15–16). The same is true implicitly as early as Aristotle. Only in late antiquity do we find Socrates credited with Platonist metaphysics (e.g. by Ps.-Plutarch, *Plac.* 878b). The absence of an ancient Socratic problem on this issue will only occasion surprise or difficulty if Plato's dialogues are treated as the standard reference-point for Socrates' philosophy, taking priority over the writings of Xenophon, Antisthenes and others' (1988: 153–4).
59 Xenophon was not the only Socratic who saw practical endeavour as the most beneficial. When asked what beautiful boys should learn, Aristippos answered, whatever 'will be useful to them when they are grown up' (Diogenes 2.80, and see 2.71). Antisthenes is said to have railed against the study of literature (γράμματα) (Diogenes 6.103).

in some way as unwise, a state which could reflect his actual status vis-à-vis the Socratic circle, so a novice on the periphery rather than an established insider. The arguments, then, for Xenophon as a marginal Socratic figure in the philosopher's lifetime could find support from Xenophon himself.[60]

Related to the subject of his immaturity, I think we can glean more from the 'Socrates episode' and from our knowledge of Xenophon's background. His formal education must not have weighed sufficiently to bear influence on the decision to disregard the advice Socrates gave him, as, rationally, such a course – not asking the basic question – was not optimal in terms of his own interests. The same could be said of his upbringing and the paternal direction to which he was subject. On the other hand, his putative ignorance on the counts of his father, Socrates and the education provided by the *polis* is counterbalanced by a spirit of independence, which may indicate a deeper level of awareness about his deficiency in wisdom. I think this potentially destructive tension between himself and the external factors seeking to shape his character reveal Xenophon as one of those whom Socrates had in mind when he spoke of being 'in love' with someone, that is, with an individual whose soul naturally inclined to excellence (*Memorabilia* 4.1.2).

The Peloponnesian War and Civil War at Athens

Close experience of violent conflict was a feature of Xenophon's life from early on. It probably accounts for his strong view on the role the gods played in human affairs and, on more earthly matters, instilled in him an appreciation of the importance of good command. Involvement in the Peloponnesian War may have afforded him his first taste of travel and philosophy.

While he makes no mention of it in his works, it is fairly certain that he fought for Athens in the Peloponnesian War as a cavalryman. Even had he been born as late as the mid-420s he would have been eligible for military service in the later stages of that war. Evidence that he did fight may lie in certain passages from his *Hellenika* that convey a sense of autopsy. An example is the detailed account he gives at 1.2.1–13 of a campaign by the Athenian general Thrasyllos in Ionia in 409; specifically, he writes of a Persian commander, Stages, who 'managed to capture one Athenian alive

---

60 But a reader for the publisher points out that Aischines makes Xenophon and his wife interlocutors with Aspasia in a dialogue arguably written in the early fourth century (the fragment appears in Cicero, *Inv. rhet.* 1.51-2). On that view we might read *An.* 3.1.5–6 in an altogether different way: Xenophon, because he was an associate of Socrates, goes out of his way to indicate that the philosopher had no responsibility for his own decision to join Cyrus.

and kill seven others' (1.2.5).⁶¹ Then there is the possibility that he was part of the fleet sent to Mytilene in 406 to rescue the blockaded Athenian force. In *Hellenika* he writes:

> When the Athenians learned of the events at Mytilene and the siege, they voted to bring help with 110 ships, manning them with everyone – both slave and free – who was of age. The ships were manned and departed in thirty days. Even many of the Knights [*hippeis*] went on board. (1.6.24)

Diogenes has nothing to say of Xenophon's military record prior to his joining of Cyrus's expedition, but another third-century AD writer, Philostratos, refers to a stay in prison in Boiotia (*Vitae Sophistarum* 1.12); Anderson associates this with the Battle of Arginousai in 406, though Wright thinks it may relate to the Boiotians' seizure of Oropos in 412.⁶² Philostratos writes that Xenophon secured release on bail to attend lectures by Prodikos, the eminent Kean sophist, adding that his famous lecture, the 'Choice of Herakles', is related by Xenophon (*Memorabilia* 2.1.21–34). If the young Athenian had indeed attended lectures, Proxenos, an aspiring Boiotian philosopher and guest-friend of Xenophon's, could have arranged the release. It was Proxenos who, in early 401, invited him to join Cyrus the Younger in Asia Minor.

Like many citizens, Xenophon was involved in the *stasis* at Athens that followed the war. After the surrender to Sparta in spring 404, under Lysander's gaze a body of thirty was chosen at Athens to write down the ancient laws, 'according to which the government would be run' (*Hellenika* 2.3.2). This group, from the elite classes, found natural support from those who formed the cavalry (see *Hellenika* 2.4.2). The fact that the democratic leader, Thrasyboulos, was only able to field seventy horsemen is an indication that the Athenian cavalry overwhelmingly supported oligarchic rule (*Hellenika* 2.4.25). It seems reasonable to suppose that Xenophon was with the majority, and again evidence from his *Hellenika* might be invoked to support this view. Yet, if this were the case, the hostility to the Thirty recorded

---

61 Cawkwell 1979: 9, Stronk 1995: 4 and Thomas 2009: xx, among others, take this as proof of autopsy. David Thomas in correspondence stresses that it is not just the vividness here that points to personal experience but the particularity of the detail in an otherwise not especially full narrative. Cf. Anderson 1986: 37–8 and, as a more general note of caution, Flower (2017b: 304): 'vividness of narration is no more dependent upon eyewitness testimony than it is in a modern novel'. It bears remarking that if indeed Xenophon was on this campaign, then he had already toured the area where he would travel to in 401 to join Cyrus the Younger.
62 Anderson 1974: 18, Wright 1922: 37.

in *Hellenika* would suggest that not long into their tyranny he withdrew or became a reluctant participant, or at least this is the impression he wishes to give in his history of the period.[63]

A major question concerning *Anabasis* is why, thirty years or more after the event, Xenophon wrote his account of the march of the Ten Thousand. A similar question might be asked of this part of *Hellenika*, published at an even greater distance (early 350s) from the events described.[64] I argue apologia shapes *Anabasis* to a substantial degree, and this may be the case too with the second part of *Hellenika*. As personal apologia, it is to Athenians and their posterity he is writing, his intention in the opening being to present his own participation in the regime of the Thirty Tyrants as comparatively benign. As Tuplin remarks of the second part, it would have been extraordinary if it had been written entirely without thoughts about Athens and what Athenians might learn from it.[65]

An episode involving Socrates strengthens the argument for a distinct apologetic flavour to *Hellenika* and highlights the presence of Socratic defence in a historiographical context (I examine a more pervasive Socratic presence in the work in the next chapter; by Socratic defence I mean throughout 'of Socrates' rather than a method of thought or argumentation). At 1.7, the author provides a dramatic account of the trial of the generals following the sea battle around Arginousai in 406. In addition to its historical content, the episode serves to show how easily the voting body can be manipulated and how this can have damaging consequences for the state. But Xenophon's principal purpose here is to show both the courage and integrity of Socrates, fearless in the face of the democratic mob, and his steadfast obedience to the laws. As Henry contends,[66] he accentuates the extraordinary courage of Socrates' action in refusing to admit an illegal motion.

---

63 Lee (2017: 25) suggests reasons why Xenophon might have participated only reluctantly: 'Family obligations, loyalty to cavalry comrades, or plain reluctance to seem cowardly could have kept Xenophon in the ranks just as much as sincere political belief.'

64 As discussed, *Hellenika* is widely considered to have been written in two parts, the first a continuation of Thucydides from where he broke off with events in 411 down to 404, the second covering the period 404–362 (1–2.3.10 and 2.3.11–7.5.27 respectively). The account of the Thirty is the focus of the second part's opening.

65 Tuplin 1993: 33. Dillery (1995: 139), who notes that Xenophon wanted to re-examine the events surrounding the Thirty at Athens, and that he did not have to, quantifies the extent of his treatment: 'Not counting the brief mention of their installation at 2.3.2–3, the Thirty's story extends (from 2.3.11 to 2.4.43) over twenty [OCT] pages or more than a tenth of the entire history which covers almost fifty years; assuming that their rule extended from the summer of 404/3 to the summer of 403/2, no other year is covered in such detail in the *Hellenica*.'

66 'Now the development of this entire scene was obviously contrived with no other object in view than to set off the adamant refusal of the great philosopher in the face of overwhelming constraint. All objections that Xenophon in according Socrates only this one line is slighting him or that he does not recognise the meaning of his life are intolerable and can

[14] Then, when some of the presiding committee refused to allow the motion to come to a vote on the grounds that it was contrary to the law, Kallixenos again mounted the platform and accused them on the same charge as he had Euryptolemos. And the crowd shouted to him to serve a summons against the presiding committee men who had refused to allow a vote. [15] This so frightened the presiding committee that they now agreed to put the matter to a vote, all of them except one – Socrates son of Sophroniskos, who said he would do nothing except in accordance with the law. (*Hellenika* 1.7.14–15)

The Exile Decree: The Philosopher Outcast

The third factor identified as significant in shaping the thought and literary output of our author is his exile from Athens. Why the Athenians imposed this penalty, and why he had earlier left Athens, are questions that may be intertwined. Both call for consideration in their own right, with the latter exercise holding out the promise as well of a better insight into the author's personal outlook. I start with the less well-investigated matter of his leaving Athens, turning then to the exile decree.

Xenophon's Departure from Athens in 401

With the restoration of the democracy in 403, and the city still coming to terms with its defeat to Sparta and the loss of its empire, Xenophon cannot have been optimistic about his future in Athens. When a letter arrived from Proxenos inviting him to travel to Asia to meet a Persian prince (*Anabasis* 3.1.4), he must have felt a life-changing opportunity was at hand. In the circumstances, it is quite understandable that he disregarded the advice of Socrates and put a leading question to the god at Delphi.

The circumstances of Xenophon's departure from Athens are traditionally framed in the above terms. Given his presumed links to the Thirty, and the ambition to which his later adventures and writings testify, this explanation seems attractive. As Cawkwell memorably wrote, 'it was time for a young man with a taste for war and a distaste for democracy to be off'.[67]

Yet it may have been that Xenophon did not have a real choice in the matter of his leaving; that either he was forced out or, as it were, saw the

---

only arise from a profound misconception of the artistry of the description.' Henry 1966: 197. Cf. *Seventh Letter* (Plato) 324d–325a. For perspectives on the Arginousai affair, see Gish 2012, Christ 2020: 17–26.

67 Cawkwell 1972: 13. Notwithstanding he had a certain distaste for it, as I show in Chapter 3, the Xenophon we meet on the retreat incorporated democratic method into his leadership style. I suggest that he was not opposed to democracy in its original form (Chapter 3 pp. 118–20), but that what produced distaste was the abuse of the developed system by political actors.

writing on the wall. The extent to which he participated in violent episodes during the reign of the Thirty would undoubtedly have been an important factor in determining his future following the restoration, but as we will see, membership of the cavalry was in itself a determining factor. Looking at the evidence for the period 404–401 in *Hellenika* and other contemporary materials, I assess the political climate in Athens at this time and how this affected citizens of Xenophon's class. I highlight the possibility that in his case, rather than leaving by choice to pursue an opportunity for self-improvement abroad, the motivation for that may have been concern for his own life.

Return of the Democracy

By September 403 the Thirty were marginalised and the democracy at Athens restored. Pausanias, the Spartan king, and a delegation sent from Sparta by the ephors, brokered a settlement on the following terms: 'that there was to be peace between both sides; that the men of the city and the men of Piraeus were each to depart to his own home, except for the Thirty and the Eleven and the Ten who had ruled in Peiraieus' (*Hellenika* 2.4.38). It was permitted as well that any of those who had been involved with the city party and were concerned their security should be free to settle in Eleusis, to where the Thirty had gone in spring 403 (*Hellenika* 2.4.38, Diodoros 14.33.6).

Agreement to these terms by the democrats, the victors, seems to have been a magnanimous gesture. Large numbers of them had suffered injustice and violence at the hands of the regime. Episodes reported by Xenophon in *Hellenika* include the arrest of those 'least likely to accept being pushed aside and kept out of public life' (2.3.14), the execution of the male citizens of Eleusis (2.4.9)[68] and the murder of people from Aixone (2.4.26). Yet much of the evidence relating to the period, including Xenophon's, gives the distinct impression that the Pausanias amnesty was remarkably effective.[69] On the basis of these testimonies, some modern scholars hold up the reconciliation as proof of democracy's inherently more civilised nature.[70] There is cause to believe, however, that the reality was less straightforward. Green writes:

---

68 Lysias (12.52) gives 300 as the number arrested and condemned to death. He says as well that citizens of Salamis were among these.

69 See, for example, *Hell.* 2.4.43, Lysias 16.8, Aristotle, *Ath. Pol.* 40, Nepos 8.3.3. Rahn (1981: 111) concludes from a study of speeches delivered to Athenian juries in the period that there is evidence of 'a continual committal on the part of the audience (i.e., the jury), to the amnesty and the agreements made with the Spartans in 403 BC'. Krentz (1995: 155–6) considers that by and large the amnesty was successful.

70 Finley (2004: 183) writes: 'Lord Acton was one of the few historians to have grasped the historic significance of the amnesty of 403. "The hostile parties", he wrote, "were reconciled, and proclaimed an amnesty, the first in history." *The first in history*, despite all the familiar weaknesses, despite the crowd psychology, the slaves, the personal ambition of many leaders, the impatience of the majority with opposition.'

Scholars tend to overestimate the impact of the official amnesty between factions orchestrated by Pausanias in 403. Wars, and civil wars above all, are not so easily written off. Greeks and Irishmen have always had a special talent for μνησικακία, the nursing of ancient wrongs.[71]

McKechnie expresses a similar view, seeing recriminations against those involved with the Thirty in the speeches of Lysias: 'The reason must be that, amnesty or no amnesty, the upheavals of 404/403 were not easily forgotten by the Athenians.'[72] The democracy, moreover, had shown itself during the war with the Peloponnesians to be equally capable of brutality, so the absence of a violent backlash against those involved with the Thirty does look exceptional.[73] In fact, there is evidence that vengeance was taken. In *Seventh Letter* (325b), the author writes of the restoration: 'it was not surprising that in some instances . . . men were avenging themselves on their foes too fiercely'.

One way of making sense of the conflicting ancient testimony – (Plato) *Seventh Letter*, Aristotle, *Athenaion Politeia* 40, Xenophon *Hellenika* 2.4, Lysias, *Mantitheos* 8 – might be to speculate that a burst of retribution attended the takeover, but that then the spirit of the reconciliation gradually took hold. However, there is evidence of serious enmity several years after the restoration at Athens. In 399, for instance, the Spartan commander Thibron, beginning a campaign against Persia in Asia Minor, asked Athens for 300 horsemen, whom he said he would support himself. The Athenians, Xenophon writes, 'sent those who had served in the cavalry under the Thirty, for they thought that it would be advantageous to the people if these men went abroad and died there' (*Hellenika* 3.1.4). In isolation this might be dismissed as Xenophon's gloss – it could be argued that the Athenians were honouring their treaty obligations to Sparta (*Hellenika* 2.2.20) and that Xenophon's comment is personal bias rather than objective report[74] – but as is apparent from a speech of Lysias,

---

71 Green 1994: 223.
72 McKechnie 1989: 23. See Lysias' opening in *Against Eratosthenes* (12.1): 'The difficulty that faces me, gentlemen of the jury, is not in beginning my accusation, but in bringing my speech to an end: so enormous, so numerous are the acts they [the Thirty] have committed . . .'. For an analysis of the post-civil war trials, see Wolpert 2002.
73 For example, execution in 421 of adult males in Skione, enslavement of the women and children, land given to Plataians (Thucydides 5.32.1); execution of Melian males in 416/15, women and children sold (Thucydides 5.116); Assembly decree to cut off the right hand of men taken in battle (*Hell*. 2.1.31). See also *Hell*. 2.2.3, 2.2.10.
74 Gray (2007: 17–18) characterises these men as criminals, though there seems to be no clear basis for such a judgement, other than that they are said to have served under the Thirty, just as Xenophon likely did. See Lee 2017: 25 (cited above) on reluctant participation. The number sent out amounts to almost half of the Athenian cavalry size as it stood at the end of the war with Sparta (Krentz 1995: 140).

even down to the late 380s the democracy regarded cavalry service under the Thirty as a mark of untrustworthiness.⁷⁵

I suggest a tentative interpretation of the varied testimony. In the democratic faction agreeing to and, according to several contemporary reporters, broadly upholding the reconciliation of Pausanias, there was a strong element of pragmatism. The democrats could not afford to irritate Sparta (which would show its willingness to act in subjecting democratic Elis in the Elean War [ca. 403–401?]), and they needed stability if their system were to flourish again. Relevant to this last point is the fact that the oligarchs maintained a base at Eleusis, and with or without Spartan support they remained an existential threat to the democracy.⁷⁶ That the democrats were acutely aware of this danger is clear in the action of Archinos, who, in clear contravention of the Pausanias agreement, moved to limit the numbers from the city party who were readying to go there pursuant to the amnesty (Aristotle, *Athenaion Politeia* 40.1). Even if its capacity was limited, Eleusis remained a credible centre of opposition and as such acted as a check on the excesses of the democracy, whose supporters lived now in the knowledge that pogroms could provoke a renewed civil war or even a full-scale Spartan invasion. More from circumstance than by choice, then, did they confine their collective retribution to recalling the *katastaseis* (loans) from the cavalry, now the symbol for democrats of oligarchic repression.⁷⁷ The *hippeis*, together with those from the city party who remained under the democracy, and who had not been involved in criminality during the war, can have felt a degree of security, though not much.

---

75 In his speech *On the Scrutiny of Evandros*, dated to 382, Lysias writes: 'Suppose that he were now under scrutiny for admission to the Council, and he had his name registered on the tablets as having served in the cavalry under the Thirty: even without an accuser you would reject him' (26.10). See further Isokrates, *Panegyrikos* (esp. 110–14), dated to 380 or later. On animosity towards the cavalry following the amnesty, see Bugh 1988: 151, Spence 1993: 217, 219.

76 Eleusis was the Attic stronghold nearest to the Peloponnese. The link between the oligarchic faction and Sparta (or at least to Lysander) was strong throughout the post-war period. It was Lysander who effectively installed the Thirty (Diodoros 14.3.4–7) and Xenophon has their leader, Kritias, express loyalty to Sparta (*Hell.* 2.3.25). When the oligarchs began to run into trouble late in their reign, they sent for, and received, help from Sparta. Rahn (1981: 113) argues that the democrats looked to Pausanias as a counterweight to Lysander, though he may overplay the significance of the schism between the two men in terms of its effect on Spartan foreign policy. Sparta was not traditionally known for a fondness towards democracies.

77 For a consideration of social attitudes to the cavalry before and after the Thirty, see Spence 1993: 216–18. On the recalling of the *katastaseis*, see Lysias 16.6–7. A fragment from another of his speeches, *Against Theozotides*, dated to 403/2, suggests that the grain (*sitos*) allowance given to the cavalrymen was reduced at this time.

The Triumph of the Democracy

The political landscape was to change in 401/0 when the democratic side lured the remnants of the Thirty – supposedly recruiting mercenaries for a campaign – out of their bolthole in Eleusis to attend a meeting. In an episode strikingly like events involving the leadership of the Ten Thousand in Mesopotamia in the same year (see *Anabasis* 2.5), they were seized and put to death. The democrats initiated a reconciliation with those inside the town, and the civil war formally ended. 'Both parties', Xenophon writes, 'then swore oaths not to remember past wrongdoings, and to this day they live as fellow citizens and the people abide by their oaths' (*Hellenika* 2.4.43).[78] With this pocket of hard-line oligarchs removed, the immediate check on the democracy was lifted. Its show of reconciliation was doubtless intended to succour Sparta – a public gesture of reassurance now that its foothold in Attica had been removed. As Xenophon's subsequent revelation about the Athenian cavalry sent to Thibron shows, it cannot be said to have been wholly genuine.[79]

It was not long before the Eleusis reconciliation that Xenophon left Athens.[80] His departure in late spring may be unconnected,[81] but it may not have been coincidental that he left the city in the period leading up to the elimination of this last pocket of the faction he was associated with. In *Anabasis*, when he recalls how he joined Cyrus, he makes no reference to the political situation in the city at this time, other than giving us the reason why Socrates was concerned with his plan – that involvement with Cyrus

---

78 As Krentz (1995: 155) maintains, this belongs to the original 403 reconciliation but is held up until here in the narrative in order to obfuscate the recorded violation of the amnesty and to end this part of the history on a positive note. We have something similar in *Anabasis* 5, where Xenophon defers an event (an account of violence by the men towards local ambassadors) to a later point in the narrative: see further Chapter 4 p. 144.

79 Notable as well are the trials of influential anti-democrats which took place in the same year, 399, as the cavalry was sent out. Green (1994: 225) writes: 'the suppression of the Eleusis faction seems to have encouraged the democrats to take further covert action against their opponents: it is in this atmosphere that the different yet related trials of Andocides [tried for impiety] and Socrates – both early in 399, each in its own way politics masquerading as religion – should be evaluated'.

80 Aristotle gives the 401/0 dating for Eleusis, *Ath. Pol.* 40.4: '[The Athenians] also made a reconciliation with those that had settled at Eleusis two years after the migration, in the archonship of Xenainetos.' See also Spence 1993: 217, Krentz 1995: 155, Waterfield 2006: 50 and Hornblower 2011: 219. Munn (2000: 284) thinks the beginning of the archon's year (June 401) probable for the fall of Eleusis, and I share this view. Green (1994: 224–5) appears to have it at the end of the year, so allowing him to hint that the mercenaries the Thirty were recruiting (*Hell.* 2.4.43) could be Xenophon's, even though at this point in time they were in the Black Sea area (see further below).

81 For different views on starting dates for Cyrus's expedition, see Lee 2007 and Brennan 2008.

could cause him trouble with the authorities (ὁ Σωκράτης ὑποπτεύσας μή τι πρὸς τῆς πόλεως ὑπαίτιον εἴη Κύρῳ φίλον γενέσθαι, 3.1.5). While it may be unfair to imply that Socrates was used by Xenophon to obscure other factors, *Anabasis* certainly does not tell the whole story and, as I suggest below, it seems likely that at that point Xenophon, if not *already* in trouble, was a person of interest to the authorities. On the matter of the democracy's attitude to his joining Cyrus, I am inclined to think that it would have been glad to see a *hippeus* live and die in a foreign land, but of course Socrates is correct in seeing that joining the prince could provide grounds for their taking action against him in the future. One of the ironies here is that had Xenophon stayed in Athens, there is every chance he would have ended up where he did, fighting with Thibron in Asia in 399. As it was, he will have met up with the horsemen sent out by the democracy that year as he led the Cyreans into the Spartan campaign against Persia.

One of the strongest arguments against the hypothesis that Xenophon took flight is the presence of the above-mentioned cavalrymen in Athens in 399. If the period leading up to and after the decapitation of the Eleusis opposition had caused serious unease amongst the *hippeis*, many would have left in 401.[82] Had Xenophon been guilty of a serious crime during the rule of the Thirty, he would have left the city in 403 or else risked coming to a bad end, so we can probably conclude that his role and actions under the oligarchic regime were not the reasons behind his departure in 401. However, there are a couple of possibilities that complicate this. Xenophon could have been one of those who did go to Eleusis following the reconciliation brokered by Pausanias in 403 (large numbers of the 'city party' apparently intended to do so, and as noted, only an extraordinary intervention by the democrats prevented an exodus). In this scenario his role in the Thirty's tyranny could have been more compromising if stopping short of serious wrongdoing, and he would have been primed to leave Attica when there were signs that the democracy was setting its sights on Eleusis.

---

82 With the caveat that some or all of these could already have been abroad, *Anabasis* may provide indirect evidence for a modest departure of Athenian officers. The work names Amphikrates, Kephisodoros, Phrasias and Polykrates as captains, and Lykios as the commander of the cavalry (his father, Polystratos, was probably prosecuted for being a member of the oligarchic regime of 411); an Ariston is one of three ambassadors chosen by the army at Kotyora to sail to Sinope, while Gnesippos and Theopompos appear in situations that suggest them to be senior figures. There may have been other Athenians in the force not mentioned by Xenophon. The presence of these nine men (including Xenophon) in a mercenary enterprise may be unusual. Athenians are not prominent in mercenary service in the fifth century, this presumably due to the strength of their economy and the stability of the democracy. It is tempting to imagine that these men thought service with a prince, even a barbarian one, was preferable to life after the restoration (see Bugh 1988: 151, Roy 1967: 307–8), although it is possible they could have joined for financial reasons, or because of ties of guest-friendship (3.1.4: Xenophon as guest-friend of Proxenos).

Assuming he did not leave the city, and considering his relationship with Socrates, he might have been seen as a potential opposition figure following the 403 restoration, and pressure might gradually have built on him. His statement in *Hellenika* that the Athenians heard that 'the men at Eleusis were trying to hire foreign soldiers' (2.4.43) is indicative of an escalation in tension which, despite his own consecutive linking of the hiring and the marching out in arms of the democracy, will probably have grown over a period.

We can now remark that by early 401, Cyrus the Younger was in the final stages of recruiting for his attempt on the Persian throne. Recruitment of Greek soldiers was his priority and Eleusis, populated with disenfranchised anti-democrats, must have been regarded as fertile ground; notably, as Munn points out, it was the place where 'less than two years earlier Lysander had assembled a mercenary force to protect his allies in Attica'.[83] Is Xenophon hinting obliquely in 2.4.43 that the democratic side used Cyrus's activities as a pretext for marching against Eleusis, or have we two mercenary recruitment drives taking place there at around the same time? In either case the democracy must have felt threatened. A further inference from this is that Cyrus's links to the oligarchs and his role in Athenian geopolitical affairs were greater than usually thought, a possibility that in turn casts sharper light on Socrates' reservations about Xenophon joining him (*Anabasis* 3.1.5).

To sum up, Xenophon could be disguising the real reason why, and how, he came to join the expedition. As a compromised figure at Athens by dint of his varying relationships, or perhaps because he had grown to prominence amongst the Eleusis faction, he felt obliged to leave Attica when the end for the anti-democratic pocket seemed near. Rather than it being an invitation and a subsequent visit to Delphi which saw him on his way to Sardis, it was Cyrus's agents who paved the way. Such a reading of events does not necessarily imply that his account of his consultation with Socrates about the expedition is a fiction, though the historicity of the episode, which may already be in doubt given Xenophon's taste for paradigmatic writing, does become more suspect.[84] One thing that is certain is that we do not know enough to be able to say with any confidence why Xenophon left Athens when he did.

---

83 Munn 2000: 283, drawing on *Hell.* 2.4.29. The friendship between Cyrus the Younger and Lysander is significant here (see *Hell.* 1.5.1–7, 2.1.13–14, *Oik.* 4.20–5).
84 According to the terms of the original amnesty, it was 'not lawful for those at Eleusis to go into the city, nor for those in the city to go to Eleusis' (Aristotle, *Ath. Pol.* 39.2). If Xenophon were at Eleusis, just as Proxenos wrote to him, he in turn could have written to Socrates. I examine the subject of paradigm shaping Xenophon's historical writings in the next chapter. Speculatively, some support for Xenophon having limited knowledge of life inside Athens after 403 might be found at *Hell.* 2.4.43, where there is an apparent temporal lacuna: with the words ὑστέρῳ δὲ χρόνῳ – 'later' – the author moves from the victory speech of Thrasyboulos in 403 to the showdown with the oligarchs at Eleusis in 401.

The Exile Decree

At some time in 399 or later, a decree was passed in Athens banishing Xenophon.[85] That the Athenians took this measure raises again the question about his profile and standing in the city. It could be that, as just argued, he was a more significant figure at home than has been assumed, or that events on the retreat of the Cyreans or immediately afterwards in Asia Minor elevated him to a level of prominence that made treatment by a public order desirable. The reason(s) for the decree (of Euboulos: Diogenes 2.59) is not known, though if we could establish its date, the matter would be clearer. Broadly, banishment in the early 390s would point to Xenophon's associations with Cyrus, and Socrates, while the late 390s would point to involvement with the Spartans. Some scholars have tried to square the evidence by suggesting intermediate dates in which more than one of these factors might have played a part.[86] In any event, some form of *prodosia* (betrayal) is likely to have been the basis of the charge laid against him. The subject of Xenophon's exile, impinging as it does on the interrelationships between Athens, Sparta and Persia on the one hand, and on his personal writing motivation on the other, is an important one. As I show in later chapters, there is a good case to be made that in *Anabasis* Xenophon confronts the matter of his banishment from Athens.

Dates and Causes of Exile

Notwithstanding the paucity of ancient evidence for his exile there has been much written in modern times about the subject (ancient writers who refer to it include Diogenes Laertios 2.51, 58, 59, Dio Chrysostom 8.1, Plutarch, *De exilio* 10, Pausanias 5.6.5). Tuplin lists seven combinations of date and cause for Xenophon's exile, with the most commonly favoured of these being: Date – 399, Cause – association with Cyrus's rebellion against Artaxerxes, and Date – 394/3, Cause – association with the Spartans, especially participation in the Battle of Koroneia in August 394. His own study, however, leads to: Date – late 395/4 or beginning 394/3, Cause – supporting Cyrus

---

85 A passage in *Anabasis* gives the *terminus post quem*. Xenophon is in Thrace getting ready to return home and remarks, οὐ γάρ πω ψῆφος αὐτῷ ἐπῆκτο Ἀθήνησι περὶ φυγῆς ('for no motion regarding his exile had yet been put to the vote at Athens', 7.7.57). Several scholars have interpreted this as meaning that the decree was then imminent (Erbse 483, Anderson 1974: 148, Higgins 23), though Tuplin (1987: 60) does not think the 'not yet' carries this meaning: 'Xenophon is merely giving an incidental explanation (for the benefit of readers who know him as "the Athenian exile") of how he could even think of going home'; and see also Rahn 1981: 118. For an overview of the process of how decrees were voted on and passed, see Woodhead 1981: 39.
86 David Thomas has briefly stated his belief that the decree dates to 396, shortly before the outbreak of the Corinthian War (2009: xviii).

and Laconism.[87] While the cause he gives, or one of them, is very likely true, I argue that the 399 dating is the most persuasive.

Later studies of the problem by Green and Badian are worth noting. Badian dismisses Xenophon's joining Cyrus as the cause of exile on the implied grounds that the decree should have been passed when, or soon after, he had left for Asia in 401.[88] To his mind, 'it was only when it became clear that [Xenophon] intended to stay at Sparta, after his going there with Agesilaos, that the Athenians were seriously upset'.[89] Badian's establishment of the Battle of Koroneia as a *terminus post quem* for the exile rests on the belief that Xenophon could not have made an offering at the Athenian treasury at Delphi, where he (probably) went with Agesilaos following the battle in August 394, had he been an exile.[90] I do not share this view, on the practical ground that in the company of a victorious Spartan king no one was likely to stop Xenophon enriching the sanctuary. A more convincing argument might be that, with a decree by the Athenians against him in place, Xenophon would not have been inclined to honour the sanctuary.[91]

Green settles on the earlier date, 399. While he takes care to scrutinise the context and background, the resulting hypothesis is undermined by his argument that the democracy believed Xenophon might lead the Cyreans to Attica to support the remnants of the oligarchic faction.[92] He writes of their demise that 'it would be extraordinary if an approach was *not* made to Xenophon at this point'.[93] Even if we suppose, as Green seems to do, that their elimination took place at the end of the archon year in question (401/0) rather than, as I do, at its beginning, it is difficult to see how such an approach could have been made. In early summer 400 the Ten Thousand were away in a corner of the Black Sea with many obstacles ahead on their way home.[94] The earliest juncture at which deployment of the Cyrean force

---

87 Tuplin 1987: 59–60, 68. Dillery (1998: 4–5) shares this view.
88 Badian 2004: 41.
89 Ibid. p. 42. See also Lesky 1963: 664, Lipka 2002: 3–4, Whitehead 2019: 1.
90 Badian 2004: 41.
91 On Xenophon's offering at Delphi, it bears notice that Diogenes implies he had already made it by the time of his supposed visit with Agesilaos. He writes that of the money which Xenophon had in Ephesos in 399 (see below), he gave half to the temple priest for safekeeping, with the other half being 'sent in votive offerings to Delphi' (ἔπεμψεν εἰς Δελφοὺς ἀναθήματα). 'Next,' he continues, 'he came to Greece with Agesilaos' (2.51). On the use of temples for the safe depositing of objects and funds, see Casson 1974: 73. Scott (2010: ch. 2 *passim*) discusses the control and management of Olympia and Delphi and suggests that dedicators had greater flexibility as to the placement of their votives in Delphi.
92 Green 1994: 224–5. Rop (2019) argues that Cyrus's mercenaries were in fact political agents, and on this line in this case Xenophon could have been seen by Athens as a potential, if remote, threat: see further Chapter 5 n.55.
93 Green 1994: 225.
94 See the comparative chronology table in Brennan 2021b. It must be questionable whether anyone at Athens in the early part of 400 even knew where they were.

could have been considered as a possibility was October 400, after they had arrived in Byzantium, but by then surely the opposition movement had collapsed, as Green himself notes.[95] To come at the matter from the other end, that is, the start of 401/0, it might not have been unrealistic for the oligarchic leadership to have approached Xenophon with a plan before he left Attica for Asia in May 401. Granted such a situation, it is open to serious question whether Xenophon would, and could, have led the mercenaries back out from under Cyrus's nose in his own satrapy, although admittedly an opportunity to do so did arise in Tarsus in August (401) when the troops mutinied against Cyrus and there was talk of a return.

Green rightly draws a link between the political climate at Athens in the tumultuous period following the rule of the Thirty and the decree issued against Xenophon. He concludes:

> Xenophon's exile thus falls into the same general category as the exactly contemporaneous trials of Andocides and Socrates, as part of a vengeful anti-oligarchical backlash that sought to circumvent the terms of the amnesty, and was fuelled by a very real fear (whether justified or not) of a military-backed counter revolution.[96]

I do not think myself that the exile was part of a vengeful backlash, but rather part of a systematic exercise in uprooting the longstanding anti-democratic tradition at Athens.[97] We can add to the famous trials Green mentions the infamous dispatch of cavalry to Asia: three hundred citizens who, at least as Xenophon saw it, were sent away to die fighting in a foreign land. Since the restoration, Athens had been following a course of compliance with Sparta (see *Hellenika* 3.1.4, 3.2.25: supplying troops), but while doing so it patently had an eye to taking opportunities to lessen the hold

---

95 'The separatist movement collapsed': Green (1994: 224) on the outcome of the democracy's action at Eleusis in 401/00.
96 Green 1994: 226. See also Higgins 23–4.
97 As I argue at several points in this monograph, I do not believe Xenophon was an anti-democrat, not an avowed one anyway. But his membership of an elite class associated with opposition to the democracy was sufficient to mark him in governing eyes. Ober takes a more benign view than the one proposed here or by Green. 'By 399 BCE,' he writes, 'the immediate political crisis had passed, but so had public euphoria at surviving the war, averting endless civil war, and reuniting the polis under a re-established code of law. The realization sunk in that reunification was only the beginning of a costly and uncertain rebuilding period, and that Athens remained fragile and vulnerable to its enemies. The Athenian willingness to tolerate potentially dangerous behavior and apparently irresponsible public attitudes reached a low point. And so, for Meletus the time was ripe: he could prosecute Socrates for impiety on relatively novel grounds with little concern of incurring the penalty for failing to gain a fifth of the votes' (2011: 173).

which the Spartans exerted. My view, then, is that the decree was passed in 399 as part of an ongoing drive by the democracy to re-establish itself and to remove internal threats permanently. Its elimination of the Eleusis faction in 401 was a major step towards this end, and it in turn paved the way for action against prominent figures and movements perceived as anti-democratic. By the end of 400, as news of the Cyreans' remarkable retreat and their exploits in Thrace filtered back to Greece, Xenophon's profile, if it had been prior to this, ceased to be obscure. The decree against him in 399 was an interdiction that closed down the possibility he might become a focal point, the philosopher armed, for elite and intellectual groups' questioning of the democracy and its suitability for rule.

As to the official cause of the decree, prior agreements between the factions and the desire to avoid a new *stasis* ruled out pro-oligarchic sympathies, and Laconism was politically awkward at this date. Association with Cyrus, whose cause was lost, would have been a convenient charge.[98] I think we can rest this supposition on a relatively firm footing. In his invitation letter to Xenophon, Proxenos wrote that he believed Cyrus was better for him than his own *patris* (3.1.4), and this hint at tension between the individual and his *polis* is picked up by Socrates, who sees that associating with Cyrus, who had supported Sparta in the war, could ultimately lead to Xenophon's separation from his own *patris* (3.1.5). The philosopher is the embodiment of wisdom in Xenophon's writings and his foresight is proverbial: would the author, in his Socratic enterprise, allow him to be wrong? Any doubt on that score would seem to be dispelled shortly on in the narrative by way of a dream which 'Xenophon' has wherein his father's house is hit by lightning and set ablaze (3.1.11).[99] I remark that Socrates must have been conscious that association with himself was dangerous for the young man; what he has in mind is the most expedient ways for the democracy to deal with opposition.

Xenophon sheds little light on the subject in his writings, referring to the decree only in *Anabasis* and only in passing (5.3.7, 7.7.57), though as I argue in Chapter 4 he indirectly engages with it in the same work. I suggest there that Xenophon's silence on the matter could be interpreted as disdain, a measure of his contempt for the action against him, but it could also

---

98 Rahn (1981: 115) writes: 'the evidence from the law courts, the politics of Athens' leading men and the accounts of the ancient historians all imply that between 403 and 395 BC no one could be or was condemned for pro-Spartanism'. Several later writers – Diogenes 2.58 (but cf. 2.51), Dio Chrysostom 8.1, Pausanias 5.6.5 – cited Xenophon's association with Cyrus the Younger as the reason for his exile from Athens. Anderson, who similarly considers the official cause to be association with Cyrus, thinks that Laconism was an element of the real one (1974: 149).

99 For the link between the burning house and his exile, see Bradley 2011: 296–7, Flower 2012: 126–7. Cf. H-R 80–1.

reflect the circumstances at the time of writing and be a pragmatic decision not to reopen or challenge the historic narrative.

Another possibility is that his silence communicates his obedience to the laws, a Socratic value he emphasises in his writings. Most vividly, as we saw earlier, there is the Arginousai trial of 406, where Socrates, who was serving on the Council's presiding committee, alone resisted popular clamour to admit an illegal motion to judge the Athenian generals collectively not severally (*Hellenika* 1.7.9–15). In *Memorabilia* Xenophon writes: 'All his private conduct was lawful and helpful: to public authority he rendered such scrupulous obedience in all that the laws required, both in civil life and in military service, that he was a pattern of good discipline to all' (4.4.1). The link between obedience and good character carries across the *oeuvre*. In *Agesilaos* the author praises the king more than once for being obedient to Sparta's laws (1.36, 7.2), and in *Kynegetikos* (12.14) a good education is said to teach 'a man to observe laws'.[100] From this perspective I do not think there was much room for Xenophon to follow a different course if he did not wish to undermine himself as a Socratic. I argue at length later in the book that he does, indirectly, contest the charge, but by this mode he does not openly confront the system.

---

100 We might detect in Xenophon's silence about his exile a cultural resonance with the famous inscription on Spartan obedience at Thermopylae (Herodotus 7.228).

CHAPTER 2

Anabasis *in Historiographical and Literary Context*

Xenophon was unique among all of the philosophers in that he engaged not only with words [en logois/logoi] but with actions [ergois/ erga] as well; for he writes about virtue in his discourses and histories, while excelling himself in actions. And moreover he produced military leaders by means of the examples he gave; for instance, Alexander would never have become great had Xenophon never been. And he says that we should record even the everyday acts of distinguished men. (SB)

Eunapios, opening of the *Lives of Philosophers and Sophists*

In this chapter I consider historiographical and literary aspects of Xenophon's *Anabasis*.[1] Long regarded as his most popular work, in more recent times it has come to be seen as one of his richest as well, a fact that has brought into relief questions of intent and classification. This issue of the book's nature is looked at in the second part of the chapter, which, having described it as a 'Socratic history', concludes with a consideration of the term in the context of Xenophon's historiographical (broadly defined) writings. In the third part I look at literary features of the text, focusing on how exemplars shape the narrative, and in the fourth, following a preview of Xenophon's apologetic *Tendenz*, I highlight and explore the presence of what might be termed 'literary apologia'. I begin the chapter by looking for the work's audience.

---

1 *Kyrou Anabasis* in full, usually translated as 'the march upcountry of Cyrus'. Scholars regularly point out that the title only covers the events of Book 1; however, what follows is naturally a direct consequence of these, and so there seems no need to ponder the matter too much (cf. Strauss 1970: 84, Buzzetti 2014: 299–300). The *Kyroupaideia* offers a formal parallel in that only the first book covers the education proper of Cyrus the Great. On the textual history of *Anabasis*, see Thomas 2021a.

Listeners and Readers

I suppose that, like every writer, Xenophon imagined his potential audience as large. Considering his links to important historical figures, his adventures out in the world and the range of themes which he addresses in his works, in his case that expectation was not unrealistic.[2] The subjects dealt with in *Anabasis* indicate that Xenophon may have had a few distinct audiences in mind. The question I seek to answer here is, in addition to his everyman listener, to whom did he wish to speak? Was there a particular *polis*, social class, intellectual or professional group? By identifying one or more of these, by the degree of inflection we may gain insight into the writing motivations behind the text.

It is the case that in other of his works Xenophon speaks to certain audiences, and we should look to those as potential ones for *Anabasis* as well. To start at the end, in *Poroi* he prescribes ways to improve the economy of Athens, and as we saw in the last chapter, the second part of *Hellenika* is concerned to a significant degree with key events at Athens and events affecting Athenians.[3] Then we can assume that the treatises on horsemanship and hunting (*Peri Hippikes, Kynegetikos*) were principally for the landed class. Sparta is a further distinct category: *Hellenika, Agesilaos* and *Lakedaimonion Politeia* are all in varying degrees relevant to this *polis*.

Although today we regard Socrates as an outstanding Hellenic cultural figure, from the literary record and evidence from law courts we know that not all of his fellow Athenians were enamoured of him. Xenophon's structuring of two of his formal Socratic works (*Apologia, Memorabilia*) around the charges levelled by the Athenians, and the fact that the other two (*Oikonomikos, Symposion*) are set in and close to Athens, would seem to be an indication that the cycle was aimed at this audience. Considering that we have a particular representation of the philosopher and his teaching in them, another certainly was those anywhere interested in ethics and justice and in the figure of Socrates himself. Perhaps we should even see

---

2 In the fourth century we should probably think listeners rather than readers. Knox (1985: 7) observes: 'early and late, ancient reading was predominantly reading aloud, performance in fact – before a smaller audience than at the Dionysia or at Olympia but still performance. The book, at this early stage of transition from a fully oral to a fully literate society, serves as a script for recital rather than as a text for individual study.' Nonetheless, copies would have been circulated, typically to influential figures and people close to the author: see Pelling 2013: 41–2 citing Turner 1952: 19.
3 See Chapter 1 p. 34, with reference to Tuplin (1993: 33), who comments that 'it would be singular if it [part two] were written entirely without thoughts about Athens and what Athenians might learn from it. Indeed it is a virtually inescapable assumption that Xenophon expected the work to have, at least *inter alia*, an Athenian audience.'

Socrates' own audience in these works – young men of ability and leadership potential – as the intended one.[4]

While, on the face of it, without a preface and with a physical setting outside of the Greek world, *Anabasis* does not have an obvious target in the way other of the author's writings do, nevertheless we can match narrative strands in the book with several of the named groups above. In broad terms, its Socratic and panhellenic flavours, and the fact that it deals with politico-military events in real (linear) time and place, make it of interest to a cross-section of Greek readers. Given the risk of circularity and of an ultimately unsatisfactory conclusion it might be enough, even sensible, to stop with this every-group; on the other hand, making the effort to cycle through key thematic elements in *Anabasis* might reveal one or more groups that stand out.

One of the dominant themes is leadership, which in terms of audience points to men with the ambition to assume high office and military command. We meet several such in dialogue with Socrates in *Memorabilia*. Notably these need not originate from any special background: he himself indeed emphasises the transferability of skills, which leads to his argument that successful businessmen are likely to make successful military leaders (3.4.2–6). Although he never read any of his writings, Xenophon's guest-friend, Proxenos of Boiotia, who from his youth 'wanted to become a man capable of achieving great things' (*Anabasis* 2.6.16), would be a typical example of who he might have had in mind (see further 2.6.16–20). Vivienne Gray names others outside of the Socratic circle: Prokles of Phleious (*Hellenika* 6.5.38), Polydamas of Thessaly (*Hellenika* 6.1.2–3) and Agesilaos and his son Archidamos.[5]

Another dominant theme in *Anabasis* is personal apologia, and a main audience here would be Athenians. His fellow countrymen are signalled in different ways at numerous junctures in the text (for example 3.1.45, 4.6.16, 7.6.33, 7.7.57), and as I argue in Chapter 4, the work acts as a defence against his exile from Athens. We can note too that his style of leadership is Athenian, and in his vital speeches to the army by the Zapatas (Greater Zab) River he alludes to the military triumphs of Athens and to Athenian democratic practice. From still another perspective, the appearance of Socrates with Xenophon at 3.1.5 and the talk of getting into trouble with

---

4   Kelly argues that Xenophon had in mind his peers when writing (1996: 161–2); Christ (2020) similarly contends that we should see elite Athenians as the main intended audience for Xenophon's writing. Buzzetti envisages 'high-minded and talented youths with some political ambition' (2014: 293).
5   Gray 2011a: 54.

the city must have been pointed reminders of historical events at home for Athenian listeners.[6]

Sparta is a further important presence in *Anabasis*. Given the focus in the final book on its governance around the Propontis, the text could even be read to some extent as commentary on Spartan hegemony of the Greek world in the aftermath of the Peloponnesian War.[7] Such a treatment would of course be of interest to others, but the focus on their activities must have drawn and been intended to draw the attention of Spartans. The view (Chapter 1 p. 25) that Xenophon finished *Anabasis* after Skillous and after Spartan hegemony was at an end encourages us to imagine that he was not constrained in his treatment by ties to the *polis*.[8] With regards to panhellenism, in Chapter 1 I indicated that this was a theme Xenophon did not need to advertise to attract readers interested in the subject. Later in this one I show how it is worked carefully into the narrative with both positive and negative slants detectable, so although a reader would come to the story of the march expecting food for thought on the subject, and receive it, anyone looking for unequivocal support for the idea – or a basis for outright rejection – would be disappointed.

Going back to the non-Greek setting of the story, it may be worth asking if Xenophon had in mind any foreign audience. Leaving aside matters of reading cultures and language barriers, it is not out of the question that he did have an expectation of outside interest in the text. Indeed, when we think of the cosmopolitan and open nature of Athens, it seems likely that in this local sense a foreign audience was envisaged. Beyond that, the non-Greeks Xenophon encounters on the expedition could conceivably learn from his own experiences and from the leadership exposition offered in the work. Cyrus the Younger exemplifies this possibility being a barbarian whose openness to Greek values – presumably arising from contact with Greeks

---

6 I have in mind both the trial of Socrates in 399 and, quite possibly around the same time, Xenophon's exile, mentioned later at 5.3.7, 7.7.57. Gera (1993: 24) reports but is sceptical about the notion that in the story in *Kyroupaideia* (3.1.38–40) of an Armenian sophist who is killed by the king for corrupting his son, Xenophon is making a conciliatory gesture to the Athenians following their repeal of his exile. See McCloskey 2017 for further discussion of this interesting episode.

7 Krentz in his commentary on the second part of *Hellenika* (1995) writes that Xenophon's detailed treatment of the Thirty, 'a model of rulers who fail', is also intended to highlight the failure of Spartan imperialist methods as, although the oligarchs are thirty, 'their rule is essentially the same as a dekarchy' (122). This idea expands the range of the theme of critique of Spartan power during its ascendancy.

8 Powell (2020: 24–7) highlights a number of areas which he argues are suggestive of a Spartan audience, for example, the author's usage of Spartan military terms (ἐνωμοτάρχης, 3.4.21; ἐνωμοτία, 3.4.22), telling exchanges between Xenophon and Kheirisophos (3.1.45, 4.6.14–16) and the former's self-representation as a willing servant of Sparta (3.2.37).

during the period of his satrapal rule in western Anatolia, c. 407–401 – contributed to his stature as a leader (for Cyrus represented as a Greek, see Chapter 3 pp. 98–9). While such could be read as a form of cultural panhellenism, in light of Xenophon's Socratic mission it seems more apt to regard his lessons in virtue and leadership as transcending ethnic and sociopolitical boundaries. I visit this subject again in the next chapter.

Two further audiences that may have been on the author's mind deserve notice. We should, I think, consider posterity as something Xenophon was very conscious of during his writing career. Traces of this are apparent in several works, for example at the closing of *Hellenika*, where he writes: 'To this point, then, let it be written by me. Perhaps someone else will be concerned with what happened after this' (7.5.27). In the case of *Anabasis* I argue that a function of the march record is to inscribe the journey in cultural memory. The fixed register of parasangs and *stathmoi* serve as an enduring literary monument to the army – and not just to the Greeks but to the remote tribes, such as the Taochoi, who they encountered along the way.[9] Another less obvious if not remote audience could be a female one. In her study of *Kyroupaideia* Due speculates that the interest in food and drink, everyday life and pomp and splendour shown in the text may suggest Xenophon was thinking of a female audience. 'I do not say this', she writes, 'in order to be condescending to my own sex, but I am trying to explain why the Xenophontean works and world seem to me to be much more open and wide than, say, those of Thucydides or Plato.'[10]

What Is It?

The existence of fundamental questions about the nature of *Anabasis* is certainly in part the result of the absence of any statement or indication of purpose in the work.[11] Xenophon may have thought his intention was obvious, but he may have preferred too to leave this matter open, perhaps with the aim of maintaining the curiosity of his readers. At any rate he was at odds with prominent predecessors such as Hekataios, Herodotus and Thucydides, who each open their works with programmatic statements. Nor, for that matter, and for all the durability and influence of *Anabasis* through the ages, was this authorial decision to find many imitators. We

---

9 On posterity as an audience for the work, see Flower 2012: 44; *contra* Powell 2020: 43. I discuss the case of the Taochoi later in the chapter.
10 Due 1989: 234.
11 Like *Anabasis*, *Hellenika* begins *in medias res*, though in that case the fact is consistent with the first part of the work being, as most consider, a continuation of Thucydides. Defosse (1968) argued for 'une lacune' at *Hellenika* 1.1.1 but the case for such has been demonstrated to be weak (see MacLaren 1979). For thoughts on beginnings in Xenophon, see Dillery 2017: 201, and on the topic generally, Dunn and Cole 1992.

only need look to Ammianus Marcellinus (31.16) at the other end of antiquity to see that the programmatic statement retained its prominence in historiography.[12]

Not unrelated to this, there is, as Rosie Harman has pointed out, an issue with confounded expectations. We start off with Cyrus the Younger and the Persian Empire and expect the story to be about a rebellion, yet it ends with the prince's death in Book 1. The struggle of the Greeks to return home then suggests a *nostos* narrative, but the army never does return home (at least not to mainland Greece) in the frame of the text; then there is contradictory talk of founding cities, though these projects are never seen through. 'This lack of resolution of expectations leaves the reader unsure what to make of the narrative: what sort of story are we left with?'[13]

A third unsettling element in the story is the presence of multiple thematic strands, with none apparently sufficiently pronounced for it to be a story about that. These include moral and political philosophy, horsemanship and the benefits of cavalry, mercenaries, memorialisation, friendship, panhellenism, Spartan hegemony over the Greek world, self-defence and defence of Socrates. Measuring their comparative importance has not proved to be easy, a circumstance explained by their artful integration into the narrative, by the above-mentioned absence of a prologue to the work and by the complex configuring of the narrative.[14] In this last regard, Xenophon has three – or four – presences in *Anabasis*: as the author, as a character in the story and, behind this, the historical participant in the march; the fourth would be as the narrator of the story, though there is a view that s/he is a third figure, independent of author and character but is still of course Xenophon. This mix is further complicated by Xenophon's

---

12 Ammianus' statement comes at the very end of his work, and interestingly bears a strong similarity to the close of Xenophon's *Hellenika*, both authors hinting that their narratives should be taken up by others capable of the task. The first thirteen books of Ammianus are lost, so it is unknown whether there was a prologue as well: for the historiographical context of the work, see Sabbah 2003. On the influence of *Anabasis*, Arrian named his account of Alexander's campaigns *Alexandrou Anabasis*, and arguably Caesar's commentary on the Gallic War (*Bellum Gallicum*) reflects Xenophon's work in important ways, being for instance structured around seven books and written in the third person.
13 Harman 2016: 133–4. I add to this catalogue the anti-climactic participation of the Greeks at the Battle of Cunaxa. After the setting of a tense, even epic stage for the conflict between Cyrus and the King, we finish the main battle phase with the Greeks chasing off some of the enemy with no clashes to speak of (I discuss this episode below, pp. 65–6).
14 Tamiolaki's observation on the challenge of genre identification with *Kyroupaideia* could just as well be applied to *Anabasis*: 'an attempt to single out only one element in defining its genre collides with the multifarious character of this work; on the other hand, naming it simply a blending (or mixture) of different genres is an easy (but rather unsatisfactory) way to get away from the problem' (2017: 181).

attributing of authorship to another, one Themistogenes of Syracuse, who is not mentioned in the text but is referred to in *Hellenika*. This Themistogenes may be the narrator of the story.[15]

> The story of how Cyrus gathered an army and with it marched upcountry against his brother, how the battle between them turned out, how Cyrus himself was killed, and how after this the Greeks made their way safely back to the sea – all this has been written by Themistogenes of Syracuse. (3.1.2)

Writers in antiquity seem to have viewed the text more straightforwardly, with most taking it as a narrative of events on the march.[16] Even so, those coming to the work from a more literary perspective showed awareness of deeper waters: Lucian berates Xenophon for omitting a preface (*De historia conscribenda* 23) while Plutarch, owing to the Themistogenes passage, emphasised a personal agenda (*De gloria Atheniensium* 345e). In terms of a prevailing theme, we could highlight military leadership, as ancient readers certainly saw *Anabasis* as a resource for armies on campaign. Alexander refers to the Ten Thousand as his men prepare to face the Persians (Arrian, *Anabasis Alexandrou* 2.7.8–9), as does Antony amidst a desperate campaign in the east (Plutarch, *Life of Antony* 45.6). Bearing in mind that Xenophon was known through antiquity as a philosopher, we have another important way of understanding the text. As an illustration of this I suggest in Chapter 5 that the key episode in *Anabasis* where Socrates is introduced to the story alongside Xenophon (3.1.5–7) would have been read in a philosophical light by contemporaries, thereby imbuing the remainder, and indeed the whole of the work, with a Socratic flavour.

For modern readers it was not until the revival of interest in Xenophon in the later part of the twentieth century that *Anabasis* began, figuratively, to shake the crust off its parasangs. As new readings and interpretations revealed underlying connections between his works, the exceptional character of the text emerged. The extraordinary number of descriptions applied in our time attest to the difficulty of defining it; that the work can be simultaneously defined by labels as diverse as 'apologia', 'travelogue'

---

15 On the different presences of Xenophon in the text and their interrelationships, see Bradley 2010, Grethlein 2012 and Pelling 2013. Grethlein (2012: 37) links questions about the work's purpose to the relationship between character and narrator in the text. McCloskey argues that Themistogenes is the narrator (2017: 622–5), an idea I look at in Chapter 4. Along with most readers I think that Themistogenes is a pseudonym; however, as I argue later, I think it is used as a means of signalling that the work is not formally autobiographical rather than, as many believe, a means of enhancing the credibility of the account.
16 See Arrian, *Peripl. M. Eux. passim*; Polybius 3.6.9–12; Diodoros 14.19–31, 37; Diogenes 2.50.

and 'political philosophy' is a measure of its richness in meaning rather than necessarily a failure to grasp what that essentially is.[17]

Two monographs from the 2010s tackle the question about its nature, one claiming to have uncovered 'the authentic plan of the *Anabasis*'. Adopting a Straussian approach to the text (reading the author between the lines), Eric Buzzetti seeks to reveal it as a work of political philosophy whose aim is to analyse the nobility and goodness of the political life and, more specifically, to show that *Anabasis* 'makes the freedom of Hellas more accepting of the highest manifestation of civilization – philosophy'.[18] Original a reading as this is, it feels to me as if the author's three-stage plan shoehorns the narrative into his idea of what it is. This is a sense reinforced by there being arguably insufficient attention to the geographical, personal and literary contexts in which the story is set.[19]

---

17 Descriptions and labels proposed by scholars include: *work of personal apologetics*, Schwartz 1889, Mesk 1922/3, Erbse 2010, Azoulay 2004; *autobiography*, Momigliano 1990, Gera 1993, Gray 2011b; *an autobiographical history*, Purves 2010; *autohistoire*, Dan 2014; *auto-eulogy and apology*, Nicolai 2018; *didactic work on leadership and military practice*, Tuplin 1991; *an enlightenment narrative which elucidates the seductive charms of the nexus of despotism, economy, and voluntary servitude*, Diken 2021; *eyewitness account of a military campaign*, Waterfield 2006; *guidebook*, Bell 1911; *monograph on a historical event*, Grethlein 2013; *irregular work of history*, Lendle 1995; *military handbook*, Boucher 1913; *military memoir*, Westlake 1987, Luce 1997, LaForse 2005, Lee 2007; *military theory*, Spaulding 1937; *novelesque autobiography*, Bradley 2010 (or more specifically, a shift during the story from history to this form, which is defined as 'a prose narrative that exhibits narrative structures and characteristics typical of the novel in presenting the author as a fictively wrought character at the centre of recent historical events'); *polemic against other generals*, Calvino 1999; *political philosophy*, Ambler 2008, Buzzetti 2008 and 2014; *response to other accounts of the expedition*, Tarn 1927, Cawkwell 1972 (restated 2004); *response to Spartans' attempts to dominate their fellow Greeks following the King's Peace*, Millender 2020; *story of philosophical self-discovery interwoven with a military adventure*, Howland 2000; *story of temporary polis of fighting men on campaign*, Nussbaum 1967; *story of trust and deceit*, Hirsch 1985; *literary travel*, Higgins 1977; *travel narrative and political analysis*, Rood 2010; *traveller's memoir*, Roy 2007; *travelogue*, Adams 2007; *reflective autobiographical travelogue*, Cartledge 2002. Although it seeks to represent them fairly, this list does not claim to be precise in terms of its categorisation of opinions, which, moreover, may have changed. Apart from *Kyroupaideia*, the genre assignment of Xenophon's other works presents fewer challenges to modern scholars (for a discussion of the problems of describing *Kyroupaideia*, see Gera 1993: 1–13 and Tamiolaki 2017: 180–9). The number of explanations for *Anabasis* makes an evaluation of each here impractical, though a number are engaged with during the study.
18 Buzzetti 2014: 171 and 227.
19 For an evaluation of the work, see the reviews of Tamiolaki 2015, Günther 2015 and Gish 2016. Rood (2015) offers a strong critique of Straussian readings of *Anabasis* although in this piece he does not engage with Buzzetti's monograph (presumably published only after Rood submitted his article). Flower (2017a: 7) defines the Straussian method as 'a reading according to the principle that what Xenophon says is consistently

In his monograph on *Anabasis*, a highly accomplished engagement with the text, Michael Flower is more cautious about committing himself to a single view, citing instead that of John Marincola, which he describes as the 'most sensible generic description of the *Anabasis*':[20]

> a narrative history of recent events, focalized around an individual group, which tells of dangers, survival, and return against enormous odds and powerful foes. Here adopting the 'story' format eschewed in the *Hellenica*, Xenophon writes a contemporary account with a unity of plot, imposing a beginning and end on a set of events.[21]

Considering the detailed and largely accurate march record that underpins the story, it seems to me that a relation to historiography is certain.[22] That said, in comparison with the engagements of Herodotus and Thucydides, Xenophon often seems lacking as a historian. For example, arguably we would not say of *Anabasis* what Baragwanath concludes about Herodotus' histories: 'the work of an author acutely aware of the problems of historiography; of one possessing the extra perceptions available to the careful analyst, who is deeply mindful of the contested nature of the past, and sensitive to the opposing views it provokes'.[23] In comparing him to Thucydides a commonplace is to charge Xenophon with moralising rather than event analysing, and another, again not unjustified, is that he has a tendency to omit details or events which do not suit his own narrative.[24] While this characterisation is usually ascribed to *Hellenika*, such historiographical weaknesses are manifest too in the *Anabasis* narrative, as for instance in the lack of transparency concerning the role of Sparta in the expedition of Cyrus.[25]

---

the opposite of what he means for those clever enough to read between lines or to perceive the tension between passages that convey conflicting messages'. Cf. McCloskey 2017: 632. For the Straussians speaking for themselves, see Burns 2015.

20 Flower 2012: 44. However, he is less cautious in a later piece, describing it as 'the first memoir' (2017a: 2. Cf. H-R 14).

21 Marincola 1999: 316. But one might wonder about the imposition of a beginning and end given, as we have seen, both are not wholly satisfactory; nor is the author strictly writing about recent events, given he writes some thirty years after them. On the difficulty of fitting *Anabasis* into a category, see further Marincola 2017.

22 On the march record, see Brennan forthcoming. H-R (15) write that the closest antecedent to *Anabasis* as a whole is Thucydidean historiography.

23 Baragwanath 2008: 323.

24 For a particular treatment of moralising in Xenophon, namely the dangers posed by *eros* for a military commander, see Hindley 1994. For discussion of remarkable omissions in *Hellenika*, see Henry 1966: 3-5, 7, Grayson 1975: 31-2, Krentz 1989: 6-7, Flower 2017b: 305-8, Powell 2020: 13-23.

25 Powell (2020: 25), quite plausibly, thinks that Xenophon's inclination to downplay Sparta's role was to avoid associating the state with a failed enterprise, and one which made it more likely the Persians would strike out at eastern Greeks.

In this respect Cartledge is surely right to hold that Xenophon was not 'a historian in the proper sense'.[26] An explanation for this might be at hand if, firstly, we allow for the distinctive fourth-century historiographical trend wherein a greater emphasis was laid on the moral value of history,[27] and secondly, we acknowledge and appreciate the fact that to a degree Xenophon followed his own path, developing effective approaches to realising his writing aims. One might then see his omission of a preface or statement of intent as consistent with these factors, being a deliberate positioning of his work away from those of predecessors and an encouragement to readers to pay attention to its multiple a-historic thematic strands.[28]

A second generic affinity is to the travelogue, a variant on Marincola's 'story' above. Facilitating both global and personal perspectives, this allowed a range of concerns and interests to be integrated into the narrative while not unduly diminishing the intrinsic power of the journey to hold an audience. It is tempting to imagine Xenophon reflecting on his extraordinary journey, perhaps even having already sat down to write, and gradually realising that he could deal with events lying outside its scope and give expression to his apologetic *Tendenz* and didactic leanings through a travelogue format. It might not be an exaggeration to claim that his success in doing so in *Anabasis* laid the ground for the longevity of the travel narrative in Western literature.[29]

A third defining feature of the work, as Buzzetti emphasises and I argue through the course of this book, is the connection with Socrates. Although the respective ways in which this is worked out are different, I share Buzzetti's view that the philosopher is a key presence in *Anabasis*.[30] As he does in a number of his other writings, Xenophon here I believe looks to

---

26 Cartledge 1987: 67; see also Powell 2020: 43. Marincola 2014 and 2017 takes the discussion forward, in the latter with a comparison of Xenophon to his predecessors, a subject also treated in the same volume by Michael Flower (2017b).
27 See Marincola (2007: 1–8) for the broader picture of historiographical development in Graeco-Roman culture and Pownall (2004) and Parmeggiani (2014) for the fourth century in particular. 'It seems', the latter writes, 'that intellectuals of this period ... looked for new modes of writing, deliberately crossing the boundaries between genres' (2014: 3).
28 Marincola (2017: 103) lists the techniques used by Xenophon in *Anabasis* (and *Hellenika*) which his predecessors, Herodotus and Thucydides, had developed; H-R (15) highlight important ways in which Xenophon is similar to and different from Thucydidean historiography.
29 See further Burgess 2010, Humble 2011, King 2012.
30 On Socrates in *Anabasis* with Xenophon represented as an outstanding pupil, see Brennan 2011. Buzzetti does not give much weight to the apologetic argument I am concerned with (2014: 35–6) and adopts an approach – the *logos* of *Anabasis* as an introduction to philosophy – that in my opinion diverges a bit too far from the historical aspect of the work. I note specific points of difference with his readings during the monograph.

promote the value of *his* Socrates' teaching and to defend him against the charges brought at his trial. Unlike in those works where Socrates is made to demonstrate his own worth and innocence, in *Anabasis* his student's exemplary conduct and leadership performance achieves these ends. In the sense that the narrative thus perpetuates the values of the philosopher and is shaped by them, we could in a meaningful sense describe it as a 'Socratic history'. Substituting this term for 'narrative history of recent events' and 'travelogue' for 'story' in Marincola's formula above may yield a description of the work that is closer to its true nature.

'Socratic History'

While scholars have explored the idea of Socratic history, a fuller and more tractable basis for the term remains a desideratum. Such would enable the output of Socratics individually and collectively to be considered from that perspective in a more meaningful way. I offer here a limited contribution to this discussion, one not intended to be a history of the term or a methodical exercise in producing a definition for it. As a starting point, I look at how the idea plays out in other of Xenophon's writings; specifically, I look in summary detail at a selection of studies which discern substantial Socratic influence in his other major historiographical-type works, *Hellenika* and *Kyroupaideia*.

It is worth reminding ourselves of the context for the production of historical and Socratic writing in the fourth century. In Chapter 1 I highlighted Xenophon's personal background and the turbulent political environment at Athens which may have been the spur for him to leave the city. Pownall argues that the instability and upheaval of the late fifth century paved the way for a change in the way the past was used in historical writing. In this, she writes that the influence of Socrates (among others) was significant:

> [His] search to elicit from his interlocutors the definitions of basic moral virtues in order to help them see the best method to achieve right conduct in their given sphere of life thus seems to have induced both Plato and Xenophon, the two of his circle whose works containing historical material are extant, to use the past as a means of moral instruction of the elite.[31]

---

31 Pownall 2004: 21. The author points to Isokrates as being another prominent figure in the change she argues for. The Athenian had his own school of philosophy/rhetoric, and his students included the historians Ephoros and Theopompos. Although Isokrates' influence on Xenophon was far less than that of Socrates, it was not negligible in terms of his writing. Xenophon, for instance, seems to engage with *Panegyrikos* in *Anabasis*: see Chapter 4 pp. 159–61.

Tuplin and Hobden, in their consideration of Xenophon's desire to encapsulate the past, centre Socrates in his thought and motivation for writing. The natural result of this is a degree and type of manipulation of the past that is distinctive. More broadly, the death of Socrates, 'perhaps the most contested event in Athenian history',[32] is the catalyst for the literary-philosophical industry that begins to turn out promotional works about Socrates in the first half of the fourth century. 'The written record . . . has to exist to combat the idea that Socrates' life ended in failure and to extend his capacity to exert a good influence.'[33] This leads to what they term 'a species of history-writing'.[34] Their conception of this class is broad and goes beyond conventional historiography to become history staged in the literary world. This inclusive understanding enables much of Xenophon's output, and by extension that of other Socratics, to be so categorised, but ironically marginalises those writings that conform to a more recognisable historical description. I return to this distinction later but first touch on some of the ways other scholars see Socratic influence in the two historiographical works under discussion.

Hellenika

A number of readers coming from different perspectives have argued for the influence of Socrates in *Hellenika*. Ludwig examines Socratic themes in the work and what happens in historiographical terms when a Socratic considers political events.[35] He brings into relief Xenophon's distinct focus on 'the human things' and in particular his engagement with the problem of justice. This is framed within a consideration of realism in Thucydides and connects with the explorations of other theorists such as Dobski. The latter, proceeding from his opinion that in Books 1–2 Xenophon implicitly corrects Thucydides' judgement about what the best regime at Athens instituted during his lifetime had been (8.97), put forward an argument that these books are informed by Socratic thinking. I do not comment on his conclusion about Xenophon's preferred regime but highlight his view that Xenophon's impetus originates in Socrates and that the putative correction in the continuation is 'a Socratic response'.[36]

---

32 T-H 7.
33 Ibid. p. 23.
34 Ibid.
35 Ludwig 2017.
36 Dobski 2009: 317. Similarly, Ludwig (2017: 529) envisages 'a dialogue' between Thucydides and Xenophon, with Xenophon foregrounding a Socratic approach. Rood shows that in the first part of *Hellenika* the author is not only concerned with ethics but is interested in politics as well, and that 'his political analysis is thoughtfully linked with Thucydides" (2004b: 359).

In the same volume as Dobski, Gish argues that the account of the Kinadon conspiracy in Book 3 invites parallels to the trial of Socrates. Contending that Xenophon's reflections on politics and justice are indebted to his teacher, he goes on to write that 'Xenophon's critique of the Spartan regime, and its vulnerability to corruption, is profoundly Socratic.'[37] I add to this Krentz's view (note 7) about the failure of Spartan imperialist methods and the idea that the second part of *Hellenika* presents us with models of rulers who fail.

Paul Cartledge touched upon the possibility of the philosopher's influence in *Hellenika* in considering the big question of why Xenophon wrote the book. Remarking that 'its choice and treatment of material are esoteric, sometimes almost capricious', he characterises it as among the author's most puzzling productions.[38] One of the possible answers he offers to the question – but does not prefer – is an implicit Socratic agenda. 'Or did [Xenophon] perhaps aim to conflate the two, that is to manipulate history to teach philosophy by examples, employing a deceptively simple but in fact subtly allusive literary manner for the purpose?'[39] Cartledge furthermore remarks on the indisputable moralising tendency of the author, and to the extent that this shapes the narrative more than analysis and systematic reporting of important events, the case for a type of ethical-based history is reinforced.[40]

Kyroupaideia

Attempts to categorise Xenophon's telling of the life story of Cyrus the Great are invariably contentious, with opinions tending to cluster around one or a blend of labels such as fiction, drama, biography, historiography and political philosophy (see references to the discussion at the end of note 17). Many discern a Socratic influence, and not many would argue against the work having some real historical relevance, for example as a resource for Achaemenid history. Some are prepared to see a historiographical character.[41]

---

37 Gish 2009: esp. 359–63 (quote from p. 363).
38 Cartledge 1987: 61.
39 Ibid. p. 62. He prefaces the discussion with a question about whether Xenophon had remained from his youth to his later years a Socratic (61).
40 Moralising: ibid. pp. 64–5. See also Krentz (1989: 6–7), who comments on Xenophon's distinctive approach to history ('more influenced by Herodotos than Thucydides, and better illumined by reading [his] other writings than by studying his predecessors'), and elsewhere (1995: 4) that Xenophon's philosophical interests resonate throughout his writings.
41 E.g. Tamiolaki 2017: 182–9. See also Hirsch 1985.

Starting with the premise that the 'pervasive influence of Socratic thought on the theological and narrative aspects of Greek historiography is a fundamental but little noted aspect of the development of the genre during the Classical period', Ellis seeks to show that in *Kyroupaideia* Xenophon rewrites a Herodotean *logos* in light of Socratic thought.[42] The rewriting of the Croesus story (Herodotus 1.6–91: *Kyroupaideia* 7.2) is, he argues, 'in accordance with theological principles expressed by Socrates in Xenophon's *Memorabilia*'.[43] In this way Xenophon is said to reject the historical principles of Herodotus in favour of a more optimistic vision of human agency. Approaching the text from a slightly different angle, Tamiolaki chooses to emphasise its historiographical elements – the prologue, narratorial comments, subtle intertextuality with the historiographical tradition – concluding that, as the narrative is regularly interrupted by Socratic-type conversations, 'it would be tempting to consider this work as historiography of a Socratic type'.[44]

Other writers, though, while recognizing the historiographical affinity, have sought to minimise this and lay emphasis on didactic and philosophical aspects of the work. Due writes that 'the Persian surroundings and the historical setting are just an exemplification, a cover, so to speak, for a discussion and an analysis of Xenophon's own time and its problems',[45] while Gera, in what is the fullest attempt to date to explore Socrates in *Kyroupaideia*, takes as her starting point Cicero's statement that Xenophon described Cyrus 'not according to historical truth but as the pattern of a just ruler' (*Letters to Quintus* 1.1.23).[46] Cizek, in examining depictions of Cyrus the Great in the Greek historians, observed that Xenophon 'writes the history of Cyrus having in view an illustration of a Socratic model, ethical and pedagogical'.[47] Of the three authors in his study, Herodotus, Ktesias and Xenophon, he places Xenophon the furthest from 'recorded data', with the *Kyroupaideia* the 'furthest removed from the historiographical structure'.[48] This leaves us in the end with the life of Cyrus converted into an ethical, philosophical and political paradigm.[49]

---

42 Ellis 2016 (quote from p. 73). Due (1989: 121–8) provides an insightful comparison of the treatments of Croesus and Cyrus by Herodotus and Xenophon respectively.
43 Ellis 2016: 89.
44 Tamiolaki 2017: 182–9 (quote from p. 189).
45 Due 1989: 10. She adds, however, that she does 'not hereby intend to say that the *Cyropaedia* is of no value as a source for better understanding of Persia and Persian institutions, but that was in my opinion not Xenophon's main aim'.
46 Gera 1993: 1; on 'Socrates in Persia', 26–131. See further Chapter 5 p. 200.
47 Cizek 1975: 538.
48 Ibid. pp. 548, 549.
49 Ibid. pp. 551–2. On the representation of Cyrus the Great by Herodotus and Ktesias, see also Gera 1993: 6.

In a more recent study, McCloskey dwells on the philosophical aspect of *Kyroupaideia*, contending that Xenophon's writings 'should be primarily approached as philosophy, not historiography'.[50] This leads to this conclusion:

> If the *Cyropaedia* is historiography-in-form-only which is, on different narratorial levels, both non-ironically and ironically focused on philosophical truth (rather than historical truth: could we call the *Cyropaedia's* genre 'Socratic historiography?'), it may provide a model for new, philosophical readings of the *Hellenika* and *Anabasis* that would address their generally negative assessment as works of historiography.[51]

This seems to go further than Tuplin and Hobden, who as I noted envisage a species of history-writing, albeit one with broad parameters for inclusion.

Does this short synopsis bring us any closer to a fuller framework for Socratic history? Arguably in one respect, in opening up space for a distinct subcategory of the genre, it does. Proceeding from the general characterisation of Tuplin and Hobden – 'scenes from the past intended to illuminate (ethical) thought and behaviour in the present'[52] – I think we can form a subcategory that draws on traditional historiography and can accommodate *Anabasis* as well as the two other Xenophontic works considered. Whereas the main category in this scheme is liberal as regards to what constitutes Socratic history writing, this more orthodox one reserves its use for writings that have greater affinity to the Classical historiographical model, marked in these three cases by their chronological framing, biographical interests and non-fictional physical settings.

To unpack this more, I think we can agree that Xenophon has produced three substantial works that conform in varying degrees and ways to a historical form. It furthermore looks as if each of these has been influenced to some notable extent by Socratic thinking; that is, Xenophon has shaped both historical material and the context in which it is set in order to facilitate illustration of Socratic precepts. I recall now my earlier idea (Chapter 1 p. 22) that certain works have a common conception, and suggest that these three were conceived as historiographical. In this frame, the distinction between them is modest, with the earliest, *Anabasis*, written in line with a traditional paradigm. *Anabasis* and *Hellenika* share similar didactic and apologetic characters, with a difference that the former's more compact

---

50 McCloskey 2017: 606.
51 Ibid. p. 631.
52 T-H 25.

chronology and the presence of a march framework situate it in closer proximity to the historical record. *Kyroupaideia* is the furthest from this but is still in important ways a work of historiography: Xenophon has chosen a historical setting with a prologue and real characters as a platform to enable a further expression of Socratic ideals. This brings us to a particular understanding of Socratic history as referring to a recognisable historiographical text that is influenced at a fundamental level by an implicit effort on the part of the author to perpetuate Socratic values.

Finally, I suggested at the start of the section that a more informed basis for understanding the term would offer us a different perspective to consider the output of other Socratics. As we do not have complete works from these apart from Plato, for whom history was not a primary interest, this exercise, it has to be admitted, is quite speculative. One author worth touching on nonetheless is Antisthenes, a close companion of Socrates. Antisthenes is thought to have written a *Cyrus* based on the life of Cyrus the Great (but conceivably it could centre on Cyrus the Younger) and is known to have written Socratic dialogues.[53] Although we just have fragments from the *Cyrus*, when we combine the interest in a figure from the past and the common agenda of the Socratics, it becomes reasonable to conjecture that this was of the type we are concerned with. The general opinion that *Cyrus* probably preceded *Kyroupaideia* may even suggest a template for the latter; *Cyrus*, or its predecessor, in turn might be the prototype for our subgenre.

The Exemplary Author

Xenophon's output of fourteen works incorporates numerous literary innovations. Hallmarks of his writing include experimentation with form, vividness in place and event descriptions,[54] and extensive use of literary devices. The range of the last in *Anabasis* especially is notable. Among others, in modern narratological terms we have foreshadowing, immersion, flashforward and flashback, use of the narrative gap, paradigm and literary apologia.[55] In this and the next part of the chapter, I look at these last two.

---

53   See the informative discussions in Due (1989: 139–41) and Gera (1993: 8–10).
54   Plutarch, referring to *An.* 1.8, applies the ancient rhetorical concept of *enargeia* (*Artax.* 8.1). 'The central idea of *enargeia*', write Allan et al., 'is that the story world appears so clearly to the listener that he experiences the illusion of being present at the events reported in the narrative' (2017: 36). See further Huitink 2019: 209–13 and, on *An.* 1.8, Wylie 1992: 131.
55   *Foreshadowing*: the loss of Menon's men in the crossing of the Taurus Mountains into Kilikia speaks to the danger of being in mountains and looks forward to the trials which await the army on its journey (1.2.25); the destruction of Tarsus by comrades of those lost in the crossing (1.2.26) warns of the dangers which mercenaries pose to cities and anticipates the storming of Byzantium (7.1.7–17); Xenophon's departure from the line

On a certain level *Anabasis* is a paradigmatic text. The details of events on the journey habitually resonate with thematic elements in the work, and the main protagonist, the character Xenophon, is a particular model of leadership. To show how Xenophon uses exemplars and to highlight their pervasiveness in *Anabasis* I examine a selection of passages from the text. These illustrate how, through incidents and people, and even physical locations, he shapes the narrative in order to serve an assortment of themes and interests. While, of these, I look only at panhellenism and morality, in following chapters on leadership and apologia the same process is evident (some of the episodes below are engaged again if with different emphases). I remark that while the highlighted passages have almost certainly been lightly adapted to achieve a desired (often didactic) outcome, they are embedded in a historic fabric, reflecting real events, people and places.

A major function of exemplars in *Anabasis* is instructional.[56] Considering Socrates' preference for teaching through dialogue, this might at first be unexpected; however, we should not overlook the ubiquitous tradition of teaching by example. As a boy Xenophon would have been introduced to the Homeric heroes and other figures considered suitable models to emulate, a pedagogical conditioning that likely affected his own didactic approach, and that of other Socratics, who were keenly aware of the power of example to affect human behaviour. Eukleides remarked, 'they learn the most beautiful things, those who imitate the most beautiful things' (SB) (Stobaios, *Anthology* 2.31.52), and Phaedo contended that wise men do not need to teach to bring about positive effects in those around them (Seneca, *Letters* 94.41 = Phaedo 12). Xenophon referred to Socrates' living example in *Memorabilia* (1.2.3), while, notably, in the *Kyroupaideia* he writes that, having witnessed it in their rulers, the inhabitants of Asia turned to wickedness: 'For, whatever the character of the rulers is, such also that of the people under them for the most part becomes' (ὁποῖοί τινες γὰρ ἂν οἱ προστάται ὦσι, τοιοῦτοι καὶ οἱ ὑπ' αὐτοὺς ὡς ἐπὶ τὸ πολὺ γίγνονται, 8.8.5; see also 8.1.8, *Lakedaimonion Politeia* 8.2 and *Agesilaos* 10.2, where

---

to speak with Cyrus on the battlefield at Cunaxa prefigures his own leadership role on the retreat (1.8.15). *Immersion*: evocative description of landscape and natural environment on march through 'Arabia' (1.5.1-2). *Flashforward* to Skillous: 5.3.7-13. *Flashback* to Athens: 3.1.4-8. *Narrative gap*: Xenophon is a master of conjuring a space for his readers to fill for themselves and of avoiding revealing more than he has to about a situation. We experience this at the very opening of the book (1.1.1) with the story beginning in such a way as to invite a reconstruction of the preceding history. For other literary devices identifiable in *Anabasis*, see Tsagalis 2009. For a more complete look at Xenophon as writer, see H-R 36-8, 69.

56 For functions which exemplars could have in an ancient literary text, see Marincola 2014: 56. Kelly, in his monograph on Ammianus, provides a detailed consideration of the term (2008: 258-66). Needless to say, not all of the models given in *Anabasis* are positive, and in the opposite case they function as lessons in how not, or what not, to do.

Xenophon holds up the Spartan king as a universal model of goodness). In *Anabasis*, pointedly at a time of crisis, Xenophon's character tells the generals and captains:

> The soldiers here all have their gaze fixed upon you, and if they see you being faint-hearted, they will all be cowardly; but if you show yourselves to be making preparations against the enemy and you summon the others to join you, there's no doubt about it: they will follow you and try to imitate you. (3.1.36)

A striking feature of Xenophon's use of exemplars in *Anabasis* is his rooting of these in a real context. His detailed and largely accurate march record provides the foundation for the lessons in leadership and virtue he wishes to provide. In this way one form of truth complements another, and consequently the impact of the individual episodes is greater. The factual strata, moreover, keep his audience engaged by playing on their knowledge of the expedition's historicity. We might draw a contrast here with Ktesias' *Persika* and *Indika*, which inhabit a terrain between fact and fiction, and with Xenophon's formal Socratic works, where anachronism and lack of specificity place us almost on the same plane.[57]

Exemplarity in Anabasis: *Panhellenism*

Xenophon never directly broaches the subject of panhellenism, though as noted earlier, as the storyline of the book is distinctly relevant to the idea he need not strictly have done so even if his intention were to contribute to the discussion. I think this was one of his intentions in *Anabasis* and that at several junctures he inserts telling comment or presents an event in a way that speaks to the theme. This may constitute an encouragement, or a discouragement, to panhellenic action.[58]

---

57 Marincola 2014 discusses 'rhetorical history', one of the characteristics of which he describes as 'the composition of speeches and even of actions based not on any historical record but on the criteria of probability and appropriateness' (41). By way of comparison, the approach in *Anabasis* is more grounded. On the veracity of Xenophon's march record, see Brennan 2012 and forthcoming.

58 On panhellenism and *Anabasis*, see further Chapter 1 p. 20. Examples in addition to the two examined in this section include: 1.5.8: discouragement – discipline of Persian elite class on display; 1.5.9: encouragement – nature of the empire, 'strong in the magnitude of its territory and the number of its people, but weak from its extended lines of communication and the dispersal of its forces if someone mounted a swift attack'. LaForse (2013: 32 n.15) further points to 1.3.1–21, 1.7.3–5 and 5.5.8–23. For *Anabasis* as a negative paradigm for panhellenism, see Rood 2004a, Flower 2012, Gray 2021. I recall Peter Wiseman or Claude Kananack in a discussion about Valerius at Exeter (research seminar, 12 March 2009) asking if the author could be inviting his readers to disagree with him. Perhaps Xenophon is doing the same on this subject, or at least looking to complicate the debate.

Battle of Cunaxa (1.8)

The events on the battlefield in Babylonia where Cyrus fatally clashed with his brother have long been the subject of scrutiny and debate. With more than one eyewitness account surviving, there is unique scope for discussion.[59] A remarkable feature of Xenophon's is his report that not a single Greek was killed in the encounter (οὐδ' ἄλλος δὲ τῶν Ἑλλήνων ἐν ταύτῃ τῇ μάχῃ ἔπαθεν οὐδεὶς οὐδέν, 1.8.20). The supplementary information that 'on the left wing someone was said to have been shot by an arrow' affirms the extraordinary outcome and assures readers that they have not misunderstood what happened in the battle. The fact that almost every clash on the ensuing retreat results in casualties, with less than half of the force ultimately surviving (though some of this loss is down to attrition rather than action), accentuates the oddness of Xenophon's report here. Moreover, we have a contradictory report in Diodoros, who refers to Tissaphernes on the Persian side as killing 'great numbers of the enemy' (14.23.6: see note 60 for complete sentence), but these need not have been Greeks.

However, if we are to take its substance to be true, which following from my view about the work's historical fidelity I believe we probably should, then there should be an explanation available for the outcome. I think there is, and that it lies in a combination of two factors: Klearchos' disobeying of Cyrus's order to attack the enemy centre and, on the other side, the nous of Tissaphernes, who deliberately gave way in order to ensure the Greeks moved still further away from the battle theatre.[60] But Xenophon, who must have been able afterward to reconstruct approximately the battlefield

---

59 In addition to Xenophon's, we have preserved in Plutarch and, later again, in Photios, fragments from Ktesias, who was the King's physician and was on the battlefield (Xenophon mentions him at 1.8.27: I discuss Ktesias' *Persika* in Chapter 4 pp. 161–3). We also have the account of the first-century universal historian Diodoros Siculus (14.22–4). Diodoros mentions one of his important sources, Ephoros, who may or may not be the indirect source for the battle, but the eyewitness might well not be Xenophon or Ktesias, as some of the detail in Diodoros is inconsistent with their versions. One possibility is said to be Sophainetos (Wylie 1992: 120); another is that an eyewitness account is preserved in the fourth-century historian Deinon, who some think reflects an Achaemenid court tradition (see Bassett 1999: 475). A brief summary of the battle (and expedition) is contained in the third-century AD *Epitome* of Justin (5.11), but there is not enough to make any connection to an earlier source.

60 On argument for such a ploy by Tissaphernes, see Ehrhardt 1994, and before that Wylie 1992. In the account of Diodoros, which as just remarked may ultimately derive from an eyewitness independent of both Xenophon and Ktesias, Tissaphernes' performance on the battlefield is singled out for praise: 'Tissaphernes, a Persian noble, now succeeded to the supreme command held by the King [after he had been wounded], and not only rallied the troops but fought himself in splendid fashion; and retrieving the reverse involved in the wounding of the King and arriving on the scene everywhere with his elite troops, he slew great numbers of the enemy' (14.23.6). Lee 2016b surveys Tissaphernes' long and successful career in Anatolia as, more reservedly, does Hyland 2018.

flow, chooses not to take his narrative along this analytical line; doing so, Plutarch condemns Klearchos for his action:

> [3] if he sought safety above everything else and made it his chief object to avoid losses, it had been best for him to stay at home ... [5] ... the caution of Klearchos rather than the temerity of Cyrus must be held responsible for the ruin of Cyrus and his cause. (*Artaxerxes* 8.3, 5)

Xenophon instead, keeping to his field of vision, reinforces a general (Greek) view of Persian military weakness, telling us that the King's army did not stand the mercenary charge: 'When they were almost a bowshot away, the enemy broke and fled' (1.8.19). This, and the statement on casualties, which may be especially open to scrutiny in light of Diodoros' report, speak to a panhellenic theme, the aim being not to discourage the formation of later expeditions. The fact that not all the Great King's forces were present on the battlefield (1.7.12) furthermore bears out the earlier panhellenic-flavoured assertion that he was vulnerable to a swift advance (1.5.9).[61]

Kalpe Harbour: An Ideal Colony (6.4.1–6)

On their journey along the southern Black Sea coast, the army stays on a beach by a natural harbour. Xenophon describes it as follows:

> [3] Kalpe Harbour lies in the middle of the voyage between Heraclea and Byzantium, from whichever way one comes, and is a promontory in the sea, forming a stronghold. It consists partly of a sheer cliff extending out to sea, at its lowest no less than 120 feet in height, partly of a neck which reaches up from the stronghold to the mainland, about 400 feet across; inside the neck, there is a natural stronghold large enough to house ten thousand people. [4] There is a harbour under the cliff, with a beach facing west, and there is also a spring of fresh water that flows abundantly, right by the sea and commanded by the stronghold. There is a large amount of timber of various kinds, and especially a great deal of fine shipbuilding timber right by the sea.

---

61 Depending on one's views about Xenophon's intentions in his account of the battle, other interpretations are possible. Wylie (1992: 124–6) makes a defence of Klearchos, arguing that 'the order of battle had in all probability been decided earlier (*An*. 1.7.1)', and the Spartan would have been justified in resisting any last-minute change. David Thomas in correspondence remarks on the potential effect of confused testimony from eyewitnesses about whether Tissaphernes had remained with his cavalry or gone to the King, adding that if Xenophon pushed away a different view of the battle, one much less flattering to the Greeks, that does not mean he made a conscious choice to prefer propaganda to analysis of the facts. On the battle, see Wylie 1992, Thomas 2021c.

[5] The hilly country extends into the interior for about two and a half miles, and is rich in soil and not stony, and the area along the coast for two and a half miles or so is thickly wooded, with many huge trees of different kinds. [6] The rest of the countryside is beautiful and extensive, and there are many well-inhabited villages in it, for the earth here yields barley and wheat and all kinds of pulses, foxtail millet, sesame, a sufficiency of figs, many vines producing agreeable wine, and everything else except olive trees. (6.4.3–6)

It is clear from the exceptional amount of detail and the qualities of the location that the author is signalling it would be ideal for a settlement, another Hellenic colony to complement those to the east – Sinope, Kotyora, Kerasous and Trapezous. Earlier, at Kotyora, he had spoken of how such would 'add both territory and strength to Greece' (5.6.15), and this prepared us to hear about other potential sites further along the coast.[62] Notably, the strength of the force prompts the idea at Kotyora, whereas here it is the landscape and location which induce desire for colonisation. The suspicion of the soldiers that some in the leadership were intent on founding a colony implicitly confirms the merits of the site (6.4.7). While in both cases the army preferred to continue homeward, privileging the possibility of quick gain over the longer-term benefits of being colonists, the message might be that more loyal (or savvier) Greeks could have benefited themselves and their country by availing themselves of an outstanding opportunity to add to the established Hellenic archipelago in the Black Sea region.

Given the detail of Xenophon's description, it may be surprising that the site has not been securely identified.[63] It bears mention that unlike his reports about Larisa (3.4.7–9) and Mespila (3.4.10–12) in Mesopotamia, where he likely had not the leisure to produce himself the detail he provides about those cities, here he would have had the time to record physical features (I remark that to believe he did make notes about the site at the time

---

62 The notion of colonisation surfaces earlier in the text, at 2.4.22 and 3.2.21–6, when the Greeks are in the heart of Persian territory and Xenophon argues that if all else fails they could stay and prosper. However, as Grethlein (2013: 70) observes, in these passages Xenophon 'adduces the possibility of a colony as an argument that is meant to encourage and instil hope into the Greeks' (i.e., we have encouragement to press homeward rather than to settle).

63 Many commentators plumb for locations around the modern seaside resort of Kerpe (Manfredi 1986: 241–5, Lendle 1995: 385–9, Stronk 1995: 82, Waterfield 2006: 167–9, Aslan 2014: 131–2). Arrian's placement, too, may be in this area (*Peripl. M. Eux.* 12–13). Other possibilities are Ağva and Şile further west along the coast. Although none of these sites fully evinces the description, my view is that, by dint of the given locational indicator (halfway between Herakleia and Byzantium), the area around Kerpe is the most likely.

does not require us to subscribe to the existence of a systematic travel diary). One plausible explanation for the uncertainty resides in the coastal topography, which is replete with jagged coves that approximate to his sketch; even applying a fairly strict interpretation of the given parameter – halfway between Herakleia and Byzantium – several locations are possible. Another could be down to the fact that seismic activity regularly affects the area. The explanation I prefer lies with the description itself, which I suggest incorporates adjustment of the natural features to fit with the prevalent notion of an ideal colony. Thus, the physical setting of the place, which might still be identifiable from a careful ancient depiction, is by minor adjustment to its scale and features effectively transformed beyond recognition. The knowledge that the soldiers indirectly vouch for its quality as a settlement is, perhaps, meant to assure us that any amplification on the author's part is not excessive.

Exemplarity in Anabasis: *Morality*

Character and leadership in Xenophon are closely intertwined. In *Anabasis* we see this relationship most clearly in the obituaries provided by the author for certain commanders on the expedition, a subject I look at in the next chapter. His concern for virtuous behaviour, though, extends to all the men, and is not just an element of his leadership didaxis. This is marked by his description of some of them anyway as virtual *kaloikagathoi* (6.4.8) and exemplified in his periodic calling out of bad behaviour among the ranks (5.7.12–33, 5.8.6–12). The first episode I look at falls into this last category, albeit treated in typically subtle fashion, while the second speaks of the benefit that accrues from the virtuous life.

Aineias and the Precious Robe (4.7.13–14)

During their crossing of eastern Anatolia, the Greeks encounter a number of local tribes, among them the Taochoi. Needing supplies, the force besieges one of their strongholds and eventually succeeds in taking it. Amidst a distressing scene of mass suicide, Xenophon hones in on one of the Greek officers:

> [13] Here too Aineias of Stymphalos, a captain, seeing a Taochian wearing a fine robe [στολὴν ἔχοντα καλήν] make a run to throw himself down, grabbed him in order to stop him. [14] But the Taochian dragged Aineias after him, and both went flying down the rocky cliff and were killed. (4.7.13–14)

Whether Xenophon was near this event or heard about it afterward, the detail of the 'fine robe' seems to alert us to a particular authorial interest in it. There must have been much that was unforgettable about the disturbing encounter with these people, and I suggest that his selection of this episode from amidst the carnage marks it as significant for his agenda.

We might be tempted to read this recording of his death as a sort of tribute to Aineias, yet he has not featured in the drama that led to the capture of the place and has not appeared before in the narrative. Xenophon, I think, is far from eulogising him. While he avoids openly condemning the captain for attempted theft, he is equating such an action with negative, deadly consequences (with the robe being his motivation for trying to stop the man, any other interpretation of Aineias' action would be perverse). The implied judgement on Aineias, moreover, and more strikingly, seems to extend to the army as a whole. Following what he terms the 'terrible spectacle' (δεινὸν ἦν θέαμα) of mothers hurling their children from the top of the stronghold and the women and the men jumping after them, there is the closing comment that 'from this place only a very few people were captured; but they acquired cattle and asses in great numbers, and also sheep'. Through his clinical reportage, Xenophon compels us into a moral consideration of the army's actions. In this reflective space he establishes too a covert memorial to the Taochoi, who refused at any cost to compromise their freedom.

Skillous: Xenophon in Paradeisos (5.3.7–13)

At some time following his return to Greece with Agesilaos in 394, the Spartans settled Xenophon in the Peloponnese. He describes his later life on his estate by way of a prolepsis in *Anabasis*, and there is a clear sense of this being idyllic:

> [8] It happened that through the plot of land flowed the river Selinous; and in Ephesos also, close to the temple of Artemis, there flows a river Selinous. There are fish in both rivers, and mussels; and in the plot of land in Skillous, there are also opportunities to hunt every kind of beast that is hunted . . . [10] . . . Xenophon's sons and the sons of the other townspeople used to organize a hunt for the festival, and there also hunted along with them those grown men who wanted to do so. Their quarry – boar and roe deer and fallow deer – was taken partly from the sacred precinct itself and partly also from Mount Pholoe. [11] . . . In the sacred precinct, there is a meadow and tree-covered hills, sufficient to support pigs and goats and cattle and horses, so that the draft animals of those coming to the festival have their feast too. (5.3.8, 10, 11)

The Skillous vignette has been read in a variety of ways by scholars, many of whom comment on the contentment portrayed. Dillery thinks it evokes the colonial space which Xenophon hoped he might enjoy somewhere on the shores of the Black Sea: 'the quiet and ordered life we see in this bucolic description is a capsule or miniature of the life he had hoped to lead as a prominent settler leader in Asia. Scillus, like Cotyora and [Kalpe Harbour], is described in glowing terms – a place blessed by nature.'[64] In his analysis, Rood writes that Xenophon describes the estate 'to show that it was modelled on the goddess' [Artemis'] own sanctuary at Ephesus and to stress its plentiful produce'.[65] I take this divine parallel further and suggest that Xenophon's aim is to indicate an earthly paradise. The prolepsis situates readers in future time, enabling a moral exemplar that alludes to the benefit that flows from a noble and pious life. The idyllic estate is divine reward for just action and due reverence to the gods; the abundance of meat (fish, mussels, boar, deer, gazelles), Xenophon hunting with his sons, celebrating with his neighbours, is a portrait of what could be described as a heaven on earth. As Xenophon himself indicates in his speech to the generals and captains of the army on the banks of the Zapatas River, this is the life which accrues to brave men:[66]

> I see that those who have learned that death is common to all and unavoidable for human beings, and who compete for the prize of an honourable death, are the ones who somehow or other reach old age and enjoy a happier existence as long as they live. (3.1.43)

As remarked in Chapter 1, the reality of life at Skillous would have been more mundane, and possibly quite uncertain – scholars point out that the location of the estate in a geopolitically sensitive area made it unstable and potentially dangerous.[67] Nevertheless, as with Kalpe Harbour, the essential description is likely to be fairly accurate, and there is no reason to think that Xenophon, who had endured much in his life and lived through many dangers, would not have felt himself to be in a peaceful environment.

The author's placing of the flashforward at a juncture where some in the army murdered friendly ambassadors underscores the exemplar's didactic function. The incident at Kerasous where a group of the men acting on their own attempted to raid a friendly stronghold and, afterward, stoned to death three ambassadors who had come from there to ask the Greeks why they had attacked them, is actually recalled by the author at a later point in

---

64   Dillery 1995: 90. Mahaffy (1895: 45) envisages it as a retreat where Xenophon 'combined religion, sport, and literary work'.
65   Rood 2012: 91. Christopher Tuplin in discussion at Liverpool 2021 observed that the inscription which Xenophon sets up at the temple in Skillous (5.3.13) marks the temporal end of *Anabasis*.
66   While it is very likely that Xenophon in the end was forced to leave his estate, as we know nothing concrete about what he did afterwards, that change in itself does not upend the moral truth.
67   Powell (2020: 4–5) furthermore notes that Xenophon was vulnerable to changes in the Spartan order and was subject to the unpredictability of its policymaking.

the text, 5.7.12–25, where it serves to provide a suitable background for his own actions in disciplining men. But its natural place is at 5.4.1, just after the flashforward. I refer to the episode in the next part and examine it more fully in Chapter 4 p. 144.

We can note the counterpoint to the Skillous exemplar in Menon's end. According to Xenophon, the Thessalian was about the worst human being ever to have lived. Lies, deceit, betrayal and exploitation were among his usual ways of conducting his relations with others, not to mention his habitual participation in the injustices of his soldiers. Xenophon concludes his withering obituary with the outcome of this extraordinary life. 'He is said to have met the end befitting a villain, after being tortured alive for a year' (2.6.29).

Menon's cruel end prompts comparisons with other deaths in Xenophon, which I suggest often encode the same message about the virtuous life. A striking one is the passing of Cyrus the Great in *Kyroupaideia* (8.7). Contrary to accounts in other Greek historians (see Herodotus 1.214), his death is orderly, peaceful and dignified. Surrounded by his sons and friends, he speaks of his successes and the happiness he was blessed with in each stage of his life (8.7.5–8). One of Xenophon's intentions in this portrait of the king as a dying man is surely to emphasise that a noble life ends nobly. The event incidentally brings into relief the different historiographical approaches not only of Xenophon and Herodotus, but also of *Kyroupaideia* and *Anabasis*. Going back to the Battle of Cunaxa as detailed in *Anabasis*, I suggest we have another exemplary death involving a Persian royal, except in this case a violent one.

Although it is an exception to the general truth of 3.1.43 that brave men survive battle and live happily thereafter, the end of Cyrus the Younger is stamped with nobility. Pointedly, Xenophon does not claim to have witnessed what he describes artfully at 1.8.24–9, so allowing him to retain his historical gaze.[68] While, as we garner from the narrative, the prince is still growing as a leader and his virtue is on occasion suspect, the manner of his death is heroic, and in the terms of 3.1.43, he earns the prize of honourable death at Cunaxa. The prelude is his sudden attack on the King, prompted by fear that the Greeks under his own charge would be encircled by his

---

68 An eyewitness account may survive in Ktesias, to whom Xenophon refers in his version (for the different accounts, see note 59). In some respects, their versions are alike, but the character displayed in each is very different, with the one of Ktesias arrogant and driven by a thirst for power (see *Artax.* 11). Another report survives in Deinon and may derive from the Achaemenid court tradition, which some think Xenophon could have had access to (Bassett 1999: 475–6). In this Cyrus is also portrayed negatively, showing lack of control and precision (see *Artax.* 10). The interrelationships between these accounts is discussed by Bassett 1999, Almagor 2018 and Thomas 2021c. Unlike the other two, Bassett assumes that Diodoros' version is a contracted one of Xenophon's (1999: 478). While my reading differs from hers on this and other points, I agree that Plutarch's epitomes of Ktesias and Deinon are negative as regards Cyrus (477) and that Xenophon's depiction of his death is in some way shaped by his own personal apologetic agenda (475).

brother. Cyrus's valour and that of his 600 guards succeed in scattering the 6,000-strong contingent shielding the King, with Cyrus himself said to have slain their commander, Artagerses, with his own hand. His own death in the midst of fierce combat – a javelin strikes him under the eye – is, moreover, implicitly linked to the prince's decision alone of all his men not to wear a helmet for the battle (Κῦρος δὲ ψιλὴν ἔχων τὴν κεφαλὴν εἰς τὴν μάχην καθίστατο, 1.8.6). This choice symbolises his fearlessness and the transparency of his claim to be King. As a confirmation of his worthiness, the eight best of his men die fighting to protect his body (1.8.27). The subsequent callousness of his brother, decapitating the corpse and severing Cyrus's right hand (1.10.1), serves to accentuate the nobility of the prince.

The Apologetic Author

A prominent feature of Xenophon's writing highlighted in modern scholarship is a strong apologetic *Tendenz*. In addition to self-defence, his subjects range from individuals – most notably the philosopher Socrates – to communities and social groups. In the first section I look at one such community, the Ten Thousand, and in the second a social group, the *hippeis* at Athens. Turning then to his self-defence, I show how the author makes effective use of apologetic contexts by leveraging accusations made in his narrative.[69] I start with some prefatory remarks.

Four distinct strands of apologia are apparent in *Anabasis*. The character Xenophon explicitly defends himself to an internal audience on three major occasions: the colony plan, the review of generals (Book 5) and the accusation of corruption (Book 7). Second, the author Xenophon has been held to be fending off criticisms from external audiences, for example other accounts that diminished or removed his role in the successful retreat of the Ten Thousand, condemnations of mercenaries (the Ten Thousand included) and aspects of his life history such as exile from Athens. Third, the good and pious performance of 'Xenophon', framed as a Socratic by 3.1.4–7, redounds to Socrates' credit and so implicitly rebuts the charges that Socrates corrupted the young and had unorthodox religious views. Lastly, there is an assortment of third-party defences in addition to those already mentioned. For instance, ones of Klearchos and Cyrus, and on the plain of ideas, of the notion that Greeks could successfully attack the empire.[70]

---

69 Potential factors explaining Xenophon's apologetic mindset were discussed in Chapter 1, and the subject of apologia is considered in detail in Chapters 4 (self-defence) and 5 (Socrates).
70 Bassett (2001: 7–11) argues that Xenophon is writing apologia for Klearchos, and Diken (2021: 36) that he defends Cyrus: 'Xenophon's ambition is to reconcile economy (Cyrus) and philosophy (Socrates). To do this, both men must be defended, and hence

Defence of the Ten Thousand

This is a subject that is often passed over, probably because, as one of them, Xenophon's own defence is considered to apply in many ways to the army, and in some ways it does. There is also, I think, a willingness on the part of posterity to overlook certain actions by this iconic group that might call for defence. But Xenophon himself, if he overlooks or plays down certain aspects, does not seek to justify the actions of the army, even if he explicitly defends the men on a small number of occasions. His own position here is delicate, not least as he is a part of the army – and a significant one at that. In a later chapter I explore the ways in which he separates himself in the narrative from the mercenary body.

Silence and obfuscation, the hallmarks of Xenophontic apologia, are evident in the author's representation of the Ten Thousand and serve to produce what on the surface appears to be a fairly respectable image. Moreover, the heroic circumstances of the retreat's beginning, predicated by the author on a brazen act of barbarian treachery, adeptly set the psychological tone for the external audience, who settle into the story braced for drama and willing the wronged underdog to succeed against seen and unseen enemies. In this way, Xenophon controls our perception of the journey and establishes an ostensibly favourable impression of it. We might come away thinking that if the men were roguish in moments, overall and in consideration of what they faced, they seem to have acquitted themselves admirably.[71] Yet if we allow ourselves to be enclosed in what one could term an Orientalist-type mindset, we

---

Anabasis can be read as an apology for Cyrus as well as for Socrates.' Powell (2020: 48) suggests that 'the more important apologia implicit in the *Anabasis* is for a principle: that the expedition in support of prince Kyros had not been impractical, that the Persian empire could be defeated on its own ground in future'. We can note that the speeches of others also furnish evidence for the author's apologetic mindset, with many of those being centred on defence of their own actions. For example, Klearchos' address to the soldiers at Tarsus (1.3.3–6), and in succession Klearchos to Tissaphernes (2.5.3–15) and Tissaphernes to Klearchos at the Zapatas (2.5.16–23).

71 Perhaps capturing the prevailing sentiment of his age, Horn in the 1930s envisages young Greeks on a character-building outing. 'Much is said of their games, their eating and their drinking, their experiences with novel foods and drinks, their discovery of new peoples and new ways of living and doing things, their delight in the novel experiences afforded by the expedition. We see cleverness in meeting new situations and resource-fulness on the part of the common soldier as well as on the part of the officer. These qualities should appeal to young men (perhaps more than to young women), just as they certainly appealed to the Greeks for whom Xenophon wrote' (1935: 156). Fiona Hobden (2021) offered a much different contemporary take in her thought-provoking paper at the Liverpool Xenophon conference, 'Xenophon War Criminal? Or, Reading *Anabasis* Otherwise'.

risk missing the author's own nuanced stance, one which a critical view brings into relief.

The shift in perspective already enables us to see events in a more balanced light. The tribes who line up on a mountainous ridge north of the Aras River basin before the advance of the army, rather than savages bent on thwarting the efforts of the Greeks to get home to their families, are communities trying to defend their own families. The fear which the mercenaries instilled in nearly all those they encountered is communicated to us by Xenophon in shocking reports: a Kardouchian prisoner of war refusing to divulge his knowledge of routes even when his life is threatened has his throat cut; villages in the mountains in eastern Anatolia in mid-winter are thoughtlessly burned to the ground; a collective of Armenian settlements are held captive by the Greeks, who work through their winter supplies while subjecting youths to humiliation for drunken entertainment; an entire community which tried to defend its members and property throws itself from a height to avoid the fate of capture by the Greeks; along the Black Sea coast, cities are plundered and some completely destroyed by the passing army. Demonstrating explicit condemnation, on several occasions Xenophon intervenes to try to stay the damage and to remind the men of their culture and values. At Kotyora on the Black Sea he addresses them uncompromisingly on the recent outrage in which local ambassadors were killed:

> [32] 'if you think that such deeds are characteristic of wild beasts rather than of human beings, look into some way of putting a stop to them. Otherwise, in the name of Zeus, how shall we perform sacrifices to the gods with glad hearts when we are carrying out impious deeds? Or fight our enemies, seeing that we are slaughtering each other? [33] What friendly city will take us in if they see us display such utter lawlessness? Who will dare to provide a market for us if we show ourselves to be guilty of such offenses as regards the most serious matters? And where we thought we would obtain praise from everyone, who would praise us if this is the sort of people we are? Indeed, I know we ourselves would say that those who commit such acts are scum.' (5.7.32–3)

His defence of the Ten Thousand, such as it is, is characteristically subtle, achieved largely through concentration on the challenges overcome by the men. The primary aim is to dampen criticisms made by others, ones that also of course tarnish himself. There are exceptions whereby he positively extols the merits of the men, but these are usually responses to external criticisms. Outside the frame of the story there is, for instance, the slight Isokrates sees fits to level about the men and to which Xenophon is probably responding at 6.4.8,[72] while within the story a charge by a Sinopean ambassador at Kotyora draws a sharp defence (5.5.7–23).

A telling passage that should be included in this discussion is *Hellenika* 3.2.6–7. Early in their service with the Spartans in Asia Minor, the Cyreans plundered lands belonging to their allies (*Hellenika* 3.1.8), a circumstance that may have led to Thibron, the overall commander, being replaced. The Spartans later warn the Cyreans about their conduct. 'If, then, in the future the soldiers acted unjustly, the ephors would not tolerate it, but if they behaved with justice toward their allies, they would commend them' (3.2.6). Xenophon stands up and pushes back, but he does not actually refute the charge against the men, pointing the finger of blame instead at the commander in the field, Thibron:

> 'See here, Spartans, we are the same men now as we were last year. But there is a different commander now from the one we had before. You yourselves, therefore, can figure out quite easily why we do not now act unjustly, whereas back then we did.' (3.2.7)

While, in the end, my sense is that Xenophon stops short of disowning the band so as not to undermine his writing agenda, it would be unwarranted to argue that he was solely about self-interest. If we place any store in his own Socratic background, then his interventions and efforts to moderate the behaviour of the mercenaries deserve assessment in this light too and should not be seen as manoeuvres to paint himself in a better shade.

Defence of the Hippeis

On his very first appearance in the story, Xenophon is on horseback.[73] Leaving the Greek line, he rides forward to consult Cyrus before the showdown with the King (1.8.15). The moment is surely meant to be auspicious – the hegemony of the empire is about to be decided, and Xenophon literally inserts himself into the centre and into the central narrative of the battle. It is also his departure point from it, as we saw above in the respective discussions of his account of Cyrus's death and his treatment of the Battle of Cunaxa.

---

72 At *Paneg.* 146 Isokrates says that Cyrus's Greek mercenaries were 'not picked troops, but men who, owing to stress of circumstances, were unable to live in their own cities'. I discuss this passage in Chapter 4 and argue that Xenophon is responding at *An.* 6.4.8.
73 Farrell (2012: 78–9) argues that Xenophon was in fact on foot here and that the tendency to have him on horseback in this scene arises from the long-standing view that he belonged to the Athenian cavalry class. While he makes a cogent case for this, given the indelible association between Xenophon and horses on the expedition, it is tenable to have him mounted for this moment.

This pre-battle set piece furthermore foreshadows Xenophon's character's own leadership role, and alludes to his identity as a *hippeus*, a member of the elite Athenian class of horsemen. Following their association with the Thirty at Athens (404–403), the public standing of the *hippeis* had fallen; as we saw in the previous chapter, one result was the dispatch by the democracy of 300 horsemen to Asia to join the campaign of Thibron against Persia in 399. Xenophon remarks sardonically that the Athenians 'sent those who had served in the cavalry under the Thirty, for they thought that it would be advantageous to the people if these men went abroad and died there' (*Hellenika* 3.1.4). The event may have been a spur to his representation in *Anabasis* as a horseman – the link between 'Xenophon' and horses persists through the narrative (3.3.19, 3.4.46, 4.5.35, 4.7.24, 6.2.16, 7.3.45, 7.8.2, 7.8.6) – and the book's testimony might be intended to show *inter alia* that members were virtuous and capable of doing good for those around them. Xenophon would have served alongside the 300 as part of Thibron's force in Asia and quite likely knew a number of them even before the campaign. It bears mention that Mantineia (362), where the action of the Athenian cavalry was later commemorated in the home city, so marking a positive rehabilitation of the class, happened after the publication of *Anabasis*. Xenophon's ongoing allegiance to the *hippeis* is amply evidenced by his works on cavalry command and horsemanship and by the fact of his sons serving in the Athenian cavalry in the 360s. But even if the Mantineia commemoration marked a turning point, or confirmed an earlier one, we should keep in mind that the telling *Hellenika* (3.1.4) comment on the 300 horsemen was published after 362, as was the statement in *Poroi* (6.1) about the importance of restoring ancestral payments and privileges to the *hippeis* among others (καὶ ἱππεῦσι τὰ πάτρια ἀποδώσομεν).[74]

After having brought the image of the *hippeus* to centre stage at Cunaxa, one of Xenophon's first initiatives in his later role as a leader is to form a cavalry. After crossing the Zapatas River in upper Mesopotamia, the Greeks came under severe pressure from harrying Persians and were unable to initiate any effective counter-attack. 'This was because the Greeks had no cavalry and the rearguard could not catch the enemy infantry within a short distance, since the enemy turned in flight while still a long way off; to carry on the pursuit very far from the rest of the army was impossible' (3.3.9). Perhaps tellingly, it is an Athenian, one Lykios, who is appointed commander of the new force (3.3.20) (on Lykios' father, see Chapter 1 n.82).

Through the course of the arduous retreat, the cavalry plays a prominent part in securing the survival of the army. Its capacity to scout and skirmish proves especially beneficial to the greater body of the force. Typically, at

---

74 On the history of the horsemen at Athens, see Bugh 1988, Pritchard 2018.

the moment when the Greeks sight an end to their ordeal on the march down to the sea, the horsemen are fending off attackers at the rear of the column (4.7.21–4). The many militaristic qualities which Xenophon, rarely off his horse, displays on the retreat – riding skill, valour, initiative, cunning, selflessness – are those that he wishes also to associate with the *hippeis*.[75]

Aspects of Xenophon's personal defence, a subject I examine in Chapter 4, can also be interpreted as defence of the knights. I suggest there is a conspicuous and sometimes even heavy-handed effort to show that the class are not as inherently anti-democratic as popularly held. As I show in the next chapter, Xenophon on the retreat adopts the Athenian style of leadership with, for instance, his regular calls for voting on proposals in assembly recalling the democracy in action. Strikingly, in Thrace, he draws a sharp contrast between himself and a pair of Spartan officials (sent to bring the Ten Thousand back to Asia). The Spartans are looking to recover the monies owed to the mercenaries by the Thracians, and address a warlord who is aggrieved at the ravaging of villages by the men in his newly acquired territory:

> [17] 'Well, then, we would go away as you wish,' the Lacedaemonian delegates said, 'if and when those whose actions have achieved your present position for you receive their pay. But if they don't receive it, we are even now coming to help them, and to take revenge on men who wronged them, contrary to their oaths. And indeed, if you too are people of that sort, we will begin here and now to exact what justice requires.' [18] Xenophon added, 'Medosades, you might want to turn the decision over to the people in whose land we are – since you say that they are friends of yours – for them to vote whether it is appropriate for us to leave their land or for you to do so.' (7.7.17–18)

Literary Apologia

The last feature of Xenophon's writing I look at in this chapter is 'literary apologia'. One might think of this as a sort of organic rhetorical genre which emerged from the functioning of Athenian civil institutions. Gray, in a study of classical autobiography, writes: 'The courtroom and assembly often forced orators to autobiographical defence of their past careers in real life, and this gave rise to a literature that could mimic real life for

---

75 Providing a wider context for cavalry prestige, in the earlier narrative Xenophon emphasises the elite character of the Persian one. 1.7.11 (narrator): 'People said that the enemy numbered 1,200,000, plus 200 scythed chariots. There were 6,000 cavalry as well, which Artagerses commanded: these were stationed in front of the King himself.' 2.4.6 (Klearchos): 'And of course, if we did have to fight at all, there would be no cavalry to support us, while the enemy's cavalry is very numerous and should be rated very highly.'

autobiographical purposes.'⁷⁶ The defensive stance of the author in his recounting of life events is said to be a response to cultural resistance to, even a taboo against, self-praise in talk about the self.

In this study I apply the term to a demonstrable tendency in Xenophon to present defences against charges in a way that not only exonerates him but clearly points as well to merits in his character, or leadership, or both. The primary intention in these instances, then, need not be apologia; instead, an apologetic situation can be used as, say, a means of showcasing good leadership. This is not to say that some or any of the charges are fictitious, though they might be, or that the circumstances portrayed would be unrecognisable to the internal audience, but rather that the narrated events may have been adapted to facilitate the author's agenda. This idea is like what I argued for with exemplars, events and places being adapted in some (small) measure to facilitate didactic ends.

Although it appeared well after the publication of *Anabasis*, the thinking Isokrates expresses in his *Antidosis* (late 350s) serves to provide us with an insight into the sort of ideas Xenophon may have been exposed to from other sources – or generated independently – on the subject of apologia.⁷⁷ In the *Antidosis* (8), explaining his apologetic method, Isokrates writes:

> If I were to attempt a eulogy of myself, I should not be able to cover all the points which I proposed to discuss, nor should I succeed in treating them without arousing the displeasure or even the envy of my hearers. But it occurred to me that if I were to adopt the fiction of a trial and of a suit brought against me – if I were to suppose that a sycophant had brought an indictment and was threatening me with trouble and that he was using the calumnies which had been urged against me in the suit about the exchange of the property, while I, for my part, cast my speech in the form of a defence in court – in this way it would be possible to discuss to the best advantage all the points which I wanted to make.

---

76 Gray 2011b: 15. Analysing Socrates' defence speech in Plato's *Apologia*, Ober (2011: 145) writes: 'Plato's "Socrates on trial", like many actual Athenian litigants, spent a relatively small part of his allotted time answering the prosecution's charges; like other Athenian defendants, the bulk of his defense speech was devoted to a discussion of the conduct of his life and an assessment of his behavior and attitudes in respect to the democratic culture of the polis. The choice to use much of the water in the clock on self-presentation was not inherently peculiar.' On courtroom oratory see further Johnson 2021: 30–1.

77 It cannot be ruled out that *Anabasis* (or *Memorabilia*) gave Isokrates pause for thought on this subject and that this is reflected in *Antidosis*. Comparisons of individual works suggest there was engagement between the two contemporaries, for example, *Panegyrikos* and *Anabasis*, and the encomiums of *Evagoras* and *Agesilaos*. Tuplin sees a distant parallel in terms of life-history writing between *Anabasis* and *Antidosis* (2003: 154). For Plato's *Apologia* as the literary model for *Antidosis*, see Ober 2011: 147. See Marincola 2014 for a study of Isokrates and his relationship to fifth- and fourth-century historiography.

Except that its focus is a third party and not the author, a more obvious affinity to this than *Anabasis* may be *Memorabilia*, which opens in a formally apologetic way but arguably is not fundamentally an apologetic work: the charges frame what turns out to be a statement by the author on the true nature of Socrates. When we consider the context for authorship this becomes a still more compelling reading, for by the 360s when *Memorabilia* (and *Anabasis*) were published, it seems probable that the struggle to rehabilitate Socrates had been displaced to a notable degree by the contest over his legacy.[78]

In *Anabasis* Xenophon's character in the story is subject to an assortment of accusations. Some, as we will see in Chapter 4, are met with elaborate defence speeches; others, as below, are processed almost seamlessly within the course of events. In many instances the response, either in *erga* or *logoi*, highlights certain key personal or professional qualities, and we may suspect that this is the author's principal intention, whether as a means of promoting 'Xenophon' or part of his didaxis on leadership. Analysis of apologetic episodes involving Xenophon's character show some interesting similarities, and within the sphere of literary apologia it may be admissible to talk of a scheme involving the presentation of charges made against him. Often the accuser is a person of dubious moral standing (vindictive, a talker) and one who, following their own interest instead of the wider community's, lacks the nous to see the bigger picture; the internal audience, if they are ready to entertain the charge as truthful, are invariably turned by the defence and applaud the speaker.

The relatively brief analyses of the episodes which follow, all from the initial period of Xenophon's command, aim to bear out this argument. I remark that if we take 'literary apologia' as a widespread phenomenon in the text, that in turn impacts on our understanding of the degree to which it should be seen as 'genuine' self-defence whereby answering charges is real and paramount and any merits showcased in the course of the author's defence are incidental.

Xenophon Talking Nonsense (3.1.26)

After Xenophon has delivered a rallying speech to the captains of one of the commanders seized by the Persians, one of the group pipes up, saying that 'it was nonsense for anyone to say he could achieve safety other than by persuading the King, if that were possible'.

It suddenly feels as if Xenophon's credibility is on the line: he has literally just stepped forward to make a claim for a leadership role and a

---

78 T-H (24) are more assertive on this: 'the weight here and in Socratica as a whole (and not only Xenophontic ones) was on evoking Socrates at work, not fighting and refighting a court-room battle that he himself had been scarcely interested in fighting'. On the similarity with *Antidosis*, see Gray 1998: 60–73.

captain calls him out for talking nonsense (φλυαροίη). But as the latter starts to recount the difficulties of their predicament, Xenophon cuts him short and reminds everyone that, as they have learned through their own recent experiences, they cannot trust the King. 'You most extraordinary person, you do not understand what you see or remember what you hear.' The decisive manner of his summary dismissal of the captain, which earns the emphatic support of the internal audience, quickly reassures us that this pupil of Socrates has not stepped in over his depth, which may be one intention of the episode. Another, in the didactic frame, is to point to the need for a commander to be able to recognise and promptly act when dissent threatens to disrupt planning or undermine morale.[79]

Guilty of Tactical Error (3.3.8–11)

In an episode touched on earlier, we saw the Greek rearguard come under pressure from the pursuing Persians in the vicinity of the Zapatas River. Xenophon, one of the two commanders at the back, decided to lead out a contingent in response, but the force was unable to overtake the enemy and was rendered more vulnerable for having detached from the main body. The action in addition retarded the progress of the army as a whole.

Cheirisophos and the oldest of the generals afterward blame Xenophon, 'because he had gone away from the phalanx in pursuit and put himself in danger without being able to harm the enemy to any greater extent at all' (3.3.11). While this is really reprimand – unless we wish to read that Xenophon is being accused of stupidity – the unflattering dress-down does enable the author to show himself in positive light. 'Xenophon', in fact, does not seek to defend himself, but acknowledging his error (ἀκούσας δὲ Ξενοφῶν ἔλεγεν ὅτι ὀρθῶς αἰτιῷντο, 3.3.12) goes on to point out that the episode has exposed the army's acute need for cavalry and slingers. The Greeks adopt the measures he proposes to remedy this and, as a result, can fend off a sustained attack the following day. In the didactic scheme, the key professional and personal life skills highlighted – owning errors and building on what one has learned – enable the commander to enhance his credibility and enrich his field experience.

Xenophon Not Pulling His Weight (3.4.46–9)

Xenophon leads a race against the Persians to capture a strategic height which overlooks their way. He is on horseback, and is urging on the men with him, when one of them, named as Soteridas the Sicyonian,[80] complains

---

79 For a detailed analysis of this episode, see H-R 91–4.
80 For the possible significance of this ethnic, see LXA 3.4.47a.

that they 'are not on equal terms'. Although, as we soon learn, this is not a common sentiment, Soteridas' intervention serves to alert us to one of the basic conditions for willing obedience: that the commander should lead by example, especially in difficult circumstances (see *Agesilaos* 5.3; in *Memorabilia* Socrates identifies other attributes a leader must have if he is to induce men to obey him, for example, being the best and knowing the best course to take, 3.3.9, and being a good speaker, 3.3.11). Realising what is needed, Xenophon at once dismounts, grabs the man's shield, and presses onward on foot. The rest of the men castigate Soteridas and compel him to take back his shield, whereupon Xenophon remounts and continues until the terrain forces him to complete the last stretch of the successful operation on foot.

In this testing early stage of his leadership, Xenophon, through the agency of Soteridas, highlights his presence of mind and brings into relief at the same time a key leadership lesson. Together with our preceding example the vignette acts furthermore to establish an index, preparing us to appreciate Xenophon's character's growth as a commander in the rest of the retreat. Notably, towards the end of it, as they prepare for a raid in Thrace, he dismounts his horse so that he can lead the men on foot. In a rare instance of explicit didacticism, he tells his Thracian counterpart, Seuthes, 'the hoplites will run more quickly, and willingly, if I too am on foot when I lead them' (7.3.45; see further Chapter 5 p. 236). In the next chapter, I examine Xenophon's leadership style in detail and draw a comparison with the other styles showcased in *Anabasis*.

CHAPTER 3

Xenophon Didaskalos: *Leaders and Leadership in* Anabasis

Kings and rulers, [Socrates] said, are not those who hold the sceptre, nor those who are chosen by the multitude, nor those on whom the lot falls, nor those who owe their power to force or deception; but those who know how to rule.

Memorabilia 3.9.10

Political philosophy, the problem of how to rule, pervades Xenophon's writing. Time and again, whether by way of households, armies, kingdoms or oneself, it surfaces in his works. We need only look to his experience of war and civil war at Athens on the one hand and to his early association with Socrates on the other to appreciate how such a deep-seated concern developed. In the comparative scheme presented by the author in *Anabasis*, 'Xenophon' serves as a paradigm for an ideal leader, and in this chapter I seek to show how this ideal derives from Socratic and Athenian elements. The representation serves at the same time to obliquely defend the author, as the historical figure behind the model, and Socrates, Xenophon's mentor and teacher, against accusations made against them respectively. The cases for *Anabasis* as personal and Socratic apologia are examined in the following chapters.[1]

---

1 The subject of leadership in *Anabasis* has been a focus of interest for scholars since Breitenbach's 1950 study, which brought out the concern in Xenophon's historiographical works for portraying model military commanders. Notable subsequent studies which cover *Anabasis* include Breitenbach 1967, Nussbaum 1967, Dillery 1995, Humble 1997, Gray 2011a, Sandridge 2012, Tamiolaki 2012, Ferrario 2014a, Buzzetti 2014, Buxton 2016, Millender 2020. Humble in her dissertation showed that Xenophon's representation of himself as a leader in *Anabasis* approximates to an ideal (1997: 46). It is worth remarking that Xenophon's engagement with leadership issues has attracted significant interest from modern management scientists and thinkers on organisation: see, for example, Drucker 1954, Aupperle 1996, Humphreys *et al.* 2011, King 2013, Hayek *et al.* 2014, Wilson 2016, Blok 2019.

As *Anabasis* is the story of an army on campaign written by one of its commanders, it should not be surprising that it encompasses the subject of military leadership. The fact that the author is a Socratic furthermore sets up an expectation that guidance on the subject may be provided. Yet it is not immediately obvious from the narrative that the treatment has a function beyond the storytelling itself; it does not, of course, follow from the presence of leadership content in the narrative that it must be didactic. Carried along by the trials of the Greeks, a reader who had not been drawn to the text by an interest in leadership could be excused for not registering the force of that underlying theme. This is a mark of Xenophon's talent as a writer, and we can see his artful approach as a way of transcending the often tedious style of military treatises of the day. To take the surviving work of Aineias Tacticus (*Techne Taktike*) as an example, although the author has frequent recourse to historical events to illustrate his detailed instructions, the whole has an undeniably dry feel and, one thinks, would only have been read cover to cover by those especially interested in the subject matter.[2] In this chapter I address two interrelated questions: how do we establish that *Anabasis* is didaxis on leadership, and what does it have to say on the subject?

The first question was partially answered in the previous chapter where I showed that exemplars reflecting core themes shape the narrative to a notable degree; in this one I provide examples of events on the march which, I argue, have been lightly shaped to form leadership instructional material. Further elements of the answer lie in the evident abbreviation of the travelogue in order to showcase events with leadership content, and in the regular focus on the (in)action of leaders in different situations.

In the broader view, the fact that many of Xenophon's works have decided didactic characters hints that *Anabasis* too could offer instruction on one or more of the author's central themes.[3] And then, given his

---

2   Another parallel might be the putative *Kyrou Anabasis* of Sophainetos, the surviving fragments of which provide only bare geographic detail. While these are too few to enable any assertions about the nature of the work, if it existed, some speculate that the fragments might have been part of a military handbook. See further Chapter 4 p. 152.

3   *Cavalry Commander* (*Hipparchikos*) and the treatises on hunting (*Kynegetikos*) and horsemanship (*Peri Hippikes*) are explicitly concerned with practical instruction; in *Kyroupaideia* the author outlines an ideal education and proceeds to demonstrate its worth in different situations. *Poroi* advises Athens on the management of its economy. Of the standard Socratic works, *Memorabilia* offers direction on a range of moral and practical questions, including military command (3.1–5), while *Oikonomikos* focuses on household and agricultural management. A concern for good military leadership is evident in *Hellenika* commander descriptions and anecdotes (for example Teleutias in Book 5, Iphikrates in 6).

Socratic background and the concern of Socrates to improve those around him, it is natural to see Xenophon wishing to pass on his own learning in those areas in which he had ample experience. We know from personal detail that these included horses, hunting, estate management and military affairs. In *Anabasis* Xenophon either commands or is in joint command of the army for the greater part of its arduous journey back to Ionia, and indeed it is largely down to his leadership that a substantial number of them manage to return.

On the question of what it has to say on the subject, in consecutive parts of this chapter each of the principal leaders in the story – Cyrus the Younger, the Spartans Klearchos and Cheirisophos, and Xenophon the Athenian – are showcased in action. I argue that, in addition to a range of practical situational lessons, Xenophon presents different styles of leadership and implies that the optimal is that which is informed by both democratic principles and moral philosophy – the style which he himself embodies on the retreat. Before turning to the individual commanders, I look at dynamics of the leadership theme in *Anabasis*.

The Leadership Theme

One measure of the importance of this is the extent to which the *Anabasis* narrative is taken up describing the characters and actions of commanders in the story. We will see shortly how this displaces travelogue, but here I draw attention to the ratio of coverage with non-commanders. The large Asian contingent is almost completely ignored except for Cyrus and a handful from his inner circle,[4] while of the 14,000 or so Greek mercenaries who Xenophon travelled with for two years only a small number are mentioned (c. 65), the majority of these being officers (c. 50).[5] Although

---

4 There is no really reliable basis for an estimate of the size of this force, though I am inclined to think the number would have been greater, but not much greater, than that of the mercenary total: see further Brennan 2021a: xxx–xxxi. Cf. Lee (2016a: 103), who estimates the number of Asian troops as roughly 28,000.

5 Roy (1967: 303–6) provides a list of individuals whose name and nationality are given in *Anabasis*. Sixteen of these are generals (στρατηγοί), twenty-nine captains (λοχαγοί), seven are other officers (ταξίαρχοι, ἵππαρχοι) and fourteen non-officers. H-R explore the meaning and functions of several of the officer ranks given in the text. Manning's (2018) prosopographical study of Cyrus's inner circle includes Glous and Pigres, the Persian nobles who free Cyrus's wagons in the episode featured below. Buzzetti (2014: 7 n.10) observes that the occurrence of the word 'king' (*basileus*) at least 144 times in the work reflects the theme of kingship. 'This number is substantially larger than the number of occurrences of the word in the *Education of Cyrus* [*Kyroupaideia*] (at least one hundred), a work longer than the *Anabasis* by perhaps 25 percent. And of course, the *Education of Cyrus* is unquestionably focused on the theme of kingship and its establishment.'

it is fair to say that this focalisation was not untypical of contemporary historiography, and in any event the naming of over sixty individuals is notable, the case of Xenophon himself bears notice. Up until the events on the banks of the Zapatas River, when he ceases to be merely a part of the entourage, the character of Xenophon appears only three times (1.8.15–17, 2.4.15, 2.5.37–42) whereafter he is mentioned over 250 times.[6]

In the first section of this part, I bring out how events on the march are shaped to provide exemplary leadership material. Episodes centring on mud involving Cyrus in Book 1 and Klearchos in Book 2 are examined, and following this, with more emphasis on the abbreviation of the travelogue, examples from Books 1 and 3 are looked at. In the second section I analyse what we might call the author's teaching method in *Anabasis*, and in the third I consider in more detail his pedagogy and the particular case of the obituaries.

Leadership Events

Wagons in the Mud (1.5.7–8)

While travelling through the desert region north of the Middle Euphrates, the narrator reports that wagons in the train became stuck in mud. He says that Cyrus ordered them to be dragged out, and eventually a group of Persian nobles freed them. Although this episode takes place in the closing stages of the march to Babylonia and the circumstances are challenging, the event could not be said to have any substantial significance in the story. In a straightforward account of the march, we might expect it to warrant no more than a mention, yet it receives the same amount of space (a half page of the Oxford Classical text (OCT)) as the rest of the description of the long stage (ninety parasangs) during which it occurs.[7]

Analysis of the event reveals its exemplary character, if not yet its principal lesson, which Xenophon artfully holds up in order to underline the point he wishes to make. Upon arriving at the place where the train had become

---

6 Coming from a different perspective, Kingsbury (1956: 163) identifies the roles of Cyrus, Klearchos and Xenophon as significant within the architecture of the work. In her view these characters are framed by the genre of tragic drama, with the rank and file being a massed chorus. 'The spectacle of drama or epic is that of a single large action carried on by a few major characters with a chorus of individuals more or less affected by the actions of the main characters.'

7 It was remarked in Chapter 2 that incidents such as this are probably based on actual events which the author adapts to his own end. The mud incident, or something close to what is described, would have occurred in the west of the modern Anbar province of Iraq. See Figure 3.1 for the river. For more on the location and the chronological value of this episode, see Brennan 2008.

Figure 3.1 Euphrates River, western Anbar, Iraq. (Author)

stuck, he tells us that Cyrus, who is accompanied by the most privileged of his men, ordered two of them to take some of the native troops and help to free the wagons:

> When they seemed to him to be taking their time about it, he gave orders, as if in a temper (ὥσπερ ὀργῇ), to the Persian nobles in his entourage to help get the wagons going. Then indeed one could see a bit of good discipline (εὐταξία). Each nobleman threw off his purple robe wherever he happened to be standing, and they rushed down an extremely steep hill, like people running for victory in the Games, with their expensive tunics and their embroidered trousers, some of them wearing necklaces and bracelets. They immediately leapt into the mud with these on and, more quickly than one might suppose, brought the wagons out onto higher ground. (1.5.8)

Xenophon is highlighting features of Cyrus's leadership that he wishes to draw attention to. One is his apparent lapse into anger, a trait which Xenophon associates with undesirable results (see 4.6.2–3, and *Hellenika* 5.3.7), and although here the result is desirable, the prince's less than sure grip on himself foreshadows trouble, even disaster. However, it should be remarked that the literal reading is that Cyrus feigned anger, presumably to effect the desired result, so it may be that Xenophon is actually drawing attention to the range of his leadership skills. We might think it would have been hard for him to have judged the leader's real disposition if he had witnessed this event, though perhaps the prince's demeanour immediately after the order suggested it and is what made the episode stick in the author's mind. In any case it has to be acknowledged that if he had meant to convey actual anger unambiguously, he should have put it differently.

A second feature on display is Cyrus's ability to produce good order (εὐταξία) on the march, a point needing emphasis lest the more indelible image of disorder that shortly follows (1.7.19–20) should come to define Cyrus's leadership. A third feature only becomes clear in the second book, when Xenophon chooses to highlight another incident – again, not a particularly obvious one to dwell on – involving Cyrus's successor as leader of the army, Klearchos the Spartan. This threading of didactic material through the narrative is, as we saw in the case of panhellenism in the last chapter, characteristic of Xenophon's thoughtful teaching approach.

Klearchos in the Mud (2.3.11)

As the Greeks begin their long march homewards from Mesopotamia, we are told that the route they were led along by the Persians was criss-crossed by ditches and canals full of water. To cross these, they had to make bridges from palm trees. Xenophon describes how Klearchos, leading the army, would take his staff to any shirkers, 'while at the same time he himself went into the mud and lent a hand, so that they were all ashamed not to be working hard along with him' (2.3.11). We are not told that Klearchos is angry, but it seems reasonable to infer from the circumstances that it was this emotion that spurred him to use his staff, though like Cyrus perhaps it was feigned (on his anger, see further 2.6.9).

While the Spartan deploys his βακτηρία, he complements his use of physical discipline with exemplary action: in doing as he himself orders, the leader inspires – or in this case, to the same effect, shames – those around him. His descent into the mud pointedly recalls Cyrus's failure to do so when his wagons had become stuck and marks a key distinction between their leadership styles. The implicit linking of the two episodes gives both a sense of the subtlety of Xenophon's narrative and the degree to which it is subject to paradigm.

The Trial of Orontas (1.6)

Towards the end of the arduous march through the desert west of Babylonia, Cyrus arrests and tries a traitor. Xenophon tells us how the man, a Persian noble, was detected, and provides an account of the trial. Although the treachery of Orontas would have been damaging if realised – his plan was to desert to the King with as many horsemen as he could – it would probably not have had a critical impact on the outcome of the battle. The episode nonetheless receives two and a half pages of OCT, almost the same as the account of the thirteen-day, ninety-parasang, stage during which it takes place. As the showdown with his brother looms, Xenophon clearly wishes to place further focus on Cyrus's leadership, in this case his careful exercise of justice. Within Achaemenid royal ideology the Great King, deriving his authority from the supreme Persian deity, Ahuramazda, was judge over all his dominion, and his ability to deliver justice was crucial both for his own legitimacy and the social order in his kingdom.[8] Cyrus's competent display at this juncture advertises his suitability to assume the mantle of power and reinforces the earlier indicator of divine approval for the campaign; we recall that at the ford of the Euphrates River, Cyrus and the army cross on foot, something absolutely extraordinary which the local inhabitants had not witnessed before. 'It seemed indeed that it was a divine sign, and that the river had clearly drawn back for Cyrus as the future King' (1.4.18).

In prompting readers to reflect on Cyrus's judgement as a leader, Xenophon also exposes a weakness, for Orontas, as we learn in the report of the trial, had already betrayed him twice before (1.6.6–7). Granted his forgiveness on those occasions could be seen as a way of making Orontas a stronger ally and would suit claims for kingship, it should be concerning that after two betrayals Cyrus included him in such a high-stakes venture – and Klearchos tells him as much when asked for his judgement (1.6.9). Nor up until this point has Orontas been the first to deceive or plot against Cyrus. Tissaphernes (1.1.2–3), Megaphernes (1.2.20), Pasion, Xenias (1.4.7) and, as we see when looking more closely at Cyrus's rule in the next part of the chapter, Klearchos (1.3, 1.8.12–13) each in their turn call into question Cyrus's capacity to know those 'well-disposed toward him' (1.9.20).[9]

On the theme of political philosophy, we could furthermore see the trial as part of a pattern intended to show the current Achaemenid house as lacking the wisdom necessary to rule, or, in Socratic terms, lacking the know-how to do so (*Memorabilia* 3.9.10). The extraordinary influence of the queen mother, Parysatis, is one factor in this, another the superior nous of other courtly figures. Thus, Cyrus's pretext for raising his army deceived his brother but did not take in Tissaphernes (1.2.4); Syennesis (1.2.12, 21–7) and, subsequently, Abrokomas are able to avoid their armies becoming a part of the fraternal feud by shrewd manoeuvring (1.4.5, 1.7.12).

---

8 Kuhrt (2007: 471) writes: 'Auramazda has equipped [the King] with the ability to distinguish right from wrong, which enables him to act fairly and thus maintain the social order. He only acts after due consideration, never hastily. As a result, he metes out punishment and reward as appropriate.' On Cyrus's justice, see also 1.9.13.

9 On the Orontas episode, see further Keaveney 2012. Marincola (2017: 107) draws attention to a Socratic resemblance in Cyrus's dealing with the traitor. Through the prince's systematic questioning, Orontas is led, 'like a Socratic interlocutor, to convict himself'.

Crossing the Zapatas River (3.3.6)

After their generals have been seized by the Persians on the banks of the Zapatas, the Greeks must reorganise and get across the river before the enemy attacks. Xenophon devotes considerable space to this critical period, most of it taken up with speeches which he himself makes to rouse and ready the men (3.1.15–25, 35–44; 3.2.7–32, 34–9). These addresses serve to establish his importance as an actor in the story, and to emphasise his own style of leadership, in which speech is the preferred method of persuasion. In his treatment of the episode at the Zapatas, however, he neglects to tell us how the army actually crossed the river, a significant tributary of the Tigris. We may contrast his silence here with the detail he later provides on the crossing of the Centrites River, where the army found itself trapped between two enemies (4.3.3–7). Presumably pontoon bridges spanned the Zapatas as they had the Tigris (2.4.17) and Physkos (2.4.25), and while it is possible the Persians had blocked access to these, or even destroyed them (see 1.4.18), it seems likely that to avoid a showdown with desperate men they did not obstruct the route onwards.[10] Such an outcome may well have rendered the episode un-noteworthy in Xenophon's eyes, it affording little ground for didaxis on leadership. He would, in short, rather dwell on the difficulties they overcame than the difficulties they did not have to face. The omission thus reflects how the dominance of the leadership theme has displaced, in this case historically important, journey detail.

Teaching

While a number of leaders feature in *Anabasis*, we could say that the most prominent are those who head the Greek force during the course of its long march. These are Cyrus the Younger, the Spartans Klearchos and Cheirisophos, and Xenophon the Athenian. The arrangement of the narrative reflects this order, with Cyrus the focus in Book 1, Klearchos in Book 2, and Cheirisophos and Xenophon in Books 3–6; following the death of Cheirisophos (6.4.11), Xenophon comes to dominate the stage in Book 7, though, as I suggest at the end of the chapter, this terminal segment may be intended to complicate, if not stand apart from, the others in terms of the leadership theme.[11]

---

10 As H-R suggest (144), it could be that the Persians considered it would have been easier to strike them in the plain beyond the river, which they did.
11 Waterfield proposes that the arrangement is part of a mixed constitutional model that Xenophon has used to structure his narrative; so, in the case of Books 3 and 4 the other leaders are suppressed in order to highlight Xenophon and Cheirisophos, at the front and rear respectively, as 'monarchs' in these realms (2011: 145).

The actual leadership arrangement on the retreat is less straightforward than this scheme indicates. After the seizure of generals at the Zapatas River in Book 3, we know the leadership resided in a collective of seven: Sophainetos, who was not among those seized, Cheirisophos, Xenophon, Kleanor, Timasion, Xanthikles and Philesios (3.1.47; 3.2.37). However, from Xenophon's account the impression is that the others had little involvement in the conduct of the retreat. On the crucial march down to the sea Sophainetos only appears once (4.4.19) and Kleanor twice (4.6.9, 4.8.18), with none of the others bar Xenophon and Cheirisophos being mentioned by name at all. Indeed, without close reading it would be hard to take it any other way than that Xenophon and Cheirisophos are in joint command, with the latter in the portrayal as *primus inter pares*.[12] But the closer reading does call into question this impression, and I agree in principle with Roy that the seven *strategoi* managed the army's affairs by majority decision 'until Cheirisophoss was elected sole commander'.[13] Given what we know about Xenophon's aims in *Anabasis*, and the number of instances in which collective decisions are made (see note 13), the case for a wider controlling group is convincing. This highlights again how an important historical stratum is overshadowed by the presence of thematic elements.

The paradigm of leadership revolving around the nexus of Cyrus and the Greek commanders could be expanded, though, being more complex, such might undermine the essential value of this mode of presentation. In any expanded treatment we would certainly identify as additional actors the Persian satrap, Tissaphernes, the King, and the Thracian chieftain,

12 See 3.4.38: Cheirisophos orders Xenophon to the front, but cf. H-R 172. In his account, Diodoros (14.27.1) writes that Cheirisophos was made supreme commander at the Zapatas. This statement could reflect his source's conclusion on Xenophon's narrative (i.e., from reading Xenophon, where Cheirisophos is to the fore on the retreat to the sea, he formed the judgement that the Spartan was sole leader from early on), or derive from a different account of the march, or it could be the product of some carelessness on Diodoros' (or his source's) part: H-R (127) think that it most likely arises from misinterpretation of the verb 'to lead' (ἡγεῖσθαι) in 3.2.36 or 3.2.37. On the matter, see further Roy 1967: 293–4, and Erbse 495–9, who seeks to show that Diodoros' report is not reliable. I examine the question of Diodoros' source(s) for the expedition in the next chapter.

13 Roy 1967: 289. Collective decisions on the retreat: 3.4.21, modification to march formation; 3.5.12, rejection of proposal to build floating bridge on Tigris; 3.5.17, march north into Kardouchoi lands; 4.6.7, blocked pass; 4.7.4, Taochoi stronghold. The discussions leading up to Cheirisophos' election at Sinope (6.1.18) confirm a form of collective rule. We should note as well that there is evidence for this in the period from when Cheirisophos departs at Trapezous to his return and election at Sinope, albeit, as I argue in the next chapter, this is inferred through a power struggle between several of the generals, including Xenophon.

Seuthes. But I think their function is principally as foils for their counterparts rather than as separate models (whether positive or negative) in their own right. The shadowy nature of Tissaphernes' presence in *Anabasis*, from his riding upcountry alongside Cyrus to see the King when he was ill to his tracking of the Greeks along the Tigris River on their retreat, places him somewhere next to rather than in a progressive line with the other main leaders. And then in Book 7, Seuthes, who is named over 100 times, should certainly be seen as a foil for the leader (Xenophon) under focus: the story wouldn't be disrupted were the notices of him a fraction of this.

Method

The author's focus on top commanders is indicative of his intention to provide exemplary material. In his treatment of their actions, one of his concerns is to highlight their respective strengths and weaknesses and thereby to make his record serve as thought-provoking and instructive material for aspiring commanders. His teaching method can be formulated in the following terms:

- Leader is confronted with a problem/opportunity
- Leader implements a course of action, or does not act at all
- Lesson.

The impact of the (in)decision is occasionally commented on (see 2.2.13), but more often the reader, who is a witness to the unfolding events, is left to reflect themselves on its implications for the leader, for his command and for the army as a whole.[14] As I remarked earlier in the chapter, this subtle approach might mean some readers who cared did not benefit, but most who did, knowing of Xenophon's interest in the problem of how to rule, will have come to the story primed to learn something about military leadership or about problem-solving more generally.

A further aim of Xenophon's in his focus on the selected four individuals is to critique different styles of leadership. Cyrus is royalty and rules on what we might term an absolute model; Klearchos and Cheirisophos are products of the Spartan militaristic tradition, and Xenophon himself

---

14 In *Hellenika* Xenophon seems more inclined to offer authorial judgement (e.g. 6.5.51), something more exceptional in terms of earlier historiography than the *Anabasis* tendency. Note for instance Mitchell's (2008: 30) reference to Hornblower in her conclusion about Thucydides: 'As Hornblower [1987: 160–1] observes, Thucydides very rarely uses the language of political theory and his theorising is implicit and allusive rather than explicit, and worked out through action and event. He presents the case, but he leaves his readers to draw their own conclusions.' In similar vein, see Hobden 2005: 105.

is an Athenian citizen with a philosophy background.[15] The treatment of leadership in the work, then, is as much about highlighting the effectiveness of leadership styles as it is a practical exercise in learning from the successes and failures of outstanding men. In the following parts of the chapter, addressing the question of what Xenophon has to say on the subject, through a study of selected events I seek to unpack some of the lessons which he embeds in the narrative.

Two final points, briefly. Instruction on leadership is not solely expressed through character (in)actions: Xenophon as author provides examples of recommended tactical and strategic approaches and on occasion as character offers advice. Second, it bears emphasising that we should see the goal of his presentation in light of an overarching political philosophy, the substance of which he has Socrates spell out in *Memorabilia* 3.9.10 (see opening quote).

The Obituaries: Teaching and Remembering

Anabasis incorporates several obituaries or short biographies. We get one of Cyrus immediately after his death at the end of Book 1 (1.9) and five more at the end of Book 2 following the seizure of Greek commanders (2.6).[16] The notices complement the character portraits built up in the course of the narrative but also, as I argue here, complicate them. Their placement may indicate a further purpose, as the locations serve as interludes following dramatic action and underscore the transitions to a new phase of the story.

Taken together, the obituaries have evident didactic purpose as a succinct digest of the leadership styles featured in Books 1–2; they furthermore prime us for the new leadership style that follows in the remaining ones. A danger in reading them just as records of the individual performances is that we may come away in the belief that, say, Cyrus's leadership was exemplary; that is, since the obituary portrays him as nearly ideal, his actions on the march

---

15 Buzzetti (2014) argues that the author intends the presentation of the different styles to show how each one deals with the problem of reconciling morality with advantage in rule. Buxton (2017: 324) does not think that Xenophon is interested in surveying leadership styles and instead seeks to show that the author pushes a single approach (to leadership) in all his works.

16 For discussion, see Momigliano 1993: 51–2, Gray 2010: 12 and 2011a: 71–9, Ferrario 2014a: 190–3, Marincola 2017: 113–14. Touching on their exceptionality, Wylie (1992: 133) writes of Cyrus's obituary: 'Xenophon breaks off halfway through a graphic account of the battle to insert a long and not over-interesting panegyric on Cyrus, which takes up as much space as the battle. Is this mere "padding", to obscure his paucity of information, or has it a purpose?'

are retrospectively seen through this glowing lens.¹⁷ Yet, for example, the desertions of commanders close to him at Myriandros (1.4.7) undermine the report in the obituary of the esteem in which he was held by those around him (1.9.28; and they negate a similar report in the *Oikonomikos* 4.18–19). Conversely, in the case of Klearchos, who has the second longest of the obituaries, undue weight on the notice would leave us with an impression of a more limited leader than is borne out by the narrative. The tone in this case may reflect the ambivalence, and even coolness, towards Sparta which we witness through the narrative.¹⁸

Granted the obituaries impinge directly on the men as leaders, and as an axiom for Xenophon good character and good leadership go hand in hand, the discernible tension between these and the narrative which they abut seems to warn those interested in learning from remarkable leaders to exercise caution when looking for lessons in a *laudatio/vituperatio* mode. Xenophon's treatment in his writings of Agesilaos and Cyrus the Younger respectively illustrates this. In the *Agesilaos*, an encomium, the character and achievements of the Spartan king are praised, with divisive issues and episodes overlooked or explained away, whereas in the history-oriented *Hellenika* there is a more balanced evaluation of his life and deeds.¹⁹ In the *Anabasis* obituary, Cyrus, hailed at the outset as 'the most kingly ... and the one who most deserved to rule' (1.9.1), is roundly praised for his range of skills and virtues, whereas again in *Hellenika* we receive harder detail about his life and conduct, for example his execution of two royals who had apparently failed to show him due respect vis-à-vis court protocol (2.1.8–9).²⁰ But we do not have to look this far to see the principle under discussion demonstrated: Cyrus's manifest leadership failings in his preparations for the expedition and his management of the campaign stand in notable contrast to the obituary.

---

17 The obituary is not a flawless picture at all points: for instance, at 1.9.20 it is apparent that friendship for Cyrus was a conditional relationship, with his own benefit paramount. As Flower (2012: 188) says of the obituary, '[p]raise predominates on the surface, but those who read carefully and critically may feel some disquiet'. Some scholars though, placing weight on the notice, regard Xenophon's portrayal of Cyrus's leadership as ideal: see Delebecque 1947: 97, Azoulay 2004: 299, Millender 2012: 388.

18 Roisman (1985–8) brings into relief the incongruity between obituary and narrative in the case of Klearchos, concluding that the 'lack of harmony between them is probably the result of the different kinds of evidence used by the author as a basis for each' (51).

19 On the respective treatments, see Momigliano 1993: 50–1, Cartledge 1987: 55–73, LaForse 2013: 29–30.

20 This passage may be an interpolation, but even if it is, its inclusion may hint at some widespread view about the prince's behaviour. It is also the case that shortly after this incident Xenophon reports that Cyrus is recalled to Persia (2.1.13).

Bringing out further the utility of the obituaries for the author, the painting of Cyrus in noble colour serves an apologetic function, furnishing as it does a suitable context for Xenophon's joining him on the march.[21] Menon's moral infamy, overshadowing his successes as a leader, and Proxenos' training with Gorgias the Sophist, hint that their obituaries, too, have a foot in the apologetic dimension of the work and form part of its fabric as a Socratic history. I look at both of these characters in the final section of Chapter 5.

I consider that Xenophon also intends the obituaries to work as memorials. I suggest that recognition of memorialisation as an important concern in his writing reduces the inclination to take them as solely, if not primarily, didactic. One effect that can be illustrated is the result of the absence of one for Cheirisophos, which downgrades him in importance in the story.[22] In this way we can see the notices as a means for Xenophon to configure, through inscribing a summary of characters in the story, the way that he wishes them to be remembered.

Cyrus the Younger

Cyrus, the son of Darius and Parysatis, is the principal actor in Book 1. He assembles the expeditionary force, leads it upcountry to Babylonia, and directs the attack against his brother. As with the other main characters in the story, the picture which Xenophon draws of him may not be so much an accurate historical portrait as a composite of selected individual traits and, in this case, the stereotype of a monarchical ruler. Several of the examples given below illustrate this, Cyrus showing an enlightened tendency towards those serving under him while also being capable of exercising absolute command. Through the same process of blending in *Kyroupaideia* Cyrus the Great is similarly made to appear decidedly less barbarian. We might conjecture that this approach, leaving us with a Cyrus (in both cases) who bears resemblance to the conception of an ideal Greek leader, would have surprised many of his readers (Xenophon meets the more traditional expectation through his encomium of the Spartan king, *Agesilaos*).[23]

---

21 As Azoulay writes: 'Posthumous praise of Cyrus goes hand in hand with justification of the author' (2004: 299).

22 Other readings are possible. David Thomas has pointed out to me in correspondence that, unlike the six who do receive obituaries, Cheirisophos did not die at the hands of the enemy. I argue elsewhere in the monograph that one of Xenophon's favoured ways of putting down an individual is to ignore them (see Chapter 4 p. 172).

23 For reflections on the use and depiction of Cyrus the Great, see Due 1989: 22–5, Tamiolaki 2017: 190–3; Sandridge observes that choosing a non-Greek 'allowed Xenophon to study and celebrate him in ways that would be less politically controversial than if he had written, say, *The Education of Pericles*' (2012: 9–10). For the wider subject of identity in *Anabasis*, see Briant 1995, Tuplin 1999, Humble 2011, Harman 2016. In this monograph I adopt the post-Persian Wars meaning of 'barbarian', which, if not pejorative, is arguably less neutral than its original sense.

In Xenophon's representation of him, Cyrus's potential to be a great king (1.9.1; *Oikonomikos* 4.18) essentially resides in his appreciation of Greek values, epitomised in his lauding of 'freedom' (ἐλευθερία) in his address to the officers in the run-up to battle (*Anabasis* 1.7.3) and before that his resolution of a crisis through the power of speech rather than arms (1.5.11–17). This contrasts starkly to the antithetical image of slavery which the Persian King is indelibly linked with in Greek eyes (Xerxes intends to enslave the whole of Europe: Herodotus 7.8) and with the habitual use of force to express royal will (Xerxes orders the Hellespont to be lashed and shackled: Herodotus 7.35). As we see through a consideration of selected episodes, while Cyrus's route to virtue and enlightened rule is problematised by the deeper roots of his upbringing, it is not at all ruled out.

A Crisis over Pay (1.2.11–12)

On the Kaÿstros Plain in western Anatolia, the soldiers approach Cyrus about their pay: he owes them more than three months. Xenophon reports that 'it was clear he was distressed (δῆλος ἦν ἀνιώμενος), for it was not Cyrus's way to fail to hand out what he had' (1.2.11). While they are still encamped on the plain, the Queen of Kilikia arrives, and soon after the men are paid. Xenophon writes: 'it was said that Cyrus even slept with her' (1.2.12).

In this vignette Xenophon highlights Cyrus's concern for the soldiers and his resourcefulness. The first of these leadership traits, an early example of Xenophon's individualist representation of the prince, distinguishes him from typical mercenary employers, who often withhold pay deliberately or pay only in part, in order to keep men tied to their enterprise (see Polyaenus, *Strategemata* 3.9.51);[24] his concern, furthermore, separates him from the stereotype of a monarchical enslaver (for Persians behaving as slave drivers, see Herodotus 7.22, 7.56; but there is an echo of this from Cyrus, as we see below).

However, the episode itself serves as a reminder of one of the dangers of being a φιλοστρατιώτης (soldier's friend), the extraordinary disregard for Cyrus's status shown by the men in approaching his tent foreshadowing their later mutiny at Tarsus (1.3). Pointedly in his obituary of Klearchos, who successfully dealt with that mutiny, Xenophon emphasises the value which he laid on strict discipline:

[9] [Klearchos] always used to punish troops severely and sometimes in anger, which on occasion even he regretted. [10] But he also punished on principle, for he thought that there was nothing to be gained from an undisciplined army; on the contrary, the story was

---

24 There may be an implied contrast here as well to Spartan disregard for men owed money: see 7.1.7, and Thucydides 8.84.

that he even said that if a soldier was going to be on sentry-duty, or avoid squabbles with his mates, or advance unhesitatingly against the enemy, it was necessary for him to fear his commander more than he feared his enemy. (2.6.9–10)

Cyrus's resourcefulness, the second feature spotlighted, is apparent in the manner of his securing of substantial funds from the Kilikian queen. The clear potential of the cash crisis to derail the enterprise underlines the importance of this quality. But while Xenophon is surely pointing out that good leaders are prepared to put their bodies on the line for their men, we are implicitly prompted as well to wonder how, hardly having begun, Cyrus has already run out of money. Despite the care he shows for his men, he has very nearly failed in his duty to provide for them, a basic requirement of leaders (see *Memorabilia* 3.1.6, *Hipparchikos* 6.2–3). Given his straitened financial circumstances, his decision while preparing for the march to offer more to one of his commanders (Aristippos of Thessaly) than he had requested seems in this new light not to have been well thought out (1.1.10). It could have been that the meeting with the Kilikian queen (Epyaxa) had been long arranged, but Xenophon would hardly then have described Cyrus as being 'distressed' (ἀνιώμενος) when the men came to him looking for their pay. The sudden, unexpected shadow of disorder which comes over the expedition is reinforced by the suggested image of the barbarian royals copulating on the dusty Asian plain.

The Wagons in the Mud (1.5.7–8)

In the previous part of the chapter, I brought out the paradigmatic character of this episode. To recap, while marching through the desert, wagons in the train became stuck in mud and Cyrus ordered two of his best men to take soldiers and help free them; dissatisfied with their efforts, he ordered others from his entourage to go down (1.5.8). In terms of the teaching formula outlined earlier, Cyrus encountered a logistical problem which he resolved at the second attempt by committing extra, higher-quality resources. His successful approach additionally revealed the loyalty which he commanded among those close to him (see, too, 1.9.31), and, by calling to mind a contrast with the mercenaries whom he has hired – Tarsus 1.3, Thapsakos 1.4.11–12 – emphasised the truth that by nature such men cannot be relied on.

In the fuller leadership exposition, the episode does nonetheless raise a critical question about Cyrus's style. Why did he not himself take part in the action and lead by example as later Klearchos (2.3.11) and Xenophon (3.4.48, 7.3.45) respectively see fit to do? But perhaps in the context of absolute monarchies like the Persian it does not matter as much. The men seem to do well enough without an inspiring example. Their colourful attire and adornments and instant obedience remind us that the leadership dynamic

Figure 3.2 Detail from Persepolis bas-relief showing *proskunesis*. National Museum of Iran. (Author)

in this culture is different. Instead of loyalty we witness the performance of hierarchy, with Cyrus literally above everyone else (see Figure 3.2 for an illustration of *proskunesis*, the Persian practice of showing deference towards superiors). One undoubted concern, though, in terms of leadership is that Cyrus's motivation for sending down the nobles may have been anger. This lack of self-control – if this was in fact an instance of it – will emerge on the battlefield at Cunaxa, fatally, as impetuosity (1.8.26).

Defusing a Dispute (1.5.11–17)

Opposite the city of Charmande on the south bank of the Euphrates, a serious quarrel arose involving Klearchos and the soldiers of Menon the Thessalian.[25] Earlier, at the halting place, Klearchos had adjudged that one

---

25 The broader antagonism between these generals should be considered, one pointed event being Menon's crafty action at Thapsakos, where he led his men across the Euphrates first, so guaranteeing favour with Cyrus but undermining Greek unity (1.4.13–17). Prior to this, at Tarsus (1.3), Klearchos did the same, winning the favour of Cyrus by resolving the impasse with the soldiers but undermining the unity of the army, in this case by leaving two of its commanders – Pasion and Xenias – with depleted contingents, a situation that subsequently prompted them to desert. Klearchos' actions

of Menon's men was at fault in a dispute and beat him; the victim reported his mistreatment to his comrades, who, on subsequently seeing Klearchos passing through their camp, hurled stones.[26] A stand-off between the two contingents ensued, and Proxenos attempted unsuccessfully to placate the Spartan commander, being told by him to get himself and his men out of the way (ἐκέλευσέ τε αὐτὸν ἐκ τοῦ μέσου ἐξίστασθαι). At this point Cyrus arrived at the camp and learned what was going on. Xenophon writes:

> [15] He immediately took a light spear in each hand and rode forward into the middle with those of his trusted advisers who were there, and said: [16] 'Klearchos and Proxenos, and you other Greeks who are here, you don't know what you are doing. If you take to fighting with each other, you should realize that on that day I shall be cut down and you too, not long after me, since if our affairs go badly, all these barbarians whom you see will be more hostile to us than the King's troops.' [17] When he heard this, Klearchos came to his senses, and both parties broke off and put their weapons away in their proper places. (1.5.15–17)

Cyrus's intervention is at once decisive and critical. Seeing the great danger confronting his enterprise, he reacts instantly and places himself, armed, between the two sides. Proxenos had done this too (interjecting with a company of hoplites), but his words, instead of defusing the crisis, inflamed the situation (Klearchos claimed that he 'spoke mildly of what had happened to him', 1.5.14). Cyrus has thus achieved this result through a combination of action and judicious words, with his speech the key. As evidence of his rhetorical skill, we have his earlier speech at Myriandros (1.4.8), which follows the desertion of two officers and has the effect of encouraging the whole army to go on.

It is noteworthy that Xenophon here casts Cyrus as a Greek: 'if our affairs go badly,' he has him tell the Greeks, 'all these barbarians whom you see will

---

at Tarsus indeed saw him supplant Menon as the most prominent general among the Greeks: that Menon had enjoyed this role is evident at 1.2.15, where he led the right wing, and at 1.2.20, when Cyrus selected him to take the Kilikian queen across the Taurus mountains. On the march into Babylonia it is Klearchos who alone of the Greeks is invited to witness the trial of Orontas (1.6.5), and at the Battle of Cunaxa he receives the instructions from Cyrus (1.8.12). While this suggests that his service at Tarsus ranked higher than Menon's at the Euphrates in the mind of the prince, perhaps the episode under discussion was significant in this regard.

26 Hornblower, in an illuminating study of Spartan violence (2000), does not refer to this episode, though it may offer additional circumstantial evidence for his thesis that free Greeks were enraged by Spartan use of the βακτηρία (staff) for beatings, on account of its demeaning quality – 'both a weapon in a crude sense and also not quite a weapon' (70) – and its regular use against helots. Xenophon does not mention Klearchos' staff here, but when we see him striking soldiers later on (2.3.11), it is with his βακτηρία.

be more hostile to us (ἡμῖν) than the King's troops'. Although he attributes to him presence of mind and the power of speech, Xenophon may be suggesting that these key leadership qualities derive from the prince's strong affinity with Greek ways. This cultural influence, which we can probably date to the period of his governance in western Anatolia and friendships with individuals like Lysander, is brought out in different ways in the narrative, for example by Cyrus's using the arguments of a Greek commander when preparing troops for battle with non-Greeks (1.7.2-4), and by the contrast with Tissaphernes, whose character as portrayed is the embodiment of barbarian treachery. This opposition is signalled at the very outset when, summoned to the court by his father, Cyrus takes Tissaphernes as a friend (ὡς φίλον) but is then defamed by him and nearly loses his life (1.1.2-3). In *Anabasis* Cyrus's open nature and sense of honour (τīμή) are repeatedly emphasised, as is the treachery of Tissaphernes.[27] Yet neither does Xenophon deny Cyrus's own heritage or, as we see in the obituary, its worth. One of the aims of his representation of the prince may be to blur the boundaries between stereotypes in order to show that education and the capacity to learn are the key determiners of a leader's quality.

The Battlefield (1.8)

The episode at Charmande touches on another important concern of Xenophon's in *Anabasis*: the problem of how to manage mercenary soldiers. He engages with the issue throughout the march upcountry, cuttingly at the critical moment when the armies of Cyrus and the King line up for battle. Cyrus orders Klearchos to lead the Greeks against the enemy centre, but instead the Spartan holds them by the river, and they charge the facing wing (1.8.12-13, 18). In a poignant irony, it is to prevent the King getting in behind the Greek force that, with just his own 600 cavalrymen, Cyrus launches his fatal attack on the Persian centre. The heroic action fought by Cyrus's own men, epitomised by the destruction alongside him of 'the best eight of his supporters' (Κῦρος δὲ αὐτός τε ἀπέθανε καὶ ὀκτὼ οἱ ἄριστοι τῶν περὶ αὐτὸν ἔκειντο ἐπ' αὐτῷ, 1.8.27), contrasts with the simultaneous movement of the mercenaries away from the battle epicentre (1.8.19). With the barbarians mirroring the Spartan ethos of glorious death (*Lakedaimonion Politeia* 9.1-2; Herodotus 7.228), and the Greeks skirting along the fringes of the battle, without a single loss, Xenophon again confounds the stereotypes. (For an exemplary reading of Cyrus's death, see Chapter 2 pp. 71-2, and note 61 (p. 66) for a defence of Klearchos.)

---

27 Cyrus's noble nature: sends extra funds to guest-friend (1.1.10); holds a trial for a commander suspected of treason on campaign (1.6); charges directly against the King while Tissaphernes makes to plunder the Greek camp (1.8.24, 1.10.8).

The battle, however, also serves as a reminder of Cyrus's poor judgement, the commander whom he relied on for the success of the expedition, Klearchos of Sparta, disobeying his final order.[28] To appreciate the failing here we can recall the earlier events at Tarsus, where Cyrus, alarmed at the mutiny unfolding before him, sends for Klearchos; he refuses to come but secretly sends a messenger to the prince to tell him not to worry and that things will turn out as they should (ὡς καταστησομένων τούτων εἰς τὸ δέον, 1.3.8). At the decisive moment when Cyrus issues his orders for the battle at Cunaxa, Klearchos handles him in a strikingly similar way, disobeying but saying he will take care that things go well (τῷ δὲ Κύρῳ ἀπεκρίνατο ὅτι αὐτῷ μέλει ὅπως καλῶς ἔχοι, 1.8.13). The repetition of insubordination, ultimately with fatal consequences, affirms the lesson in hand, that a general should be careful about entrusting command to any who have defied his will. I think Xenophon is suggesting too that if Cyrus had been a better leader, seeing the pattern and foreseeing its potential consequence, he would have doubled down on his order or even replaced Klearchos.

Returning to the subject of the obituaries, a further relevant context pointing to Klearchos as a liability emerges. In the notice for him, Xenophon writes that he had disobeyed the ephors much earlier, an act which earned him the death sentence at Sparta (2.6.3–4): it was at this point Klearchos went to Cyrus, who therefore, Xenophon implies, knew before hiring him of his propensity for disobedience. The penultimate remark in the notice seems especially damning: 'they said that he did not at all like it when others gave him commands' (ἄρχεσθαι δὲ ὑπὸ ἄλλων οὐ μάλα ἐθέλειν ἐλέγετο, 2.6.15).[29]

---

28 See Plutarch's condemnation of this action in his *Artaxerxes* (8.3–7, partially cited in Chapter 2 p. 66). Other evidence from later antiquity suggests similar responses – though they may have been influenced by Plutarch's. In a poem to the emperor Leon VI (AD 886–912) included in a copy of *Anabasis*, the anonymous author refers to the affair: δοκεῖ δέ μοι Κλέαρχος ὁ κλεινὸς Λάκων / σφῆλαι τὰ πάντα συσχεθεὶς ἀτολμίᾳ / Κύρου σοφὸν βούλευμα φαυλίσας τότε, 'But it seems to me that Klearchos, the famous Spartan / ruined the whole affair by cowardice / so crippling Cyrus's wise plan' (SB: for a complete translation of the poem, see Kaldellis 2015: 26–7). Modern scholars are more divided on the question of Klearchos' role at the battle. Notably, Wylie (1992: 124–6), alluded to above, makes a defence of the Spartan's actions.

29 The use of 'they said' (ἐλέγετο) distances Xenophon from the remark, leaving perhaps a sense that he is reluctant to openly criticise Klearchos' role (or that of a Spartan commander) in the battle. I add to my argument that he is critical by pointing to one of his own (character's) speeches by the Zapatas, in which he says: 'Where people are willing to take the lead in flight, it is far better to see them drawn up alongside the enemy than in our own ranks' (3.2.17). I am tempted to read this as an oblique reference to Klearchos, both his action at Cunaxa and the undertone of his fatal visit to Tissaphernes. Cf. Bassett 2001, who argues that Xenophon is defending Klearchos in his portrayal of the background to the Spartan's joining Cyrus's expedition.

Looking beyond Cyrus's individual leadership failing, the unsettling outcome of the expedition is a clear warning to ambitious princes and states alike about the dangers of relying on mercenary armies.[30]

Conclusions

Cyrus displays several of what, from the Greek perspective, are typical weaknesses of barbarian rule. There is lack of forethought in his planning of the expedition (he runs out of money early and does not include in his force an adequate cavalry component), loss of self-control at its conclusion (on seeing his brother, 'immediately his self-control vanished', 1.8.26), and disorder in his advance into Babylonia (1.7.20; see Herodotus 3.25 for similar barbarian impetuosity). He cannot exert full control over his mercenary contingent – in the end a failure which cost him his life – and the obedience of his own troops, if not his companions, is down to systemic subservience rather than loyalty (1.5.8). His inability to secure willing obedience is a critical leadership weakness which leaves him vulnerable throughout the march. The achievement of his goals relies on money and the craftiness of commanders, for example Klearchos at Tarsus and Menon at the Euphrates.

In situations where Cyrus displays effective leadership, as when he intervenes between Klearchos and Menon and their armies by the Euphrates (1.5.11–17), Xenophon seems to represent him as a Greek, thereby questioning the possibility of truly successful barbarian rule. As argued, however, Xenophon also clouds the boundary between Greek and barbarian with the (Socratic) purpose of showing that both have the same capacity for leadership. Cyrus's accreting of Greek values (presumably while he was in western Anatolia, but conceivably as well through Greeks attached to the royal court) demonstrates the fact that first culture background is not an exclusive determiner of character. We might see this enlightened view and the aforementioned one on leadership capacity as further ways in which the work reveals itself as a Socratic history (and note *Oikonomikos* 4.4, 4.18; *Memorabilia* 4.1.2).

While Xenophon's obituary of the prince is, appropriately for the genre, flattering, the reality of his rule as depicted in Book 1 shows that his style of

---

30 The subject was topical in the Classical period. Aristotle (*Eth. Nic.* 3.8.9) offers a critical assessment of the use of mercenaries. 'But professional soldiers prove cowards when the danger imposes too great a strain, and when they are at a disadvantage in numbers and equipment; for they are the first to run away, while citizen troops stand their ground and die fighting, as happened in the battle at the temple of Hermes. This is because citizens think it disgraceful to run away, and prefer death to safety so procured; whereas professional soldiers were relying from the outset on superior strength, and when they discover they are outnumbered they take to flight, fearing death more than disgrace.'

leadership, despite purple patches, is inefficient and ultimately ineffective. The success of the retreat will supply a proof of the comparative superiority of Hellenic leadership. But equally, through what I have argued is his implicit damning of Klearchos at Cunaxa, Xenophon reinforces the notion that capacity for successful leadership is not determined by ethnicity. In *Anabasis* we see this yet more prominently with Menon the Thessalian, who, through his lack of virtue (2.6.21–8) is in effect a barbarian, as are the mercenaries who murder the Kerasountian ambassadors on the Black Sea (5.7.13–19).

The Spartans: Klearchos and Cheirisophos

Following the death of Cyrus, Klearchos the Spartan became de facto leader of the Greek mercenaries (2.1.4, 2.2.5), remaining so until his capture some seven weeks later by Tissaphernes. His unofficial elevation was due to a combination of his Spartan background, age – he was around fifty at the time of the expedition – long experience of warfare and his privileged position under Cyrus.[31] Of these, bearing in mind the truth of *Memorabilia* 3.9.10, we should doubtless look to his experiences as the prime factor in bringing about his rule. From his obituary we learn that Cyrus was sufficiently impressed by him to part with money for a force to be maintained in the Chersonese (2.6.4; 1.1.9). Xenophon goes on to tell us of his fondness for war:

> When it is possible to live in peace without suffering shame or damage, nevertheless such a man chooses to be at war. When it is possible to live at ease, he wants to work hard, so long as it involves waging war. When it is possible to retain his money without danger, he chooses to diminish his wealth by going to war. Other people want to spend their money on boys or some other kind of pleasure; Klearchos wanted to spend his money on war. (2.6.6)

There is a sense in this description, and through the obituary, that Xenophon is alluding to the state and has in mind the militarised Spartan mode of life which he describes in *Lakedaimonion Politeia*. This inclines us to see Klearchos' representation as like Cyrus's, a blend of stereotype and real character traits. We can extend this way of reading, too, to Cheirisophos, who takes over his compatriot's role following his seizure by the

---

31 Spartan background: 3.2.37; age: 2.6.15 (for longevity conferring authority, see 2.1.10); war experience: 2.6.2, 15; position under Cyrus: 1.6.5, 3.1.10.

Zapatas River and may be, moreover, an official Spartan representative, having been sent out with 700 hoplites.[32] I suggest that Xenophon may be using the status of Cheirisophos to distinguish between the calibre of their respective leaderships. His character recommends to the Greeks at the Zapatas that Cheirisophos should lead the vanguard, since he is a Lakedaimonian (ἐπειδὴ καὶ Λακεδαιμόνιός ἐστι, 3.2.37). The usage of that sole attribute seems to equate to a limited evaluation of the Spartan at the outset, and while it is true the opposite effect might have been intended (see Plutarch, *Lykourgos* 30.5), his chequered performance on the retreat speaks to limitation. As historical context it may be relevant that he does not feature in the surviving histories of the Peloponnesian War (see further note 41). Internally, it is notable that when at Sinope on the Black Sea Cheirisophos does become the leader, and recalling again *Memorabilia* 3.9.10, it is by way of election, with a strong reaction from the men to the assertion by Xenophon that they should choose Cheirisophos instead of himself because he is a Spartan. 'Agasias of Stymphalos said that it would be ridiculous if things were as Xenophon had indicated. Or would the Lacedaemonians also be angry if when people got together to have a party, they didn't choose a Lacedaemonian to be the master of ceremonies?' (6.1.30).

In the selections which follow, key characteristics of the Spartan leader emerge, linking the two commanders under focus and enabling assessment of their leadership style. As in the case of Cyrus, the reader is implicitly invited to contemplate the reasons behind positive and negative outcomes arising from leadership decisions.

Managing Crises 1: Dealing with a Mutiny (1.3)

At Tarsus, realising they have been deceived and suspecting the true scale of Cyrus's ambition, the men refuse to continue (1.3.1).[33] Klearchos attempts to deal with the crisis by using force to get his own troops to move, but they

---

32 Xenophon is vague on the subject of Spartan support for Cyrus (1.4.2–3), and though in *Hellenika* he is more forthright (3.1.1), he does not say there either that Cheirisophos was sent out by Sparta. Diodoros (14.19.2–5, 21.1–2) is clear that Cheirisophos and his contingent are an official, if clandestine, Spartan contribution to the expedition. Roy (1967: 300) believes that the hoplites were Peloponnesian mercenaries hired by Sparta for the purpose. Spartan support would have been a repayment for Cyrus's backing of Sparta in the Peloponnesian War (*Hell.* 1.5.2–9, 1.6.18, 2.1.11–14; Thucydides 2.65.12). Some think that Klearchos too was sent by Sparta: Plutarch, *Artaxerxes* 6.3; Isokrates 8.98, 12.104.

33 Although this event occurs in Book 1, when Cyrus is leader, the prince has at this point suffered temporary leadership paralysis, leaving Klearchos in effective control.

in turn react violently, throwing stones at him and the pack animals as they try to go forward.[34] Later he changes tack and calls an assembly of his men: standing before them, as they look on in amazement he begins to cry, and continues doing so for a long time (πολὺν χρόνον, 1.3.2). By virtue of the emotive speech which he subsequently makes about his personal loyalty, Klearchos secures the trust of his men, and a large number of others (some 2,000 soldiers) leave their own commanders (Pasion and Xenias) to join him (1.3.7).

Klearchos' instinct when confronted with a mutinous situation is to act as a disciplinarian, using force to bring about order (see *Lakedaimonion Politeia* 2.2, 6.2). On first sight, his response to the failure of this approach seems very un-Spartan – this impression reflected in the reaction of the men to his tears. But in fact another key trait of his training is apparent in this action: the art of deception, taught to Spartan youths from an early age (*Lakedaimonion Politeia* 2.6–9; and see *Anabasis* 4.6.14–15). In manipulating the men and playing false with his true loyalties (1.3.8), he is drawing on this training. One outcome is that Cyrus is pressed into offering an increase in pay, and the crisis is averted, for the time being at least; a second is that Klearchos has succeeded in strengthening his own position in the army.

The ability of leaders to respond effectively to adverse circumstances is undoubtedly one of the episode's instructive features. So too is the power of speech to bring about desired results. Perhaps less obviously, an implicit concern is raised about the impact which the decision of 2,000 soldiers to transfer their allegiance to Klearchos from the commands of Pasion and Xenias might have on the unity of the army; that concern is realised not long after when one consequence of the failure of either Klearchos or Cyrus to address the transfer manifests itself in the desertion at Myriandros of the two disaffected commanders (1.4.7).

Xenophon uses the episode at Myriandros, where Pasion and Xenias sail off with their booty, to illustrate leadership successes and failings. On the one hand it reveals an important consequence of Klearchos' self-interested leadership and on the other, through his measured reaction to the desertions (1.4.8), Cyrus's skill in restoring the morale of the men and his own standing among them; the fact that he had taken the precaution of holding the families of the deserters at Tralles furthermore shows that he possesses some foresight.

---

34 Referring again to Hornblower's study of Spartan violence (note 26), the angry reaction may have been triggered by the use of the βακτηρία, probably carried by all Spartan officers (2000: 58). Regardless, there is evidently a link with the circumstances of its usage: in the canal case (below) there is no adverse reaction from the men when Klearchos uses his staff to strike. Stoning was not an unusual response to bad commanders and tyrants; Xenophon himself nearly suffers this fate in Thrace (7.6.10).

Crossing Canals: Leadership in the Field (2.3.11)

Following the battle at Cunaxa, the Greeks conclude a truce with the King, whose heralds lead them off to a location where they can secure provisions. Even though a truce is in effect, Klearchos keeps the army in order and himself commands the rearguard (2.3.10). His control invites a contrast with Cyrus's laxity on the approach into Babylonia (1.7.20). Xenophon reports that the route along which they were led by the Persians was crisscrossed by ditches and canals full of water and that to cross they had to make bridges from palm trees (this episode featured earlier in the chapter, where I looked at the force of exemplars in shaping Xenophon's narrative):

> Here one could readily see how Klearchos led his troops, with his spear in his left hand and his officer's baton in his right. If ever any of those posted to this task seemed to him to be slacking, he would pick out the right person and hit him, while at the same time he himself went into the mud and lent a hand, so that they were all ashamed not to be working hard along with him. (2.3.11)

The disciplinarian in Klearchos is again prominent, though in this episode he complements his use of physical punishment with exemplary action: in doing as he himself orders, the leader motivates those around him. This is another key feature of Spartan leadership (*Lakedaimonion Politeia* 8.2, *Agesilaos* 5.3). As already noted, Klearchos' descent into the mud recalls the Persian prince's failure to do so when his wagons had become stuck. In his marking of this episode as a lesson in leadership (καὶ ἐνταῦθα ἦν Κλέαρχον καταμαθεῖν ὡς ἐπεστάτει) Xenophon is stressing the importance of this quality in a leader.[35] In the mirroring of the episodes there is a hint too of a strong similarity in attitudes towards subordinates, that the use of the staff and the lash linked Spartans and Persians in an important way.

As we see later in the narrative when he is accused of *hubris* for beating a man (5.8.1), Xenophon (as an Athenian?) appears to be subject to a different code. In that case, as with the one under discussion, the army was under threat of imminent attack, yet Klearchos' striking of men not pulling their weight does not result in the same reported reaction at the time or after. On flexibility being a valuable leadership quality, it may be notable that one commander reverts to the method of the other when his own approach fails: Klearchos using speech in Kilikia, Xenophon violence in Armenia.

---

35 He himself displays this leadership quality on several occasions through the retreat: 3.4.47–8, 4.4.12, 7.3.45, and note also *Kyr*. 1.6.8, and *Hipp*. 6.4: 'To put it shortly, a commander is least likely to incur the contempt of his men if he shows himself more capable than they of doing whatever he requires of them.'

The Ass among the Weapons: False Reporting (2.19–20)

One night in Babylonia, in the tense atmosphere that prevailed following the battle, a panic threatened to descend on the Greeks:

> [19] Nevertheless, as the night went on ... there was a hubbub and a din such as readily happens when a panic descends. [20] Klearchos ordered Tolmides of Elis, the best herald of his day, who was, as it happened, in his quarters, to call for silence and proclaim that the generals had an announcement to make: that whoever gave information as to who had let the donkey loose among the weapon stacks would receive a talent of silver as a reward. (2.2.19–20)

Although he does not explicitly mark this as a lesson in leadership, it is apparent that Xenophon intends it to be an exemplum for commanders in tense situations. Aspiring military leaders should cultivate the ability to think and produce effective solutions on the hoof, as the experienced Klearchos instinctively does. Recalling his tears in Tarsus, this is a further instance of the Spartan's use of brazen deception on his own men to achieve a favourable outcome.

Zapatas River: Leadership around the Table (2.5)

Following agreement of terms for a return to Ionia (2.3.26–8), the Greek army together with a Persian one led by Tissaphernes set off northwards along the Tigris. However, mutual suspicion between the two sides grew steadily and threatened to develop into serious conflict (2.4.9–11). At the Zapatas River, on the initiative of Klearchos, the two leaders met to discuss the volatile situation (2.5.3–26); as a result, the Spartan agreed to return to the tent of Tissaphernes the next day with the other generals in order for those suspected of being responsible for fomenting hostility to be identified. Not all in the Greek camp were convinced of the wisdom of this, but five of the generals and twenty captains were prevailed upon by Klearchos to go (2.5.29–30). The Persians seized him and the generals and cut down the captains (2.5.31–2).[36]

While the initiative of Klearchos in approaching Tissaphernes to clear the air was commendable, he did not have the requisite level of political skill to carry it through successfully.[37] Superior in this field, Tissaphernes

---

36 An irony here is that Klearchos himself several years before had used a similar ruse at Byzantium to eliminate the city's rulers and take control of it (Diodoros 14.12.2–3; Polyaenus, *Strat.* 2.2.7).

37 Danzig (2007: 35) remarks: '[t]he fact that some Greeks guessed Tissaphernes' intentions shows that his actions were not as shocking as Clearchus' were foolish'. Rood (2006: 51) sees one of the roles of the advisers ('some of the soldiers', *An.* 2.5.29) as pointing up the rashness of the person (Klearchos) who neglects their warning.

turned the situation to his own advantage by exploiting the naivety, rashness and ambition of the Spartan. From Xenophon's reconstruction of the dialogue between the two men at their fateful meeting, we witness how the Persian outwits his adversary. At the start Klearchos assumes that his counterpart shares his implacable faith in the sanctity of their oaths – 'First and most important, the oaths we swore to the gods prevent us from being enemies to each other' (πρῶτον μὲν γὰρ καὶ μέγιστον οἱ θεῶν ἡμᾶς ὅρκοι κωλύουσι πολεμίους εἶναι ἀλλήλοις, 2.5.7; see also 2.4.7) – thereby leaving himself open to be exploited on trust. He goes on to reveal personal ambition by suggesting that he would be willing to lead the mercenaries in any number of campaigns that would benefit Tissaphernes (2.5.13–14); in his reply, Tissaphernes says that 'you yourself have mentioned some of the ways in which you and your troops are useful to me, but I myself know the greatest: for only the King can wear the tiara upright on his head, but perhaps another, with your assistance, might readily wear it upright in his heart' (2.5.23).[38] Klearchos must, then, have left the meeting with heady prospects in mind.

Xenophon next reveals that Klearchos was anxious to purge the army of elements in it hostile to himself (2.5.29). Given his arrangement with Tissaphernes that each of them would identify the troublemakers (2.5.24–6), it is apparent that he also saw the detente as an opportunity to strengthen his own control over the army. Notably, his need to cajole officers to go to Tissaphernes speaks to his inability to secure an enduring willing obedience. Once again, as at Tarsus, and on the battlefield at Cunaxa where the mercenaries lined up as one with the native force, Klearchos failed to act in the interest of the whole army. His actions now not only proved fatal to himself but endangered the very survival of the Greek force. This theme of Spartans pursuing individual self-interest continues throughout the narrative and is especially marked in Xenophon's depiction of the behaviour of senior officials (Anaxibios, Aristarchos) in European Thrace (Book 7).[39]

This episode is a good example of how Xenophon uses the figure of Tissaphernes to point up deficiencies in the actions of the expedition commanders. Notwithstanding his portrayal in roundly negative terms across Xenophon's writings, his prominence and effectiveness hint that

---

38 Readers debate what precisely Tissaphernes means here. Some think he is hinting to Klearchos that he has ambitions to be king, others that he wishes only to secure a practical independence from the monarch. Roisman (1985–8: 46 n.40) offers another reading: 'As the context of the remark makes clear, it meant that the King leads by virtue of his rank and office while Tissaphernes leads because of the affections he stirs among his followers. Such a claim did not constitute an ambition for the Persian throne.'

39 Cf. Roisman 1988, who seeks to undermine Xenophon's treatment of Anaxibios and Aristarchos, offering a different perspective on the Spartans' actions.

in historical terms the Athenian recognised Tissaphernes as one of the outstanding statesmen of the age.[40]

Managing Crises 2: Speech versus Action (3.1–3)

On the initiative of Xenophon, following the events at the Zapatas, Cheirisophos the Spartan becomes commander of the army vanguard. As I argued above, Cheirisophos' primacy arises from his status as a Spartan (3.2.37), whereas Klearchos' derived from experience in the field. That Cheirisophos was not among the generals who went to Tissaphernes could, as David Thomas suggests, point to a minor role in the old command, although it might as well indicate that, as a fellow Spartan, Klearchos trusted him more than the other commanders: it is he whom Klearchos sent to Ariaios following the battle at Cunaxa to offer him the throne (2.1.4–5).[41]

Compared to Klearchos, Cheirisophos is more limited in terms of speech-making. His longest address is twelve OCT lines (6.1.32–3). In contrast to the elaborate speeches made by Xenophon in Book 3, his words to the men in Mesopotamia are sparse, and may seem to be inadequate in light of the desperate circumstances in which the army finds itself.[42] Yet, with their reputation for military prowess and tradition of military success, the men look to the Spartans for decisive action rather than inspirational words and gestures (recall, for instance, their amazement when Klearchos wept at Tarsus before going on to speak at length). Cheirisophos, in his pragmatic response to the crisis, meets this expectation. When Xenophon has concluded his speech (one and a half OCT pages long) to an assembly of surviving generals and captains, Cheirisophos instructs the officers to go and choose new rulers where this is needed in order that a full assembly of the army can be held: 'no sooner had he said this than he stood up, so that there should be no delay and they would carry out what was necessary'

---

40 For readings of Xenophon's representation of Tissaphernes, see Danzig 2007, Jansen 2014, Lee 2016b. Hyland (2018) presents a picture of Persian affairs in the west 450–386 and argues that Tissaphernes and the other satraps were less autonomous than others have thought; their success, he argues, was limited in some part by the apparent reluctance of the King to commit resources to achieve objectives but also, especially in the case of Tissaphernes, by missteps.

41 The suggestion by David Thomas (in correspondence) that Cheirisophos may have been a relatively junior officer would help account for the facts that he was not known from the Peloponnesian War, was not one of those who went to the tent of Tissaphernes and had no real clout with the army when elected their leader on the Black Sea. Millender (2020: 233) dismisses Cheirisophos in the text 'as a rather colourless foil for Xenophon'.

42 Cf. H-R (35), who seek to show through analysis of the short speech at 3.2.2–3 that Cheirisophos is not without rhetorical effectiveness. Similarly, Powell (2020: 26) calls attention to the Spartan's repartee in a (humorous) exchange with Xenophon in Armenia.

(3.1.47). Following Xenophon's subsequent speech to the full assembly (five OCT pages), for which he dresses himself in his finest armour, Cheirisophos urges the measures spoken of to be voted on 'as soon as possible' (3.2.33; and see Thucydides 5.69). After, then, the brief, in some ways colourful lead of Klearchos, with his compatriot we have a return to a more typical Spartan leadership style. We might even see Cheirisophos as a corrective to the individualism of Klearchos, this symbolised by the latter's status as an exile.

Cheirisophos impresses his stamp in the crucial period which sees the army cross the Zapatas River and re-establish its viability. It is he who answers Mithradates – an old ally of Cyrus who appears claiming to be well disposed towards the Greeks – on the morning they set out (3.3.3), and the subsequent decision not to admit heralds so long as they are in enemy territory bears the hallmark of his militaristic training (3.3.5). Once on their way, he leads from the front and is quick to point out and admonish even high-level errors (3.3.11: Xenophon at fault).

We could easily overlook the quiet but effective pragmatism of Cheirisophos amidst the drama of Xenophon's introduction to the story and the stirring series of speeches which he delivers on the banks of the Zapatas River. It is tempting to see this in the Spartan's favour as a negative contrast between words and deeds – talking about doing and doing. Yet, in the wider picture, the inspirational speeches are an equally important ingredient for survival. In the despair and danger of the predicament there is the unmistakeable impression that the laconic contribution would not be sufficient of itself to bring about the rebuilding of morale that Xenophon at least sees as a prerequisite for escape from Tissaphernes' grasp (3.1.39–42; and see *Kyroupaideia* 1.6.13). In this regard, Xenophon's leadership brings into relief the limits of Cheirisophos' when dealing with a non-Spartan army and points to the desirability of an equilibrium between speech and action, 'a speaker of words and doer of deeds'. Xenophon's character marks this in the conclusion to his major speech to the assembly at the Zab: 'it is now time to bring my speech to a close and put it into practice' (3.2.32).

Military Expertise (1–4 passim)

Not surprisingly, both Spartans show a high level of competence in military matters. Numerous instances highlight tactical proficiency (1.8.13, 4.3.17), proficiency in the art of deception (2.3.9, 2.4.26), strategic foresight (2.3.13), maintaining order and obedience (2.2.20, 2.3.11), the ability to obtain supplies and logistical nous (2.3.4–6). The quality of the Spartans' training and its more or less successful application invites comparison with the styles of Cyrus and Xenophon respectively. While demonstrably capable, both are shown as being conspicuously lacking in one or more important facets of military leadership: Cyrus, for example, in running out of money (1.2.11) and in leaving his forces vulnerable on the approach to battle by not keeping their order (1.7.19–20), Xenophon through failing to grasp the limitation of pursuing enemy cavalry on foot (3.3.8–10; and see *Hipp*. 5.1) and in his poor handling of a foray to secure supplies from an enemy tribe (5.2). However, quite apart from Xenophon's steep learning curve, what comes through from the narrative is the Socratic view that military expertise, while an essential part of good military leadership, is not sufficient by itself to make a good commander. Xenophon's skill in speaking and his cultivation of willing obedience show themselves to be arguably more vital in this regard.

Incident with the Guide: The Angry Spartan (4.6.2–3)

After a week sheltering from winter weather in the Armenian highlands, the Greeks continued their journey, taking with them as a guide the headman of one of the villages where they had stayed (the Armenian villages Xenophon writes of may be situated north of the Euphrates around Bulanık; Figure 3.3 shows a village in the region). On the third day's march, still not in sight of any settlements, Cheirisophos confronted the guide, who insisted that there were none in the area. Becoming angry with him (αὐτῷ ἐχαλεπάνθη) the Spartan struck him (αὐτὸν ἔπαισεν), and that night, not having been bound, he fled. The narrator states that this incident – the harsh treatment

Figure 3.3 Snowbound village in eastern Anatolia. (Author)

of the guide and the neglect that led to his escape – 'was the only thing about which Cheirisophos and Xenophon had a serious disagreement during the whole journey' (4.6.3). By this explicit disapproval he is underlining the importance of the need for commanders to manage key assets properly. Later in the march, 'Xenophon' exemplifies the correct approach, placing informants under strict guard (ἐφύλαττεν ἰσχυρῶς), 'so that they could act as guides to wherever there might be a need to go' (6.3.11).

The author is surely being ironic when he says that this was the only thing the two men disagreed on (see 4.1.19), and in relating this incident he is pointing up two serious failings in Cheirisophos' leadership, both of which may be attributable to his Spartan background. The first is his arrogant attitude towards the guide. Given the prudence of his leadership up to this point, and notwithstanding the fact that the man's son had been taken along as a hostage, it is hard not to read his failure to ensure that the guide was bound as a form of arrogance, deeming him to be so insignificant as not to warrant detention.

The second, and perhaps more severe fault in Xenophon's eyes is the event that led to the guide fleeing – Cheirisophos, in his quickness to anger, striking the man. His flight during the night left the Greeks lost in a harsh environment; they may subsequently have gone on to follow a river, the Phasis, in the mistaken belief that it emptied into the Euxine, an error that lengthened their journey and occasioned additional hardship. Nor is this the first time that Spartan rage has endangered the expedition. As described earlier, Klearchos, after Menon's men threw things at him, ordered his own to arms to redress the humiliation, with only the intervention of Cyrus preventing disaster (1.5.11–17 and see 2.6.9). It is notable that *Hellenika* too highlights Spartan propensity to anger: for example, at 1.6.6–7, 2.4.32–4 and 6.2.19. At 5.3.7 Xenophon interjects an explicitly didactic paragraph warning of the danger of acting out of anger:

> Now I claim that men can learn from such experiences [the fate of Teleutias], and they can learn especially that it is not right to punish anyone in anger – even a slave, since masters who are angry often themselves suffer greater evils than they inflict on their servants. And it is a complete and utter mistake to attack an enemy with anger rather than judgement. For anger acts without foresight, whereas judgement has in view a way to harm one's enemy without suffering any hurt from him in return. (*Hellenika* 5.3.7)

Xenophon has evidently learned from first-hand experience that Spartan commanders are prone to angry outbursts and can exhibit arrogance in their attitude towards non-Spartiates. He shows that this temperament undermines the effectiveness of their leadership on the retreat and, by extension, raises an implicit question about their suitability for governing Greece. Xenophon does not venture an explanation for these character faults, but possibly there is a hint in the episode under review that they are a consequence of their social system, with its underclass of helots: the guide, a functionary in a village which supplies the stables of the Great King (4.5.34), is in a similar type of relationship to the Persians as the helots are to the Spartans. Referring to the Teleutias episode mentioned above, Thomas writes: 'the reason Spartans are addicted to outbursts of temper may be the high proportion of unfree people within Spartan society, whom upper-class Spartans can attack without restraint'.[43]

Conclusions

Klearchos, Book 2, and Cheirisophos, Books 3–6, are the main representatives of the Spartan style of leadership. As we would expect, they are both portrayed as highly capable in military matters, and they display competence in statecraft and speech, with Klearchos showing an impressive turn of oratory to achieve a success for his leadership. When they need to, then, Spartans can deploy the power of speech too (which may be a more positive assessment than found in other ancient writers: see for instance Thucydides 4.85–7, with the author's prefatory comment that Brasidas was not a bad speaker 'for a Spartan', 4.84.2). Yet, markedly so in the performance of Cheirisophos, we see that they do not do so enough to be effective in an army of non-Spartans. Xenophon demonstrates convincingly that there are other factors as well which make them unsuitable for all but parochial leadership: notably, they are quick to anger, corruptible and selfish (these traits are even more in evidence in the representations in Book 7 of Anaxibios and Aristarchos).

In addition to being a key part of the leadership theme in *Anabasis*, the exposition of Spartan leadership serves as a critique of Spartan hegemony over the Greek world in the aftermath of the Peloponnesian War. In terms of its control of peoples and resources, Sparta reached the zenith of its power around 400, making Xenophon's commentary in *Anabasis* especially relevant. This in my view is the author post-Leuktra (371) offering a reflection on the nature of Spartan power as it manifested itself across the Hellenic space. I think there is an implicit question for the reader: 'Could this have changed?' So, the pattern of rule that the Spartans

---

43 Thomas 2009: xli. See further Hornblower 2000: 60–1, 69–71, and on 71 citing Redfield's (1995: 173) explanation for the phenomenon of Spartan violence: 'Spartiates, he [Redfield] notes, "were raised predominantly by women, then evicted into the male world of asceticism and competition, and we may attribute to the abruptness of this change the rigid and yet uncertain self-control of the Spartans; for all their discipline, they were certainly (as we meet them in the histories) more than other Greeks subject to fits of rage and violence".'

employed in their relatively long period of hegemony was inset, and predictable, from the beginning.[44]

As a counter to the formation of an unequivocally negative judgement on their rule, late in the narrative we encounter the more positive figure of Kleandros, the harmost (Spartan term, literally, 'fixer') at Byzantium and a guest-friend of Xenophon. Featuring prominently in Books 6–7, he is portrayed as showing wise judgement in a case against two of the Cyreans and in seeing through accusations that had been made against Xenophon himself.

Xenophon the Athenian

At the Zapatas River, as already seen, the surviving officers elect new generals to replace those seized by Tissaphernes. The march order subsequently sees Cheirisophos command the vanguard, with other generals marshalling the flanks and rear.[45] It is Xenophon who proposes this order, saying that Cheirisophos should go in the lead position as he is a Spartan (3.2.37). Nonetheless, it is clear from Xenophon's own role that, from the beginning, he himself is prominent in directing the march. In his own account he is the one who stirs the army from its torpor (ἀθύμως) following the devastating decapitation strike by Tissaphernes: his speeches, first to the captains of the contingent to which he is attached, then to the wider officer corps, and finally to a full assembly of staff and soldiers, succeed in rallying morale and producing a plan for an ordered retreat out from under the shadow of Tissaphernes. So effective has been Xenophon's intervention, and despite his youth and hitherto near anonymous role in the expedition, we feel almost no surprise when it is he who orchestrates the key practical decisions about march formation and assignment of commander roles.[46]

---

44 Gish (2009: 367), in a study of Spartan hegemony in *Hellenika*, comments that 'the rule of the Spartans at home and abroad imitated the despotic rule and tyranny of their severe souls over their own bodies'. Millender, in a more substantial study of relations between Xenophon and Sparta in *Anabasis* than I have provided here, sees a more concrete motivation for Xenophon's treatment of Sparta in the work. 'The *Anabasis* rather provides a focused critique of the foreign policy that the Spartans pursued after the ratification of the Peace of Antalkidas – or King's Peace – in 386' (2020: 244). This view is linked to Millender's belief that Xenophon wrote the bulk of *Anabasis* in the late 380s – indeed wrote it as a response to Spartans' attempts to dominate their fellow Greeks following the peace (224) – and that the text parallels Isokratic literature of the same period (244–5).

45 New generals (3.1.47): Cheirisophos, Xenophon, Timasion, Xanthikles, Philesios, Kleanor. Cheirisophos is in the vanguard, with Sophainetos, one of the original commanders (1.1.11, 1.2.3), Xanthikles, Philesios and Kleanor on the flanks and Xenophon and Timasion in the rear. This structure appears to have operated until Sinope on the Black Sea, when Cheirisophos is elected sole commander (6.1.32; see also 6.1.18, 21).

46 See the earlier discussion (pp. 89–90) on the leadership arrangement as it likely was versus how it is portrayed by Xenophon. As argued, the elision of other leaders in the account can convincingly be explained by the degree to which the narrative is subject to the author's agenda.

Xenophon's achievement in extricating the Greeks from their predicament and ultimately getting them back to Asia Minor invites comparison to other successful historical figures involved in military conflict. I argue that he himself purposefully alludes to several in the Athenian democracy in order to situate himself within this tradition and to create for his internal audience an expectation about his own style of leadership and the success that it may bring to the army. One reference would be to Themistocles, who persuaded the Athenians to leave their city in the face of the King's advance and inspired their subsequent improbable military triumph (Plutarch, *Themistocles* 10.1–2; Herodotus 7.143). Arguments in Xenophon's speeches indeed suggest specific connections to leaders of the early fifth-century Persian resistance; for example, his contention that the King would gladly build roads to assist the Greeks in leaving his territory (3.2.24) calls to mind the plea Plutarch reports Aristides as making to Themistocles not to destroy the bridges over the Hellespont but instead to seek ways to speed Xerxes' departure from Hellas, 'lest, being shut in and unable to make his escape, from sheer necessity he throw this vast force of his upon the defensive' (*Aristides* 9.4).[47]

With more contemporary resonance, the eloquence and thrust of Xenophon's speech to the full assembly recalls the famous funeral oration which Thucydides ascribes to Pericles at the outset of the Peloponnesian War (2.35–46). I show in the first section that Xenophon's outstanding performance on the retreat maps on to the key values which Pericles extols in the speech. It bears mention that with a relatively small number of Athenians in the army, an Athenian model of leadership is not what we, or presumably the men themselves, would have expected, so its adoption is indicative of both its appeal and of Xenophon being an adept exponent of democratic practice. And although a number of the practices and underlying values in question would be common to other *poleis*, it would be odd to argue that Xenophon was following anything other than an Athenian model of governance.[48] I add that the evocation of the Athenian system also forms part of the work's Socratic dimension, this being the environment in which the philosopher operated.

In the second section I turn to explore this other dimension and seek to demonstrate how Xenophon's leadership draws on his association with the philosopher Socrates. As with his depiction of the other leaders, we

---

47 However, the report may be late and unhistorical, so probably not an allusion intended by Xenophon, though he may have known an oral tradition of the same.
48 Cf. on Xenophon and Athenian democratic ideology Seager 2001, who argues that 'it is at least possible that Xenophon, the (qualified) admirer of Sparta, was not averse to pointing out that Sparta sometimes provided a better exemplar than Athens of those values that Athenian democrats claimed to prize' (396). Hornblower (2004: 244) points out that Cheirisophos also calls for a vote of hands (*An.* 3.2.33).

should not regard Xenophon's own representation of himself as wholly historically reliable;[49] rather than Xenophon qua Xenophon, the character we have in *Anabasis* is at once an exemplar of a young Athenian citizen and a student of Socrates. It is these democratic and philosophy backgrounds which inform his character's leadership throughout. In the treatment, I highlight distinctive features of Xenophon the character's style and, where relevant, draw a contrast to the Persian and Spartan approaches to leadership. While there is a focus on highlighting links to the military advice given by Socrates in Xenophon's *Memorabilia*, in practice Xenophon's own training and experiences as an Athenian cavalryman are equally important ingredients in his successful performance.

Xenophon the Democrat

Rhetorically accomplished speeches are the hallmark of Xenophon's leadership. From his formal introduction to the story in Book 3, he makes over twenty substantial speeches, invariably at times of difficulty either for the army or for himself. Although Xenophon's character does not sideline action, the author emphasises the primacy of the spoken word and its power to influence and even to change decisively the course of unfolding events.[50] While Xenophon's facility as *rhetor* owes itself in part to his association with Socrates (see *Memorabilia* 3.3.11, discussed in the next

---

49 I argue elsewhere in the monograph that although *Anabasis* has an autobiographical character it is not at the same time a reliable source for detail on Xenophon's life, even for the period 401–399. It is worth noting Cicero's comment (*QFr*. 1.1.23) that in *Kyroupaideia* Xenophon describes the figure of Cyrus the Great 'not according to historical truth but as the pattern of a just ruler'. Articulation of the gap between Xenophon's role on the march and his own representation of that role in *Anabasis* is unlikely to be possible in the absence of another participant account. A particular concern would be what he does not tell us.

50 The power and charm of speech: 3.2.8–32, Xenophon rallies and motivates the men to save themselves; 5.7.5–33, defuses tense situation arising from rumours that he plans to lead the army back towards the Phasis; 5.8.2–26, successfully defends himself against charge of *hubris*; 7.1.22–32, prevents sack of Byzantium; 7.6.11–38, defends himself against charge of corruption (7.6.9, internal audience acknowledgement of Xenophon's skill in persuasion). Dio Chrysostom (*Or*. 18.15) writes of Xenophon's speeches: 'If it is needful for the statesman to encourage those who are in the depths of despondency, time and again our writer shows how to do this; or if the need is to incite and exhort, no one who understands the Greek language could fail to be aroused by Xenophon's hortatory speeches.' On his speech to the general assembly at the Zapatas, Erbse (491) writes: 'These familiar tropes of Athenian rhetoric provide scarcely any grasp on how to deal with the present situation. But they do give the exhausted troops the will to live again: Xenophon manages to *get something* to happen, and demonstrates that only he, the educated and rhetorically trained Athenian in the midst of the rough mercenaries, has access to the means for this success.'

Figure 3.4 Fourth-century BC Boiotian helmet recovered from Centrites River in the mid-nineteenth century. Gts-tg, CC BY-SA 4.0, Ashmolean Museum.

section), it must also owe a debt to his Athenian roots and upbringing. For any young citizen interested in political advancement at Athens, acquiring skills in argument was a prerequisite, and while to do so many sought expert tuition, turning, for example, to the sophists, participation in the democratic process was itself a powerful mode of learning.[51]

In his first address to the assembled army (3.2.7–39), Xenophon exemplifies the tradition of public oratory at Athens. Before he even begins, he accoutres himself in his finest armour: in the absence of a recognisable physical forum, this act symbolises the formality and importance of the occasion for both his internal and external audiences.[52] The speech itself

---

51 On the meaning of *rhetor* in the Athenian political context, see Hansen 1983: 39–42.
52 Xenophon is doubtless also keen to impress; see *Kyr.* 8.1.40. Erbse (491) writes that his dressing up allows his personality to cast its spell on his audience, while, in contrast, Waterfield (2006: 183) thinks it reveals a pretentious side to Xenophon's character. On what he might have worn, Aelian (*VH* 3.24) talks of an Attic breastplate and a Boiotian helmet (κράνος Βοιωτουργές): one such was discovered in the nineteenth century in the Centrites (Bhotan Su), a river crossed by the Ten Thousand while under great pressure on both sides. See Figure 3.4. Though he makes no mention of his on the march, Xenophon the author does write enthusiastically about this type of helmet: *PH* 12.3. Schachner and Sağlamtimur (2008) suggest the one found in the Centrites is the only archaeological evidence for the historical event.

is engaging and inspiring, raising the spirits of the men. Replete with references to sacrifice and freedom, it is, as Sarah Ferrario remarks, close to the genre of funeral oration, the delivery of which was reserved for eminent political and military leaders of the democracy (Thucydides 2.34.6).[53] Xenophon is thus representing himself as being in a line of successful Athenian leaders and, by way of the democratic setting – full assembly, speech, inclusive decision-making process – is signalling that his leadership on the retreat ahead will be according to the same principles as those espoused by his forebears. I suggest that he intends his leadership performance to be viewed especially against the background of Pericles' famous funeral speech. On the march Xenophon embodies ideals expressed by Pericles at the Kerameikos, and his success lends real substance to the case for democratic leadership being more effective than the two styles he has already showcased. The examples given below demonstrate how echoes of the Thucydidean speech reverberate throughout the retreat and how Xenophon links himself to it via his character's actions.[54]

On the ground it is debatable of course whether the internal audience, which as remarked consisted of only a relatively small number of Athenians, cared as much for the operating principles of Xenophon's leadership as they did for the success which it promised. Perhaps we should also question Xenophon's fidelity to democracy in both its literal sense and as an ideology. On the retreat it becomes apparent that his interest in this form of government owes itself to a considerable degree to its efficacy as a means of achieving leadership goals. We see this in what *appear* to be instances of his being directed by an empowered *demos*: on numerous occasions he calls for proposals to be put to a show of hands, but notably these are ones where the course being put forward will surely be approved. As Nussbaum points out,

---

53 On Xenophon's speech, Ferrario (2012: 364) writes: 'The recollections of the victories over the Persians (3.2.11–13), of the *eleutheria* ("freedom") that the Greek states enjoy (3.2.13), and of the achievements of the soldiers' *progonoi* ("ancestors", 3.2.13–14) are all also traditional themes of the Athenian *epitaphios logos*.' H-R remark that it is 'largely made up of topoi familiar from battle exhortations and Athenian funeral orations (especially Lys. 2.20–47; Pl. *Menex*. 240a–41d), here adapted to remove the exaltation of specifically Athenian glory and so appeal to Xenophon's diverse audience' (106).

54 Tamiolaki argues that Xenophon draws on Pericles' funeral oration in *Hellenika* (2008) and in *Kyroupaideia* (2017). Rood (2004a: 328) remarks that Xenophon in *Anabasis* 'is at times Thucydides' Pericles, a model leader, inspiring the despondent' (328). Cartledge (2021: 278) identifies echoes of Pericles at Thucydides 2.13 in Xenophon's speech to the Ten Thousand at Byzantium, where he enumerates the resources which Athens drew on in the Peloponnesian War, but to opposite effect (see *An*. 7.1.27). On the relation between Thucydides' Pericles and Xenophon's self-presentation in *Anabasis*, see further Nussbaum 1967, Rood 2006, Christ 2020. Xenophon's embracing of the ideals outlined does not necessarily mean he was uncritical of Pericles himself, or that Pericles' speech as reported by Thucydides is uncritical of Athenian democracy.

no proposal put to the army is ever rejected.⁵⁵ Conversely, in cases where a proposal may pass, and he does not want it to do so, he is able to intervene to have it shelved (see 6.1.25–31, where Xenophon dissuades the men from a course that would have him elected as leader).

We see a good illustration of the dynamics of the first situation (no proposal rejected) at Trapezous, where the army faces the possibility of there being insufficient ships to ferry them onwards. Xenophon's suggestion that they order the cities along the coast to have the roads rebuilt as a precaution is received negatively:

> As [he] perceived that they were being gripped by folly, he did not put anything to a vote on this topic, but instead persuaded the cities to mend the roads voluntarily, saying that they would more quickly be rid of the army if the roads were made passable. (5.1.14)⁵⁶

Another episode that seems to be revealing of Xenophon's attitude to democracy is worth looking at. This concerns the emergence of Klearchos as leader of the Greeks following the death of Cyrus at Cunaxa. 'When they heard [Klearchos say] this,' he writes, 'the generals and captains went away and did as instructed. And from then on Klearchos acted as the commander and they obeyed, not because they had elected him their commander but because they saw he alone understood what the commander must understand, while the others did not have enough experience' (2.2.5). This seems to be a critical comment on the nature of democracy, in that what confers genuine legitimacy on a leader, Xenophon asserts, is his ability to perform his role effectively, not the process of how he came to be in that role, a point repeated expressly at *Memorabilia* 3.9.10–11.

The question of Xenophon's attitude towards democracy is one less studied than it might be, and before turning to the Periclean comparanda I digress further on it. A preliminary comment is that the focus on leadership in *Anabasis* may give the impression of the soldiers being blindly led and the democratic system as a powerful means of realising voluntary servitude – a view indeed held by some in the elite of the time (see, for example, Thucydides 6.89.5, where Alkibiades speaks of 'others, formerly as now, who

---

55 Nussbaum: 'not a single proposal which is recorded as being once moved is rejected' (1967: 58). See 3.2.9; 5.1.7, 8; 5.7.35; 7.3.3–6. Note also 7.7.18, where Xenophon confidently invites an opportunist Thracian court figure, Medosades, to allow the inhabitants of the land they are in 'to vote whether it is appropriate for us [the Greeks] to leave their land or for you to do so'.
56 For discussion of this episode, see also Rood 2004a: 325, Brennan 2011: 128–9 and 2021a: xx. It would count as well as an occasion when the army exercises its sovereignty: see further below.

tried to lead the multitude astray'). But I do not think such an impression is wholly consistent with the picture of the quasi-democracy Xenophon provides in the text. The Ten Thousand, transformed into a rudimentary *polis* under his tutelage, duly exercise their sovereignty on a number of occasions, for instance in offering Xenophon the chance to become leader at Sinope (6.1.17–19) and Byzantium (7.1.21) and in discarding their leaders at Herakleia (6.2.9–12). The meeting at Trapezous discussed is also singular in this regard, as the constituency displays its independence and exercises its ability 'to judge proposals' (Thucydides 2.40.2).

The general lack of noise around the topic of Xenophon and democracy may be partly explained by a modern assumption that has him fixed as an anti-democrat (it should be noted that direct democracy has traditionally been thought of as crude and unpredictable, so making ancient elite aversion to it understandable regardless of ideological leaning).[57] The basis for the assumption about Xenophon presumably lies in his personal background and the association of elites with oligarchic, or at least not democratic, power. In his biography, Anderson writes that his 'political ideas reflect the inherited traditions and prejudices of his class'.[58] For (arguably) anti-democratic sentiment in the *Memorabilia* see 1.2.9, 2.6.27, 3.7.5. But it seems worth suggesting that for both Xenophon and Socrates proto-Hellenic democracy, wherein the weight of decisions was felt profoundly by those making them, was something of an ideal.[59]

---

57 For Xenophon as anti-democrat: Luccioni 1947, Anderson 1974: 42, Vlastos 1983: 502–6, Goldhill 1998: 109, Brock 2004: 253–4, Pownall 2004: 82, 112, Waterfield 2006: 50. For studies pushing back on the anti-democratic Xenophon, see Gray 2007, Kroeker 2009, Gish 2012 (161, for the perception of direct democracy), none of whom, however, looks in detail at *Anabasis*. Tuplin 2017 and Christ 2020 take the subject forward with examinations of the relationship between Xenophon and Athens. Christ, who characterises Xenophon's perspective on the democracy as moderate, presents him as an internal critic who seeks to improve rather than overthrow (2020: 6–7). My general view, as outlined in the paragraph, embodies more of a tension than this.
58 Anderson 1974: 40.
59 I would not be alone in holding the opinion that the origins of democracy lie in the agonistic culture that came to define early Greek societies. The numerous tribes holding plots of defensible agriculture succeeded by way of their individual members' reliance on one another, a factor which gave those members a real voice, one that carried over time and when on a large enough scale ultimately developed into a system defined by law and the ballot. For expert views on this subject, see Rhodes 2004, Cartledge 2016. Cartledge (2016: 51) would see a less harmonious background to the emergence of democracy than the one I outlined: 'Already in Homer, indeed, in the conspicuously ill-favoured shape of the agitator Thersites, there are signs of plebeian, anti-aristocratic thinking, even perhaps political thought ... the very fact that it was spelled out in this way likely hints at a subtextual anxiety, at an at least vague sense of popular discomfort with or even resistance to the rule of those who are both in Homer and later also in Hesiod called "kings" (*basileis*).'

The difficulty with the system that eventually grew out of this was that it diluted individual responsibility and was open to manipulation by influential actors who might seek to profit at the expense of the community, or lead it in a dubious direction, as for instance was the case with the generals' trial following Arginousai (*Hellenika* 1.7). We get a sideways glimpse of this system in *Anabasis* in what, in a memorable exchange between Xenophon and Cheirisophos, is presented as a Spartan's attitude to democracy. Xenophon's character, who ribs the Spartan about their practice of stealing, receives this response:

> But on the contrary... what I hear is that you Athenians are terribly clever at stealing public money, even though it's an especially terrible danger that the thief is running – and indeed I hear that this is especially true of the best among you, assuming that with you it is the best who are thought fit to rule. (4.6.16)

I think, then, that Xenophon had no liking for this democracy but that he recognised it offered advantages in the practice of leadership and, with the failure of oligarchy at Athens, it was, as Christ argues, the system Athenian leaders were obliged to work within.

Thucydides 2.40.2. 'Unlike any other nation, we regard the citizen who takes no part in [state affairs] not as unambitious but as useless, and we are able to judge proposals even if we cannot originate them; instead of looking on discussion as a stumbling-block in the way of action, we think it an indispensable preliminary to any wise action at all.'

Xenophon's initiative by the Zapatas exemplifies this ethic. Although he has had no role in the command structure of the army, as part of the army he stands up to act in the public good. He looks at the outset to earn position through this positive initiative instead of seeking for it through personal networks and connections. The symbolic and literal references already remarked upon make a strong link to the Periclean funeral speech: Xenophon's dressing up is meant to mark the formality of his address – the sartorial equivalent of Pericles' mounting a specially constructed platform (Thucydides 2.34.8) – while his statement immediately prior to the speech that, if he is to die now, he wishes himself to be adorned nobly, prompts the reader to call funerary speeches to mind.[60] Then his careful articulating of the predicament and his various proposals for action evince the imperative

---

60 I owe the point about the link between Xenophon's reference to his death and funerary oration to Ferrario 2012: 364. For further comparison between Xenophon and Thucydides see her thoughtful monograph on historical agency (2014a).

of talking things through, or planning; a proposal of particular note is that all should be involved in the process of administering justice, not only the rulers (3.2.31).

Thucydides 2.37.1. 'Our constitution ... favours the many instead of the few; this is why it is called a democracy. If we look to the laws, they afford equal justice to all in their private differences.'

On each occasion that a participatory assembly is held, the Athenian form of government is emulated, with the ordinary soldiers empowered through voting and given voice through the freedom afforded to air their views.[61] Although assemblies have been held prior to the establishment of the new leadership, they have either been limited in terms of participation (1.3.2, 1.4.13), or intended only to report information (1.4.12).[62] From the crossing of the Euphrates at Thapsakos up until the Zapatas, there are no assemblies at all recorded, whereafter through to Thrace twenty or more are.[63] Indeed, Xenophon, from a tense episode at Kotyora (5.6.37), leads us to believe that there would have been still more had his view always prevailed. In light of the discussion above on his democratic stance, we need not stop short of endorsing him as a leader who governed in the interests of the majority on the ground that he did not always yield to the sentiments of the crowd.

At Kotyora on the Black Sea, trials of soldiers and officers for wrongdoing over the course of the retreat take place. While Xenophon does not say he was behind the initiative, he has made the accompanying suggestion to purify the army (5.7.35). The availability of legal recourse for all was typically Athenian and, more specifically, the subjecting of the generals to justice mirrors the practice of *euthuna*, the public audit of officials at Athens at the end of their service (for generals, see Aristotle, *Athenaion Politeia* 59.2). Again, then, Xenophon's Athenian heritage appears to form an integral part of his leadership style. The accusations of *hubris*, a prosecutable offence at

---

61 Voting: 3.2.9, 33, 38; 5.1.4, 7, 8, 11, 12; 5.6.11, 33; 5.8.1; 6.1.32; 7.3.5–6, 14. Voices: 5.1.2; 5.8.2; 6.2.4, 5; 6.4.18; 7.3.13; 7.6.8. See Nussbaum (1967: 48) for a definition of the general assembly of the army.
62 It is notable that Klearchos calls an assembly of his own men only after his use of physical force to achieve his end has failed (1.3.1–2). He does not call any assemblies during the critical period after Cunaxa in which he commands the army.
63 Assemblies/army gatherings on the retreat: 3.2.1; 5.1.2; 5.4.19; 5.5.7; 5.6.1, 22; 5.7.3; 5.8.1; 6.1.14, 25; 6.2.4, 11; 6.4.10, 17, 20; 6.6.11, 29; 7.1.24; 7.3.2, 9; 7.6.7. H-R (6) point out that there are no meetings between the Greater Zab River and the Black Sea, though it seems to me that the circumstances of this critical phase of the retreat do not make that extraordinary, bearing in mind as well that the assembly at the river did decide about matters for the journey ahead.

Athens, made against him by soldiers and his own successful defence serve to demonstrate his proficiency within the system and the system's provision of justice for all.[64]

Thucydides 2.37.2. 'We are open and free in terms of our public and private conduct' (SB).

Accessibility, visibility and transparency are constants in the performance of Xenophon's character on the retreat. These qualities are not only important in obtaining voluntary obedience, but also serve to enhance organisational effectiveness, with relevant information and solutions more likely to be brought to the attention of decision makers. The importance of accessibility in particular as a leadership feature is underlined at several junctures. Notably, when enemies simultaneously block the army from behind and on the opposite bank of a river which they must cross, Xenophon's reputation induces two youths to bring him critical information, so enabling the army to find a way out of its tight predicament:

> As Xenophon was having his morning meal, a couple of young men ran up to him, for everyone knew (ᾔδεσαν γὰρ πάντες) that they could approach him at the morning or evening meal or indeed, if he were asleep, could wake him up and speak to him if anyone had something to say relevant to the campaign. (4.3.10)

A similar situation arises later in the march down country when, with the army again faced on the opposite bank of a river by warriors, one of the peltasts approaches Xenophon. This man had been a slave at Athens and believed he knew the language of this tribe. 'I think', [he said], 'this is my native country. And unless there is something to prevent it, I would like to talk to them' (4.8.4). As a result, a misunderstanding about the motive of the Greeks on the part of the tribe is cleared up and the army can continue on its way.

Xenophon's approachability contrasts markedly with what he says about Klearchos in his obituary: '[Klearchos] even said that if a soldier was going to be on sentry-duty, or avoid squabbles with his mates, or advance unhesitatingly against the enemy, it was necessary for him to fear his commander more than he feared his enemy' (2.6.10).[65] Looking ahead to the argument about Xenophon's character behaving as a model student of

---

64 Lendle on 5.8.1 notes the Athens *euthuna* link (1995: 356–8). In the next chapter, I look at the *hubris* episode as part of an apologetic context.
65 But as Xenophon shows elsewhere, all Spartans are not like this, and accessibility as a leadership quality is not exclusive to democracies: see *Hell.* 5.1.14, *Ages.* 9.1–2, *Kyr.* 7.5.37–40, and note that the mercenaries were able to approach Cyrus the Younger about their pay in the march upcountry (1.2.11).

Socrates, a reader for the publisher remarks that 'Xenophon's' openness on the retreat could count as a version of how Socrates lived his life. '[He] always lived in the open. Early in the morning he went to the walking areas and gymnasia; in the afternoon he was visible in the *agora*, and for the rest of the time he was wherever people gathered' (*Memorabilia* 1.1.10 (SB)).

On transparency, Xenophon is seen to encourage and facilitate open dialogue about affairs on the retreat, largely through the mechanism of assemblies: 'Now if anyone sees any better plan, let's do it differently' (3.2.37), and then 'if anyone sees another, better plan, let him speak up' (3.2.38) are early instances of the approach. The contrast with others and their leaning towards private deliberation is clearly made at Kotyora, where he recommends that an assembly be called to discuss a plan to sail back towards Trapezous. In response, Timasion the Dardanian 'gave it as his opinion that they should not call a full assembly but each should first try to persuade his own captains, and so they went away and set about doing this' (5.6.37). The conducting of collective business publicly reflects the Athenian habit and the greater accountability to which its leaders were bound.

An exception to normal democratic process is the suppression of dissenting voices, something more usually associated with authoritarian rule but which may be regarded as admissible in given circumstances. The exemplar here is the handling of Apollonides, an officer who expresses concern about the wisdom of trying to escape from the King following the seizure of the generals by the Zapatas (3.1.26). Xenophon cuts the man off in mid-speech and, after a detailed response, proposes to demote him and use him as a baggage carrier (3.1.27–30). Howland writes that the 'political understanding displayed here is profound: The freedom of speech that characterises the community of soldiers after Xenophon's ascent (see esp. 4.3.10) is made possible only by the prudent use of force to suppress dangerous speech at the moment of founding.'[66] A similar situation arises much later in the retreat, this time involving one of the generals, Sophainetos. He dismisses the idea of crossing a wooded hollow with the enemy at hand, but Xenophon retorts that they must, outlining exactly why to the officers on the ridge. 'As a result, the captains told him to lead the way, and nobody dissented' (6.5.22). While such exchanges between leaders are not unusual, Sophainetos is not heard of again in the narrative, outcast by the author as well as the character.[67]

---

66 Howland 2000: 886. This episode was one of those looked at in the previous chapter in the context of literary apologia.
67 Tension here and maybe previously (4.4.19, 5.3.1, 5.8.1) between the two commanders has been put forward as an explanation for the apologetic quality of *Anabasis*. I examine this in the next chapter.

Xenophon the Socratic Commander

There is a further important dimension to Xenophon's leadership in *Anabasis*, albeit in the Athenian context, as Hansen showed in bringing out the 'orator and general' as a paradigm of political leadership, there is nothing exceptional in this multifaceted character.[68] As I show in this section, there are strong links between what 'Xenophon' does on the retreat and what Xenophon reports Socrates as saying on the subject of military leadership. Although other of his Socratic writings touch on the subject, I take the most important to be *Memorabilia*, which has several continuous sections devoted to the ideal commander. Socrates' teachings in 3.1–5 constitute therefore a source of instruction to inform Xenophon's leadership on the retreat, and to make the argument that 'Xenophon' is an exemplary Socratic commander we should be able to draw a clear correlation.

While the instruction itself might seem to be plain, owing itself in some part to 'wisdom literature', the force of Socrates' personality and his style of questioning serve to ensure that what are in fact key tenets of generalship are not overlooked.[69] This idea of the paramount importance of mastering basic skills is reinforced in other works, and where the same, or similar, advice occurs in another part of the corpus, I try to mark the place(s). As remarked in the previous section, when appraising Xenophon's command capacity we should as well bear in mind his training and experience as an Athenian cavalryman. The tension between the Socratic commander and Xenophon the democrat as just discussed is considered in Chapter 5 p. 226.

Memorabilia 3.1.6. A general must be capable of supplying military equipment and provisions. (*In this, and in the following three examples, Socrates is conversing with a youth who aspires to become a general.*) See also *Kyroupaideia* 1.6.14, *Hipparchikos* 6.3.

In his opening lesson on the subject of military leadership, Socrates eschews field tactics, which he points out are only a small part of generalship,

---

68 Hansen 1983.
69 Tuplin (Xenophon Liverpool 2021) in discussion remarks that Socrates invariably talks about 'ordinary stuff' yet gets us to a place where he wants. On wisdom literature and *Memorabilia*, see Gray 1998. Johnson (2018) seeks to reveal the thought which Xenophon brings to bear in developing these passages (*Mem.* 3.1–7). As part of his consideration he adopts an opposite approach to what I do here. 'Can we', he asks, 'identify a significant distance between Xenophon's treatment of leadership in the *Memorabilia* and his treatment of that topic in his non-Socratic works?' (488). Considering his statement that Xenophon would presumably include himself among the successful leaders produced by Socrates (489), it may be surprising that he does not look at *Anabasis* in the study. Looking at *Memorabilia* 3 from a different perspective, Fallis 2015 claims that it catalogues forms of human ambition.

in favour of logistics. Reflecting this emphasis, much of Xenophon's early activity on the retreat is concerned with meeting the military needs of the beleaguered force. Plugging serious vulnerability in its defensive capacity, in the first stage in which he has a commanding role he organises and equips both a corps of slingers and a makeshift cavalry (see *Agesilaos* 1.23). For the former, he exploits the fact that there are Rhodians in the army. The islanders have a tradition of using the sling, and their missiles carry further than the Persian sling-stones: '[theirs] reach only a short distance, because in their slings they use hand-sized stones, but the Rhodians know how to use lead pellets as well' (3.3.17). Recognising that volunteer numbers for the corps would rise if the men were incentivised, Xenophon suggests that they pay them or offer them some exemption from other duties (see *Agesilaos* 1.24). For the cavalry, he draws on horses already part of the army, some belonging to the officers, some in use as carriers and others captured from the enemy. Once a sufficient number are rounded up, riders are supplied with the necessary equipment. 'That same night two hundred slingers were identified, while fifty horses and horsemen passed inspection the following day. Leather jerkins and breastplates were provided for these, and a cavalry commander was appointed, Lykios the son of Polystratos, an Athenian' (3.3.20).

As for the requirement to 'be able to supply provisions to the soldiers' (SB), understanding the vital importance of provisioning, Xenophon has researched the matter even before they break away from the Persians at the Zapatas. 'It is clear that we have to make our way to where we shall have food supplies (τὰ ἐπιτήδεια), and I hear that there are fine villages not much more than two miles from here' (3.2.34). Later, when they arrive at the Black Sea and are discussing the remainder of their journey, he prioritises the procurement of food supplies: 'So I will tell you what it seems to me it is appropriate to do while we're waiting. First, we must obtain our food supplies from enemy territory . . .' (5.1.5–6). Although it is a basic function of generalship, not every leader in the story performs well in the critical task of supplying the men: we saw how Cyrus on the Plain of Kaÿstros was unable to pay the men (1.2.11–12), who as a result could have been prevented from purchasing their supplies in the market.

Memorabilia 3.1.6. Key personal qualities.
In the same dialogue Socrates names seventeen personal qualities which a good general should strive to possess:

> he must be resourceful, active, careful, hardy and quick-witted; he must be both gentle and brutal, at once straightforward and designing, capable of both caution and surprise, lavish and rapacious, generous and mean, skilful in defence and attack; and there are many other qualifications, some natural, some acquired, that are necessary to one who would succeed as a general. (3.1.6)

Through the course of the retreat, 'Xenophon' displays every one of the qualities named. We would indeed expect this to be the case more or less with any successful general, yet it seems worth identifying instances of these to underpin the *Memorabilia* connection. I take the qualities in order from the first, noting that an example (I generally give a single one) might often as well be assigned to more than one category, or arguably even be a better fit with another one. This suggests that many, if not all, of the concepts are less tractable to modern readers and require more consideration as to their ancient meanings.

Resourceful (μηχανικός)
- formation of slinger corps and cavalry (as above) (3.3.16–20)
- to protect those overcome by the winter conditions and unable to continue, Xenophon orders the rearguard to run at the enemy and the sick to produce a din by clashing their spears; as a result, they frighten off those stalking the train (4.5.17–18)

Active/industrious (ἐργαστικός)
- while waiting for ships in Trapezous, persuades cities along the coast to repair roads so that the army can travel on foot if needs be (5.1.14)

Careful (ἐπιμελής)
- management of the army tail through the dangerous crossing of Kardouchian territory (4.1–2)

Hardy (καρτερικός)
- half-dressed, chops wood in the snow (4.4.12)

Quick-witted (ἀγχίνοος)
- exchange with Cheirisophos in the mountains (4.6.14)

Warm-minded, gentle (φιλόφρων)
- seeks out food and drink to give to soldiers incapacitated by the cold (4.5.8)

Brutal (ὠμός)[70]
- one of two men who Xenophon has captured is slaughtered in front of the other when he refuses to give information (4.1.22–3)

---

70 Brutality as a desired characteristic may raise a difficulty for seeing *Mem.* 3.1.6 as genuinely Socratic, since at 4.8.11 Xenophon writes that Socrates was 'so just that he did no injury, however small, to any man'. But that does not necessarily mean he would not have done had he needed to, as arguably Xenophon does in this situation. Dorion (2018b: 498–500) argues (against Johnson 2005) that Xenophon did not agree with Plato that Socrates was committed to never harming anyone (see *Mem.* 2.6.35, 4.2.15).

Straightforward (ἁπλόος)
- answer to Seuthes' agent when asked by him for help in bringing the army across the Bosphoros (7.1.5–6)

Designing (ἐπίβουλος)
- puts a leading question to the oracle at Delphi (3.1.5–6); does not put a matter concerning the retreat to a vote (5.1.13–14)

Cautious (φυλακτικός)
- probing Seuthes on the campaign he is seeking to co-opt the Greeks for ('How far from the sea would you expect the army to follow along with you?') (7.3.12)

Thievish (κλέπτης)
- figuratively, proposes to try to steal (κλέψαι τι πειρᾶσθαι) a stretch of mountain from enemy hands (4.6.11–13)

Lavish (προετικός)
- puts on finest armour to address the army (3.2.7)

Rapacious (ἅρπαξ)
- seizure of wealthy Persian (Asidates), his wives, children, horses and all his possessions (7.8.22)

Generous (φιλόδωρος)
- giving share of booty to other commanders (7.5.3)

Mean/taking sneaky advantage of/grasping (πλεονέκτης)
- ploy to induce Asidates to let his guard down (7.8.20)

Skilful in defence and attack (ἀσφαλῆ καὶ ἐπιθετικόν). Multiple examples.

As for the 'many other qualifications' necessary for the good general, we can name Xenophon's attentiveness towards the men (looked at in Chapter 5 pp. 233–5), his willingness to do what he asks of others (see note 35) and his ability to bring prosperity (inferred from the men's choosing him as their leader at 6.1.17–19), each of which advances the key end of securing willing obedience.

Picking up on an argument in the previous chapter for an underlying connection between the texts on the basis of a common Socratic conception, there are ways to nuance this relationship, for example, one work being complementary to the other. In this reading the later would to some extent have been driven by the nature of the earlier one and/or influenced by its outcome. Xenophon might, say, have meant *Anabasis* to reveal itself to the attentive reader as practically Socratic but found from his audience's reaction that he had not given enough clues and so adapted *Memorabilia* 3 to put *Anabasis* more clearly into a Socratic frame of reference.

Another mode of complementarity could lie in their respective characters. In the opening of his *Lives of Philosophers and Sophists*, Eunapios pays tribute to Xenophon as a philosopher distinguished in words and deeds (see opening of Chapter 2 for translation of 1.1.1–2.3). Kaldellis interprets this *logoi–erga* distinction with reference to Xenophon as possibly referring to 'discourses about virtue' versus 'accounts of virtuous actions', which it seems to me could well characterise the relationship between *Memorabilia* and *Anabasis*.[71] We might then extend from this and the previous idea and consider whether one book functions as an implicit control over the other. If, for argument's sake, we assume that a function of *Memorabilia* was to act as a check on *Anabasis*, then we would conclude that any absence or weak showing of the qualities in 3.1.6 in Xenophon's character's performance would constitute criticisms of his leadership in (Xenophontic) Socratic terms.

Memorabilia 3.1.7–8. Tactics I: Optimal marching order. See also *Kyroupaideia* 7.5.2–6, *Hipparchikos* 2.2–4.

Turning to field tactics, Socrates uses the analogy of a physical structure to convey the critical need for an army to have an effective moving arrangement lest, like a poorly built dwelling, external elements destroy it. His interlocutor responds with high praise: 'Your analogy is perfect, Socrates ... for in war one must put the best men in the van and the rear, and the worst in the centre, so that they may be led by the van and driven forward by the rearguard' (καὶ γὰρ ἐν τῷ πολέμῳ τοὺς ἀρίστους δεῖ πρώτους τάττειν καὶ τελευταίους, ἐν μέσῳ δὲ τοὺς χειρίστους, ἵνα ὑπὸ μὲν τῶν ἄγωνται, ὑπὸ δὲ τῶν ὠθῶνται). Xenophon applies this arrangement to the letter at the key juncture of the Zapatas River, proposing to the army that they form a hollow square with the hoplites, placing inside of this the baggage carriers and camp followers (3.2.36); he goes on to propose that Cheirisophos the Spartan should lead the van while the younger commanders, including himself, should take up the rear (3.2.37). Especially in the earlier stages when they are subject to attack on the plain by the Persians, the formation proves its worth (3.4.13–14).

Memorabilia 3.1.11. Tactics II: Flexibility in the field. See also *Hipparchikos* 9.1.

Here Socrates stresses the need to adapt formation and tactics to circumstances. During the retreat, Xenophon acts to do so with decisive

---

71 Kaldellis (2015: 24) writes: 'The *logoi–erga* distinction that he [Eunapios] makes in the case of Xenophon may not strictly refer to "words" versus "deeds" but possibly to "discourses about virtue" versus "accounts of virtuous actions", both of which can be found in the works of Xenophon.'

effect a number of times. I look at one example of each. When the vanguard led by Cheirisophos is unable to take a fortress on the army's route – essential as supplies have run out and the local tribe has taken all its goods up to the stronghold – Xenophon is invited to try himself on his arrival with the rearguard (4.7.3). Mirroring Socrates, Xenophon establishes through questioning and observation what is hindering the assault; having digested the detail of the situation, he proposes a different way, which proves to be successful (4.7.4–7). The outcome prompts us to reflect that Cheirisophos' direct, head-on tactic is the same as he has earlier advocated in similar situations (4.1.20–1, 4.2.8).

Later in the journey, as they approach the Black Sea and a local tribe blocks their way, Xenophon argues for a change in the arrangement of the attacking force. 'We should dissolve the line of battle and form the companies into columns', he tells the other generals. 'The line would be immediately broken up, for we will find the mountain has no paths in one place and good paths up in another, and it will immediately lower morale for troops drawn up in line to see the line broken' (4.8.10; for continuation of the argument see 11–13). They adopt the formation, and are successful, bringing the Greeks to within only a short distance of their goal. Again, we are left to reflect on the performance of the other generals, who evidently have not considered the particular circumstances before them, a precondition for flexibility. As with the first, the episode serves to remind us as well of the cognitive discipline required in the performance of generalship.

Memorabilia 3.3.7. Exhortation in the field leads to more effective action. (*The interlocutor here and in the next passage is a young man who had been elected as a cavalry commander.*) See also *Hipparchikos* 8.22.

Xenophon's character in the story regularly exhorts the army. Most famously there are his addresses by the Zapatas River, which succeed in giving the men hope when they have all but given up, but there are other notable instances too. One occurs during the trek up along the Tigris when he leads a group to seize a height before the enemy can get there. His encouragement pushes the men towards their goal: 'Xenophon was riding on horseback alongside his troops and calling out encouragement' (Ξενοφῶν δὲ παρελαύνων ἐπὶ τοῦ ἵππου παρεκελεύετο, 3.4.46). Another occasion is when they face the Kolchians just before the Black Sea:

> As Xenophon was going back from the right wing to his position on the left, he said to the soldiers, 'Men, those you see over there are the only thing still keeping us from already being where we have long been striving to be. If we possibly can, we must eat them raw.' (4.8.14)

We then have situations where the confidence of the army has been shaken or is shaky. In the territory of the Mossynoikoi, following the first occasion on the march when men had fled from an enemy, morale is low, but Xenophon, summoning the Greeks together, lifts it by pointing to positive outcomes (5.4.19–21). Further along the Black Sea coast, where they must overcome a significant physical obstacle and engage the enemy or risk a damaging counter-attack, the psychological challenge is marked, as one of their generals, Sophainetos, has dismissed any suggestion of attacking the enemy on account of the terrain – but Xenophon's exhortation inspires them and, through discipline and boldness, they succeed (6.5.14–32).

Memorabilia 3.3.11. Speech an essential quality for a good commander.

Underlining its supreme importance, when his interlocutor wonders if speech is a necessary leadership quality, Socrates is shown to be taken aback. 'Did you think a cavalry commander should keep silent?' (mod. SB) (Σὺ δ' ᾤου, ἔφη, χρῆναι σιωπῇ ἱππαρχεῖν; 3.3.11). He then encourages the young man to reflect on the critical role speech plays in training and education. Drawing on his own association with Socrates and his Athenian cultural background, this is an area in which Xenophon excels. The power and charm of his speeches was earlier shown to be a key distinguishing feature of his leadership, his ability with words arguably more than any other capacity accounting for his success. There is no need to rehearse the speeches save to mention such highly effective ones as given on the banks of the Zapatas River (*Anabasis* 3.2.8–32), at Kotyora on the Black Sea (5.7.5–33) and inside the city of Byzantium (7.1.22–31). Although they have their moments, Cyrus's speech to the officers prior to the battle being one, Klearchos persuading the men to go on at Tarsus another, the other leaders do not match Xenophon either in the accomplishment of their speeches or the frequency with which they address the army. The high standard necessary for persuasion and the fine line between success and failure in terms of the desired outcome is palpable where Xenophon succumbs to anger (καὶ τελευτῶν ἐχαλέπαινεν, 4.5.16) when all his efforts at persuading soldiers to move in the snow failed (in this case, 'doing' – going out against the enemy and frightening them off – succeeds in achieving the objective of saving the sick). A further example worth mentioning, this time from *Hellenika*, is the speech which Xenophon has Euryptolemos give at Athens in defence of the generals in the Arginousai trial (1.7.16–33). Its failure serves to remind that rhetoric has its limits even when deployed by highly competent speakers.

Memorabilia 3.4.3–12. The winning habit. (*Here Socrates waylays a downbeat commander, Nikomachides, who has just failed to be elected a general by the Athenians. Of Antisthenes, the man chosen, Nikomachides complains that he 'has never served in a marching regiment nor distinguished himself in the cavalry and understands nothing but money-making', 3.4.1.*)

Socrates does not seek to underplay the importance of military experience, but in the face of his interlocutor's upset he takes pains to demonstrate that the qualities which make a businessman successful apply equally well to the military sphere. 'Antisthenes also is eager for victory, and that is a good point in a general. Whenever he has been *choragus*, you know, his choir has always won' (3.4.3). He has earlier said that 'human beings are most willing to obey those whom they believe to be the best' (3.3.9).

Doubtless conscious of his junior status and lack of experience in warfare, Xenophon, as I have argued, invokes his Athenian background at the outset, so implicitly aligning himself with such illustrious forebears as Pericles, Kimon and Themistocles. At the Zapatas River he recalls the valour and success of his city against the Persians earlier in the century (3.2.11), thereby creating an expectation that under his leadership the army will enjoy similar success against the same enemy. This is duly met from early in the retreat, for example in his group winning the race to the height against the Persians (3.4.44–9). It may already be that prior to his speech to the army his Attic origins and the Athenian winning habit had made him a desirable leadership option: the officers in Proxenos' contingent seemed to need little persuasion to have him as their former commander's replacement despite the fact that Xenophon is young and has had no military role to date (3.1.25–6, and see *Memorabilia* 3.5.3 and *Hellenika* 2.2.20 for what may be a wider perception of Athenians viewed positively; but there is evidence to the contrary too, for example *Hellenika* 3.5.10).

Further Considerations

I end the discussion of the Socratic commander by briefly touching on three questions. The first concerns the extent to which Xenophon's own experiences of military leadership influence his reporting of Socrates' teachings on the subject. Or more starkly, and expanding the question to include his whole Socratic output, how much of Xenophon's voice are we hearing in his own reporting of Socrates? This is a debated matter and crosses over with the same underlying issue with other Socratic authors: are we hearing Socrates' views or those of his followers in Socrates' mouth? In Chapter 5 I provide a limited overview of scholarly positions, suggesting that to some degree the Socratics' portraits are informed by their own agendas and backgrounds (p. 197). On the particular question of the *Memorabilia* military instruction, I am inclined to believe this was by and large what Xenophon heard, as he claims. I would like to emphasise that for one important aspect of this monograph, Xenophon's defence of Socrates, the question is not crucial. What is at issue is showing that Xenophon is defending Socrates, not whether what he has him say is faithful or not. Granted the defence would be stronger had it happened that the teacher independently recorded his thoughts and Xenophon's representation generally mapped on to these, by simply showing that his character's moral behaviour and leadership actions led to positive outcomes Xenophon is presenting a defence of his teacher.

Second, there is the question of the relative dating of *Anabasis* and the Socratica. I addressed this in Chapter 1 where I argued that, while the latter in the main probably postdate the former, there is not likely to have been a significant gap in time between the publication dates of *Anabasis* and *Memorabilia*. I built on the case for that by seeking to bring out a literary closeness between *Anabasis* and *Memorabilia*. Recalling my view about a common conception lying behind them, taking as an example the key personal qualities which a commander should have as named in *Memorabilia* 3.1.6, according to this view the author would already have had these clearly in mind before beginning. This enables us to see *Anabasis* as open to the teachings in *Memorabilia* even if the relevant part of the latter postdated our text. The closeness of the two in their writing is hinted at in *Memorabilia* 3.5.26, which mirrors *Anabasis* 1.1.11 and 2.5.13, though both are based on what must have been a widely known historical fact; arguably with more force we could read the opening of 3.5.26 (Τί δέ; ἐκεῖνο ἀκήκοας, 'have you heard') as a hint that *Anabasis* has recently been published. Earlier in the chapter I also remarked on a strong intertextual link between *Anabasis* 2.2.5, where Xenophon talks about the nature of true leadership, and *Memorabilia* 3.9.10–11, where Socrates dwells on the same (see chapter opening quote and p. 118 for the discussion). The apparent linking of the two works points to a less rigid divide than often comes across in modern scholarship, where the notion of a fixed Socratic cycle is ingrained. I add that so long as we accept Xenophon had a contemporary profile as a Socratic (see Chapter 5 pp. 202–3), the assumption that informed readers could relate his performance on the retreat to their understanding of the philosopher's body of teaching should not present great difficulty.

Lastly, I pick up on Gera's perplexity about Xenophon's choosing not to make use of Socrates' own military experiences as exemplary material. There is doubtless a method in this, for as she points out, Plato (*Apologia* 28e; *Laches* 181a; *Symposion* 219e, 220e; *Charmides* 153a) does refer to his teacher's exploits on the battlefield, and we know from him that he stood out for valour.[72] My explanation would be that Xenophon considered their inscribing in his contemporary's accounts as sufficient. If we consider, as I am inclined to do, that Xenophon's Socratic writings are on an important level a corrective vis-à-vis Plato's, that does not compel us to believe that he could not or did not make use of material in Plato's works that complemented or was consistent with his own, even if that was implicit.

---

72 Gera 2007: 37 n.14.

Moreover, as I argue in this monograph, *Anabasis* is in a different mould to those works that typically feature Socrates and his absence is consistent with this character.

Conclusions

Xenophon's character embodies the third style of leadership presented in *Anabasis* – Athenian, with a distinctively Socratic flavour. In conventional terms we can map this on to the contemporary paradigm of 'orator and general'. I suggest that there is a special link between *Anabasis* and *Memorabilia* 3.1–5, which brings together in a single tract advice on generalship, including the paramount importance of speech (3.3.11). The intertextuality in turn prompts us to appreciate the underlying relationship between the protagonists, Socrates as Xenophon's mentor and Xenophon as the aspiring leader who finds himself in desperate straits in Mesopotamia.

Xenophon's leadership style on the retreat conforms in many ways to that of a leader of the democracy. Lest that might not have been what his readers expected, the image is impressed through his character's regular engagement with processes that recall the working of government at Athens. Another way to interpret this would be to argue that his 'Athenianness' emerges in his relationship, both in thought and in action, with the quasi-democratic processes through which the army responds to its leaders.[73]

Xenophon's integration of Socratic precepts is intended to enhance this model. From the evidence of the narrative, the result proves to be the most effective style of leadership, its outstanding features being the use of speech and personal example to motivate and direct action and, as we will see in detail in Chapter 5, its rooting in a practical, ethical philosophy which serves to foster willing obedience. The failure of both Cyrus and the Spartans to exert decisive control over the mercenary body, and Xenophon's success in leading the expedition back to Asia Minor, is the ultimate measure of the effectiveness of the respective management approaches. The fact that the task of leadership became more difficult after the army had reached the Black Sea and the attendant pressures of survival that had bound the Greeks together receded makes Xenophon's achievement the more impressive.

---

73 Waterfield (2011: 139–40) rejects the idea that the model for the mercenaries' *politeia* was Athenian on the ground that few of the men were Athenian. However, this would not have precluded them from adapting to the system; indeed, as I have suggested, the men might well have been attracted to the Athenian model for the success the citizens enjoyed under it. We see today how youth in countries under despotic rule agitate for democratic reform believing democracy would enhance the quality of their lives. On the army resembling a *polis* on the move, see Nussbaum 1967, Dalby 1992, Dillery 1995, Hornblower 2004.

For all that, his leadership is not perfect. His handling of the expedition to procure supplies from the Drilai when the army is no longer able to source them on forays from Trapezous illustrates this (5.2). Notably, he fails to reconnoitre the enemy position, or to keep control of his men, twice suffering breakdowns of discipline (5.2.4, 16), and it takes an accident to prompt him into setting fires as a defensive manoeuvre (5.2.24–5). I read these indicators of weakness as being intended to remind that, while optimal, individual imperfection limits the leadership style in question (I discuss the limits of wisdom and human knowledge in the last part of Chapter 5). I see this as being underscored in the final book, where Xenophon sometimes struggles to keep his footing with external leaders, the Thracian Seuthes and assorted Spartans. The sense that he is out of his depth is reflected in this final book's physical setting outside of Asia and its singularly apologetic nature, and, on another level, in his getting drunk with Seuthes, his consequent misspeaking giving ground for suspicion against himself on the part of the men (7.3.29–32). However, I do not think we should be too ready to see a discontinuity between Books 1–6 and 7. Although the view about Book 7's exceptionality is grounded in persuasive circumstances, among them the geographical change from Asia to Europe and the appealing antiquarian view of the march ending at the Bosphoros, these factors should not obscure the successes of Xenophon's leadership in this book – notably his arresting of the mercenary rebellion in Byzantium – and the continuation of the leadership theme. I revisit this subject at the very end of the monograph.

In narrating the performance of his character, Xenophon offers guidance on important contemporary military and political matters. There is an extended engagement with the problem of controlling mercenary soldiers, a relevant and topical subject in the fourth century, and he offers insight into the operation of democracy, demonstrating by way of the 'moving *polis*' how this can be managed to contain the prime instincts of the *demos* and leave direction in the hands of its leaders. It might be that he is being ironic when he reports Seuthes' claim to the Spartans that 'Xenophon' is a φιλοστρατιώτης (a friend of the soldiers, 7.6.4), however, the contradiction between his supposed concern for the interests of the men and his pursuit of leadership aims that are sometimes against their wishes (as for example at Trapezous, where he has roads built) is resolved by his acting in (what he considers to be) the best interests of the army as a whole. Throughout his performance on the retreat there is a discernible tension between expediency and self-interest on the one hand and the desire to pursue just and ethical means towards leadership ends on the other. Xenophon's stance seems to me to be that the success of democracy in terms of its ability to benefit the individual and the *polis* is dependent on politically and morally responsible leadership. Where these qualities are absent, the result is potentially calamitous for all.

While he does not explicitly set up an expectation that we should judge the other leaders on the march by Athenian, or Socratic, standards, we are nonetheless left to measure their performances against his own template. In many respects the differences between them are slight, but such, as we learn from the story, can be crucial to successful outcomes. As I go on to show in Chapter 5, his adherence to underlying ethical principles such as self-control (ἐγκράτεια) and self-sufficiency (αὐτάρκεια) completes the profile of the Socratic commander.

Finally, two closing comments touching on the literary side. The first is that we should strive to see our Socratic commander in the overarching frame of Xenophon's writings on leadership. Huitink and Rood summarise the essential features of Xenophontic leadership as ability to secure willing obedience, transferability to different realms and securing order and prosperity.[74] If we accept the argument made that Xenophon brings a broad Athenian style of rule to the march, so marking his leadership as transferable to a different realm, then we can I think map him on to this profile. Secondly, recalling the discussion in the first part of the chapter, the paradigmatic character of the narrative registers for a second time on the macro level. In dealing with the subject of leadership styles, Xenophon chooses to present different models; his choosing of three (arguably there are more embedded in the narrative) perhaps betrays the influence of Herodotus' three-sided constitutional debate (3.80–2). Moreover, and more interestingly from the viewpoint of intertextuality, both writers here are concerned with the problem of how to lead, and dwell on similar models. What Herodotus presents – first democracy, then oligarchy and monarchy, with the last decided on as best by the Persians – is inverted by Xenophon, who introduces his styles in order of their effectiveness, the first being represented by the Persian prince, Cyrus the Younger (Book 1), the second by the Spartans Klearchos and Cheirisophos (Books 2–6) and the final and optimal by Xenophon the Athenian (Books 3–7). A further difference between the two writers is that whereas Herodotus' treatment of the rulership problem takes the form of an open discussion of the merits and deficiencies of each of the three types, Xenophon fashions his material into the storyline.

---

74 H-R 22.

CHAPTER 4

Xenophon's Self-Defence

Consequently death, which because of the changes and chances of life is daily close at hand, and because of the shortness of life can never be far away, does not frighten the wise man from considering the interests of the State and of his family for all time; and it follows that he regards posterity, of which he is bound to have no consciousness, as being really his concern.

Cicero, *Tusculan Disputations* 1.38

It would be reasonable to maintain that after the expedition Xenophon was not universally seen as having played a saviour role in it and that there was continuing criticism of his leadership style. If those circumstances were not to hold, then, while we may well still have had an *Anabasis*, that would likely have been a different book; in the one we have, Xenophon is at pains to represent his role on the retreat of the Ten Thousand as highly significant. From obscurity in the march upcountry, he emerges on the banks of the Zapatas River as a formidable leader of men. Until the army leaves Thrace some fifteen months later, he is involved in almost every major action described and is constantly on hand with sound advice. The fact that he appears to have used a pseudonym – Themistogenes of Syracuse – reinforces this view, there being an argument at least from the time of Plutarch that he 'assigned [Themistogenes] the honour of authorship in order to make his account more credible by having himself described in the third person' (SB) (*De gloria Atheniensium* 345e).

This reading, adopted by many as an explanation for the work, is nonetheless complicated by the evidence of Xenophon's other writings. Where he features at all, he is a retiring presence, and much of his writing besides is concerned with ethical philosophy. On a fuller view of his life and works, he was not a man we might expect to be given to self-aggrandisement.[1]

---

1 Where Xenophon does touch on events that involve him, he does not usually seek recognition or sympathy. For example, in *Hellenika*, rather than name himself as the leader of the Cyreans in service to Sparta, he refers to 'the leader of the men who had fought

A resolution to this contradiction – a reconciliation between Xenophon the author and historical figure and the foregrounding of his character in *Anabasis* – can be brought about if we take account of the extensive apologetic theme, in particular the mission to promote the worth of Socrates the Athenian. In the previous chapter, I argued that Xenophon in the story is an exemplar, a hybrid model of a young Athenian and a pupil of Socrates, and in the next I argue that this form of representation effects an original and powerful defence of Socrates. As he signifies by his use of a third-person voice and by his embedding of Socrates in the heart of the story, the main protagonist in it is a model Socratic officer whose name is Xenophon.[2]

In this chapter, I examine a number of the personal apologetic strands in the text. I categorise these into two distinctive types: those relating to Xenophon's character in the story and those relating to the author. While both are intended for the external audience, the first type naturally includes the internal one as well. The two overlap in that, for instance, defence of the character Xenophon also reflects on the author (and, as we will see in the next chapter, on his teacher).[3] In the first category, 'Xenophon' explicitly defends himself on at least three major occasions: in Book 5, the plan to establish a colony and the review of the generals' conduct, and in Book 7, accusations of corruption and collusion with Seuthes. In the second category, the author Xenophon has been held to be fending off criticisms from external audiences on a number of scores: other accounts that diminished, or overlooked, his role in the rescue of the Ten Thousand; condemnations of mercenaries (the Ten Thousand included); his relations with Sparta; and other aspects of his life history, notably his exile from Athens.

> with Cyrus' (ὁ τῶν Κυρείων προεστηκώς, 3.2.7). Later in the same account, coming to the battle (of Mantineia) in which one of his sons died in a preliminary skirmish, by all accounts bravely, Xenophon confines himself to the comment that 'brave were the men among them who died' (7.5.17). Even if we assume, as some do, that he is not the narrator, that figure respects the author's reticence. The broader literary context is informative too. Diogenes Laertios opens his biography by describing Xenophon as 'a man of rare modesty' (2.48), a distinction not afforded by him to any other of the Socratics. More generally, Demosthenes (*De cor.* 3–4) underlines the natural disposition of men to resent self-praise.
> 2 As I remarked in the Introduction, the character of the work is autobiographical in the sense that the author of the story stands behind its lead actor, and Xenophon would certainly identify with the latter as a figure reflecting his younger self as an aspiring Socratic. Nonetheless, even on this level there are obstacles to classifying the work as such, for example the short time span of the story and the fact that 'Xenophon' is virtually absent from the opening books.
> 3 Any exemplary narrative about someone who also exists in the outside world (and in this case that person is also the author) has a potentially apologetic effect; so, in many of the instances looked at in this chapter, instead of our witnessing consciously designed apologetic episodes there may merely be the impression of apologia. While uncovering the distinction is not always at all straightforward, by setting the analysis in the wider context of Xenophon's personal background and writings, the picture of the apologetic author becomes clearer.

The analyses presented aim to bring out the nature and pervasiveness of the personal apologetic element in *Anabasis* and the extent to which it shapes the story.⁴ To appreciate this fully, we need to take into account as well the broader apologetic landscape in Xenophon. There are the Socratic works, which go beyond mere defence against the charges to promotion of the philosopher, and the strong defensive element in *Hellenika*, where Xenophon justifies his role in the rule of the Thirty and highlights the virtue of Socrates.⁵ From the historiographical perspective we can discern apologia as a common dynamic in *Hellenika* and *Anabasis*. To give one example of intertextuality, at two places in *Anabasis* set in time two to three years after the restoration of the democracy, Xenophon is at pains to emphasise both his immaturity (3.1.5–7) and his youthfulness (3.1.25). In so doing he furnishes a sympathetic contextualisation for his actions under the Thirty as a *hippeus*, whatever these may have been in fact.⁶

Charges Made against 'Xenophon'

Speeches given by 'Xenophon' dominate the later books of *Anabasis*. Examination of these shows that a number bear a decided apologetic character, engaging in an elaborate way with charges made against him. We are bound to believe that these were serious enough to endure beyond the frame of the march, or else it would seem odd for them to feature in the account, even where they have some historiographical value. One or more may have been contained or hinted at in another published version, though as I show in the next part of the chapter, evidence for an account of the expedition that was hostile to Xenophon is not compelling. An alternative is that these charges featured in the prevalent oral accounts told at home; as a natural process, common strands amongst the myriad of stories told by the participants would have formed the basis of durable oral versions.⁷ In

---

4 For foundational scholarship on this subject, see Schwartz 1889, Dürrbach 1893, Mesk 1922/3, Breitenbach 1967, Cawkwell 1972, Erbse 2010.

5 Bringing out the depth of apologia across his works, Dorion (2017: 38–9) shows how in *Memorabilia* Xenophon steps in to defend Socrates over what might be seen as undesirable links: for example, decoupling him from Alkibiades at 1.2.12–17, 1.2.39–47. 'Xenophon makes every effort to dissociate Socrates from anyone ... who might damage the reputation of his teacher and stand in the way of his apologetic enterprise' (2017: 39).

6 See Cuniberti 2011 on links between *Hellenika* 3–4 and *Anabasis*. The second part of *Hellenika* postdates *Anabasis*.

7 See 2.1.17, where Klearchos envisages advice given by a Greek in the King's service being spoken of back in Greece: 'You know that whatever advice you give us will necessarily be reported in Greece' (λέγεσθαι ἐν τῇ Ἑλλάδι). I owe this reference to Stylianou (2004: 73). Waterfield (2006: 190) draws a comparison between the Ten Thousand and the survivors of the Chinese Long March, noting that many stories would have circulated afterwards about the expedition.

the Peloponnese especially, where literary culture was slower to take hold than in other parts of Greece, the oral record retained its primacy through the fourth century.[8] Many of the Ten Thousand were from the region, and those who eventually did return to Greece will all have had their own stories to tell about the adventure.[9] In this environment it would have been harder for Xenophon, living there in his later life, to ignore what was being said. A problem with this argument, as Michael Flower has pointed out, is the length of time between event and defence.[10] It seems for instance unlikely, if not out of the question, that a dispute with a baggage carrier in the snow some thirty years before prompted Xenophon to justify in writing his action in striking that man (5.8.1–11). On the other hand, as suggested, it is plausible that some stories persisted and remained prominent, pushing him to respond in the end. It could also be the case that Xenophon delayed publishing his story until very late to minimise the chance of challenges to his narrative from other eyewitnesses or reporters.[11]

Another possibility is that lengthy speeches which stem from particular charges owe themselves to 'literary apologia'. In Chapter 2, examples where Xenophon had been accused on one ground or other were provided, with the suggestion that the circumstances in each case were selective and that behind each a common scheme could be discerned. The difference with 'authentic apologia' would lie in the intent, with the literary episode designed not only to defend against the accusation in question but to speak as well to some other element of the author's agenda. One could envisage this on a scale, with an authentic defence against a real charge at one end and a false charge and fabricated circumstances at the other. I do not believe the charges in *Anabasis* are made up, though in responding to them Xenophon may be adapting events to fit better with his agenda. Where it looks like we have an apologetic background being used for a didactic purpose, then typically we are properly in the realm of the leadership theme.

To illustrate this feature of the narrative, I refer to the episode involving Xenophon striking a baggage carrier. His action resulted in a charge of *hubris*, which I look at in detail later in the chapter. As remarked, the length of time between the event and its reporting make it stand out: on the surface we have authentic apologia (defence against the charge made) but, given the time lapse,

---

8 See Harris 1989: 89, 112–14.
9 On the question of the mercenaries' origins, see Roy 1967 and 2004, Lee 2007, Brennan 2008. Roy (2004: 280–8) argues, though, that most never returned home, their main objective being to 'stay in employment in or near Asia Minor' (288).
10 Flower 2012: 33. Dillery (2017: 196) remarks that 'apologetic works are written close to the attack upon the person concerned, or the circumstances on the basis of which an attack can be anticipated'.
11 See Tsagalis 2009: 454. Cf. Erbse 498: 'He surely must have counted on the fact that, even thirty years after the events, his account would be checked by the participants.'

it must be more than that too, unless we are to suppose enduring animosity between the men owing to, say, both residing in proximity to one another or being connected by some common cultural network. Taking that not to be the case, we could have two or more possibilities. One is that Xenophon aims to show he was not a person prone to common vices such as *hubris* (see note 14), a reading which would fit with the thesis that the work was in part a means to enhance his standing as a Socratic. It may be notable that prominent followers of Socrates, Kritias and Alkibiades among them, had been widely regarded as guilty of *hubris* ('for Kritias above all those in the oligarchy became the most greedy and violent, while Alkibiades of all those in the democracy became the most intemperate and insolent' (SB), *Memorabilia* 1.2.12). A second possibility is that we really have a leadership lesson. I referred to this idea above (and in the Introduction), arguing that the author is using an apologetic situation as a means of emphasising the need for discipline in an army.[12]

Before turning to look at the speeches, by way of a brief excursus I consider the practical matter of their delivery. While Xenophon likely did give answers to the men about the charges, these were surely not on the scale or level of detail which he includes in his narrative. From the practical side, it would have been difficult for him to deliver complex speeches to the greater body of the army; in theatre, these must normally have been quite brief and communicated down the line by word of mouth (see *Lak.* 13.9). However, Thucydides does make a point of telling us how Pericles at the Kerameikos mounted a specially constructed high platform (ἐπὶ βῆμα ὑψηλὸν) 'in order to be heard by as many of the crowd as possible' (2.34.8), and speeches in the Athenian assembly were typically delivered to over 6,000 people. It is likely that, wherever possible, meetings took advantage of favourable landscape features, so in principle Xenophon may have been able to reach fairly large numbers, even if for many the experience would have been limited. Aldrete outlines impediments in the hypothetical case of a force not greatly dissimilar in size to that of the Cyreans plus camp followers:

> Consider an ancient army of 20,000 or more soldiers gathered together to hear their general's speech. Assuming that the men were not muttering among themselves, could even the most quietly attentive hoplite or legionary situated somewhere in the middle of these massed ranks have really heard anything but intermittent snatches of his general's words over the incessant background noise of the clinking and jangling of the men's armour and weapons as they shifted uncomfortably in their full battle equipment ...? Finally,

---

12 See Rood 2006: 56, cited in Introduction. We can note that the episode also showcases Xenophon's rhetorical skill, turning the tables on his accuser, who is forced on to the defensive.

how many of his men could the general reach with his unamplified voice? The usual limit on projecting coherent complex speech with the human voice is around 100 yards in the direction in which a speaker is facing.[13]

Deceiving the Soldiers (5.6.17, 27; 5.7.5–12)

While the army encamps outside the Black Sea city of Kotyora awaiting the arrival of ships from Sinope, Xenophon is accused of planning to found a colony with the aim of furthering his own name and power. Initially, when word of the venture circulated, the prospect of settling in the Pontus divided the men (5.6.19), but when they learned that Xenophon had been sacrificing about the matter in private, the mood turned against him. 'Philesios stood up, as did Lykon, both Achaeans, and they went on about how dreadful it was that in private Xenophon was trying to persuade people to stay and was performing sacrifices with a view to remaining, but in public he said nothing about it' (5.6.27).

Xenophon has already explained to the reader his reason for considering a colony (taking advantage of the ample and skilled manpower on hand) and has stated that the aim was 'to add both territory and strength to Greece' (καλὸν αὐτῷ ἐδόκει εἶναι καὶ χώραν καὶ δύναμιν τῇ Ἑλλάδι προσκτήσασθαι, 5.6.15). He now justifies himself to the internal audience, claiming that he performed the sacrifices to learn 'whether it was better to start to speak to you on this subject and set it in motion or not to touch the matter at all' (5.6.28). He accuses the soothsayer, source of the rumour, of slandering him, this because he himself is anxious to return to Greece (5.6.29, 18). As there are ships from local cities en route to take them homewards and two of the other generals, Timasion the Dardanian and Thorax the Boiotian, have secured pay for the men, he recommends without reservation that they pursue this course. 'It seems to me a fine thing for us not only to get safely to where we want to be, but also to be paid for achieving our own salvation' (5.6.31).

However, the matter is not laid to rest. Those who had promised the men money discovered that, because the army had decided to sail away anyway following Xenophon's recommendation, the Herakleians had gone back on their promise to send money as well as ships. Now they only sent the ships, and Timasion and Thorax, 'panic-stricken [and] afraid of the army's reaction' (5.6.36), went to Xenophon and proposed that they should arrange for all to sail east to Phasis. Xenophon answered that he would say nothing of the sort to the army; but another general, Neon the Asinaean,

---

13 Aldrete 2008. See also MacDowell 2009: 5, and Anson 2010 with focus on the delivery of pre-battle speeches. On human sound propagation, see Meyer 2008: 70–3.

spread a rumour that he had persuaded the commanders to this end and was planning to deceive the soldiers. A menacing atmosphere developed in the camp and, sensing the danger, Xenophon summoned an assembly. In an emotive but methodical speech (one and a half OCT pages) he defended himself against this charge of deception (5.7.5–12).

The byzantine machinations surrounding the army's onward plans at Kotyora hint at an even more complex picture of events than Xenophon paints. A number of elements are worth bringing into the frame. Firstly, we are not given any context for the whole Phasis idea. The notion that they should start to go backwards seems odd to say the least. A brief mention of the grandson of the Kolchian King Aietes does little to illuminate the circumstances, though we may suspect some discussion with the Herakleians and Sinopeans on the scheme.

Then there is the fact that existing tensions between commanders have intensified. Several factors account for this, chief among them the creation of a partial vacuum by the earlier departure of Cheirisophos at Trapezous. There may well have been a determined attempt by one, or a group of them in concert, to gain effective control of the army. Xenophon's comprehensive defence against the charge of deceiving the army should be set against this background of a power struggle in which he, Timasion, Thorax ('who was always clashing with Xenophon over the management of the army', 5.6.25) and Neon, acting in the place of Cheirisophos, were the principal protagonists. It is only at Sinope that the army decides on a sole commander, this itself in controversial circumstances (6.1.18, 30–2).

I point next to a piece of personal history that might add to our understanding of the Kotyora episode. As we know, prior to joining Cyrus and on the recommendation of Socrates, Xenophon went to Delphi to take the advice of the god about the journey. However, he put a leading question to Apollo, annoying Socrates but earning divine approval for what he himself wanted to do. It looks as if the same stratagem has surfaced at Kotyora, in that Xenophon is engaging with the gods in a way calculated to further his own ends: here his case for speaking with the men about a colony will be the stronger for having a divine stamp as, if it is forthcoming, a positive response might in turn seem to validate the idea that is being broached. It could be that the soothsayer, and even the soldiers, were aware of Xenophon's previous form on this count (recalling the earlier discussion about orality, we can readily imagine that over the course of the journey the men exchanged their own stories about how they came to be there). Their apparent readiness to call him to account may then be explained by some distrust of his character, which recurs on the same subject at 6.4.14.

To round this up, the Kotyora episode is historically important as it reflects, however dimly, a power struggle for control of the army. Xenophon seeks to influence this in his favour, but the attempt as reported in his account, whether consciously or not, is not a clean one. The episode furthermore connects with a wider apologetic agenda, portraying the Athenian as a panhellenist wanting to acquire land and power for Greece, an image he might wish to project if his credentials on that score had been doubted and that mattered to him; with more certainty the speech strives to distance him from markedly un-Socratic behaviour: disputes over leadership, hints of vainglory in the establishing of a city and putting his own interests above that of the men.

Hubris (5.8.1)

As we saw in the last chapter, following purification of the army the generals were brought to account for their conduct on the retreat (5.8). Xenophon himself is accused by several of the men of *hubris*, violent assault intended to humiliate the victim ('Some laid accusations against Xenophon, asserting that he hit them, and they set about prosecuting the case on the basis he had acted through arrogant wilfulness', Ξενοφῶντος δὲ κατηγόρησάν τινες φάσκοντες παίεσθαι ὑπ' αὐτοῦ καὶ ὡς ὑβρίζοντος τὴν κατηγορίαν ἐποιοῦντο, 5.8.1).[14] Such a charge, if proven, would doubtless have damaged his standing as a leader in the eyes of the men. While Klearchos before him seems not to have suffered any diminution in his ability to lead on account of his proclivity for beating soldiers, his obituary confirms that this trait ultimately did not breed loyalty among those he was in charge of (2.6.12). Xenophon, cultivating willing obedience from the outset, must have sought to defend himself against the accusation, considering as well that the task of leading would otherwise then have become even more difficult.

The author does deal comprehensively with the charge made against his character. In Socratic fashion, 'Xenophon' systematically questions one of his accusers and demonstrates that he acted justly (the man, who turned out to be a mule-driver, had tried to bury another man alive in the snow rather than carry him as ordered by Xenophon: for the context, see 4.5.15–21). He then proceeds to justify to the open gathering other cases where he beat men on the grounds that discipline was necessary for the good of the army as a whole (5.8.13–22). He does not recall the case of Apollonides, who, on his instigation, was driven away for defeatism at the Zapatas River (3.1.30–2); notwithstanding that he was not beaten there is a strong hint of heavy intimidation against a subordinate, and Apollonides, if he had hung on, would, one thinks, have been among those clamouring for action at the review of the generals' conduct.

---

14 Dover (1974: 54) defines *hubris* as 'behaviour in which a citizen treats a fellow-citizen as if he were dealing with a slave or a foreigner'. A charge of *hubris* was indictable under Athenian law. Ober (2011: 140) offers a concise summary of the law and its application.

Yet, as remarked earlier, unless we suppose that the charge reverberated long after the march, it may be curious that he should pick up this matter in his book many years later. One explanation could lie in its didactic message – the need for discipline to be maintained in perilous circumstances. Another could be that in the account he is positioning, or reaffirming, himself as an important follower of Socrates; as suggested in the earlier discussion on literary apologia, the author may have underscored such a charge precisely to show that his character was beyond reproach on the matter.

A rhetorical feature of Xenophon's defence is worth highlighting. In a passage between the deception and *hubris* episodes, he tells us of a series of disgraceful events at Kerasous, a Greek city through which the army had passed after leaving Trapezous. He describes at length (5.7.13–25) how some of their men had attempted to plunder a friendly stronghold with the intention of making off with booty on a ship: the survivors of the failed raid subsequently stoned to death ambassadors of the stronghold who came to inform the Greek commanders about the wrongdoing. We would have expected the recounting of this villainous affair to have come at Kerasous (5.3), but Xenophon delays it in his narrative in order to set a background against which his own actions on the retreat seem not only appropriate but of the sort that are absolutely necessary if the army, as he puts it, is to 'avoid displaying ourselves as the worst and most dishonourable of men in the eyes of both gods and men' (5.7.12).[15]

The success of Xenophon's defence against the *hubris* charge at Kotyora, evident from the shouts that he had struck the man who is accusing him 'less than he deserved' (5.8.12), is affirmed again shortly after at Sinope (6.1.18–19), when the men approach him to be their sole leader, though we should probably take it that his capacity for securing resources is a major factor here too. Reminding us of the personal apologetic element, at Sinope we again see the author's concern for his own reputation in his calculation that by accepting the leadership, 'there would be a danger of throwing away even the reputation he had already achieved' (διὰ τοῦτο δὲ καὶ κίνδυνος εἴη καὶ τὴν προειργασμένην δόξαν ἀποβαλεῖν, 6.1.21).

Corruption (7.6.9–10)

Equally as damaging a charge as *hubris* for Xenophon would have been that of corruption: Xenophon the commander and philosopher enriching himself

---

15 Gwynn, describing the passage as a 'long and ill-proportioned digression' (1929: 39), believes that the author originally had it in the natural sequence of events, i.e. at 5.4.1, when the army was leaving Kerasous, but that he later altered the arrangement as part of a response to Sophainetos, who is another of the generals brought to account by the men at Kotyora (the argument that Xenophon in his *Anabasis* is responding to a work by Sophainetos is looked at in the next part of the chapter).

at his soldiers' expense. Such an accusation was levelled at him in Thrace in spring 399 after the army, which had spent the winter in the service of a local warlord, Seuthes, received an offer to enlist with the Spartans in their campaign against Tissaphernes.[16] Perhaps significantly given Xenophon's residence there, the first accuser was from the Peloponnese:

> [9] 'You know, Lacedaemonians, as far as we are concerned we would have been in your service long ago if Xenophon had not used his persuasive powers to bring us away here, to this place with its dreadful winter, through all of which we have never ceased to campaign both by day and by night. He has the fruits of our labours: Seuthes has enriched him personally but deprives us of our pay. [10] So,' he said, 'if I could see him stoned to death, paying the penalty for the way he has dragged us around, it seems to me that I would then have my pay and not be at all weighed down by the toils we have endured.' (7.6.9–10)

Xenophon's defence against the charge is, again, methodical and thorough. His speech is divided into two consecutive parts (7.6.11–32, 7.6.33–8) and covers all of four and a half pages of OCT. This does seem to be first and foremost self-defence, probably prompted by a wish to leave his own record for posterity of what we can infer from the circumstances was a major event of the journey; in contrast to the *hubris* charge, which concerned directly only a handful of men, it was more likely to outlive the march itself. But, as we will see, it is also true that the defence serves to advertise (Socratic) qualities in the accused and to reinforce principles from the leadership theme. I add that it could be that the accusation is intended to provide Xenophon with an opportunity to defend himself against subsequent widespread charges which may not have been voiced on the journey. Plausibly, information later surfaced that cast his role in negative light. This need not mean that the staging is fictitious, but rather points to the literary development of a real episode. It may be notable that, as in the *hubris* and other cases, the unnamed accuser is a negative type, vindictive and cruel.

On the defence, in its initial part (7.6.11–32) Xenophon focuses on the army's situation, arguing persuasively that even without pay they benefited from their association with Seuthes: without his cavalry they would have been ineffective and vulnerable, but with him they have been able to secure sufficient supplies to survive the winter. Swearing by all the gods and goddesses (θεοὺς ἅπαντας καὶ πάσας), he repudiates the charge of profiteering at the soldiers' expense (7.6.18–19). In the second part (7.6.33–8) he shifts the focus on to himself. Having already stated that he had turned back to

---

16 Seuthes II, a paradynast of the Odrysian king, Medocus: see Stronk 1995: 140–3. See *Hell.* 3.1.3–6 for the beginnings of the Spartan campaign against Persia.

help the army when he heard they were in difficulty (7.6.11),[17] he recalls how, when he had left the men to go home at Byzantium, 'I started on the ... journey much praised by you' (7.6.33). The present result of his decision to return and help them is that he has earned the enmity of the Spartans, whom he has disobeyed, and of Seuthes, who has been angered by his persistent advocacy of the soldiers' interests. And now he faces the death penalty at the hands of the soldiers.

This lengthy speech represents Xenophon's immediate defence of himself, its elaborateness both a reflection of the gravity of the charge and a measure of his concern for his reputation. Its success is measured by the response of one of the Spartan envoys present: not one of the army, and probably not well disposed to Xenophon, he is nonetheless moved to stand up for him.[18] 'Now by the Twin Gods, men, you don't seem to me to be angry with this man with any justice at all' (Ἀλλὰ μὰ τὼ σιώ, ὦ ἄνδρες, ἐμοὶ μέντοι οὐ δικαίως δοκεῖτε τῷ ἀνδρὶ τούτῳ χαλεπαίνειν, 7.6.39). Yet, in a certain sense, for the reader the second part of the defence is almost redundant, for it is set within a framework of personal transparency that the author has assiduously built up in the preceding narrative. By the time the charge of corruption is made against him, Xenophon's innocence is already virtually beyond doubt. As Azoulay puts it, 'Xenophon the author carefully stages the incorruptibility of Xenophon the character'.[19]

---

17 *Contra* 7.2.8–9, where Xenophon says that Anaxibios pressed him to return to the army. See Stronk's comment 1995: 260.
18 Xenophon's relations with Spartan officials, rarely represented as more than professional on the journey, became notably strained following the arrival of the Ten Thousand at Byzantium. I explore the relationship later in the chapter.
19 Azoulay 2004: 291. The author argues that not only Book 7 but the entire work is one of apologetics (ibid. pp. 289, 291, 296). We can outline three separate contacts with Seuthes which mark the construction of Xenophon's personal transparency:
  Approach by Seuthes (7.1.5–6). At the outset of Book 7, Xenophon recounts his brief encounter at Chrysopolis with Medosades, Seuthes' ambassador, who asks him to help persuade the army to cross to Thrace. 'But the army will be crossing over in any event,' Xenophon responds, 'so Seuthes should not reward either me or anyone else on that account' (7.1.6). Later, in the presence of Seuthes and two Greek officers, Xenophon asks the ambassador to confirm the details of the encounter. 'Having said this, he asked Medosades whether he had just spoken the truth. Medosades agreed he had' (7.2.25).
  Second approach by Seuthes (7.2.10). 'When Seuthes heard that Xenophon had come back again, he sent Medosades to him by sea to ask him to bring the army to Seuthes, making him whatever promises he thought would persuade him. Xenophon answered that nothing of that kind could be done, and when Medosades heard this, he went off.' Again, at the meeting with Seuthes just referred to, with Phryniskos the Achaean and Polykrates the Athenian present, Xenophon seeks corroboration. 'At this point, he again asked Medosades if that had been his message. He agreed that it had been' (7.2.26).
  First meeting with Seuthes (7.2.19–38). On the Thracian's order, Xenophon is only allowed to bring two men into his tower. But before they come to business, Xenophon

A key dimension in this, as outlined in note 19, is Xenophon's construction of his relationship with Seuthes. In his account of their first meeting, he has him refer to the kinship between Athenians and Thracians (7.2.31), so establishing a filial basis for the friendship between the two men. This link is subsequently emphasised when they adopt 'Athena' as the watchword for the two forces (7.3.39). Xenophon affirms the appropriateness of the bond at the individual level by representing Seuthes as a noble figure: a man who is in search of justice and who has taken measures to be self-sufficient (7.2.32–4). Other qualities attributed to him by Xenophon include the ability to hold drink (7.3.35) and a knowledge of Greek (7.6.8). At the conclusion of their first meeting, the men exchange handshakes, establishing a guest-friend relationship (7.3.1).[20] Yet Xenophon's problems may begin here, with the possibility that he received more than just the handclasp of Seuthes. Towards the end of the Thracian narrative, after the Cyreans have enlisted with Sparta, the new employers send Xenophon to Seuthes to try to recover the pay due to the mercenaries (7.7.19–20). In a lengthy speech (four and a half OCT pages) he dwells on the fact of their friendship and details how he has acted properly in Seuthes' interests throughout. However, during the speech, he seems to own up to receiving gifts from Seuthes: 'before any service was done for you, you gave me a pleasant welcome, in your looks, your tone of voice and your *xeniois*' (σὺ δὲ πρὶν μὲν ὑπηρετῆσαί τί σοι ἐμὲ ἐδέξω ἡδέως καὶ ὄμμασι καὶ φωνῇ καὶ ξενίοις, 7.7.46).

Azoulay argues that *xeniois* here should be translated as 'hospitality gifts' and that in the passage Xenophon is admitting he has received many from Seuthes.[21] Such gifts, though, need not have been substantial, being rather part of the local culture of exchange we learn about at 7.3.16–18 (for this Thracian custom, see also Thucydides 2.97.4, who remarks it was 'impossible to get anything done without a present') and being within the normal exercise of guest-friendship. With this in mind, I suggest that the gifts Xenophon received from Seuthes were 'tokens of friendship' (LXA translation), of no great intrinsic worth.[22] Clues that he did not receive

---

requests that the others with him be called in: 'outside there are delegates from the generals, for each general the person he regards as the most trustworthy – each general, that is, except Neon the Laconian. So if you want our dealings to be yet more reliable, have them called in too' (7.2.29–30).
20 See Herman 1987: 50–1, Stronk 1995: 198. Regarding his representation of Seuthes, I remarked in the previous chapter on Xenophon's tendency to blur the identity boundaries between Greek and barbarian.
21 Azoulay 2004: 294.
22 Flower (2012: 157–9) in his consideration of the passage came to a similar conclusion, the gifts according to him being those ordinarily provided to a guest by his host – food and drink. Note also Dillery's translation of *xeniois* as 'hospitality' in the Loeb *Anabasis* edition.

substantial gifts come at several places in the text, notably when he crosses back to Asia from Thrace and the outcome of sacrifices affirms that he is virtually penniless (7.8.3). It bears mention too that the major gifts – an estate, and Seuthes' daughter – promised to him when he first established friendship with Seuthes (7.2.38) never materialise. Elsewhere (7.5.8), he says that Seuthes had regularly spoken of transferring forts to him but that after he had fallen out with a corrupt aide of the Thracian's, no further mention was made of these. At 7.6.18, in an address to the men, he states explicitly that he did not receive anything:

> 'But on the contrary, I think I am far from having what is yours, for I swear to you by every one of the gods and goddesses that the real truth is that I have nothing of what Seuthes promised to me for my personal reward. He himself is present and, as he is listening, he can bear witness as to whether I am swearing false oaths.'

That might be enough to close the question of *xeniois*, but loose ends remain. One is that, notwithstanding their justification in the terms above, it is questionable whether accepting gifts at all was appropriate for a Socratic, who might feel compromised by the benefits. Here we can note Socrates' denouncing of those who took a fee for their company, 'since they were bound to converse with all from whom they took the fee' (*Memorabilia* 1.2.6).[23]

A more pressing matter in terms of the gift question is that the men, for whom the etiquette and practice of *xenia* culture admittedly may not have meant much, remained convinced that Xenophon had received gifts from Seuthes (ἔφασαν δέ με καὶ δῶρα ἔχειν παρὰ σοῦ, 7.7.44); that these were more than just token in their eyes is implied by the earlier accusation of corruption against him. Xenophon himself, in what is perhaps a vindictive swipe, has previously named other commanders who did receive what might be regarded as substantial gifts, so there is real reason for the men to be suspicious about the goings-on with Seuthes.[24] His plea to Seuthes to pay the men's wages through him (7.7.49), an act that would improve his standing among the soldiers, and indeed this long, final speech in general,

---

23 Xenophon's meeting with the philosopher prior to the journey marks his status as a Socratic. On the wider issue, Herman (1987: 7) remarks: 'when seen from the perspective of the community, gift-exchange with an outsider – the essential characteristic of guest-friendship – could appear as bribery. The antithetical notion of abstinence from accepting gifts became the mark of the ideal citizen.'

24 'At this point the generals were divided into factions. Kleanor and Phryniskos wished to lead the army to Seuthes as, in an effort to persuade them, he had given one a horse and the other a woman' (7.2.2). For interest, Xenophon and Seuthes probably crossed paths one more time after the Cyreans had left: in the spring of 398 the Greeks travelled back to Thrace with Derkylidas, who was hosted there by Seuthes. See *Hell.* 3.2.9.

seems to show that his earlier elaborate efforts at defusing the bribes issue have not ultimately had the desired effect. The persistence of suspicion against him in the face of fulsome defence prompts us at this late stage to review the narrative. I choose two episodes, the first in Thrace, and the second prior to that on the Black Sea coast, which place the dissatisfaction and unease of the men in fuller light.

Early on in the Thracian adventure Seuthes hosts a dinner (7.3.15). Herakleides tells Xenophon and the other guests that they should give what gifts they can to gain the warlord's favour (7.3.16–20: the custom is referred to above). Xenophon is dismayed, 'for he had crossed over from Parium with nothing except a slave-boy and enough money for the journey' (7.3.20). When his turn comes at the banquet, he stands up, slightly drunk (ὑποπεπωκὼς), and declares at length that he is enthusiastically placing himself and his companions at Seuthes' service (7.3.29–31). This declaration might not have been well received by the other Greeks at the dinner, who, if they were willing to disregard the initial grandiosity, were compelled to take notice by Xenophon's elaboration:

> 'My gift, Seuthes, is myself and these companions of mine here, to be faithful friends to you; and none of them are unwilling, but all want to be friends with you even more than I do. And here they are now, not asking you for anything further but freely offering themselves to labour on your behalf and to go ahead in danger.' (7.3.30)

The men were not subjects and were not their leader's to gift. Xenophon may be acknowledging a mistake by recording the embarrassing episode, excusing it on the grounds of inebriation, but it would understandably linger as (another) basis for suspicion and irritation on the part of the soldiers towards Xenophon. I add that in the didactic context it serves as a blunt paradigm for how not to cultivate willing obedience.

The second episode is at Kalpe Harbour, where Xenophon is suspected of 'persuading' a soothsayer to pronounce an unfavourable reading of victims ('There were some who dared to say that Xenophon, wishing to found a settlement in the stronghold, had persuaded the seer to say that the sacred signs had not been forthcoming in favour of departure', 6.4.14). Does this hint at a widespread suspicion of improper financial conduct on his part, whether arising from this episode or from previous ones? Inserted into the narrative before this, when the army is at Kerasous on the Black Sea (5.3), is the flashforward to Skillous, in which Xenophon appears to address a doubt about what he did with funds from the sale of captives intended as tithes to the gods. In the end, one is left with the impression that the author may have exposed himself where he did not intend to and that his inclusion in the narrative of detail that impinges on his financial behaviour could be said to raise more questions than answers. If we prefer an author too self-aware or too clever for such a misstep, we could alternatively read this as part of the story's self-development theme, mistakes and misjudgements the inexperienced 'Xenophon' made in the intense circumstances of the retreat.

Criticisms of Xenophon from External Audiences

For this second category of Xenophontic defence I look at instances in the text which are thought to be responses to external criticisms of the author. In the first section I evaluate a traditional view about the reason Xenophon wrote his account of the expedition – as a response to another published version – with a conclusion that the evidence for an account at odds with Xenophon's is not compelling. I go on to examine the matter of his involvement in a mercenary enterprise, a circumstance which, considering his social background, and discreditable actions by the army on its retreat, he will have been keen to explain. In the final section I look at his relationship with Sparta and argue that its presentation is intended to provide key context for any judgements on his loyalty to his own *polis*.

Anabasis *as a Response to Other Accounts of the Expedition*

A setting straight of the record has, in modern times, been one of the most common explanations offered for *Anabasis*. Xenophon's near flawless achievement in helping to lead the Greeks homeward is believed by many to be a response to (what he at least saw as) unfair portrayal of his role in other accounts of the march.[25] This version of the personal apologia argument, attractive in that it excuses Xenophon of vain self-promotion, is dependent on there having been another account published prior to his, and on that not portraying him in a favourable light. There are differing views on this matter. Though Xenophon's is the only one that survives, his may well not have been the only participant story about the expedition to have been published.[26] Four fragments of a *Kyrou Anabasis* by Sophainetos – who is likely to be the Stymphalian general in Xenophon's account (1.1.11, 1.2.9, 2.5.37, 4.4.19, 5.3.1, 5.8.1, 6.5.13) – are mentioned in Stephanos, the sixth-century AD Byzantine lexicographer (Jacoby 109 FF 1–4), and Xenophon himself refers to the record of Themistogenes (*Hellenika* 3.1.2). Outside of this, there are the contemporary histories. We know that scores of historians were writing

---

25 The theory appears to have emerged in the late nineteenth century in Continental scholarship (Schwartz 1889, Dürrbach 1893) and has enjoyed a steady degree of interest since (see e.g. Anderson 1974: 83, Dillery 1998: 8, Cawkwell 2004: 59–63).

26 While it seems possible veterans wrote in the years following the return of the Greeks to Asia Minor, how many would have produced substantial tracts is debatable. Cartledge (1987: 59) writes that 'it is generally agreed that [Xenophon's] was not the first participant account to be published'.

in fourth-century Greece, and the subject of the Ten Thousand must have been of interest to some, whatever the context they framed the event within.[27] Those that we know of, and whose works – or parts thereof – were likely to have been in circulation in the early 360s when Xenophon was writing *Anabasis*, are the Knidian physician Ktesias, Theopompos of Chios and the so-called Oxyrhynchos Historian. Of note as well is Isokrates, who refers to the Ten Thousand in his *Panegyrikos*. I look at each of these potential sources for the march below.[28]

Sophainetos of Stymphalos

In Book 14 of his *Universal History*, Diodoros relates the story of Cyrus's march upcountry and the retreat home of his Greek mercenaries (14.19–31, 37). His account is likely based on that of the fourth-century historian Ephoros, whose thirty-book history covered events immediately following the Trojan War down to the siege of Perinthos in 341.[29] Scholars debate the question of Ephoros' source(s) for the march. While he relied for much of his material about Greek affairs for the period on the Oxyrhynchos Historian, the latter is not likely to have furnished much more than a passing reference to the expedition. Ephoros' apparently poor opinion of Xenophon, suggested by his neglect of the latter's *Hellenika* as a source for his own history, has been thought to rule out Xenophon's *Anabasis*.[30] He may have used a text of which we now have no knowledge, and there is a

---

27 On historical fragments, see Brunt 1980; Breitenbach (1970: 406–7) provides the names of some contemporary writers.

28 Ephoros of Kyme (Jacoby 70) was another writer whose work Xenophon could have been familiar with, though only if one believes that Ephoros published in instalments through his career and not only after he had finished his *Universal History*, probably in the 320s. But even in that case it is unlikely that his summary of the march, which would probably have been in Book 15/16, around halfway through the history, would have been in circulation in the late 370s/early 360s when Xenophon was writing *Anabasis*. The following notes touch on potential sources for the march that might have been used by Diodoros and Ephoros respectively.

29 Diodoros has been shown to tend to follow one source wherever he can. He mentions Ephoros as a source in his account of Cyrus's expedition (14.22.2). While it is possible he drew directly on the Oxyrhynchos Historian (Occhipinti 2016: 57–86 makes a case), or even Theopompos, as Thomas (2021d: 370–1) hints may be the case for the events around 400, since the nineteenth century the general view is that his source for material on Greece and the East in Books 11–15 is Ephoros. See Brunt 1980: 478, Gray 1980: 308, and for newer understandings, Occhipinti 2016, Muntz 2017.

30 For discussion, see Westlake (1987: 248–9), who does believe *Hell. Oxy.* wrote about Cyrus's expedition, and Stylianou (2004: at p. 68 stating his former view but in this later consideration arguing strongly for *Anabasis* being Ephoros' main source). Erbse detects a pronounced 'anti-Xenophon' bias in Ephoros but thinks he did draw on the work, changing or reordering passages as he saw fit (498–9). Cf. Higgins (94), who suggests that, as a pupil of Isokrates, Ephoros may have deliberately avoided using the work of a known Socratic.

modern tradition which thinks he drew on Sophainetos.[31] In Xenophon's account, he is the oldest of the Greek generals (6.5.13) and one of those who survived the march down to the sea. It is plausible that he may have published his story.

Two preliminary issues concerning a 'Sophainetos *Anabasis*' present themselves, namely, the slightness of the reference to his work in Stephanos (four short fragments) and its lateness (sixth century AD). While the scanty material, appearing in the context of geographical names – Sophainetos is quoted as an authority for two tribes, a city and a river[32] – is hardly sufficient to assert that it is the basis of any substantial account of the expedition, it is not at the same time 'a desperate hypothesis': the locations referred to, all far beyond the Greek world, are all on the route of the Ten Thousand.[33] The second issue is the fact that what would have been a significant work – it would already have survived through one or more generations before being used by Ephoros – was unknown to later writers. Notably, neither Arrian, who had a special interest in Xenophon and his *Anabasis*, nor Plutarch, who dealt directly with the march in his *Artaxerxes*, refers to it. It may be relevant too that Arcadia, for all its reputation for producing soldiers, was not famed for literary exponents; Aineias Tacticus, who is said to have come from the same Stymphalos, may be the exception to the rule. Responses to the putative Sophainetos work by doubters range from outright scepticism about its existence, to a belief that it is a forgery, to a theory that Sophainetos' own march story was incorporated into a military handbook and Stephanos at his long remove inferred that he had written an actual account.[34]

---

31 For discussion and context, see Bonner 1910: 97, Parke 1933: 26, Barber 1935: 127, Cawkwell 1972: 17–19 and 2004, Stronk 1995: 7, Flower 2012: 32–3, Thomas 2021d: 372–3. Erbse (498) thinks that Sophainetos was probably one of his sources. Westlake (1987) has argued that the Oxyrhynchos Historian was Ephoros' main source, though this is speculative, as is Anderson's suggestion that a Greek confidant of the Persian king, Phalinos (*An*. 2.1.7), could have authored some form of account and that Ephoros in turn could have drawn on this (1974: 83).

32 F 109.1 Καρδοῦχοι = *An*. 4 *passim*; F 109.2 Τάοι (Τάοχοι in Xenophon) = *An*. 4 *passim*; F 109.3 Φύσκος = *An*. 2.4.25; F 109.4 Χαρμάνδη = *An*. 1.5.10.

33 'Desperate hypothesis': on the ground that virtually nothing is known of Sophainetos' work, Bigwood (1983: 349) characterises it as such. Higgins (93) writes: '[I]n the absence of significant portions of Sophainetos' work this [assertion of a substantial account] must remain a gratuitous assumption'. However, many other modern scholars, including Roy (1967: 290), Cawkwell (1972: 17–18), Dillery (2009: 406) and Pitcher (2012) believe there was a meaningful work.

34 *Scepticism*: Bigwood 1983: 343; *Forgery*: Westlake 1987: 252; *Mistaken transmission*: Stylianou 2004: 73–4. To be added to these is a suggestion by Almagor (2012: 29 n.147) that the name Sophainetos is 'the result of some later corruption and a hyper-correction of "Xenophon"'.

The gist of the Sophainetos–Xenophon hypothesis is that Diodoros makes only one mention of the Athenian, and this comes when the remnants of the army are in Thrace (14.37). His ultimate source, then, can hardly have been Xenophon, with a candidate for this being the work of Sophainetos transmitted through the history of Ephoros. On this line, Sophainetos did not think much of Xenophon's command on the retreat. Possible evidence of animosity shown towards Sophainetos by Xenophon comes from two passages in *Anabasis*: at 5.8.1 he notes that the Stymphalian had been fined for neglect (κατημέλει) by the men (although charges against three of the other generals, including Xenophon himself, are noted too); at 6.5.14, as we saw in the previous chapter, Xenophon interrupts him as he (Sophainetos) dismisses the option of crossing a ravine, declaring that in the interests of safety they must cross. They do, and are successful, and Sophainetos is not heard of again. Of his earlier handful of appearances none are markedly positive, and indeed two could be seen as unflattering: at 4.4.19 he is left behind to guard the camp, and at 5.3.1 he is sent with the ships from Trapezous instead of going on land with the main fighting force.

Xenophon's treatment of his comrade in the narrative, therefore, could support an argument that he had some axe to grind with him, but whether this was as a straightforward result of events on the march, or because of a subsequent biased narrative of the march published by Sophainetos, must be an open question. I think that if it were the latter, and Xenophon cared about it, he would have responded in a different way, probably through silence, so that the name and character of Sophainetos would be doubted by history itself.

Two final observations before turning the focus on Diodoros. It should not be overlooked that Sophainetos' last appearance in the text occurs in Book 6; this could be suppression by Xenophon, but might imply that either he was killed late in the campaign or, more likely, left the army at Byzantium (see 7.2.3). Any account by him, therefore, may not have covered the events in Thrace. This suggests another Ephoran source, though Xenophon's limited appearance in Diodoros could as well be down to the method of that author, which I look at next. Second, I suggest in the later discussion of Ktesias that it is conceivable the latter used Sophainetos' account in his *Persika*; indeed, if there was one, we should not be surprised if he did, given his own personal involvement in the event (as the physician who attended the King on the battlefield). So, we just might be getting a glimpse of Sophainetos in this way, if not through later writers such as Ephoros.

The whole question of what, if anything, Sophainetos or another available eyewitness wrote is complicated by what we know of the quality of Diodoros' compilations. While it is likely that Ephoros is his source for the march, it is less certain that he reproduced a faithful summary of his version. A general difficulty arises with dates, as Ephoros arranged his narrative by subject and Diodoros sought to shoehorn these into his annalistic system; but other tendencies also work to degrade his history. An example is his seventeenth book, which he based on Klitarchos: while the latter's work is believed to have run to twelve books, Diodoros compressed it into just one. Brunt writes: 'If he paraphrased Clitarchus in a few places, he had to abbreviate inordinately elsewhere, and simply leave out masses of material.'[35] Xenophon's apparent dropping out of Ephoros' narrative could, then, conceivably be down to the method of Diodoros rather than the indifference or malice of Sophainetos or another eyewitness.

A related concern is the disposition of Ephoros himself. If, as some consider, he bore an 'anti-Xenophon' bias, he could have chosen selectively from his source(s). He is said, moreover, to have a tendency to rewrite his sources, a factor which could lead to significant distortion. Gray writes: 'No matter what the quality of the original, by the time it had passed through the hands of Ephorus, it was likely to have altogether lost that quality.'[36] In the situations outlined in this and in the preceding paragraph, the original(s) need not have been either hostile or indifferent to Xenophon, a fact which presents a challenge for the advocates of this version of the personal apologia argument. One other point to consider is that, granted he was one of the oldest generals on the expedition, any account of Sophainetos might have come after Xenophon's; or put another way, the former could have been responding to the latter.

Addressing the issue from a different perspective, a good case can be made for Xenophon being the ultimate source for Diodoros' narrative, this again undermining the Sophainetos hypothesis.[37] Almost all of Diodoros' account matches Xenophon's very closely, and what differences there are can mostly be easily explained. One that seemingly cannot is the Athenian's above-mentioned absence from Diodoros on the retreat from Mesopotamia to Byzantium, the greater part and heart of the journey. Another is their respective versions of Cheirisophos' leadership role: according to Diodoros he is elected supreme commander at the Zapatas River (14.27.1), while Xenophon has him formally as part of a leadership collective until an election at Sinope late on in the retreat (3.2.37, 6.1.32). I suggest that both discrepancies may have a simple explanation. Just as I

---

35 Brunt 1980: 493. See also Krentz's criticism (1989: 8). For a summary of views on Diodoros and his engagement with source material, see Rop 2019: 4 n.13.
36 Gray 1987: 73. For a modern study of Ephoros, see Parmeggiani 2011. Luraghi characterises his work as 'the most ambitious product of fourth-century historiography' (2017: 94).
37 Stylianou in his 2004 study set out a detailed and quite convincing argument for *Anabasis* being Diodoros' ultimate source, and I seek to complement this here. For an overview on the subject, though reaching a different conclusion on balance, see Thomas 2021d.

have argued Xenophon did, Diodoros, with his tendency to view history in terms of outstanding men, could be focusing on leaders as a framework for his compilation. Thus, he says that Cheirisophos was elected supreme leader by the men after the seizure of the generals by Tissaphernes (14.27.1), a reasonable inference from *Anabasis*, where the assembly assents to Xenophon's proposal that Cheirisophos should lead the front (3.2.37-8), and he says Xenophon was chosen as their leader in Thrace (14.37.1), a statement which reflects what Xenophon says at 7.2.9.[38] The understanding in the accounts which follow the respective announcements of leadership is that it resided in the named leader, and no additional command information was necessary. However stellar, or anonymous, Xenophon's role might have been, by this approach it would not anyway have registered in Diodoros.

To support this argument, I turn to the one passage in which Xenophon is mentioned in Diodoros and demonstrate that it betrays a concise and accurate reading of *Anabasis* (at the general level, few dispute that Diodoros 14.37.1-4 reflects Book 7 of *Anabasis*):

> At this same time a group of the soldiers who had served in the campaign with Cyrus and had got back safe to Greece went off each to his own country, but the larger part of them, about five thousand in number, since they had become accustomed to the life of a soldier, chose Xenophon for their general. (Diodoros 14.37.1)

The statement that some of the soldiers who had got back safely to Greece returned to their own countries (καὶ διασωθέντων εἰς τὴν Ἑλλάδα τινὲς μὲν εἰς τὰς ἰδίας πατρίδας) mirrors Xenophon's statements that Byzantium was the first Greek city which the army came to (*Anabasis* 7.1.29; and see 6.1.17, 6.5.23) and that some of the soldiers sold their weapons and sailed away (7.2.3). For Xenophon being chosen as their general, Diodoros/Ephoros is evidently drawing on his return to Thrace (*Anabasis* 7.2.8). Xenophon does not say he was then chosen as leader, but he clearly implies as much: 'the soldiers received him with joy and began following him right away' (οἱ δὲ στρατιῶται ἐδέξαντο ἡδέως καὶ εὐθὺς εἵποντο, 7.2.9). He subsequently presses this more: 'afterwards Xenophon began to lead them out, and they followed' (Μετὰ ταῦτα Ξενοφῶν μὲν ἡγεῖτο, οἱ δ' εἵποντο, 7.3.7; and note his being given the pick of the booty at 7.8.23). What is revealing is that while on two occasions before this Xenophon has been offered the

---

38 On the statement about Cheirisophos, H-R (127) believe there is a misinterpretation of the verb 'to lead' in *An.* 3.2.36 or 37 by Diodoros or his source. On the question of the leadership, see Chapter 3 p. 89-90. I discuss Xenophon becoming leader in Thrace next.

leadership (6.1.19, 7.1.21), he has declined both these opportunities, so it is only in Thrace proper that he is in sole command.

Themistogenes of Syracuse

Anabasis contains no detail about its narrator, but his perspective indicates that either he was a participant on the march or that his persona is that of an all-seeing 'Homeric Zeus' (see Lucian, *De historia conscribenda* 49). Xenophon, who is usually thought to be the narrator, is a character in the story and is formally introduced into it in the third book (3.1.4). Our assumption that he is the author of *Anabasis* is called into question by *Hellenika* 3.1.2, where the narrator of that work writes that Themistogenes of Syracuse authored (γέγραπται) an account of Cyrus's march upcountry and the retreat of his Greeks to the sea. As MacLaren noted in his study of the problem, this statement has caused considerable trouble for students of *Hellenika* and *Anabasis*.[39] Possible solutions to the problem are:

1) The *Hellenika* passage is an interpolation and does not constitute an intertextual problem.
2) Themistogenes wrote an *Anabasis*, Xenophon did not.
3) Themistogenes and Xenophon wrote accounts, but Themistogenes' has not survived.
4) Themistogenes is a pseudonym used by Xenophon.
5) Themistogenes is the narrator of the story, Xenophon its author.[40]

We can, I think, dismiss the first possibility on the grounds that writers from as early as Plutarch did not question the authenticity of the passage and editors would surely have excised it had there been any serious doubt.[41] The principal advocate for the second scenario is the author of the *Souda*, who considered that *Anabasis*, though attributed to Xenophon, was actually the work of Themistogenes.[42] It may be supposed that he based his view on *Hellenika*, though it cannot be discounted that he derived it from a source

---

39 MacLaren 1934: 240. Høeg (1950: 166) described it as 'une chose très étrange', and Rood (2005: xix) as 'perhaps the oddest passage in the whole of Xenophon'. Pelling (2013: 40) writes: 'It is certainly understandable that Plutarch should have fastened on this sentence of the *Hellenica*, as it is frankly astounding. Themistogenes of Syracuse?'
40 This argument by McCloskey challenges the assumption that Xenophon was the narrator of his writings (2017). There are other explanations for the *Hellenika* passage besides these five, for example that the name is the result of a copyist's error and that the sentence should read: 'Has been written, rightfully and dutifully, by one of Cyrus's men' (Prentice 1947: 76–7).
41 Cf. Prentice (1947: 74), who refers to modern scholars who consider the passage an interpolation.
42 The *Souda* entry: Θεμιστογένης, Συρακούσιος, ἱστορικός. Κύρου ἀνάβασιν, ἥτις ἐν τοῖς Ξενοφῶντος φέρεται· καὶ ἄλλα τινὰ περὶ τῆς ἑαυτοῦ πατρίδος.

now lost. On the weight of the antique literary evidence for Xenophon's *Anabasis* alone, it is safe to say that his belief that Xenophon did not write an *Anabasis* is incorrect.[43] The fact that several themes and concerns in the work recur across Xenophon's corpus provides further solid evidence that he was indeed the author.

The third scenario is plausible but undermined by the fact that the only pre-modern references to Themistogenes external to *Hellenika* are Plutarch (see below), the entry in the *Souda* and the twelfth-century Tzetzes' *Chiliades* (7.154). A further problem for it is that there is no record of a Themistogenes on the journey, although that does not have to mean that there was not a Cyrean of that name, and we do have a commander, Sosis, who brought as many as 300 hoplites from Syracuse (1.2.9).[44] In any event he would not have had to have been a participant to write about the historical event, though passages pointing to autopsy and personal experience suggest that he was (for example 1.5.2, 4.5.27).

The notion that Themistogenes was a pseudonym used by Xenophon, current at least from Plutarch's day, is the most widely accepted explanation for *Hellenika* 3.1.2.[45] Plutarch, as remarked at the beginning of the chapter, considered that Xenophon assigned authorship to Themistogenes in order to make his account more credible by having himself described in the third person (*De gloria Atheniensium*, 345e); this should be taken in the context of *De se ipsum citra invidiam laudando*, where Plutarch outlines the circumstances in which self-praise (περιαυτολογία) may be acceptable to an audience. Other views on the rationale for the pseudonym have been aired since, including that it signals an author who tells the truth[46] (note 'Themis'

---

43 References to Xenophon's *Anabasis*: Cicero, *Div.* 1.25; Dionysios of Halikarnassos, *Rhet.* 8.11; Dio Chrysostom, *Or.* 18.15; Arrian, *Peripl. M. Eux.* 1.1, *Anab.* 1.12.3; Pollux 10.80; Lucian, *Somn.* 17; Athenaios 11.112; Aelian, *VH* 3.24; Diogenes Laertios 2.50.

44 Strauss (1972: 178) appears to try to make some connection between Themistogenes and the Syracusan who features in Xenophon's *Symposion*, though he provides no indication of what this might be: 'As for Xenophon's choice of a Syracusan as the antagonist of Socrates, I fear that its explanation may depend on the explanation of "Themistogenes of Syracuse", the author of a book which is indistinguishable from Xenophon's *Anabasis*.' For more ideas, see Strauss 1975. Høeg (1950: 178) believed that there was an account of the expedition 'écrit par un Syracusain'; Waterfield (2006: 190) suggests that Themistogenes could have been a friend of Xenophon's, 'perhaps the one who first suggested that [he] should write up his memories of Cyrus's expedition'; Pitcher in his New Jacoby entry (108) offers arguments for a real figure. Tuplin says that the name was known only in Hellenistic-Roman Thessaly (2003: 130).

45 See Bonner 1910: 98 n.5. Pelling 2013: 40 n.4 provides a list of moderns who consider that *Anabasis* circulated pseudonymously.

46 See Krentz 1995: 157 for discussion. Erbse (494) dwells on Themistogenes, 'descendant of justice', opining, with additional reference to Xenophon's use of Theopompos at 2.1.12–13, that he had a strong liking for wordplay. I agree but suggest in the next chapter (pp. 206–7) that we do not only have wordplay here but an important literary relationship as well.

for justice; 'Syracuse', away from the Aegean hub, for objectivity); that the attribution was 'in part Xenophon's unconscious recognition that he had been uprooted by the expedition, that he no longer was who he had been';[47] and that 'Themistogenes of Syracuse, author of the Anabasis' means 'Xenophon the Socratic, author of a propaedeutic to philosophy designed to earn a measure of toleration for philosophy'.[48]

Building on a view that the narrator in *Anabasis* is separate from its author and from Xenophon's character in the story, McCloskey believes that Themistogenes is the narrator of the story. This emerges from his argument that the narrator of *Hellenika* is distinct from its author and that the best way to interpret 3.1.2 is that the narrator is not naming the author of *Anabasis* (from our perspective) as Themistogenes, 'since this is Xenophon, but rather that he is naming the narrator of *Anabasis*, who is the author of the *Anabasis* within its own fictional world, "Themistogenes"'.[49] This argument solves several enduring problems for us both within *Anabasis* and across the corpus. Its premise, that Xenophon creates distinct narratorial and authorial levels wherein the knowledge of each is different, is a plausible one for an author known for innovation. However, looking at the thesis from the historiographical perspective, some questions do arise. To touch on one, it is a crucial piece of information that the *Hellenika* statement comes after the publication of *Anabasis*. All things being equal, we are more inclined to see it as a corrective than as part of an ironic, narratorial game played by Xenophon. There were arguably places in the corpus in works written closer to *Anabasis* that would have better facilitated the embedding of the idea; one thinks for example of Socrates talking about Cyrus the Younger in *Oikonomikos*. Given the book's unhistorical texture, the introduction of the Themistogenes passage at, say, the end of 4.19 might have been more in line with the argument being made.

Whether one considers that Themistogenes was a writer of the day who filed some report on the event either separately or as part of a bigger narrative, or as the great majority do, that he was a fictive persona, the important question concerns the intention of the author in introducing him. One possibility is the narratorial one argued for by McCloskey, another the traditional explanation that Xenophon's aim was to enhance the credibility of his narrative by referring to himself in the third person. My own view is that he uses it to indicate to his readers that *Anabasis* is not autobiographical, that Xenophon in the story is likewise fictive – as it happens, a model Socratic officer. Although they certainly overlap,

---

47 Waterfield 2006: 194.
48 Buzzetti 2014: 311 (who thinks it may also mean: 'Xenophon the Socratic, a man who resists certain aspects of the Socratic path').
49 McCloskey 2017: 622–5 with references (cited passage, p. 625).

his representation is distinct from the historical role played by Xenophon on the march. On my suggestion of a corrective, this would have been prompted by the audience response to *Anabasis* following its publication, there being too much of a tendency to equate character and author. This might have become uncomfortable for him, given there were veterans of the march and perhaps senior Spartan figures who would have had different recollections. In Chapter 5, I argue for a literary connection between Themistogenes and Theopompos, the name in some manuscripts of the young Athenian who appears in Book 2.

Concerning the question of a response to another account, this would be relevant only in two of the scenarios I have given, and as I have dismissed the first (2), it would apply just to the second (3); as this posits the Themistogenes version was lost, we can infer that it did not have any widespread circulation or content of durable interest. We may doubt as well that Xenophon would have given any oxygen to this version had he been misrepresented in it.

Isokrates

A contemporary of Xenophon's, Isokrates published his famous treatise on panhellenism around 380 or later, and in this, not surprisingly, he makes several references to the Ten Thousand.[50] Passages in *Anabasis* have been convincingly linked to ones in the *Panegyrikos*, suggesting that Xenophon had some form of engagement with this work.[51] Notably, at *Panegyrikos* 146, Isokrates says that Cyrus's Greek mercenaries were 'not picked troops, but men who, owing to stress of circumstances, were unable to live in their own cities' (οὐκ ἀριστίνδην ἐπειλεγμένους, ἀλλ' οἳ διὰ φαυλότητ' ἐν ταῖς αὐτῶν [πόλεσιν] οὐχ οἷοί τ' ἦσαν ζῆν). This suggestion of a ragbag, rootless army could well have irked Xenophon, and he may be responding at *Anabasis* 6.4.8:

> Most of the soldiers were not the kind of people who, in need of a livelihood, have sailed overseas for the pay (τῶν γὰρ στρατιωτῶν οἱ πλεῖστοι ἦσαν οὐ σπάνει βίου ἐκπεπλευκότες ἐπὶ ταύτην τὴν μισθοφοράν), but they had done so on hearing of the personal merits

---

50 Dating: *Paneg.* 126: καὶ νῦν Ὀλυνθίους καὶ Φλειασίους πολιορκοῦσιν ('and now they are laying siege to Olynthos and Phleious'). From *Hellenika* it is clear that both sieges, which lasted more than a year, were going on in 380.
51 See further Dillery 1995: 80 and Gray 2021. Millender (2012: 415) considers that owing to the 'strong resemblances between their accounts of the Cyreans and their mutual interest in the issue of "friendship" with the barbarian (especially of the Spartan variety)', the authors were in conversation. Another point of contact between the pair may be their encomiums, with some seeing Isokrates' *Evagoras* shaping Xenophon's later *Agesilaos*: see Humble 2020: 295–6.

of Cyrus: some actually brought men with them, and others had even spent their own money. Beyond these, there were yet others who had run away from their fathers and mothers, and some, hearing that people in Cyrus's following were doing very well, had left children behind, intending to come back when they had acquired money to spend on them. These being the kinds of person they were, they longed to get safely back to Greece.

An earlier statement about the mercenaries as a group also represents them in positive light and could also be taken as a response:

> by the time that they reached Kilikia, it seemed clear to everyone that the expedition was against the King. Unwilling though they were, and fearful of the journey, the majority still followed along from a sense of shame toward Cyrus and toward each other. (3.1.10)

However, the actual events at Kilikia as narrated by Xenophon in Book 1 – the men refuse to go on and agree to do so only after Cyrus has increased their pay – contradict this claim of a noble motive defining the majority at Tarsus. In the second half of the first cited passage above, there seems to be acknowledgement too that some of the participants joined for money, though that could conceivably be read Socratically as individual initiative towards becoming self-sufficient.

It bears mention that in the *Panegyrikos* passage Isokrates goes on to comment favourably that, when the Persians seized the Greek High Command, 'hoping by this lawless act to throw their army into confusion (147) . . . the soldiers not only stood together but bore their misfortune nobly (καλῶς)' (148); and then at 149: 'Let me sum up the whole matter: these men did not set out to get plunder or to capture a town, but took the field against the king himself.'

Yet the stain of his earlier disparaging remark is not fully removed, and with Xenophon's propensity for apologia there must be a strong possibility that he took *Panegyrikos* 146 hard and is responding to it at *Anabasis* 6.4.8. It is the fact that he does not generally portray the mercenaries in glowing light that makes the passage stand out.[52] Through his narrative, providing

---

52 Mercenaries behaving badly: 1.2.11, demanding money from Cyrus; 1.4.12, refuse to proceed unless given more money; 4.4.14, burning houses in Armenian villages; 5.4.16–18, unsanctioned raid; 5.7.12–25, murders at Kerasous; 6.2.4–7, threatening a Greek city (Herakleia); 7.1.15–17, storming of Byzantium. A relevant extratextual reference discussed in Chapter 2 as part of a treatment of Xenophon's defence of the Ten Thousand is the episode in *Hellenika* (3.2.6–7) in which 'the leader of the men who had fought with Cyrus' defends the army against a charge of plundering allied lands in the campaign against Tissaphernes; however, Xenophon does not actually refute the charge, but rather assigns blame to the Spartan commander, Thibron.

guidance in a typically quiet way on the handling of mercenaries, Xenophon demonstrates that the paramount driving force behind their behaviour is self-interest; furthermore, he takes trouble to distance himself from them on the march, emphasising at several points that he is not driven by the desire for profit, this being the guiding light of the mercenary body. Contradicting this line, 6.4.8 would have him in a community of virtual *kaloikagathoi*, a hard-working body of men who, if not seeking personal development, are pursuing the important virtue of self-sufficiency.[53] This incongruous quality of the passage (and, it can be added, of the earlier one at Tarsus), when taken with the apologetic *Tendenz* in the work, indicates that it could very plausibly be a response to the *Panegyrikos*, and while we must doubt this alone was the impetus for Xenophon to write *Anabasis*, it could be the moment that spurred him to start.

Ktesias of Knidos

Ktesias, having been captured in a campaign, is said to have spent seventeen years at the Persian court, in that time becoming the personal physician of the Great King.[54] In addition to an *Indika* (one book), *Geography* (three books) and some medical treatises, he wrote a multi-volume history (twenty-three books) of the Persians down to 397.[55] This would have encompassed the attempt of Cyrus on the throne, and indeed Xenophon references Ktesias in his own account of the battle with the King (1.8.26–7); although it cannot be

---

53 McKechnie (1989: 80) prefers what Xenophon says in 6.4.8 to the characterisation of Isokrates. Azoulay (2004: 297) too thinks there is something in the honourable depiction, arguing that Xenophon is distinguishing between two categories of Greeks, one which followed from noble motives, the other only out of desire for profit. Rop (2019: 20–1) thinks that the majority were politically interested. Still, my own view is that there must be little doubt that those joining Cyrus for the promise of wealth formed the largest group, notwithstanding Xenophon's implying the opposite in 6.4.8. Roy's (2004: 287–8) argument that the ultimate aim of the mercenaries was to secure long-term employment in Cyrus's garrisons is consistent with this view. Neither is it affected by the status of the men prior to their joining Cyrus: that they might have come from modestly prosperous backgrounds is not a proof that they did not seek to increase their material means. See further Van Soesbergen 1982/3: 134–5, McKechnie 1989: 79–80, Roy 2004: 271, 275–6.

54 Diodoros 2.32.4. He seems to have left the court around 397 to act for the King in affairs on the seacoast (see Plutarch, *Artax.* 21.1–3). A tradition of Greek healers at the Persian court can be traced back to Demokedes of Croton, who tended to King Darius (Herodotus 3.129–30).

55 Epitomes of the *Persika* and *Indika* survive in Photios (*Bibl.* 72); fragments of Ktesias are collected in Jacoby (688), added to by Lenfant 2004. Besides Photios, the major transmitters are Nicolaus of Damascus, Diodoros and Plutarch, through his *Artaxerxes*. Kuhrt (2010) believes that we do not really have Ktesias at all, and she draws attention to the view of some scholars that his work may be a fiction, or at least was written without him ever having left the surroundings of Knidos. While such would make it a peculiar work, it need not invalidate its content. Historians today write about places they have never visited, and the bustling port of Knidos would have provided a wealth of research possibilities.

discounted that this reference might be an interpolation, on balance it seems likely that *Anabasis* postdates *Persika*.⁵⁶

While without the complete work we can only draw up a limited catalogue of comparable subject material between the two authors, it is clear that there are intersections. From Xenophon we know that Ktesias gives an eyewitness account of events on the battlefield at Cunaxa in 401, our author, as noted, referring to this in his own battle report (1.8.26–7).⁵⁷ Ktesias further provides detail of the fate of the generals captured by Tissaphernes on the Zapatas (*Anabasis* 2.5), claiming to have had contact himself with Klearchos at Babylon – even being given his ring as a sign of friendship.⁵⁸ It is probable that Ktesias learned from him a variety of detail about the march, and he could have included this in his *Persika*, though there is no evidence in what survives to support such a hypothesis. And as Xenophon did not emerge as a significant figure in the march until after the seizure of the generals, Klearchos will not have had much to say about his role.

It could be argued that Ktesias learned details of the retreat from another source, there being ample time for him to do so (the *Persika* was published no earlier than the late 390s), and on the basis of this provided a report of the march, one which was not to Xenophon's liking (as indicated earlier, this scenario provides some indirect support for the Sophainetos hypothesis, assuming that any work by him was published not long after the event). While such a report would fit in a history of Persia, it must be unlikely that Xenophon would have referred to Ktesias' account if he had felt dissatisfied with his own portrayal in it. Moreover, we know the author was not well received critically by some in antiquity, so even if Xenophon had been slighted by him, he might not have felt a need to respond.⁵⁹ That

---

56 Interpolation: Almagor 2012: 33–5. In support of *Anabasis* postdating *Persika*, Bassett (2001: 9) argues that Xenophon is referring to it at *An*. 2.6.4 where he remarks that the arguments which Klearchos used to persuade Cyrus to give him money for an army 'have been recounted elsewhere' (ἄλλῃ γέγραπται). Some consider that Xenophon's brief summary of the events surrounding the accession of Artaxerxes to the throne (*An*. 1.1.3) could be based on Ktesias (Bigwood 1983: 347 n.33), and Cawkwell (1972: 21–2) believes that Xenophon may have used a rudimentary route-guide contained in Book 23 of the *Persika* in the construction of his march record. On the dating of Ktesias' *Persika*, see Bigwood 1978, Stronk 2010, Llewellyn-Jones and Robson 2010, Lenfant 2014, Almagor 2012 and 2018. Almagor in the later work usefully surveys the tradition of Classical writings on Persia collectively labelled as *Persika* (2018: 61–8).

57 For a treatment of the relationship between the battle reports of Xenophon and Ktesias, see Bassett 1999, and note the caveat of Thucydides on eyewitness battle reports, 7.44.1. I examined Xenophon's treatment of Cunaxa in Chapter 2 pp. 65–6.

58 Plutarch, *Artax*. 18, and see Photios 72.44a.29–34.

59 For negative views of Ktesias, see Strabo 11.6.3, Lucian, *Ver. hist*. 1.3 and *Hist. conscr*. 39. Neither has his writing been highly valued in the modern era (e.g. Cook 1983: 22, Momigliano 1990: 10), although this is now changing: see Bassett 1999, Stronk 2007 and 2010, Llewellyn-Jones and Robson 2010, Lenfant 2014.

said, Plutarch reads *Anabasis* 2.1.7 as Xenophon implying Ktesias is a liar (*Artaxerxes* 13.3–4), which would be compatible with a negative account.[60]

Theopompos of Chios

The case of Theopompos is somewhat similar. He is known to have authored two substantial historical works, a *Philippika*, which covered events in the reign of the Macedonian king (360–336) in fifty-eight books and, preceding this, a *Hellenika*, a continuation of Thucydides down to the Battle of Knidos (411–394). Fragments of this work do refer to several places named in *Anabasis*, although on the conventional view of the author's birth year (378/7) it could hardly have been published prior to the latter. However, an alternative, based on the *Souda*, has Theopompos born at some time around 404–403, which would make it possible for the work to have been in Xenophon's hands before or while he was writing *Anabasis*.[61] Even if we do assume this last scenario, though, and notwithstanding he was an author who got into detail, there would not seem to be a strong case to infer that Theopompos wrote at any length on the Ten Thousand and less of a one still that what he did write might have been sufficiently hostile towards Xenophon for the Athenian to be moved to set the record straight.

The Oxyrhynchos Historian

The history of this writer probably covered the period from 411 to 386 as a continuation of Thucydides. Some scholars think he is Theopompos, but more regard Kratippos as the likeliest candidate (there is a suggestion that he was a she, the daughter of Thucydides, but few currently take the possibility seriously). The work was conceivably published by the end of the 370s, but it could have been as late as 346. An intermediate possibility is that instalments, or parts of the work, were in circulation between these dates. From the recovered papyri, it is evident that the author was well informed about Persia and that he had knowledge of the topography of Asia Minor. As an annalistic work, it could well have referred to the march, although by the same token such a format would not have lent itself to an

---

60 While not going as far as to suggest that Xenophon was writing in response to Ktesias, Almagor, in an attempt to show a substantial relationship between the works of the two authors, argues that the Athenian's report 'is linked in a special way to the *Persica*. Xenophon had to take into consideration the stories he found there' (2012: 29). Kelly (1996: 159) believes that Xenophon was set on correcting the detail given by Ktesias in his history.
61 Flower (1994: 15) thinks the date is historically useless but that the existence of the *Souda* passage suggests alternative traditions circulated. For discussion of Theopompos' birth date, see ibid. pp. 12–17.

in-depth treatment. And again, as with the other sources looked at, without relevant material in hand we cannot know how it characterised the events and its participants.[62]

In light of the analysis presented in this section, my conclusion is that Xenophon was not writing in response to a work by Sophainetos or anybody else. While other writings influenced him, none, in my view, caused him to sit down and write his own account in response. Xenophon had a brimming agenda, and the content of another's work, though it might, as in the case of Isokrates' negative characterisation of the Ten Thousand, draw a response from the author – even possibly a beginning – it could not displace his desire to share learning on leadership, thoughts on panhellenism and Sparta and to promote the value of Socrates.

The Spectre of the Mercenary

As is the case today, mercenaries in the ancient world were not highly thought of.[63] Ideally *poleis* defended themselves with their citizenry and, if they made some use of outside specialists, did not rely heavily on paid troops. Mercenaries were often associated with tyrants, who hired troops to suppress citizens and gain control of cities,[64] and were rarely regarded as virtuous. In the course of the fourth century, however, with economies monetised and ever greater numbers of hoplites taking up military service abroad, the practice came to be widely accepted as a feature of Greek society.[65] This change in attitude did not encompass the elite classes, for whom wage-earning (which implied dependence and susceptibility to corruption) was generally considered dishonourable. For a *hippeus* like Xenophon, hiring himself and his arms out for pay was a dire measure,

---

62 For further detail on the Oxyrhynchos Historian (H.O.), see Breitenbach 1970, Thomas 2009 and Luraghi 2017, who discusses the other continuators of Thucydides as well. As remarked in note 31, Westlake 1987 considers that H.O. was Diodoros' source, via Ephoros, on the Ten Thousand. Occhipinti 2016 argues that Diodoros repeatedly used H.O. directly.

63 See Plato, *Leg.* 630b, 697e; Isokrates, *Ep.* 9.9–10, *Pace* 8.46; Demosthenes, *First Phil.* 46; Aineias Tacticus 12.2–5; Aristotle, *Eth. Nic.* 3.8.9. The literature on mercenaries in the ancient world is extensive, and *Anabasis*, as a chronicle of mercenary service, is a uniquely important source for the subject. In this section my focus is on Xenophon and his self-representation. I do not seek to evaluate the information he provides about service for pay or the related networks of reciprocal friendships. For studies on the political and social history of mercenaries that include *Anabasis*, see Parke 1933, Griffith 1935, Roy 1967, Trundle 2004, Rop 2019.

64 Examples include Peisistratos, who took Athens in 546 and maintained power using a force of mercenaries until his death in 527 (Herodotus 1.63–4; Aristotle, *Ath. Pol.* 15.1–3), and Polykrates, who ruled Samos c. 535–522 (Herodotus 3.39, 3.45).

65 See Miller 1984 on the increase in mercenary numbers in the fourth century.

and he will have wanted to distance himself from *misthos* (wage) relationships with Cyrus, Seuthes and Thibron, although, as I go on to argue, the Spartan case is qualitatively different. This is therefore an important strand of his personal apologia. We can infer from its presence that the taint of paid service may have hung over Xenophon down the years. The question of his relationships with powerful outsiders also impacts on that of *polis* loyalty, the issue which most concerned Socrates when his student asked him for advice about joining Cyrus (3.1.5). We should also, then, read Xenophon's justification of his involvement with Cyrus as indirect defence against accusations of *prodosia*, betrayal of homeland being the most likely official cause of his exile from Athens. A second aspect of Xenophon's relationship with the mercenaries, his critical stance towards the Ten Thousand in the face of their discreditable actions on the retreat, was discussed in Chapter 2 pp. 73–5.

Cyrus the Younger

Xenophon deals obliquely with the nature of his relationship with Cyrus. My impression is that he is striving to strike a balance between a strong wish to be associated with the prince and awareness of the fact that this association compromises him in different ways. As I discuss in the next chapter, the moral justification for the rebellion was slight; and then, in the eyes of the Athenians, there were further wrongs: association with Cyrus, who was their enemy, and fighting against the King, who they were not on hostile terms with. Hostility between Sparta and Persia, intensified by the former's support for Cyrus and their own campaign in Asia Minor, in due course came in fact to make Athens an ally of the King. 'The diplomatic turning point', Green writes, 'only came after the outbreak of the Corinthian War in 395, which renewed Athens' old conflict with Sparta.'[66] In 395 the King's man, Tithraustes, channelled money to influential groups in the mainland cities for the purpose of warring on Sparta. Xenophon writes that 'the Athenians would not accept the money, but they were nevertheless eager to wage war against Sparta, thinking that they would again acquire an empire' (*Hellenika* 3.5.2).

In *Anabasis*, at the point of his character's introduction to the story, Xenophon indicates that he did not join Cyrus for a campaign against the King: 'In the army there was a certain Xenophon, an Athenian. He did not accompany the army as a general, nor as a captain nor as an ordinary soldier' (3.1.4). Given the placement of this statement, after rather than before the account of Cyrus's campaign, we understand that it is referring

---

66 Green 1994: 220.

to the march against Artaxerxes. This is underscored shortly after, when the narrator explains that Xenophon had been deceived as to the purpose of the expedition, its stated aim having been the subjection of the Pisidians (3.1.9–10). Yet, if it helps him on relations with his *polis*, this explicitly apologetic claim does not seem to further his case for not being a mercenary, as he appears to be admitting that he did join a paid military campaign, just not the one he expected.[67]

Looking more into the question of his status on the expedition, a notable attempt to indicate that in principle he need not have been earning a wage from his weapons occurs in a passage discussed earlier:

> Most of the soldiers were not the kind of people who, in need of a livelihood, sailed overseas for the pay, but they did so on hearing of the personal merits of Cyrus: some actually brought men with them, and others had even spent their own money. (6.4.8)

To some extent, this benign texture has been cultivated through the narrative by the author's characterisation of several of the Greek commanders serving with Cyrus as *xenoi*, the more obvious term, *misthophoros* (wage-earners), being used when speaking of mercenaries on the campaign who opposed them (1.4.3, 4.3.4, 4.4.18, 7.8.15).[68] This picture, however, if not overturned, is contradicted at several junctures, for example by soldiers demanding money from Cyrus (1.2.11), the mutiny at Tarsus (1.3) and the events at Thapsakos, where Cyrus finally declared his true purpose and the men agreed to continue with him contingent on an increase (on top of the Tarsus agreement) in their pay (1.4.12). But, notably, Xenophon adroitly excluded his character from these events. In fact, except for 1.8.15, where he approaches Cyrus on the battlefield, he is completely absent from

---

67 Buzzetti (2014: 114) highlights a mitigating circumstance, pointing out that Proxenos' invitation did not mention what Cyrus would want Xenophon to do, and then on arrival both Proxenos and Cyrus set to persuading him to join the expedition against the Pisidians – a strong hint that he did not know of it beforehand. Granted Xenophon's subtlety here, most likely he did know that Cyrus was organising a military expedition of some kind, since his recruiting agents had been active on Greek territory. But even leaving aside this circumstantial evidence, the fact that he went on campaign well prepared for such is an indication that he knew there was a military aspect – Xenophon brought a shield-bearer (4.2.20), two panoplies (3.2.7) and perhaps several horses (3.3.19).

68 Xenophon uses *xenoi* several times when referring to mercenaries in Cyrus's service (1.1.10, 1.1.11, 1.3.18). At the time of authorship in the 360s, *misthophoros* had become the common designation for hired soldiers, so any usage of *xenoi* in this context may be notable. For a study of the changing terms used to describe mercenaries in classical antiquity, see Trundle 2004: 10–21. Rop 2019: 19 contends that the usage of the term 'mercenary' in modern scholarship is misleading, the soldiers being 'political agents'.

the march upcountry. The representation of himself prior to this moment as a mere implied presence ensures that he cannot be explicitly associated with the episodes involving demands for pay. His virtual absence furthermore serves symbolically to reinforce his claim that he did not join the army for a campaign against the King.

In the key passage where he introduces himself into the story (3.1.4–5), the narrator informs us that Xenophon had been invited to join Cyrus by Proxenos the Theban, an old guest-friend (ξένος) of his. Proxenos in his turn was a guest-friend of the prince's, and we learn that Cyrus asked him to bring as many men as possible to his satrapy for a campaign against a troublesome tribe, the Pisidians (1.1.11). What Xenophon may be doing here is setting his participation on the march in the context of ties of guest-friendship, *xeniai*, one party being obliged to help the other when requested to do so. As Proxenos was a guest-friend of Cyrus, we are led further to suppose that Xenophon too might enter this kind of relationship with the prince, a belief later strengthened by Cyrus himself, who asks Xenophon to remain with them when they are introduced at Sardis (3.1.8–9). Xenophon's honouring of this wish indeed seems to imply such a relationship; in any event, as Azoulay argues, Xenophon can cite his ties of ritual friendship with Proxenos as his reason for joining Cyrus.[69]

He does not do this, however, and nor does he confirm any guest-friend relationship with Cyrus. I argue in the next chapter that a more compelling reading of the relationship between Xenophon and Proxenos and of their reason for joining Cyrus lies in their background in political philosophy. For young men interested in leadership practice, the opportunity to associate with the prince will have been a unique one. In Chapter 5, I furthermore query the nature of the guest-friend bond, pointing to Xenophon's consultation on the matter with an advisor and suggesting that it need not normally have been a strong one, although this undoubtedly depended on the quality of the underlying relationship. Xenophon's guest-friendship with the Spartan Kleandros

---

69 Azoulay (2004: 298–9). Several of the other commanders on the expedition were also guest-friends of Cyrus: Aristippos of Thessaly (1.1.10), Sophainetos of Stymphalos, Socrates of Achaea (1.1.11) and Klearchos of Sparta (1.3.3). Amongst the high-status classes there would not have been anything unusual about an association with a similar foreign figure. As Herman put it, the ancient world was 'united at its highest social level by a web of complex alliances' (1987: 162). Other remarkable personal connections of the period included Alkibiades' with both Tissaphernes (Thucydides 8.47) and Pharnabazos (*Hell.* 1.3.12), and Cyrus and Lysander (*Hell.* 2.1.14). In practice, one guest-friend might well profit from his assistance to another; indeed, it was his expectation that some material benefit – patronage, property, money, position – would accrue from his involvement. To see this, we need only look at what Xenophon says about Proxenos' expectation from the expedition: 'He thought he would [by joining Cyrus] obtain a great name, great power and much wealth' (2.6.17).

is a good example of how real benefit could flow, for instance when the latter prevailed on Anaxibios to allow Xenophon enter Byzantium so that he could sail home (7.1.38–9). The author also plays up his personal relationship with Seuthes, though this proves to be a double-edged sword.

Seuthes

Xenophon frames his relationship with Seuthes, the warlord who employs the army in Thrace, very clearly in terms of friendship. At their first meeting, he has him speak of a kinship (συγγενής) between Thrace and Athens, so invoking a basis if not an obligation for each to trust and help the other (7.2.31, and see 7.3.8–9).[70] When they establish an agreement for use of the army, the relationship is crystallised on a personal level by a handshake (7.3.1), the birthmark of guest-friendship. Once we move from the world of compromising wage-earning (*misthos*) to honourable friendship (*xeniai*), where one *xenos* is bound to assist another, Xenophon's involvement with Seuthes – as before in Cyrus's enterprise – assumes a different and, as far as his high-status audience goes, altogether more positive character. Yet, as was seen, his internal audience seems to have been less willing to recognise the nature of the relationship, and Xenophon's receipt of hospitality gifts may have been the cause of the accusation of corruption made against him, even if, as I argued, these gifts were not of any great intrinsic value.

Thibron

The army's third and final employer is Sparta. Answering a plea from the Greek cities of Asia Minor, who claimed that Tissaphernes was putting demands on them (*Hellenika* 3.1.3), the Spartans sent Thibron out to wage war. One of his first steps was to recruit the remnants of the Ten Thousand in Thrace, offering a daric per month for each soldier with 'double for the captains and double again for the generals' (*Anabasis* 7.6.1). Xenophon led the force down to Thibron, and he participated in the campaign against Tissaphernes.

The circumstances here are somewhat different from the previous cases, as it is a Hellenic enterprise and Xenophon might justify his involvement on the ground that he is benefiting other Greeks by supporting a liberation war against Persia. And then, pointedly, having recently won a substantial

---

70 The kinship which Seuthes claims between Thrace and Athens is reflected in the mythical story of the Athenian king, Pandion, who married his daughter Prokne to Tereus, founder of the Thracian Odrysian kingdom. In recent historical time (431), an alliance between the Odrysian king and Athens resulted in the king's son becoming an Athenian citizen (Thucydides 2.29).

amount of booty in a successful plundering raid against a Persian landowner in Mysia, he is not in need of the wages on offer. If he took them, this could be laid at the door of prudence, with Xenophon considering how an additional amount of money would secure his later life at home – an all the more relevant imperative if the decree of exile against him had just been passed. We can think of the advice of Socrates to an old companion of his, Eutheros, when he has returned from the war and has no property or other financial security: 'Then it would be better to take up some kind of work at once that will assure you an [income] when you get old' (*Memorabilia* 2.8.3).

Not-for-Profit Xenophon

In addition to addressing his involvement in cash-for-arms campaigns, the context Xenophon furnishes for his own character makes pursuit of profit on his part appear incongruous. This largely owes itself to his Socratic self-representation, but we may mark within this a demonstrable tendency to emphasise a distance between himself and the mercenaries. The first step he takes to achieve this is informing us of his relatively well-off status on joining the expedition, for we learn that he has come from Athens well resourced.[71] With just a few exceptions towards the end, there is no indication through the course of the journey that he is seeking money or that he is in need of maintenance. Even in Thrace, judging from the fact that he forgoes booty due to him, he is able to support himself independently.

Looking at places in the text where money features, Xenophon is showing us there that he is not motivated by personal enrichment. At Tarsus, the men continue with Cyrus when they are promised an increase in pay (1.3.21), whereas Xenophon continues because he believes it is the honourable thing to do (3.1.10; and see *Oikonomikos* 14.10).[72] A prime concern of the mercenary group once they have reached the sea is to acquire booty to take home (5.1.8, 6.1.17, 6.2.11, 6.6.38), whereas Xenophon's objective is to get the men back to Greece safely; notably, when eventually they reach the straits of the Bosphoros, in sight of what Xenophon terms the first Greek city

---

71 See note 67 for detail; cf. Farrell (2012: 73), who contests the standard view (e.g. Lee 2007: 134–5) that Xenophon owned the horses he appears with in *Anabasis*, arguing instead that these had been captured and distributed by the army (ibid. p. 80).

72 While, at 3.1.10, Xenophon writes, 'the majority (οἱ πολλοί) still followed along from a sense of shame towards Cyrus and towards each other; and amongst these Xenophon was one', this is nevertheless inconsistent with the account he has earlier given at Tarsus, where it is clear the men assented to go on only when an increase in their wage was granted (1.3.18–21). We could understand this as an influential group winning the wage concession for the larger body, whose integrity therefore remains intact, or as Xenophon being munificent or misleading, with the truth being that the statement about honour applies just to a minority group which includes himself.

170   XENOPHON'S *ANABASIS*: A SOCRATIC HISTORY

(Byzantium), he announces that he wishes to leave (7.1.4).⁷³ The objective of safety (τῆς ὑμετέρας σωτηρίας, 3.2.15; 3.2.26) which he had set down on the banks of the Zapatas River has now been achieved, and he has no further responsibility to the soldiers. The declaration at the Zapatas inscribes the nature of his association with the mercenary body. It is also the background against which his later service with Seuthes is to be read: having left the army at Byzantium, he returns to assist the force when he hears it is in trouble, finally leading it to Seuthes, whom he adjudges to afford the best chance of survival through the winter. On the matter of payment from the army's new employer, he is pointedly indifferent; typically, after Seuthes has made his offer to the men and they are digesting the terms, Xenophon is thinking of their future safety. 'How far from the sea would you expect the army to follow along with you?' (7.3.12). When Seuthes invites him to take something from the proceeds of the sale of plunder, he declines and tells him to give the pick to the officers who are with him, who duly take up this offer (7.5.3–4); again, when the Thracian finally gave the army pay, Xenophon, who is central to the transaction, did not take anything for himself or become involved in the distribution of the booty (7.7.48–57).

At the conclusion of the book, Xenophon closes his defence on the matter of his mercenary status by reference to his then straitened circumstances. His arrival at penury at the end suggests complete depletion of his initial wealth plus whatever had been distributed to him on the retreat:

> [1] From there they sailed over to Lampsakos, and there Xenophon was met by Eukleides, a seer from Phleious . . . [who] asked him how much gold he had. [2] Xenophon solemnly swore to him that in truth he would not have even enough money for the journey home, unless he sold his horse and what he had about his own person. (7.8.1–2)

The promise of neat closure is, however, seemingly denied by the odd pronouncement that the soothsayer, Eukleides, did not believe him (ὁ δ' αὐτῷ οὐκ ἐπίστευεν, 7.8.2). A number of explanations are possible. It could be a clever way by Xenophon of showing that he did have gold – and probably quite a lot of it (5.3.4; and we can note that later at Ephesos he deposits money with Megabyzos, warden of the temple of Artemis, 5.3.6) – but

---

73   First Greek city (Ἑλληνίδα δὲ εἰς ἣν πρώτην ἤλθομεν πόλιν): 7.1.29. Xenophon has referred to cities along the Black Sea coast as being Greek, but he must regard these as being outside the Hellenic world (Trapezous, 4.8.22; Kerasous, 5.3.2; Kotyora, 5.5.3; Herakleia, 6.2.1): compare 6.1.17 at Harmene, the port of Sinope, where they are 'near to Greece' (ὡς δὲ τῆς Ἑλλάδος ἐδόκουν ἐγγὺς γίγνεσθαι) and 6.5.23 in Bithynia, where they are at the very 'doors of Greece' (ἐπὶ ταῖς θύραις τῆς Ἑλλάδος ἐσμέν). Roy (2007: 75) suggests that 'Xenophon evidently understood [Hellas] in a geographical sense as the area of concentrated Greek settlement. Isolated communities outside the area of concentration were Greek but not did not form part of Hellas.'

that this was sacred money, of no significance for his own welfare. He has earlier emphasised that he had come away with nothing from his time with the Cyreans in Asia: 'for he had crossed over from Parium [to Thrace, having been on his way home from Byzantium with Anaxibios] with nothing except a slave-boy and enough money for the journey' (7.3.20).

Another possibility is a link to the corruption charge in Thrace. It could be that the soothsayer had heard about this and believed Xenophon had profited from his relationship with Seuthes; it is only following sacrifices that he does believe that he has nothing, and by virtue of their performance, Xenophon has produced divine confirmation of his poverty (7.8.3). So, after all, he was telling the truth (if any in the external audience had doubted), and this now casts our readings of the Thracian self-defence speeches in somewhat new light. The first reaction of the soothsayer may foreshadow a view that would emerge in the Greek world that the Ten Thousand had taken a substantial amount of booty on their long march home, and we might as well see Xenophon's report of the encounter and subsequent sacrifice as being intended to address this.[74]

Relations with Sparta

Like much else in his world, Xenophon's relationship with his native city was not straightforward. Most problematically, he was associated with the pro-Spartan faction which was defeated in the 404–403 civil war at Athens. Even if his role in that conflict is unclear, it is probably safe to place him in the Kimonian philo-Laconian tradition at Athens, whose adherents had not welcomed Pericles' prosecution of the (Peloponnesian) war with Sparta.

I argued in Chapter 1 that Xenophon's political orientation was a factor in his departure from the city in 401 and may well have been the underlying reason for the decree of exile passed against him at some time in the 390s. He himself refers incidentally to the decree in *Anabasis* (5.3.7, 7.7.57), and some consider that in this work he is answering the charge(s) against him, whatever this may have been.[75] I think that is right, though I consider

---

74 The matter of money from the sale of slaves on the Black Sea pledged to Apollo and Artemis might have been one which shadowed Xenophon in later years. Rood (2013: 208) suggests that the inscription which he set up on his estate at Skillous (5.3.13) could have been intended as a defence against charges 'of deriving personal advantage from his obligations to the goddess'. This would, then, add to the catalogue of apologetic material in the narrative. I note that the raid following the encounter with the soothsayer properly occurs when the men are in Spartan service, and moreover that it involves spear-won booty against a barbarian of excess wealth. I look at the episode in Chapter 5 p. 225.
75 See Erbse 486, Breitenbach 1967: 1646, Humble 2002: 80. Xenophon's statement at 7.7.57 that the decree at that point had not yet been passed (οὐ γάρ πω ψῆφος αὐτῷ ἐπῆκτο Ἀθήνησι περὶ φυγῆς) rules out the late 400s as a possible date.

his pathway is a systematic defence of his foreign relationships rather than engagement with any specific, if unnamed, charges. Contesting the decree indirectly, undermining its content with substantial contrary evidence, would also be in keeping with his general reticence on personal matters and with the Socratic principle of obedience to the law. There should not be any doubt that Xenophon would have regarded the banishment as a serious stain on his character, and its practical consequences, including possibly the seizure of his property, would have deepened his animosity. Because the exile decree is barely mentioned at all in his works, it is apt to remark that disdain was another feature of Xenophon's literary persona, being one of his favoured ways of putting down an individual or diminishing the importance of an event.[76]

Following on from the discussion in Chapter 1 about his activities at Athens in the aftermath of the Thirty's defeat, we can surmise that Xenophon had dealings with officers in Lysander's garrison and/or Pausanias' relief expedition of 403. He served alongside Spartan commanders in the retreat of the Ten Thousand, and he subsequently led the remnants of the Cyreans in the Spartan campaign against Tissaphernes and Pharnabazos: see *Hellenika* 3.2.7 (for discussion of this passage in the apologetic context, see Chapter 2 p. 75). He remained in their service until his return to Greece in 394 with Agesilaos, with whom in his writings he represents himself as being close, after which he settled on an estate in the Peloponnese. A tradition has it that his sons were educated in Sparta (Plutarch, *Agesilaos* 20; Diogenes 2.54). This close association with the rival *polis* may have been the cause of Xenophon's exile from Athens. For the re-established Athenian democracy, his Socratic links and membership of the *hippeis* already rendered him something of an enemy within; his high-level ties with the Spartans would seem to have made a return to the city problematic once the Corinthian War had begun, if not indeed before that. So, as an Athenian, the matter of his relationship with Sparta is one which he must have sought to address, whether or not it was in fact the underlying cause of the exile decree.[77] While he was probably linked to them in ideological terms at Athens, and could have had personal links to various individuals, the retreat of the Ten Thousand marked

---

76 Besides reticence and disdain and a wish to avoid tension with Socratic principle, there are other potential reasons for Xenophon's quietness on the exile. One could be restored personal relations with Athens following the later repeal of the decree, another, that he was guilty. David Thomas (2009: xviii) writes: 'it is interesting to note that [he] never expresses bitterness about his exile, so presumably he accepted that he had done something to deserve it'.

77 Among those who consider that Spartan association was the reason for exile are Lesky (1963: 664), Breitenbach (1967: 1575) and Badian (2004: 42). The subject was discussed in Chapter 1, and I revisit it at the end of this one with a suggestion that adds weight to the argument for this cause.

the beginning of his relationship proper with the Spartans and so was an apt place to ground his defence.[78]

I have argued that Sparta's post-Peloponnesian War hegemony over the Greek world is a theme of *Anabasis* and that in the work Xenophon is regularly critical of Spartan commanders on the retreat. This critique must have been intended for a broad Hellenic audience but especially the Spartans themselves and his fellow Athenians. Here I argue that Xenophon leverages the theme for apologetic purpose via his characterisation of his personal relations with Spartans on the retreat. Specifically, I show that by way of establishing a noticeable degree of competitiveness, *agon*, and mistrust, *apistia*, between himself and Spartan leaders, he clearly distances himself from them. Few Athenian readers as a result can have considered that Xenophon was an adopted Spartan, while at the same time patriotic Spartan readers would not necessarily be put out by the portrayal of their fellow countrymen. They might even have found benefit in what Xenophon says. This balancing of his own allegiances, political orientation and authorial goals is another hallmark of his writing.

Nature of the Relationship: Agon

Throughout his narrative, Xenophon represents his involvement with Spartan officials as functional, sufficient to collaborate in the goal of returning safely to Greece but rarely more. The exception which underlines this is his establishment late on of guest-friendship with Kleandros, the harmost of Byzantium.

There are, nonetheless, times at which Xenophon does seem to be bolstering Spartan power more than he need do, and by looking closely we can see how he covers over, even counters, this impression. The standout example is at Byzantium, where, having been deceived by Anaxibios, the mercenaries storm the city. Calling on his considerable rhetorical skill, Xenophon succeeds in calming the men and returning control to the

---

78 One could dismiss the view that Xenophon chose to present a defence of himself to his countrymen and argue that, on the contrary, he burned his bridges with Athens and in his writings sought to portray himself favourably to his Spartan benefactors. Powell (2020: 50) shows that in practical terms Xenophon was quite dependent on Sparta and his patrons there, and he argues that to maintain his good standing he represented himself as being potentially useful to the *polis* in the geopolitical sphere; his experiences on the campaign of Cyrus and the retreat through the empire recounted in *Anabasis* are said to situate him 'as a potential guide within the Persian empire'. But this would only take us so far. Any dependency would have dematerialised with the Spartan defeat in 371, and the 360s see Xenophon reconnected with Athens. In any event, as we saw in Chapter 3 and see again in this section, he does not go out of his way to show Sparta in positive light in *Anabasis*.

Spartans (7.1.1–32). He confronts the risk of being accused of pro-Spartanism by arguing strongly in his speech that he is acting in the interests of the men; he is so persuasive, indeed, that by the end of it we perceive the rebellion as utterly hopeless. Xenophon has furthermore, since his own rise to the high command, created in the eyes of his audience a division between himself and Sparta by sustaining a real measure of tension in the relationship; a result is that in the given situation we are somewhat off guard and do not consciously pick up on the essence of it, which is that the Athenian has acted in the interests of the Spartans as much as he has in those of the men (I examine the episode at Byzantium and its potential implication for Xenophon further below). As I demonstrate, one of the ways in which he achieves this tension in the book is by documenting a competitive relationship between himself and Cheirisophos, the leading Spartan on the retreat.[79]

Their first encounter comes late, after Xenophon has delivered his speech to the remaining Greek commanders by the Zapatas River. The response of Cheirisophos, who had joined Cyrus back at the Mediterranean with 700 hoplites (1.4.3), pointedly reveals no prior interaction and undercuts any suspicion that Xenophon was involved with Sparta at the outset:

> After him Cheirisophos spoke: 'Well, Xenophon, previously I knew you only to this extent, that I used to hear of you as being an Athenian. But now I also praise you for your speech and actions and I would wish that the majority were like you; that would be good for the army as a whole.' (3.1.45)

The encounter serves to establish a baseline for the relationship between the two men, setting this at a level of professional respect with the expectation of collaboration. From this positive departure point, however, Xenophon goes on to develop a palpable undertone of tension in his dealings with Cheirisophos and the Spartans, playing on the traditional rivalry between the two states, whose contrasting political systems were a constant point of friction. On a formal level this is symbolised by the respective roles of the two men on the retreat: Xenophon is a commander at the rear, while Cheirisophos leads, as Sparta does in the Greek world.[80] Right from the beginning Xenophon subjects this leadership to scrutiny,

---

[79] Competition was very much a defining feature of Greek society. I earlier related its origins in limited availability of farmland to the phenomenon of democracy (Chapter 3 p. 119 n. 59). I remark further that the underlying geo-economic constraint indelibly shaped Greek culture from athletic games to philosophy. In *Anabasis* we have an instance of the former at 4.8.25–8, and events presented as such at 3.4.44–9 and 4.7.8–12; see also *Hell.* 3.4.16 and 4.2.5–8. On philosophy, Dorion (2018a: 64) remarks how, as a form of *agon*, 'Greek philosophy was inherently polemical from its very beginnings'.

[80] Sparta as first among Greek states: 6.6.9, 12; *Hell.* 3.1.3, 5.

frequently pointing up its weaknesses by having his character identify a more effective way of achieving an objective. Given Sparta's high military reputation, its exposure on this front hints at more serious shortcomings in other spheres of governance. Within the frame of the march from the Zapatas to the Black Sea, I summarise below some indicative examples of Xenophon's method, beginning with one where he himself is eyed competitively by his Spartan counterpart.[81]

3.3.6–11. Not long after they have crossed the Greater Zab River, Xenophon at the rear decides to strike back against the pursuing enemy. His initiative is unsuccessful, and it both endangers the rearguard and slows the progress of the army as a whole. Cheirisophos is quick to reprimand him and leads a chorus of criticism from the other commanders. One subtext is that the Spartan is stressing his own leadership role while reminding Xenophon of his junior status. The harmonious beginning on the banks of the Zab has quickly faded, though it is not long before Xenophon pushes back.

3.4.39–41. Harrying the Greeks in upper Mesopotamia, the Persians occupy a height beneath which their enemy must pass. Cheirisophos is contemplating a frontal attack on their position with peltasts, but Xenophon, when he arrives at the front, takes in the wider picture and notices that from the summit of the mountain immediately above their own army there is a byway to the hill where the Persians are. 'The best thing, Cheirisophos, is for us to make haste to the top as quickly as we can, for if we occupy the summit, they will not be able to remain above our route.' This becomes their plan of action and is successfully executed, with Xenophon himself leading the assault group. Notably, the event plays out as an athletic contest with the Persians, both sides racing for the top and both shouted on by their comrades. The earlier tactical error is now forgotten, and Xenophon, through his success for the army, has elevated himself to a position of real authority within it.

4.6.14–27. In a switch to the realm of culture, as they are deliberating on how to take another height, Xenophon pokes Cheirisophos about the Spartan practice of learning to steal from an early age; quickly responding, Cheirisophos points to corruption among the Athenian elite and calls on Xenophon to use his own training in order that they may steal the high ground from the enemy. The colourful vignette serves to paint the pair as being in a state of enduring, if amicable (for now), competition. In terms of their head-to-head and the subsequent military operation, the Spartan enjoys a double advantage. Having bested his rival in the verbal exchange, he goes on to deny him another field success, precluding the possibility of a

---

[81] Remarking on the rivalry between the Athenian and the Spartan, Calvino (1999: 20) writes that 'Xenophon's solution is always the more astute, generous and decisive'.

repeat of the earlier win in the race for the summit by reminding Xenophon of his defensive responsibility at the rear. The Athenian duly concedes to his suggestion that others besides himself should lead the assault, and a task force is formed (4.6.19–20). The night attack, which sees Cheirisophos lead the main body of the army, proves to be successful and ends with the setting up of a trophy (4.6.27).

4.7.2–7. Cheirisophos has tried and failed to take a fortress which, on account of their lack of provisions, the army must capture. As Xenophon uncovers through enquiry after his arrival with the rearguard, the Spartan's approach, as it has been on other occasions, is a direct one which does not apparently weigh complementary stratagems. He duly assesses the situation and proposes a plan which achieves their objective, so in the process building his own authority within the army.

Nature of the Relationship: Apistia

A second defining element in Xenophon's representation of his relationship with Sparta is mistrust (*apistia*). In bringing this out he undermines accusations of Laconism and simultaneously raises the dramatic tension of his narrative. The tension between himself and the Spartans, moreover, is aggregative, so that we come to expect an eventual breakdown in the relationship. In this light I am inclined to take Xenophon's striking comment in Book 4 about his dealings with Cheirisophos following the latter's mishandling of their Armenian guide as ironic. 'This incident', he writes, 'was the only thing about which Cheirisophos and Xenophon had a serious disagreement during the whole journey' (4.6.3).

Proceeding from the initial appraisal by Cheirisophos of Xenophon at 3.1.45 (above), I offer a selection of passages from across the retreat which chart the growth in suspicion between the sides. It is worth emphasising that 3.1.45 signals a positive beginning: not only is there the Spartan's words, but our knowledge of traditional Spartan impatience with lengthy speech (see Thucydides 1.86.1, Herodotus 3.46.2).

3.4.37–9. As they march north following the events by the Zapatas River, Cheirisophos calls (καλεῖ) Xenophon and tells (κελεύει) him to bring the peltasts to the front.[82] Xenophon rides forward from the rear but does not bring the peltasts, for at his end he has seen Tissaphernes come into view with his army.

---

82 The verb used twice here does not have to mean 'to order/summon', yet it seems to have a stronger sense than 'requested', the rendering suggested by H-R (172). The relevance in our context lies in the light it sheds on the working relationship between the men at this early point.

The Spartan does not inform Xenophon why he wants the light-armed troops at the front, though the external audience knows that his order does have a tactical rationale, as the Persians have taken a height by which the army must pass (this is the hilltop discussed previously where Xenophon and a group of soldiers go on to race to the top). The Athenian, too, has cause to justify his decision to leave his men behind, given that he has just seen the army of Tissaphernes approaching. In the ensuing exchange between the two men, each questions the action of the other, revealing an unmistakeable mistrust. The use of direct speech dramatises the *hupopsia*. 'Why are you calling me?' (Τί καλεῖς; 3.4.39), Xenophon asks. Cheirisophos gives his reason in brief and then asks in his turn: 'But why didn't you bring the peltasts?' (ἀλλὰ τί οὐκ ἦγες τοὺς πελταστάς; 3.4.40).

4.1.15–21. The army comes under severe attack in the Kardouchian mountains. On one occasion, instead of slowing the march to allow the rear to stay connected, Cheirisophos presses ahead, and as a result Xenophon's men are forced into flight. We are informed that two brave men were killed (δύο καλώ τε καὶ ἀγαθὼ ἄνδρε τέθνατον, 4.1.19).[83]

When confronted by Xenophon, Cheirisophos provides an explanation for his decision to keep marching: their road led up to a narrow pass, and he sought to seize this before the enemy. 'That is why I was pressing on and why I didn't wait for you, so that I could get there first before the pass was occupied against us – the guides we have say there is no other road' (4.1.21). The explanation is reasonable (even though it turns out there is another pass), but Xenophon had evidently assumed that they were endangered without just cause: 'When they reached the end of the day's march, Xenophon, just as he was, went straight up to Cheirisophos and began to blame him because he had not waited and they had been forced to fight while fleeing' (4.1.19). We might take his subsequent comment that the front and rear 'put a lot of effort into supporting each other' (4.2.26) to be ironic, though it could as well just about fit with the pervasive theme of didaxis on leadership.

5.1.2–10. After their arrival at the Black Sea, when the army is deliberating on how it will proceed on its journey, Cheirisophos offers to go and seek ships from the Lakedaimonian head of fleet so that they can sail away, an offer that met with the approval of the men, who 'voted for him to set sail as soon as possible'. Xenophon, however, seems not to trust his intentions:

'If we knew for sure that Cheirisophos was going to come back with enough merchant ships (εἰ μὲν ἠπιστάμεθα σαφῶς ὅτι ἥξει πλοῖα

---

[83] Flower (2012: 131) considers Xenophon's own decisions were responsible for these deaths.

Χειρίσοφος ἄγων ἱκανά), there would be no need for what I am about to say. But in fact, since this is uncertain, I think we should also try to get a fleet of merchant ships ready from our base here.' (5.1.10)

His doubt is subsequently borne out (5.3.1), and the men must proceed by land, with the sick and elderly boarded on ships they have managed to commandeer while waiting. When Cheirisophos eventually does return, it is with a single trireme (6.1.15). Of course, it cannot have been assured that setting out he would be able to collect the requisite number of craft, but Xenophon does not choose to phrase his concern in that way, rather emphasising the agency of the Spartan. In other words, Xenophon might have said, 'given the scale of our requirements, we can't be sure that this number is achievable'.

6.1.16–32. It becomes apparent from later events that Cheirisophos' return has less to do with assisting the army than ensuring it comes under firm Spartan control. He has, it seems, specifically been tasked with keeping a check on Xenophon, who is evidently viewed by the Lakedaimonians as a threat to their interests in the region. In a brief speech which Cheirisophos gives to the army following his election as its leader, complimenting the men on withdrawing their offer of the same to Xenophon, he informs them that 'Dexippos said that he was of the view that Xenophon wished to share the command of Klearchos' army with Timasion, though he is a Dardanian, rather than with himself, a Lakonian' (6.1.32; see also 6.6.34).[84] Cheirisophos says that he sought to prevent his countryman from slandering Xenophon at Byzantium, though the claim should properly be seen in the context of his conciliatory acceptance speech, and against the background of mistrust that grew between himself and Xenophon in the account of the retreat which we have.

Spartan suspicions about Xenophon's influence are not without grounds. In the election just referred to, the soldiers had decided to choose him as their leader, despite the presence of the newly returned Cheirisophos. Heading off his election, Xenophon told the men that it would not be in their interests to choose him over a Spartan, and that the role could lead to

---

84 Dexippos, a Lakonian *perioikos*, had slipped away from the army at Trapezous in a trireme which he was supposed to use in the effort to collect merchant ships. A conspicuously shady character, prior to the expedition he had led mercenaries in Sicily and was suspected of taking bribes from the enemy (Diodoros 13.87). Having later rejoined the Ten Thousand on the Black Sea, he was at the heart of an incident in which some of the men were accused of robbery. He met his end in Thrace at the hands of another Lakonian, while 'carrying on some intrigue at the court of Seuthes' (*An.* 5.1.15).

a bad end for himself should he seem to be 'reducing their [the Spartans] reputation to impotence' (6.1.28). To undercut any view that personal factors lie behind the animosity, he links Spartan distrust of him to the fact of his being an Athenian. 'For I observe that the Lacedaemonians did not cease waging war against my native land until they had made the whole city agree that they were to be their leaders too' (6.1.27).

7.1. Byzantium. Having lured the men out of Asia at the bidding of the Persian satrap, Pharnabazos, the Spartans become hostile towards them, regarding the mercenary body now as a threat to stability in their own sphere of control. With Cheirisophos dead following an illness, Xenophon is under increased suspicion for the influence he wields, though by his own account his only desire is to sail away from Byzantium (7.1.4, 8). Ironically, it is he who saves the city from being sacked, convincing the Cyreans, as already noted, that it is in their own best interests to leave, as they cannot resist Spartan power (7.1.24–31). Despite this, when he subsequently requests permission to re-enter the city so that he can sail away from the port, he is informed that Anaxibios, the head of the fleet (*nauarchos*), has serious reservations about letting him in, for 'it was not expedient to have the soldiers close to the wall and Xenophon inside it' (7.1.39). Although Anaxibios relents thanks to Xenophon's guest-friend, Kleandros, at the terminal point of the retreat proper we see the Athenian virtually excluded from the locus of Spartan power.

7.2. Treachery in Thrace. A change of officials at Byzantium, and the influence of Pharnabazos, leads to individual Spartans competing against one another. Xenophon, sailing away with Anaxibios, is ordered by him to return to Thrace and bring the Cyreans back over to Asia; but Aristarchos, the new harmost, 'in obedience to Pharnabazos' wishes' (7.2.12), sails to Perinthos to prevent the crossing. In a terse exchange with Xenophon, he says: 'Anaxibios is no longer *nauarchos*, and I am the harmost in these parts. If I catch any of you at sea, I will sink you' (7.2.13). The next day he sends for the generals and captains of the army, but Xenophon is advised that if he goes with them, 'he would be arrested, and either something would happen to him there or he would be handed over to Pharnabazos himself' (7.2.14). So he seeks out Seuthes, the Thracian warlord, secures an agreement for employing the men and leads them into his service. Spartan scheming in the Propontis – notably, individuals pursuing their own interest above that of the state – justifies Xenophon's decision to take the Cyreans into barbarian service and provides yet further evidence that he has been justified in his ongoing mistrust of Spartan rule. His decision to go to Seuthes marks a decisive break in the relationship, although, owing to new circumstances, it does not prove fatal for either him or the men.

Xenophon in Spartan Service: The Exile Question Again

The important matter of Xenophon's exile is a subject I have discussed at several points in the book, and I turn to it again in this last part, suggesting a new potential cause.

Given the level of mutual distrust between Xenophon and Spartan officials on the march, Spartan mistreatment of the Cyreans and Xenophon's leading of the mercenaries into service with Seuthes, a reconciliation between the sides in the winter of 399 must have seemed unlikely. However, at the behest of the cities on the coast, Sparta had decided to launch a campaign against Tissaphernes in Asia Minor, and Xenophon and the mercenaries had a valuable use. Thibron sent for them, promising the soldiers a daric per month and more for the captains and generals (7.6.1).

Xenophon, though, consistent with his declared aim at Chrysopolis (7.1.4), prepares to leave for home. 'Xenophon did not have anything to do with the sale [of booty] but openly made preparations to go home, for no motion regarding his exile had yet been put to the vote at Athens' (7.7.57).[85] But some of his closest supporters (οἱ ἐπιτήδειοι) plead with him at least to lead the army to Thibron. Pointedly, he does not say whether he agrees to this, but he evidently relents, as he does cross into Asia with the army (7.8.1). It seems reasonable to conjecture that his plan at this point was to perform a last service for the men by taking them down the coast and to then depart from Ephesos, where he had arrived two years previously.

Yet, in spite of his stated intention to go home (7.7.57, and see also 7.1.8, 7.1.38) and his problematic relationship with Sparta, we know that Xenophon does not then return to Athens, but joins the campaign and serves under a succession of Spartan commanders in Asia Minor until his return to Greece in 394 with Agesilaos. To add to the *aporia*, we know that he held Thibron in low regard,[86] that having enriched himself at Pergamum on the journey through Aeolia (7.8.23) he had no pressing pecuniary motive for service, and that he did not apparently sacrifice about the campaign beforehand.

I suggest three possible explanations for his participation. First, allowing for the effect of his apologetic agenda, his relations with Sparta might not

---

85 Bradley makes the point that in stating his intention here to return home and mentioning the exile decree, Xenophon creates a dramatic effect: 'the important point is that its [the decree's] mention is designed to make it at least *seem* to the reader that the vote of exile was imminent and that Xenophon, had he set out when he first wanted to, perhaps could have made it home in time to defend himself. It is the dramatic effect, not the historical fact, that is key in the narrative' (2011: 290 n.18). See now Erbse 492–3. I integrate this argument into a final observation on the exile below.

86 See *Hell.* 3.1.8, 3.2.1, 3.2.7. Thibron was condemned for allowing 'his army to plunder the friends of the Spartans' and exiled (*Hell.* 3.1.8).

have sunk as low as the impression Xenophon gives, and on crossing back to Asia he might have decided to continue just as he had been doing, perhaps having reckoned too that income would not be liable to attract the same attention as monies which accrued from the march. As remarked earlier, at Byzantium he must have earned the gratitude of the state, and the fact that Sparta does seek to enlist him for the Asia Minor campaign speaks for itself. This pragmatic reading shows again how the author's personal agenda can create friction between the narrative and the reality of events on the ground as they emerge from close reading.

Second, during the period between his departure from Thrace and arrival in Ionia, the decree of exile against him at Athens was passed. Xenophon's statement, as he is readying to leave Thrace, that the decree had 'not yet' been passed (οὐ γάρ πω ψῆφος αὐτῷ ἐπῆκτο Ἀθήνησι περὶ φυγῆς, 7.7.57) seems to carry a temporal quality, and a number of scholars have interpreted it as an indication that the motion was then imminent.[87] Erbse considers that such a reading 'is certainly suggested by the words used and presumably the author counted on it that the Athenian reader would understand him'; so Bradley, who suggests that the ending of the story is intended to be anticlimactic in order that the reader is prompted to construct their own closure, namely that Xenophon's character's *nostos* has been thwarted by the exile decree against him.[88] The mention of the decree at this particular juncture thus draws our attention and, extending from Bradley's idea, offers a contingent explanation for his joining Thibron. Drawing on historical knowledge beyond the text, the reader infers that, with no way home, Xenophon's best alternative was to join Sparta and put himself to use in the campaign against Persia. This solution improves on the first too in that we do not feel as strongly a wish to know why he did not sacrifice on the subject of joining the campaign beforehand.

The third explanation is that Xenophon, as he reflected on the retreat and on his future plans, recognised that the war had the potential to liberate the Greek cities of the coast and at the same time deal a fatal blow to Tissaphernes, in his writings an archenemy of Greece. Coming to see the campaign's importance, he abandons his plan to go home, which from 7.7.57 we know he could have done, and puts aside his lack of faith in Sparta to serve the greater community. This act of selflessness is further complemented in Socratic terms by the prudence he shows in taking steps towards his own longer-term self-sufficiency (see the advice of Socrates

---

[87] See Erbse 483, Anderson 1974: 148–9, Higgins 23, Bradley 2010: 548–9. Tuplin (1987: 60), however, does not think the term (οὐ γάρ πω) carries this meaning (see Chapter 1 n.85). For the process of how decrees were voted on and passed, see Woodhead 1981: 39.

[88] Erbse 492–3, Bradley 2010: 548–51. Bradley develops this view with an emphasis on the role of Zeus Meilichios in a later article (2011).

at *Memorabilia* 2.8.3). The failure to mention a sacrifice, as I suggest in the next chapter, may be because the campaign related to the next phase of his personal life journey. In all three scenarios, the onward path out of *Anabasis* is picked up, if not seamlessly owing to the sacrifice question, in *Hellenika*, where we are told about Xenophon's role in the campaign and his later return to Greece with Agesilaos.

A New Cause for Exile?

The fact of Xenophon's entering Spartan service might have added weight to that affiliation being the cause of his exile if the decree were not passed prior to his joining Thibron, though we should bear in mind that Athens had sent a force to support Sparta in that campaign. In any case, the connection must have reached an intolerable point in Athenian eyes in 394, when Xenophon was supposed to have fought on the Spartan side against Athens at Koroneia, and accordingly some think that this was the trigger for the exile. I would like to suggest that an earlier event touching on Atheno-Spartan relations was as likely as this one to have been the cause of Xenophon's exile and so would produce a new potential solution for the question: date – 399, (true) cause – Spartan favouritism.

The event is the storming of Byzantium by the Ten Thousand immediately following their lockout by the Spartans. It is only Xenophon's actions that stay the mercenaries and prevent the seizure of the city from the Spartan authorities. A significant moment in this extraordinary episode is when one of the soldiers runs up to him after the men have successfully stormed the walls:

> 'Now,' [he says], 'you can become a big man, Xenophon. You have a city, you have triremes, you have money, and you have all these men. Now, if you wanted, you would help us and we would make you great.' (Νῦν σοι ἔξεστιν, ὦ Ξενοφῶν, ἀνδρὶ γενέσθαι. ἔχεις πόλιν, ἔχεις τριήρεις, ἔχεις χρήματα, ἔχεις ἄνδρας τοσούτους. νῦν ἄν, εἰ βούλοιο, σύ τε ἡμᾶς ὀνήσαις καὶ ἡμεῖς σὲ μέγαν ποιήσαιμεν, 7.1.21)

An Athenian hearing a report of such after news of the event had reached Athens might well feel that Xenophon had passed up an exceptional opportunity to make his own city great again. Byzantium had been a prized Athenian possession, and recovery of the strategic site might just in turn have provided a fillip to the democracy as it got back on its feet four years on from the defeat to Sparta (for Athenian ambition in 395 see *Hellenika* 3.5.2). This may explain to us why Xenophon goes to such lengths in his speech to the triumphant Cyreans on the Thracian Ground inside the city walls to convince them that there was no hope, whatsoever, of holding on to the place. In fact, he is talking as much to his external audience, specifically, as is often the case in *Anabasis*, to the Athenians.[89]

But was there really no hope of success? Xenophon had at his disposal triremes, money and all those experienced men. There would doubtless have been local support, and very possibly Persian interest too, it being a fair bet that the King would become unfavourable to Sparta. Even with a good knowledge of the political climate at the turn of the fifth century, we cannot really know, but it must be true that some would have read into the episode that Xenophon, if he had not foregone a patriotic action, had rescued Sparta. Could news of this missed opportunity/favouritism, whether in truth it was either, have irked the Athenians so much that they decided to exile Xenophon? Even taking a radically opposite view – that he was a potential megalomaniac who risked getting Athens into trouble – could lead to the same political outcome. Either way, if the decree was passed in 399, as I believe it was, then it is certainly conceivable that some citizens would have been privately influenced by the affair and voted accordingly. Just as it would have been had the real reason for the exile been, say, his links with the Thirty or with Socrates, the official cause would have been involvement with Cyrus, who was no longer an actor in regional affairs.

I make a final observation that impinges on Xenophon's relations with Sparta and the possibility he was exiled because of this at the earlier date. By the way it is told in *Anabasis*, one would think that the remnants of the army almost by chance were co-opted by Sparta into its campaign against Tissaphernes in Asia Minor (7.6.1). We should not of course expect Xenophon to provide us with a full context for the approach of Thibron, as the subject is beyond the scope of the present story. But neither does he really give us one where he should, at the appropriate juncture in *Hellenika*. Instead, the mercenaries are introduced as part of the campaign narrative, and notwithstanding their addition is militarily decisive in that it facilitates a change to an offensive posture (3.1.6), we are not given any substantial insight into the planning of the war, an ambitious venture on the part of the state.

When we think of it, Xenophon's leading of the Cyreans to Thibron runs counter to our expectations. He has told us he was keen to return home, and we know he had already turned back to help the army before,

---

89 On this idea, a reader for the publisher wrote: 'A scenario in which Xenophon and the army seize Byzantium for Athens is too implausible to be a rational basis for Athenians to take it hard when Xenophon does not do it. But B.'s assumption is perhaps that it is not a rational ground for complaint, merely a bit of fake outrage from people who would have been horrified at the implications for their (currently weak) city had it happened.' Having resisted excision, I was pleased to see McCloskey in his presentation at the Liverpool Xenophon 2021 conference make a case for the eyes of the Athenians being on Xenophon following events in the city.

so we would not be at all surprised if this time he declined the request of his closest supporters (7.7.57). How valid is the impression we form of near happenstance, or that it was only by virtue of some deep-seated instinct to help that he did so? One could certainly argue that the Spartan architects of the war had factored in the likely availability of up to 10,000 experienced soldiers, a force moreover which had fought with distinction against Tissaphernes. In this light, the return to the army of Cheirisophos at Sinope (6.1.16) and after him, further up the Black Sea coast, the arrival from Byzantium of the harmost (6.6.5), Kleandros, looks to have been more about overseeing key assets than any concern for the well-being of fellow Greeks. The winter with Seuthes may have been a holding exercise until the spring. These circumstances, together with the fact that Xenophon became a guest-friend of Kleandros and sailed away from Byzantium with Anaxibios the *nauarchos*, who sent him across the Propontis to join the army, at the least invite us to consider Xenophon's role in the, admittedly patchy, implementation of Spartan foreign policy in Asia. Bradley astutely observes that Xenophon directs us to a certain reading of the ending, but perhaps that is not really about bringing attention to thwarted *nostos* as he suggests, but is Xenophon the author's shaping of his own presence in the historical narrative. The unexpected, almost accidental path out of *Anabasis* obscures a more revealing trajectory that links Xenophon indelibly with Spartan power.[90]

---

90 Erbse's analysis is worth noting here too. 'In an apologetic work especially, statements that advance the interests of the author ought to be treated with care. And rightly so. But all these Xenophontic statements may be freely assessed only if one separates the bias of the text in front of us from the actual events and examines the characters of the two separately' (494).

CHAPTER 5

Socrates in Anabasis

I have often wondered by what arguments those who drew up the indictment against Socrates could persuade the Athenians that his life was forfeit to the state. The indictment against him was to this effect: Socrates is guilty of rejecting the gods acknowledged by the state and of bringing in strange deities: he is also guilty of corrupting the youth.

Xenophon, *Memorabilia* 1.1.1

What? A great man? I always see only the actor of his own ideal.

Nietzsche, *Beyond Good and Evil*

From Xenophon's writings it is clear that Socrates was a major influence in his life. Four of his works feature the philosopher prominently, and I argue in this book that *Anabasis* too incorporates a strong Socratic presence. This is signalled by the philosopher's appearance in the key passage of the work (3.1.5–7) where Xenophon himself is formally introduced into the story. Although Socrates does not thereafter feature again, in his actions and moral bearing throughout the retreat, Xenophon's character exemplifies Socratic principles. The purpose of this final chapter is to substantiate this argument by showing how 'Xenophon' on the retreat represents a model Socratic pupil, the author's aim being to demonstrate in real world terms the benefit of the Socratic education. In this way he both stakes a claim for the primacy of his Socrates and offers a defence of his teacher against the historic charges of impiety and corrupting Athenian youth.

Another way of framing the search for Socrates in *Anabasis* outside of 3.1.5–7 is by way of the enterprise of the author Xenophon. As we saw in Chapter 3, a major preoccupation in his writing is the subject of leadership, and a key figure in his exposition is Socrates. In *Anabasis*, Xenophon's character could be regarded as a stand-in for the philosopher, given that he is not infrequently engaged in the same sort of educational activity as Socrates was in his life. Then we have parallels to the way philosophical dialogues are typically set up, the opening of Proxenos' obituary, where he is cast as a typical Socratic interlocutor might be, excepting the fees (2.6.16), being an example. We have as well regular reflection on problem-solving, often signalled by *aporia* – a feature of Socratic dialogue – and philosophical moments, such as the case of Demokrates, sent to the mountains to learn the truth of a matter (4.4.15).

An enduring aim of the Socratics was defence of their teacher, even if this was often really a means of staging his promotion. In a work involving an ambitious young Athenian which features Socrates, we are interested in how this concern works itself out. In other of Xenophon's writings, such as *Memorabilia*, where it is foregrounded in the opening (see opening quote), the notion of defence appears prominent, but in a different type of work it might be less evident on the surface. I think the author intended that the scene in *Anabasis* in which he goes to his teacher for advice and is advised to go to Delphi should implicitly set up what follows as a challenge to the charges made against Socrates. Many of his audience, knowing of their personal connection, would, I believe, have read the encounter between the philosopher and his pupil this way and did not have to look hard at the ensuing account to see revealed in it a methodical, if subtle, defence of Socrates. This assumes that in the 360s the figure of Socrates was still in some sense a contested one and that some of those who regarded themselves as followers sought to defend him through their writings. Even if we take a sceptical view on this score and wonder how contentious his trial was after forty years, as remarked, the charges would have made for a suitable way to stage a wider treatment of the philosopher's life and teaching. We can certainly think of Xenophon as part of the active Socrates literary-philosophical industry and imagine his representation of himself in *Anabasis* as intended to weigh in for the value and benefit of the Socratic way of life as he knew it.

A question to address before moving on is how the defensive element, broadly defined, sits with Xenophon's self-defence, which I have argued is one of the major purposes of the work. Various combinations are possible; for example, apologia for Xenophon is perfectly compatible with indirect apologia for Socrates. And then, as noted in the previous chapter, there is the fact that any exemplary narrative about someone who also exists in the outside world has a potentially apologetic effect; in the terms of this chapter, that outside presence is the person's teacher, whereas in the last one it was the author himself.

With this in mind, I consider that the two defences are closely intertwined but nonetheless distinct, their relative importance dependent on the perspective adopted. The crucial matter really is how we read Xenophon's intention about his own performance on the retreat. Is Xenophon the character following in the footsteps of the historical figure or is he the actor who embodies the ideal of his teacher? The question leads us to an understanding of the work as either essentially autobiographical or as the production of what we might call a Socratic historian. From the perspective I take in this chapter and the argumentation in the book generally, it is for the most part the latter, which is to say that Xenophon has an implicit agenda to promote Socratic values in his history writing, and consequent to this that on the retreat his character acts as a pupil of Socrates should have done. By means of his performance in Books 3–7, the lessons taught by Socrates as recorded in works such as Xenophon's own *Memorabilia* are exemplified (I look at the matter of their publication dates later in the chapter, but recall my earlier argument that they are products of a common conception). As noted above, I think this is how many in his ancient audience would have read it. Any leaning towards the alternative view would have been arrested by the author's later attribution of the work to another. It is doubtful in any case that many would have taken his superhuman performance at face value. I suppose that in forming their judgements about Xenophon's intent, readers were influenced by the cultural context for self-praise (see, for example, Demosthenes, *De corona* 3–4, 128, and Plutarch, *De se ipsum citra invidiam laudando* 3) and by Xenophon's known reticence as a writer as well as his connection with Socrates. The third-party attribution also maintained the historiographical fabric of the story, the focus on the Socratic officer 'Xenophon' allowing Xenophon to keep out of his own narrative, or as Lucian would later prescribe in his treatise on how to write history, to be a stranger in his own work (ξένος ἐν τοῖς βιβλίοις).[1]

The chapter begins with Socrates, looking at his life and the lifestyle which polarised sentiment among his fellow Athenians. The charges made against him in 399 are outlined as is the impact of his trial and the enduring literary legacy produced by his followers. The literature on this subject is vast, and the discussion is not intended to add to that growing body but to set a context for what follows. The second part of the chapter is a study of Xenophon's famous introduction of his own character into *Anabasis*, showing how this key passage of the work establishes him as an aspiring *kaloskagathos* who finds himself unwittingly caught in a desperate situation.[2] The third part brings out the substance of the Socratic presence as it is conveyed through Xenophon's

---

1 Attribution to another: *Hell.* 3.1.2. The historiographical character of *Hellenika* coupled with the strong likelihood that its second part postdates *Anabasis* suggests to me that the use of a pseudonym was a corrective, or a response to the reception of the latter. On the question of Xenophon's own representation in *Anabasis*, see Chapter 1 n.4, especially the respective remarks of Most (1989: 123) and Tuplin (2003: 154). Of relevance too in the discussion is the opening of Diogenes Laertios' biography, where he writes that Xenophon was 'a man of rare modesty' (2.48), a distinction not afforded by him to any other of the Socratics. Stranger in his own works: Lucian, *Hist. Conscr.* 38–41.

2 *Kaloskagathos* (*kalos kai agathos*), 'beautiful and good'. On the term, see Johnson 2021: 26 n.44.

character. By relating Xenophon's leadership on the retreat to guidance in his Socratica, with focus now on the ethical dimension and Xenophon's embracing of Socratic method (in Chapter 3 it was on military matters), I show how he promotes the worth of the Socratic education. With the tragic story of the Taochoi in mind, I also highlight how within this we glean a further aspect of the work's understated philosophical character, namely the author's encouraging of his readers via the actions of actors in the story to consider the value of the virtues through their presence and absence.

The Philosopher and His Circle

Socrates is not believed to have written anything in his lifetime, and what we know of him derives from the surviving accounts of his life and teachings provided by students, contemporaries and the later biographical tradition.[3] The principal surviving first-hand sources, Aristophanes, Plato and Xenophon, give us quite distinct portraits: from the pretentious eccentric of Aristophanes to Plato's inquisitive intellectual and Xenophon's practically orientated ethical philosopher.[4] Aristophanes is the only one who could claim to have known Socrates as a younger man. However, because his picture was produced in a comedic context, it is less historically valuable than the other two – although it is notable that some think Aristophanes' Socrates is a Pythagorean and that this characterisation could well be a true reflection of the philosopher as a young man.[5] A further relevant source is Aristotle, who makes about fifty references to the philosopher in his works. The fact that he was born after the death of Socrates has led many to believe

---

3 Plato says that he wrote poetry in prison (*Phd.* 60–1), though if he did, nothing of this survives. The later biographical tradition is extensive, diverse and frequently contradictory. To take an example, Diogenes (2.20) refers to the author and philosopher Aristoxenos who has Socrates as a banker: 'he would at all events invest sums, collect the interest accruing, and then, when this was expended, put out the principal again'. Rowe and Boys-Stones write that we know the titles of some 200 works written by followers of Socrates, but with less than forty-five of these extant (2013: vii). It has been well put that Socrates is both the best known and the least known of ancient philosophers.
4 Brickhouse and Smith (2000: 33–49) provide an assessment of these three as sources for the life and thought of Socrates as, more briefly, does Waterfield 2013.
5 See *Birds* 1553–64 and the interpretation of this passage by Ogden 2002: 27. In saying Aristophanes' picture is less historically valuable I do not wish to imply that the pictures of Plato and Xenophon are essentially accurate. As Momigliano (1993: 46) puts it, the 'Socratics experimented in biography, and the experiments were directed towards capturing the potentialities rather than the realities of individual lives. Socrates, the main subject of their considerations (there were other subjects, such as Cyrus), was not so much the real Socrates as the potential Socrates.' On the difference between Plato and Xenophon, Johnson (2018: 497) writes that the latter provides us with 'what we might call applied Socraticism, rather than the theoretical Socraticism [the former] offers'.

he draws predominantly on Plato, but the reality may be less distinct, as in his own lifetime he would have met many who had known Socrates.[6]

Extracting the real Socrates from the literature has, not surprisingly, proven to be as contentious an exercise as it is problematic. Doubtless each account contains elements of truth, but how much can probably never be known.[7] As I seek to show, a historical sketch of Socrates can nonetheless be tentatively drawn from what appears to be common in the reports from antiquity and from what is known of the times through which he lived. In this last regard, the context for Xenophon at Athens in the closing years of the fifth century provided in Chapter 1 is relevant, notably the circumstance that both men found themselves part of a minority towards whom the restored government was not well disposed.

Turning to the historical sketch, in Plato's *Crito* (52e) Socrates indicates he is seventy at the time of his imprisonment in 399; this age resurfaces much later in Diogenes Laertios (2.44), who, naming Apollodoros (*Chronology*) as his source, places Socrates' birth in 469/8. A sculptor by trade as his father was, Socrates supposedly had works displayed before the entrance to the Acropolis during the time of Pericles (statutes of the *Charities* and an image of *Hermes Propylaios*: see Pausanias 1.22.8, 9.35.7; Diogenes 2.19). While he does not seem to have been prosperous, he was sufficiently well off to serve as a hoplite at Potidaea in 432 and in early campaigns of the war with Sparta, though conceivably a panoply could have been purchased for him (see *Apologia* 17).[8] From the reports, he was not lacking in valour (Plato, *Symposion* 220d–221b,

---

6 Ahbel-Rappe (2009: 32) writes: 'it is doubtful that much in these remarks is independent of what Aristotle found in the Socratic works of Plato'; see also Vlastos (1971: 1), who traces the Aristotelian references to Plato's early dialogues. Smith (2018: 602), though, points out that, 'as a member of the Academy and resident of Athens for twenty years, and not so long after Socrates' death, Aristotle had the opportunity to learn about Socrates from others who knew the man, and not just from Plato'. As he goes on to demonstrate (613–14), one of these sources, and an important one, was Xenophon. Dorion (2017: 49–50) argues that three passages in *Memorabilia* (1.2.9, 1.2.54, 2.6.35) are the source of Socratic material in Aristotle, although he concludes that the general portrait of Socrates that emerges from Aristotle's writings owes little to *Memorabilia* and that his conception of Socrates' philosophy derives essentially from Plato's early dialogues (2017: 52).

7 Dorion (2006: 95–6) presents seventeen differences between the Socrateses of Plato and Xenophon and asserts that 'there is no hope of harmonising their doctrines' (ibid. p. 95). Pomeroy, though, thinks that some of his ideas 'as reported by Xenophon on the one hand and by Plato on the other are ... essentially reconcilable' (1994: 23). The same sentiment is echoed by Johnson (2018: 498). On the Socratic Question, see Vlastos 1983 and 1991 (chapters 2–3), Waterfield 2004 (with references on p. 86), Ahbel-Rappe and Kamtekar 2006, Dorion 2006, Gera 2007 and Danzig 2018.

8 For possible indicators of Socrates' wealth, see *Oik*. 2.3, and Plato, *Ap*. 38a–b, where he declares he has no money but still might be able to cover a fine of one mina. Hoplite armour and equipment were comparatively expensive, though the matter of their affordability is debated: see Hanson 1999: 291–2.

Laches 181b; Diogenes 2.22–3) or stamina (Xenophon, *Memorabilia* 1.2.1, 1.6.2; Plato, *Symposion* 220a–d) and was regarded highly by those who served with him and against him.

A common theme of the biographical tradition is the philosopher's physical oddness. A thick-set frame marked by a pot belly, bulging eyes and flaring nostrils is said to have made him akin to a satyr.[9] He went about barefoot and was impervious to cold and alcohol; on his drinking prowess, no less a figure than Alkibiades is said to have enthused that he could drink anyone under the table and that nobody had ever seen him drunk.[10] Another recurring feature is his pressed marital relationship. Xanthippe comes across as an antagonistic partner, given to physical harassment – even once tearing his coat off at the market (Diogenes 2.36–7; on a second marriage, 2.26). It is quite likely that there is exaggeration in these everyday depictions, a natural tendency where a larger-than-life character is concerned. The intentions of his followers in highlighting Socrates' outward rawness may be to accentuate the inner beauty of his soul; similarly, the aversion to travel often ascribed to him in the literature (though he did in fact travel to some extent) emphasises the importance of the inner journey.[11]

From Plato and Xenophon we learn that his main approach to teaching was based on the elimination of what is not true as a path to what is.[12] Typically his method was to pose questions which probed the axioms underlying his interlocutors' assumptions about the world and their own places in it. This, as Gray suggests, was part of a process of 'taming', it being necessary to 'reduce the pride of pupils of great natural potential . . . before they are amenable to his "instruction"'.[13] While Socrates' method

---

9 On Socrates' appearance, see Plato, *Tht.* 143e, *Symp.* 215a–216e; Xenophon, *Symp.* 2.19, 4.19, 5.5–7; Aristophanes, *Nub.* 362. For a treatment of the subject including a comparison of the Silenic depictions in the *symposia*, see Stavru 2018.

10 Barefoot: Xenophon, *Mem.* 1.6.2, Plato, *Symp.* 220b, Aristophanes, *Nub.* 103, 363. Drinking: Plato, *Symp.* 220a. Gill (1973: 27) suggests that Plato's description of Socrates' controlled reaction to his poisoning in the *Phaedo* could be intended to underline his physical toughness and stoicism.

11 Primacy of inner beauty: Plato, *Phdr.* 279b–c. Non-travelling Socrates: *Phdr.* 230d; Diogenes 2.22. Denyer (2019: 2) thinks that some of Socrates' character traits could hint at schizophrenia, though this seems speculative.

12 Socrates denied that he was a *didaskalos* (Plato, *Ap.* 19d–e), but probably to distance himself from sophists who took money for their teaching services; Socrates did not (*Mem.* 1.2.5–7, Plato, *Ap.* 19e), although Aristophanes has him accept a gift in *Clouds* (*Nub.* 1146), and some of his pupils apparently did teach for money (*Mem.* 1.2.60). The subject of how Socrates regarded himself is another contentious one: see Vlastos 1971 and Morrison 2010 and 2011.

13 Gray 2011a: 51. She elsewhere writes (1986: 116): 'Socrates used irony to test the knowledge of his interlocutor, found it wanting, convicted him of ignorance and reduced him to *aporia*, clearing the way for real knowledge.'

drew many into his circle, it piqued some and intimidated others.[14] His fame, or infamy, earned him a place in the popular culture of the day. In Aristophanes' comic play *Clouds*, performed at the Dionysia of 423, he is cast as the deranged head of a school which teaches young men, among other things, how to avoid repaying their debts (1214–1302) and that it is just to beat their parents into submission (1408–46). Commenting on a passage (358–63) in which Prodikos is referred to admiringly and Socrates dismissively – 'and you, priest of the most subtle trifles' (358) – Dover writes:

> [the lines] are intelligible as comedy only if we believe that Ar. shared the popular esteem of Prodikos as an artist, and regarded Socrates, by contrast, as a pretentious parasite who inexplicably fascinated some wealthy young men but had nothing coherent to say and produced nothing of any artistic merit.[15]

Waterfield says of the portrait: 'There must be elements of [it] that are true to life if the play is satire rather than farce.'[16] This wider view of Socrates' life helps too in setting his trial in a meaningful historical and social context. Plato's Socrates' arguing at its opening (*Apologia* 18, 19c) that the poisonous image of him painted in the play endured in the minds of many is best seen as court rhetoric for the moment.

A key trait of his public persona was unwavering adherence to the law (Plato, *Crito* 51c–52a, *Apologia* 32b–d, 35c; Xenophon, *Memorabilia* 4.4, 4.6, *Hellenika* 1.7.14–15). In *Memorabilia*, writing of his 'scrupulous obedience in all that the laws required' (4.4.1), Xenophon proceeds to give examples of this behaviour, including his refusal while serving on the Council's presiding committee in 406 to allow an illegal motion concerning the fate of the generals from the Arginousai campaign (4.4.2) and, during the reign of the Thirty, to refuse to take part in the arrest of a man (Leon of Salamis) who had not committed any offence (4.4.3; Plato,

---

14 In his biography, Diogenes (2.21) writes: 'frequently, owing to his vehemence in argument, men set upon him with their fists or tore his hair out'. Even in the *logoi* there are hints that having Socrates and his companions pay a visit could be a daunting experience: see *Mem.* 4.2.1–2. Gera (2007: 44, 46) is surely right to observe that Xenophon's portrayal of Socrates is somewhat sanitised, with the rough edges that irked the Athenians smoothed in order to enhance his defence.
15 Dover 1968: lv–lvi (line 358 trans. Dover). Socrates appeared in other of Aristophanes' plays, as well as ones by Ameipsias, Kallias, Eupolis and Telekleides, in nearly all cases his portrayal being along the same negative lines as in *Clouds*. A fragment from Eupolis reads: 'I hate Socrates who has thought everything out but ignored the problem how to provide himself with food' (386 Kassel-Austin).
16 Waterfield 2021: 268.

Apologia 32c–d).[17] I suggested at the end of Chapter 1 that Xenophon's silence on the subject of the exile decree against him could mark his own honouring of the laws.

Socrates' concern for upholding the law reflected his mission to produce good citizens for the state, his major means for doing this being philosophy, whose practice was supposed to inculcate in its adherents a desire for virtue. This process of acquiring virtue was the path to becoming *kaloskagathos*, the condition which enabled men to benefit themselves and others, or in Xenophon's words, 'to do their duty by house and household, and relatives and friends, and city and citizens' (*Memorabilia* 1.2.48). A couple of points worth highlighting are, firstly, while one can say that *kaloskagathos* – and for that matter *phronimos*, *sophia*, *sophrosune* – is part of the vocabulary of 'Xenophon' in *Anabasis*, it is equally true that they do not have the currency they do in the formal Socratic works. I suggest this is of a piece with it consciously being a different type of Socratic work, something I touch on further in the Conclusions. Secondly, Xenophon did not consider that the capacity for being good was confined to any particular class: even a slave could become *kaloskagathos* (*Oikonomikos* 14.4–9).

A strong practical element distinguishes Xenophon's depiction of Socrates' education, something we see clearly in the conversations he records in Book 3 of the *Memorabilia*, where Socrates works to make his interlocutors aware of the skills which they lack, or will require, to become successful leaders. As argued in Chapter 3 in discussion about the 'Socratic commander', we should regard Xenophon himself as a beneficiary of this training. Among other outstanding figures with links to the philosopher's circle were several of the leading political figures at Athens at the close of the fifth century. In spite of his influence, though, not all turned out as we imagine he would have liked. Charmides, whom Socrates led towards a public life (*Memorabilia* 3.7), became involved with the Thirty Tyrants (*Hellenika* 2.4.19), while Kritias was one of their leaders; Alkibiades had played a major part in the oligarchic coup of 411–410 and had acted against the city in concert with its enemies on several occasions (see Thucydides 6.88.9–6.92.5). Socrates' links with these last two men in particular seem to have been a major basis for the charge laid against him of corrupting

---

17 The illegal motion regarding Arginousai was to judge the generals collectively, not severally: see *Hell.* 1.7.9–15 and also *Mem.* 1.1.18, Plato, *Ap.* 32b. Dobski (2009: 333) wonders whether Socrates is objecting to the injustice of the proposed procedure or just its illegality. With reference to the Arginousai affair he remarks that, 'while Socrates said "he would act only according to the law", his ostensible dedication to lawfulness does not compel him even to hazard a defence of the accused, as Euryptolemos does'. For a discussion of Socrates' views on law and the nature of justice in Plato and Xenophon, see Dorion 2018b. Xenophon's Socrates is more tied to the belief that the justice of a law derives from its decreeing by the state or some human legislative body.

the youth (see *Memorabilia* 1.2.12, and for broader sources of discontent, *Memorabilia* 1.2.9 and *Apologia* 19–20).[18]

Although he opposed neither side in the civil war at Athens in 404–403, Socrates antagonised both parties and was held in suspicion by many in the city (*Memorabilia* 1.2.31–3; Plato, *Apologia* 32c–d). Natural scepticism concerning the practice of philosophical enquiry on the part of the conservative majority was intensified by the turbulence that had brought Athenian society to its knees in the period of the Thirty's rule and the events that had ultimately led to their rule; that the aforementioned Kritias and Alkibiades had central roles in many controversial episodes provided a real basis for their disapproval. We cannot be far wrong in supposing that Socrates' presence following the restoration was especially unwelcome to the leaders of the *demos*. As a potent symbol of non-conformity, he would have risen to the top of the list of personalities whom the new democracy, loosing itself from the shackles of Sparta, regarded as a threat to its viability. As I have argued, his trial was ultimately a part of a determined effort to uproot opposition and clear the way for a stable period of democratic rule.

The Charges against Socrates and His Trial

In 399, three of Socrates' fellow citizens, Meletos, Anytos and Lykon, brought an indictment against him.[19] Diogenes Laertios provides the wording, supposedly from the official records, in his biography:

> This indictment and affidavit is sworn by Meletos, the son of Meletos of Pitthos, against Socrates, the son of Sophroniscos of Alopece: Socrates is guilty of refusing to recognize the gods recognized by the state, and

---

18 Morrison (2010: 196) is surely right in asserting that the Athenians did not suspect Socrates of promoting evil or of instilling a taste for greed and ambition in those following him. 'Rather, the thought was either that Socrates' probing, critical spirit had a kind of nihilistic influence on the young, relaxing the hold that traditional values might have on them and thus allowing the baser human impulses to take over, or that quite apart from the question of moral influence, Socrates gave his young associates a mental training that amounted to a powerful tool or weapon that they could then use for the good or ill of the society around them.' In this context it is worth noting that Kritias was the author of two works on Sparta (Diels–Kranz 1960–1: 88 B 6–9, 32–7); Munn (2000: 225–7) argues that he had a vision to create a 'Spartan Athens'.

19 The literature on the subjects of the charges and the trial is extensive. My aim in this short section is only to summarise the historical event and its contemporary legacy. For political and social context, see for example Strauss 1986, Munn 2000, Brickhouse and Smith 2001, Nails 2006, Waterfield 2009 and Ober 2011, who makes a case for an out-of-touch and insensitive Socrates during and after the rule of the Thirty. T-H (7) regard the execution of Socrates as being 'perhaps the most contested event in Athenian history and arguably the most pivotal in Xenophon's life'.

of introducing other new divinities. He is also guilty of corrupting the
youth. The penalty demanded is death. (2.40)

On the impiety charge, by new divinities (ἕτερα δὲ καινὰ δαιμόνια) Socrates' accusers meant non-Olympians (see *Apologia* 24).[20] The charge of corrupting the youth must have envisaged a range of former pupils, though as is apparent from a later speech by Aischines and from the pamphlet of Polykrates (see below), some were more to the fore of the accusers' minds than others. As for the accusers, Meletos and Lykon were not well-known characters, a minor poet and orator respectively, but Anytos was a distinguished statesman and an important figure in the restored democracy. This suggests that the prosecution, if not orchestrated by leading democrats, almost certainly had the support of some of them.[21] That the case likely did have its origins in politics rather than justice or personal enmity is apparent from later speeches – Aischines (1.173) wrote that the 'sophist' was put to death 'because he was shown to have been the teacher of Kritias, one of the Thirty who put down the democracy' – and the refutation of the charges by followers of Socrates. Xenophon himself comments sarcastically: 'I wonder, then, how the Athenians can have been persuaded that Socrates was a freethinker, when he never said or did anything contrary to sound religion . . . no less wonderful is it to me that some believed the charge brought against Socrates of corrupting the youth' (*Memorabilia* 1.1.20–1.2.1).

Socrates made his own defence speech at the trial, even though Lysias is said to have prepared one for him.[22] Having heard defendant and prosecutors, the jury found Socrates guilty by a clear but not sizeable majority, approximately 280 to 220 (on the assumption of 500 jury members: see Plato, *Apologia* 36a). Exercising his right to propose an alternative punishment to the death penalty, Socrates suggested that he receive his meals in the *prytaneion* at the public expense (36b–e),[23] and though he

20 On this charge and the culpability of the defendant, see Munn 2000, Waterfield 2009, Denyer 2019. Konstan (2011: 78) refers back to the clouds being deities of Socrates in the Aristophanes play.
21 In Plato's *Meno* (90b–95a) Anytos is offended by Socrates, an outcome which points to a personal animosity between the men. However, the historicity of the encounter is not assured and, in any event, does not rule out a politically motivated trial. For an informative study of Anytos and his role in the prosecution of Socrates, see Sato 2008.
22 Diogenes (2.40–1) says that he read the speech of Lysias and, though impressed, thought it not suitable for him. 'If it is a fine speech, how can it fail to suit you?' 'Well, [Socrates replied,] would not fine raiment and fine shoes be just as unsuitable to me?' While Diogenes' comment that the speech was more forensic than philosophical encourages different interpretations, the rejection surely reflects Socrates' self-sufficiency.
23 In Plato, Socrates justifies the proposed reward on the basis of the good he has done for the city. Ober (2011: 154) writes that the honour 'would have been, [Socrates] supposed, a reasonable and appropriate acknowledgement of the special educational benefits he provided, and of the risks he incurred in the process'.

also offered to pay a fine (38a–b), his uncompromising attitude through the trial doubtless assured his conviction.

There is some evidence that the Athenians were remorseful after convicting Socrates. Writing in the first century, Diodoros (14.37.7) says that after the trial, realising the stature of the man they had lost, the Athenians became angry and put to death the prosecutors without trial. Diogenes (2.43) writes that not long after the event they closed the training grounds and gymnasia, banished Anytos and Lykon and put Meletos to death. On the other hand, there is evidence of lingering unpopularity. A pamphlet by the Athenian rhetorician Polykrates usually dated to the late 390s, *Accusation of Socrates*, speaks of Socrates' malignant effect on Kritias and Alkibiades.[24] Aischines' *Against Timarchos* (1.173, quoted above) includes a negative reference to Socrates and is dated to the 340s. It is conceivable that Xenophon's own adventure with Cyrus the Younger and his subsequent links with Sparta perpetuated negative feeling in the city, this being another instance of a promising youth gone bad at the hands of the philosopher. Xenophon's publication of *Anabasis* some thirty years after, with its key episode having Socrates air concern about his pupil's plans to join Cyrus and advise that he consult, and afterward insist he obey, the oracle, reminds readers of the argument that the charges against Socrates were unjust, and might be seen in some measure as a response to current sentiment such as that which is found a little later in Aischines.[25]

Going briefly back to the trial, one possibility to consider is that Xenophon's actions at Byzantium in autumn 400 were significant: I have argued that they could have been the underlying cause of his exile, but they might as well have added to the impetus for Socrates' prosecution. This perspective in turn potentially opens up a new understanding of 3.1.5–7 (Socrates pious and giving prudent advice), which could reflect some sense of personal guilt carried by Xenophon for his mentor's prosecution. This might challenge the argument elsewhere that Cyrus the Great's response to the Armenian king's execution of his own son's tutor, a sophist, in *Kyroupaideia* (3.1.38–40) is Xenophon's forgiveness of Athens for the execution of Socrates.

Granted that in the 360s Socrates was not universally regarded as an outstanding Athenian moral and cultural figure, as indicated in the opening of the chapter a defence of him then – at least in the minimal sense of engaging with the historic charges – might still be thought peculiar, notwithstanding

---

24 The *Accusation* is lost, but its contents can be gleaned from later writers, starting with Isokrates (*Busiris*). On Polykrates' pamphlet, see Momigliano (1993: 52–3), Stokes (2012), Waterfield (2013: 17–18).

25 Some negativity towards Socrates might have continued for many generations afterward. Denyer (2019: 6) points to Maximus of Tyre (3.1b), who, in the second century AD, reports that 'not even at this date has Socrates ceased to be subject to legal denunciation and scrutiny'. For Socrates in Hellenistic philosophy, see Long 1988.

there could have been personal reasons for doing so. However, the fact that the Socrates literary-philosophical industry was active in this period provides us with a further relevant context and invites us to see that besides concern about the execution of the philosopher on a false prospectus, Xenophon was interacting with this. In literary apologia terms, the charges frame an attempt by the author to stake ground for his Socrates. While in *Memorabilia* the charges are explicit, in *Anabasis* they are implicit, Xenophon the character's performance answering to them clearly and comprehensively.

Socratics and Socratica

In the years after his death, a number of Socrates' followers set about defending his memory, giving rise to a genre of *logoi*. In these, Socrates is typically the central character, and his virtues and his value to friends and city alike are underscored.[26] The overarching aim, as Hobden puts it, was 'to provide a counter-version to the prevailing narrative involving Socrates'.[27] Known authors of such works include Antisthenes (one of the philosopher's closest friends), Aischines, Aristippos, Eukleides, Phaedo, Plato, Simmias and Xenophon.

The only writers whose output survives intact are Plato and Xenophon, each of whom developed literary forms to extend the reach of their Socratic platforms. The relationship between the men is unclear, though they were undoubtedly acquainted with one another's work. Plato does not mention Xenophon in his writings, but is thought to be criticising his *Kyroupaideia* in *Laws* 694c, published around ten years later, where the 'Athenian Stranger' says that Cyrus 'was entirely without a right education, and had paid no attention to household management'.[28] Another apparent go at the work may be in *Seventh Letter* (if that be Plato's), where Darius instead of Cyrus the Great is the pre-eminent Persian ruler. 'And thus he [Darius] left an example of the character which should belong to the good lawgiver and king; for by the laws he framed he has preserved the empire of the Persians even until this day' (332b). Xenophon names Plato once, at *Memorabilia* 3.6.1. In later antiquity, Athenaios (11.112) talks at length about their rivalry, while Diogenes (3.34), in his biography of Plato, writes that 'Xenophon was not on good terms with him'. The matter of

---

26 For the term *Sokratikoi logoi* see Aristotle, *Poet.* 1447b9–13. On the early writings on Socrates and his life, see Rowe and Boys-Stones, who as already mentioned estimate that we know the titles of some 200 works about the philosopher (2013: vii). Rossetti ventures well beyond this, putting the number of works written by Socrates' followers at over 300 (2011: 28–32). Redfield (2018a) examines the origins of the dialogues.

27 Hobden 2020: 81.

28 For a reading of Plato's remarks about Cyrus the Great in *Laws* and the allusion therein to *Kyroupaideia*, see Nicolai 2014: 72–5 with references.

their personal and literary relationship divides modern scholars. The once prevalent assumption that, where the two cross literary and philosophical paths, Xenophon was copying from Plato, is no longer accepted by everyone.[29]

There is, as I remarked in discussion about the Socratic commander in Chapter 3, a longstanding debate about the extent to which Socrates in the *logoi* serves as a vehicle for the thoughts and individual outlooks of the authors. I look at the particular case of Xenophon, but in general there must be little doubt that to some degree their portraits are informed by their own agendas and backgrounds.[30] The epistemological and metaphysical interests of Plato and the preoccupation of Xenophon with political philosophy are not likely to owe themselves exclusively to association with Himself. At any rate, the Socratics were not writing biography as we understand it even if, as Momigliano observed, they experimented with this form (note 5). As for Socrates, it seems reasonable to believe that he had interests across different fields of philosophy, perhaps above all in the ethical life. Aristotle, at an ideal distance in time and with the requisite professional background, writes that he 'occupied himself with ethical matters and not at all with those concerning nature' (SB) (Σωκράτους δὲ περὶ μὲν τὰ ἠθικὰ πραγματευομένου περὶ δὲ τῆς ὅλης φύσεως οὐθέν, *Metaphysics* 1: 987b1–2).

The historical and philosophical worth of Xenophon's Socratica is a matter of contention, with the equivalent output of Plato being more highly regarded in the modern era. The latter's early dialogues have been thought by many to contain the truest picture of Socrates and his teaching; the fact that Plato knew Socrates for longer and was 'more of a philosopher' are often invoked as support for this position.[31] A prominent basis for the suspicion, if that's the right word, that Xenophon used Socrates as

---

29 Waterfield (2004: 107–9), for example, lists eighteen instances in Xenophon's *Memorabilia* and *Symposion* where he says the author is drawing on Plato. Dorion offers a subtle explanation, concluding that 'it was quite possible for Xenophon to borrow elements from Plato and use them in ways that run counter to Plato's intentions in his dialogues. In other words, he was able to insert elements borrowed from Plato into his own original interpretation of the philosophy of Socrates in order to contest Plato's interpretation of it' (2017: 46). On intertextuality between Xenophon and other Socratics, see the thoughtful recent study of Johnson 2021: 9–13.
30 Dorion (2018a: 57) argues that the Socratics sought to promote their own respective portraits of Socrates in opposition to those of their peers. The inherently agonistic nature of Greek culture is cited to support this view (ibid. p. 64). Rowe and Boys-Stones may offer a different explanation on the question (2013: xii), but I prefer Dorion's argument myself and consider that much of Xenophon's output should be set in an agonistic context.
31 See for instance Sandbach 1985, Macleod 2008. On Plato and the historical Socrates, see Ahbel-Rappe 2009 (chapter 4) and Danzig 2018.

a mouthpiece for his own ideas is that assertions, attitudes and even situations assigned to Socrates by him often seem incongruous: for example, Socrates singing the praises of farming (*Oikonomikos* 5), learning about planting trees (*Oikonomikos* 19) and dancing (*Symposion* 2.15–21). Yet given the fact that so little concrete is known about Socrates' life, objections of this sort are not watertight. The peculiarity of Xenophon's image of Socrates to a modern reader arises from the iconic status which Plato's Socrates has assumed in our time.[32]

A part of Xenophon's mission in his time may have been to provide a supplement, even a corrective, to what he viewed as the subjective or incomplete portrait of his counterpart. This would explain why his portrait is starkly different at points – he dismisses speculations on the nature of the universe as useless (*Memorabilia* 1.1.11–16) – and why he, for example, seems to downplay the importance of Platonic features such as *elenchus* ('not only the searching cross-examination with which he chastised [interlocutors], but his daily talks with his familiar friends', *Memorabilia* 1.4.1). Johnson phrases it this way: '[Xenophon] does not reject what others have said about Socrates, but shows Socrates discussing different things, or at least taking a different approach to shared topics, sometimes by correcting or critiquing what others had said.'[33] In his view, if I understand it rightly, this constitutes a complement to an underlying 'intertextual Socrates' rather than any attempt to present 'an entirely separate, rival version of Socrates'.[34] I do consider that Xenophon was presenting a different version of Socrates, albeit a subtly different one. It is worth underlining that the pictures of Xenophon and Plato, notably in their portrayal of Socrates as an ethical actor who was a believer that rule should be left to experts and that the law was paramount, are not greatly divergent and by the same token are sharply different to that of Aristophanes in *Clouds*.[35]

On the matter of Socratic defence, one of my concerns in this chapter, the question of Xenophon's faithfulness to the 'real' Socrates is not critical.

---

32 Nails (2006: 5) remarks that through his dialogues, Plato's account of the indictment, trial and execution of Socrates has become 'philosophy's founding myth' and has immortalised Socrates in the popular imagination. This primacy, however, is mostly a modern phenomenon, Plato and Xenophon having been by and large held in equal esteem up until the twentieth century. Waterfield (2004: 79) suggests that it is 'really only with the rise of analytic philosophy, to which Plato's concerns are more akin, that Plato's stature in this respect has overtaken that of Xenophon'. See Chapter 1 n.58 on the interpretation of Socrates in Hellenistic philosophy.

33 Johnson (2021: 4). The same might be said too of Plato, who as noted appears in his *Laws* and in *Seventh Letter* to be correcting Xenophon in *Kyroupaideia*, though the subject here is Cyrus rather than Socrates. For a study of the *elenchus* in Xenophon's writings, see Lachance 2018. For observations on the contrasts and complementarities between Xenophon's and Plato's presentations of Socrates, see Pangle 2020: 173–81.

34 Johnson 2021: 12.

35 Plato on professional rulers, *Cri.* 47a–d; on the law, *Cri.* 51c–52a.

The formal intention to defend the philosopher is not unduly affected by nuances in his historical representation. For argument's sake, even if Xenophon were using Socrates as a mouthpiece to promote his own ideas, the roundly positive representation of Socrates would in any case constitute a de facto defence of the historical figure to all but those intimate with the teacher himself, who might have a different perception. It is worth noting that this group does provide a certain control over the accuracy of the portrait, for there would likely have been evidence of criticism if Xenophon's figure were well wide of the mark.

A final thought is that in his writings he could be giving us a consciously fictional Socrates, whatever his motivation for that might be. It could be argued from, say, the discussion of cavalry command in *Memorabilia* 3.3 that there is a hint towards this in his ascription of advice to the philosopher that could be taken as commonplace instead of wisdom. Putting this another way, the distance between his Socrates and that of Plato in terms of philosophical vocabulary is notable, so it may be that he did not expect his audience to understand his presentation in *Memorabilia* as intended to represent the historic figure. Then, if Xenophon's Socrates in *Memorabilia* is not merely unhistorical as a matter of fact, but is actually meant to be taken as fictional, Xenophon cannot be intending to mount an apology for that Socrates in his writings. Such a case would undermine a key aspect of my own interpretation of *Anabasis*, namely that Xenophon's character embodies precepts of Socrates' teaching in *Memorabilia* as part of a defence (see the Socratic commander in Chapter 3). The question of why he might deploy a fictional Socrates is an interesting one. Perhaps it would be to emphasise the fluid nature of the philosopher's depiction in the literature and warn against reliance on any single account. My own view is that the figure in *Memorabilia* is not intentionally fictional, though there may be fictional elements in the account, but the aim is to provide a fuller picture of Socrates than is found in Plato; by highlighting, even playing on characteristics that would not be found in his compatriot's writing, he pushes the audience to reconsider the nature of the philosopher.[36]

---

36 The modern tendency has been to see Socrates in the literature as unhistorical. Gray, arguing that Xenophon constructed Socrates' character in the *Apologia* in light of a rhetorical theory, cautions against the historicity of the figure: 'The Socrates of literature might need to be different from the Socrates of real life if he were to convince the audience' (1989: 139). Gill (1973: 28) detects in Plato's description of Socrates' death in the *Phaedo* an instance of a historical event being transformed into a representation of a philosophical idea: '[this] should alert us to the possibility that many of what seem to be authentic glimpses into the life, and death, of the historical Socrates may in fact be illustrative pictures, attached or inset, like the myths of the dialogues, into Plato's arguments'. See also Momigliano in note 5.

Xenophon's Socratica

Xenophon is traditionally regarded as having authored four works that defend and promote the worth of Socrates: *Apologia, Memorabilia, Symposion* and *Oikonomikos*.[37] The philosopher is the central figure in each, and in different ways they each present his personal qualities and teachings with the same object of underlining that he was beneficial to friends and city alike. In *Apologia* and the first third of *Memorabilia* 1 (1.1–2), Xenophon defends Socrates directly against the charges of impiety and corrupting the youth brought against him in his trial at Athens; in the remainder of *Memorabilia* and in *Symposion* and *Oikonomikos* he promotes the value of his character and teaching (in the latter, Socrates is placed in the position of learner rather than teacher).[38]

Some have argued that other of Xenophon's works are Socratic too, and in this section I consider that proposition, starting with *Kyroupaideia*. While in this the philosopher is not mentioned by name at all, it has been argued that his presence is felt throughout the narrative. Gera discerns three types of Socratic influence in the work: personal traits shared by Socrates and Cyrus the Great; reference to events related to Socrates' trial and death; and the Socratic tenor of much of the dialogue.[39] Such an interpretative model might be applied to *Anabasis*, with Xenophon's character in the place of Cyrus the Great, but in this book the author has gone further by naming Socrates at the critical juncture of the story. A point to make on this is that his appearance is not essential for the basic storyline: if Xenophon wished to show himself semi-wise by seeking high advice, he could have depicted himself as going to Delphi on his own accord and need not have named Socrates as his advisor, and there were surely others as well whom he could have had in that role. The case of *Anabasis* is looked at in more detail later.

Socrates does feature on one occasion in *Hellenika*, and this in an episode that is clearly intended to showcase his qualities. Henry's reading of Xenophon's dramatic account of the Arginousai trial shows that one of its objects was to accentuate the extraordinary courage of the philosopher in refusing to admit an illegal motion (*Hellenika* 1.7.1–15: see Chapter 1 n.66).

---

37 Xenophon's Socratic cycle: Kahn 1996: 29, Dorion 2006: 93, Danzig 2018: 21, Christ 2020: 37, Johnson 2021: 1. Socrates features twice in Xenophon's historiographical works, at *An.* 3.1.5–7 and *Hell.* 1.7.15. Besides the *Anabasis* passage, only on one other occasion do Socrates and Xenophon appear together, this at *Mem.* 1.3.8–13.

38 Nee (2009) argues that *Oikonomikos* defends Socrates against the charge of corrupting the youth, it being the city itself which is guilty of this.

39 Gera 1993: 26–7. Tamiolaki picks the last point up, speaking of the work being 'very often interrupted by Socratic-type conversations' (2017: 189). Whidden (2008: 31 n.3) contends that the plural pronouns ('we', 'us', 'our') used by Xenophon in the *Kyroupaideia* prologue are meant to refer to the followers of Socrates and concludes that it was Xenophon's conversations with Socrates that motivated him to write the work.

Others read underlying Socratic influence across the work. As discussed in Chapter 2, Dobski sees in Books 1–2 a Socratic response to the end of Thucydides' work, while Gish discerns in Book 3 a critique of the Spartan regime which is profoundly Socratic. Krentz in his commentary detects a critique of Sparta in Xenophon's treatment of the Thirty, though he does not associate any Socratic motivation with this; however, he does remark on the fact that Xenophon omits stories that might not reflect well on his mentor.[40]

The search for Socrates outside of the traditional cycle takes us next to *Hiero*, which incorporates historical content and bears out Socratic values. Although Socrates himself is not a character in the conversation, he is present, as Gray shows, through features of the dialogue such as the manner and irony of Simonides. Arguing that the work combines the appearance of a Socratic dialogue and the tradition of accounts of meetings between wise men and tyrants in Greek literature, Gray remarks that Simonides 'conducts himself just as Socrates might have'.[41] Turning to *Poroi*, we could argue that Xenophon as the author assumes a Socratic bearing. In his study of this work, Jansen contends that the author 'framed his relationships with his *philoi* Socratically by assuming the part of the wise, practical advisor. Such is his role implicit at the beginning of the *Poroi*.'[42] Then in *Agesilaos* and *Lakedaimonion Politeia* Xenophon attributes to the lead protagonists (Agesilaos and Lykourgos respectively) important qualities displayed by Socrates in the *logoi*.

Anabasis likewise is not widely considered a part of the Socratic cycle, but arguably even more than those just discussed it reflects the author's Socratic enterprise. With the starting point that 3.1.5–7 functions to establish him as one who had been close to the philosopher, I argue in the course of this chapter that the work shows Xenophon's learning playing a significant role in his character's success and consequently impacting positively on the lives of many others. Building the case for its Socratic quality, as Buzzetti directly and others such as McCloskey implicitly contend, the text has a philosophical dimension. Indeed, the former regards it as an introduction to philosophy, with the search for virtue lying at its heart.[43] I see the philosophical element as more discreet, if no less forceful. It resides in

---

40 Krentz 1995: 122.
41 Gray 1986: 116.
42 Jansen 2007: 111–12.
43 Buzzetti 2014: 2, 7, 296. Howland argues that *Anabasis* is a companion piece to the *Republic* and that Xenophon sought to engage Plato in a dialogue about the nature of Socratic philosophising: 'both works can be viewed as variations on a common set of themes and issues, as meditations that are best appreciated in tandem, just insofar as one of them takes the measure of the other' (2000: 877). The author contends that both books, in underlining the unattainability of ideal communities, show us the limits of politics (883). Danzig, Johnson and Morrison 2018 take forward the project to consider Xenophon and Plato side by side.

the images of dialogue between Socrates and Xenophon before and after Delphi, in the fact of *Anabasis* being a story about *aporia* and problem-solving, in the implicit encouragement to readers to contemplate the value of the virtues, and in the theme of human imperfection, emphasised in the final book where the development of Xenophon in 1–6 seems to stall.

As the central figure in the story is a young pupil of Socrates who finds himself caught up in a desperate situation, from the historiographical and philosophical perspectives we are interested in how this young man acquits himself. How well has he learned from his teacher, and how useful in fact are the lessons? Should we not consider his performance to be a true test of the quality of the Socratic education? Xenophon's *Memorabilia* incorporates a sourcebook for this education, a store of detail on the philosopher's teaching which includes specific advice on generalship. Assuming we take it as meant to be authentic, it is a natural starting point to turn to when wishing to understand how a 'Socratic commander' should behave and to use as a basis for evaluating his performance. As we saw from the analysis in Chapter 3, Xenophon's character's drawing on these lessons contributes in a measurable way to his own survival and that of the army he leads. In this chapter, I broaden the focus on the Socratic education and show how ethical aspects of the philosopher's teaching were a still more valuable element, indeed the very foundation, of Xenophon's leadership.

This argument would be strengthened if it could be clearly shown that the contemporary audience read *Anabasis* as a work relevant to Socratic leadership. One promising line here is the question looked at in earlier chapters about the relative dating of *Anabasis* and the Socratica. On the conservative view, if we are to take the former as exemplifying Socratic principles, then the source of those should already be available, so that the connection and its meaning can be made by readers. A part of Xenophon's Socratic cycle may have been published before *Anabasis*, and it is possible this includes *Memorabilia* or a part of it. One of the suggestions I made on this subject in Chapter 1 is that the correspondence in material between 'Xenophon's' performance on the retreat and the military advice given in *Memorabilia* 3.1–5 could furnish some evidence that *Memorabilia* came first, though admittedly this is circular, and it could as well be that the experience of writing *Anabasis* prompted the passages in *Memorabilia*. I add that I do not believe Xenophon's audience of thinkers separated the two works generically as is the modern tendency.

In a less stringent view, a point-for-point correspondence would not be necessary for the connection. Xenophon could have expected readers knowing of his association with Socrates and knowledgeable about Socrates' military experience and leadership interest to have seen the cue at *Anabasis* 3.1 and to have read the ensuing narrative accordingly, if without benchmarking (I do not think there would have been many who did not know that Xenophon had a connection with Socrates; in *Anabasis* he merely underlines the link). Worth mentioning also are the writings of other first-generation Socratics. Given that they were portraying the same figure, and presumably said some similar things about what he taught, it is plausible that readers could have mapped those discourses on military matters onto *Anabasis* (but see Dorion, note 30 above).[44] I think in this and other respects it is important to emphasise a much denser literary context and the fact that much more was known about Socrates then than now.[45]

Going against the argument for *Anabasis* as a Socratic work, if it was received in antiquity as such, should that not have registered in the literary record? I am doubtful that contemporary readers would have spoken in these terms at all, and I think we can apprehend the absence of any modern-style grouping linking the work or not to Socrates and the Socratics. Dio Chrysostom (18.13–17), choosing Xenophon as his exemplar for the Socratics, proceeds to eulogise his speeches and narrative in *Anabasis*, evidently seeing no discontinuity between it and the author's four overtly Socratic writings. Diogenes Laertios in his biography is more explicit, penning an epigram which links *Anabasis* and the philosopher to memorialise the relationship between the men:

> Not only did Xenophon march upcountry because of Cyrus,
> But to search for some way that would lead up to Zeus.
> For having shown Greek deeds were owed to his education,
> He called to mind how beautiful was the wisdom of Socrates.
>   Lives 2.58 (SB[46])

Still later readings of the work support the view that Xenophon intended his participation to be understood within a Socratic frame; for example,

---

44 Many think Xenophon's output postdates much of that of the other Socratics; see, for instance, Redfield (2018b: 116), 'the next generation', and Johnson 2021: 4–5. There seems to be a consensus as well that some of his material is taken from their work, albeit he reworks it into a form that serves his own agenda. The interconnectedness of much of Xenophon's own output is worth emphasising again, as is the proximity in time – late 370s to early 360s (though *Apologia* may be an outlier) – of publication of the Socratic cycle and *Anabasis*.

45 On the scale of the literary field, see note 26 above. Johnson (2021: 10) evokes this in a different way: 'Xenophon must have meant readers to understand something more by "Socrates" than what he tells us about Socrates. We have, in other words, a textbook case of intertextuality, where Xenophon's text is not fully intelligible outside the wider universe of the Socratic conversations.'

46 Paton translating the *Anth. Pal.* thinks that the third line, παιδείης παρ' ἑῆς Ἑλληνικὰ πράγματα δείξας, might be an attempt to allude to both *Kyroupaideia* and *Hellenika*.

much later, Francis Bacon in *The Advancement of Learning* (1605: 1.7.30). A further part of the explanation for a lack of noise about the Socratic element is probably that the implied portrait of a conventional Socrates did not quite capture the general audience enough for them to associate *Anabasis* with him primarily, that being all the harder amidst the drama of the story of the Ten Thousand.

In light of the foregoing and noting that in each work the pair engage in conversation one time, we could say that whereas in *Memorabilia* the focus is on Socrates, in *Anabasis* it is on one of his pupils. This brings us once again to the modern question of categorisation. Is it right to describe *Anabasis* in unqualified terms as Socratic? In earlier chapters I showed that behind it lies an extensive authorial agenda and that the story of the Ten Thousand itself matters. I suggested in Chapter 2 that we should understand *Anabasis* as a 'Socratic history', a historiographical text influenced at a fundamental level by an implicit desire on the part of the author to perpetuate Socratic values. Through the (hi)story of the Ten Thousand Xenophon has thus found another, powerful means to further his mission of defending the memory of Socrates and promoting his own version of the philosopher.[47]

It would be appropriate to compare the historical-type works of other Socratics to see if these too consciously seek to promote the values of the philosopher. *Seventh Letter*, which like *Anabasis* could be described as history intercut with personal apologia, would seem to provide a basis for comparison. However, even though Socrates is mentioned on a handful of occasions (324d–325c), and notwithstanding the fact of Plato's putting himself at risk to help the cause of bringing about a philosopher-king, there is not evidence of a systematic attempt to promote Socratic values. I take this on one level as an indicator of Xenophon's innovative literary style.

A question to revisit finally as a way of tying in the above strands is the standing of Socrates in the 360s, when Xenophon was immersed in his writing phase. Talk of defence against the charges from 399, just as in the case of charges made against Xenophon on the retreat, needs to be set in a fuller context. There were doubtless those who regarded Socrates as a disreputable figure, having been convicted of acting against city and gods alike, and we have evidence revealing animosity (Aischines, *Against Timarchos*) from the 340s. One might even imagine Xenophon at Olympia listening to hard talk about his teacher from younger men and returning home to his study at Skillous to redress that. Equally, though, Socrates at that stage might not have been in pressing need of defence, and much of the discussion at Olympia and Athens and elsewhere amongst those interested in the subject

---

47 In the context it may be worth mentioning 'rhetorical history', one of whose characteristics Marincola (2014: 41) describes as 'the composition of speeches and even of actions based not on any historical record but on the criteria of probability and appropriateness'.

was likely to have been centred on the philosophy and character of Socrates. In this light, Xenophon's Socratica should not be seen exclusively or even primarily as apologetic works, but also as ways of promoting his version of the philosopher.

The Framing of Xenophon in *Anabasis*: The Philosopher Armed

We know that Xenophon in his account of the retreat of the Ten Thousand comes across as being more than an average leader. His energy and daring at times verge on the superhuman, and it seems right to conclude that in his narrative he has aims additional to defending himself against personal attacks.[48] The main explanation I offer for his extraordinary self-portrayal is that Xenophon's character is an exemplar, a model Athenian and pupil of Socrates behaving as such should in this type of situation. That *Anabasis* is not intended to be 'autobiographical' is, I have suggested, signalled by the author's attribution of the work to another (*Hellenika* 3.1.2). Rather, then, than claiming a glorious role for himself, in the wider frame Xenophon is defending an individual whom he holds in the highest regard and at the same time is inscribing a version of him that may in part be a response to others in circulation. Regardless of whether or not he was, in fact, an outstanding pupil of Socrates, in *Anabasis* his character acts as such, and thus the work stands as a testament to his teacher. This second part of the chapter demonstrates how, by way of his carefully crafted introductions into the story, Xenophon constructs the framework for his innovative interaction with Socrates.

Prelude

On the day after the battle in which Cyrus was killed, the King sent heralds to the Greeks to demand they surrender their weapons. Among them was one Phalinos, a Greek in the service of Tissaphernes. Notably, as a

---

48 Modern writers regularly remark on a sense of exaggeration in the self-representation. Calvino (1999: 20) in an essay on *Anabasis* writes: 'on occasions Xenophon appears to be one of those heroes from children's comics, who in every episode appear to survive against impossible odds'. Tuplin (2003: 149): 'it would be perverse to claim there is much sign of Xenophon doing or saying anything but the right thing between the banks of the Zab and the Mysian hinterland'. Cawkwell (2004: 60): 'Indeed he never seems to make a mistake. Both in counsel and in action, Xenophon was always right.' Lee (2005: 46): 'Xenophon sometimes comes off as implausibly competent for a relatively inexperienced young man surrounded by seasoned, mostly older mercenaries.' Haywood (2016: 99–100) describes 'an intrepid leader, overcoming all manner of enervating forces: external and internal dissent; uncharted and hostile topographies; meteorological chaos; and regular interventions by capricious gods'.

professional adviser on tactics and *hoplomachia*, he is a type who attracts attention in Socratic literature. In reply to the demand that they give up their arms, a young Athenian addresses Phalinos:

> [12] After this speech, Theopompos of Athens said, 'Phalinos, as you see, nothing else is now any good to us except weapons and our own personal merits. We think that while we have our weapons, we could also put our personal merits to use; but that if we were to give up our weapons, we would also be deprived of our lives. So don't think that we are going to hand over to you the only things that are any good to us; instead, we will use them to extend the fight to the good things you possess.' [13] When he heard this, Phalinos laughed and said, 'Well, young man, you seem like a philosopher, and you speak quite charmingly, but be aware that you are a fool if you think that your personal merits and those of the others here could withstand the power of the King.' (2.1.12–13)

In the two main manuscript families (c and f) which are preserved, 'c' here names the young Athenian as Theopompos, while 'f' has Xenophon.[49] In the former tradition some, including myself, think that Xenophon is disguising himself, the name Theopompos, 'sent by god', indicative of the sort of wordplay he shows elsewhere in his writing.[50] This in turn could explain away the main philological difficulty in accepting the 'f' (Xenophon) reading, namely that if the text had originally read 'Xenophon' it is hard to see how it became corrupted to Theopompos, whereas the reverse is plausible (so in 'f' the scribe changed what he found to what he thought should be there).

On the case for Theopompos being another character in the story, Ambler, who prefers the 'c' manuscript here and elsewhere, points to 2.1.8 ('The heralds approached and summoned the Greek commanders'), arguing that it is unlikely Xenophon would have been present at the meeting in question, as he was not then one of the army's leaders (see note 49 for the reference). Nonetheless, Theopompos is not mentioned again in *Anabasis*, and on the other hand Xenophon is closely allied to

---

49 On 2.1.12, see Ambler 2008: 264 n.4, Buzzetti 2014: 80 n.6, H-R 11 n.32 and Thomas 2021a, all of whom favour 'c'. However, Dillery in the Loeb (1998) and Hude/Peters in the Teubner (1972) print 'f'.

50 Self-disguise: there may be instances in other writings where Xenophon veils himself, for example Ischomachos in *Oikonomikos*, Tigranes in *Kyroupaideia* and Charmides in *Memorabilia*. Wordplay: arguably an example of this is Themistogenes, 'descendant of justice', at *Hell*. 3.1.2: see further Erbse 494–5 and Strauss 1975: 118. I share Buzzetti's view that Theopompos is a stand-in for Xenophon (2014: 84; 84–5 adducing further evidence for the identification). I suggest below that Themistogenes and Theopompos have a significant literary connection.

one of the leaders, Proxenos, so it would not be surprising if he was in attendance in an advisory capacity. A stronger argument suggested to me by David Thomas in correspondence is that Theopompos could have been one of those subsequently seized and killed at the Zapatas River and Xenophon did not want to undermine his message here by revealing as much. I am inclined myself, though, to think that had there been another young Athenian philosopher on the march we would have learned of this from Xenophon or somebody else.

Assuming that 'c' has the stronger claim, if we take it, as I and others do, that Theopompos is meant to be a stand-in for Xenophon, one might conclude that in the episode the author disguises himself lightly in order to limit his appearances prior to his dramatic introduction at the Zapatas.[51] Yet, on the contrary, what we have, I believe, is the author laying the ground for the emergence of the character Xenophon. As I have argued, his attribution of the work to Themistogenes in *Hellenika* is intended to signal that *Anabasis* is not autobiographical;[52] now, internally, with the foreshadowing of 'Xenophon' he provides us with equivalent information: the name Theopompos suitably, if rather grandly, captures the essence of the role this character will go on to play in the retreat. I think the author embeds a further clue in the episode to complete its meaning. In his response, Phalinos refers to his interlocutor as young and being of a philosophical persuasion (Ἀλλὰ φιλοσόφῳ μὲν ἔοικας, ὦ νεανίσκε). As a Greek, it is conceivable that he knew about this young man's background and that he is referencing him as a Socratic.

I note finally that Phalinos' mild contempt for the argument being made in the passage marks the young man's inexperience rather than being a judgement on his capacity for reason, though in light of the potential Socratic angle, this could be read as aimed at his teacher. As noted, figures like Phalinos who earned off their often limited knowledge are a subject of scrutiny in Socratic discourse. In any event, Phalinos' response anticipates the challenge which the young philosopher is destined to overcome on the

---

51 Other inferences are possible. Buzzetti, for example, believes the pseudonym was used because Xenophon was not present at the discussion with the King's men and that Theopompos says what he would have said had he been in attendance (2014: 85). We can note that Xenophon's invisibility in Books 1–2 also serves to distance him from Cyrus, an enemy of Athens and the promoter of a military adventure against a legitimate authority: see further Chapter 4 pp. 165–7.

52 The strong likelihood that the second part of *Hellenika* postdates *Anabasis* offers a key context for the Themistogenes insertion. I suggested that Xenophon found that the approach in *Anabasis* was not apprehended as widely as he would have wished, and in the later text introduced this, in effect, clarificatory statement. Of course, by that time there cannot have been any real doubt that he was the author, so perhaps playful rather than formal would better reflect the tone of the insertion.

retreat. On one level his triumph, and arguably that of Socrates in his own life, is the victory of merit (ἀρετή) over power (δύναμις).[53]

There are further instances in Book 2 wherein the author prepares for his character's formal entry into the story as an exemplary philosopher armed. After the army has begun its march north along the Tigris accompanied by the force of Tissaphernes, an unnamed young man, 'after reflection' (ἐννοήσας), offers advice when a concern about the Persians' intentions arises (2.4.19–20). Likewise, just before this, this time in his own clothing, we find 'Xenophon' and his similarly philosophically inclined companion at leisure: 'After the evening meal, Proxenos and Xenophon happened to be taking a walk (ἔτυχον ἐν περιπάτῳ) in front of the weapon stacks', 2.4.15). While walking about would only later come to denote the pulse of philosophy in literary culture, it has always been a means of problem-solving, and considering the backgrounds of the young men and the tense circumstances of the march, mention of the activity invites us to imagine a conversation concentrated on the nature of the present predicament. The most interesting episode happens after the seizure of the generals at the Zapatas River. Again in his own clothing, 'Xenophon' goes out with a group of Greek commanders to receive a message from the King and to learn about the fate of Proxenos (2.5.35–7). A formal but terse exchange takes place between Ariaios on the barbarian side and Kleanor, one of the surviving generals, on the Greek side. Following their proffering of a justification for their actions, Xenophon intervenes with a measured and logical proposal which serves to expose the unjust behaviour of the Persians (2.5.41). Ariaios and the barbarians with him talk amongst themselves for a long time (πολὺν χρόνον) but are unable to provide a response. Like overambitious young men stung by Socrates, they leave in a state of *aporia*.[54]

As I go on to argue in the next section, 'Xenophon's' chief purpose in joining the expedition was to learn from Cyrus as a model of good kingship. As a practical example of the type of learning he was exposed to, we could point to Cyrus's handling of Orontas, a Persian aristocrat who is tried for treason and executed prior to the battle with the King (1.6). Xenophon's report of the trial has Cyrus engaging in *elenchus*; while he was familiar with the method from his association with Socrates, hearing of its use in the field may have encouraged him to do the same and in the same manner when he

---

53 Tuplin suggests there might be a reference here to *Odyssey* 8.236, where Alkinoos, responding to Odysseus' anger at being taunted, uses similar language to Phalinos. 'The situations *are* different ... but perhaps there is an allusion whose point is that the army's ἀρετή will turn out (like Odysseus') to prevail' (2003: 124).
54 On the number of 'Xenophon's' appearances in the text prior to 3.1.4, the matter is complicated by the manuscript variances and by the uncertainty surrounding the true identity of several actors in Book 2, for example the unnamed young man at 2.4.19–20.

himself leads on the retreat (I highlight Xenophon's use of the *elenchus* in the final part of the chapter). From this perspective, we should regard the unspoken experience of Book 1 where 'Xenophon' is only an implicit presence as part of what makes him the way he is when he emerges as a key actor in Book 3. Considering the lukewarm evaluation of Cyrus's role offered in Chapter 3, we can appreciate that he has had a mix of experiences. This standpoint in turn prompts us to understand a process of development that formally begins with Xenophon's meeting with Socrates at Athens. For the period until his emergence on the leadership front at the Zapatas we do, I suggest, have an important validation of his learning stance, that is, of his being primarily in this mode rather than a combat or advisory one. When Xenophon has finished his speech to the officers in Book 3, Cheirisophos the Spartan remarks: 'Well, Xenophon, previously I knew you only to this extent, that I used to hear of you as being an Athenian. But now I also praise you for your speech and actions' (3.1.45). This third-party comment by an authoritative figure encourages us to see the character Xenophon as someone who has up until the present moment been an observer of events.

Xenophon the Athenian

The narrator formally introduces the lead character into the story in an external analepsis at the start of Book 3. Tensions with the Persians have come to a head and, as a result of skilful politicking by Tissaphernes, Klearchos and other high-ranking Greek officers are lured into a trap and seized. That night the men lie about in despair, convinced they will never see their homeland, families or friends again.

> [4] In the army there was a certain Xenophon, an Athenian. He did not accompany the army as a general, nor as a captain nor as an ordinary soldier: Proxenos, who was a long-standing guest-friend of his, had sent for him to come from home, promising him that if he were to come, he would make him a friend of Cyrus. Proxenos indeed said that he thought Cyrus was more important to him than was his own native land. [5] However, when Xenophon read Proxenos' letter, he first discussed with Socrates the Athenian what he would advise about the journey. (3.1.4–5)

The passage contains several assertions relating to Xenophon and the expedition: he did not set off to fight against the King; in his letter Proxenos promised that, if he came, he would make him a friend of Cyrus, whom he regarded extremely highly; Socrates was consulted about the journey. In the previous chapter, one suggestion was that the passage served to invoke Xenophon's guest-friendship with Proxenos as an explanation for his involvement in a mercenary enterprise. In this section, I adjust the focus to show that on another level these assertions collectively set a different context for Xenophon's joining Cyrus and that the passage is intended to establish that he embarked on his journey with the aim of broadening his experience of the world and developing his learning and character.[55] In the search for Socrates in *Anabasis* outside of his appearance at 3.1.5–7, this bears notice as being exactly Socratic. It is a distinctive thing about Xenophon's Socrates that he was *kaloskagathos* and aimed to make others *kaloikagathoi*.

Cyrus

Xenophon's claim that he was deceived about the expedition's purpose (3.1.10) and his preceding statement that he did not follow the army in a military role dissociates him from a campaign against the Persian King. From the fact of his guest-friendship with Proxenos, we may be led to understand that he was there on account of the obligation to help that arose from this relationship. Yet the strength of the bond in this case – and if it is representative, then perhaps generally for guest-friendship – is questionable. Before committing, Xenophon consults with another, while in emphasising the high quality of Cyrus's character, Proxenos' letter seems to strive to sweeten the summons by hinting at further reason for Xenophon to undertake the journey to Asia. What this is is apparent to the reader at this stage of the story, for we know from Xenophon's obituary of him that Proxenos, through his links with Gorgias the Sophist, is concerned with political philosophy, and before this, in his obituary of Cyrus, Xenophon has spoken at length of the qualities which the prince possessed. Significantly, he is said to have stood out at the royal court for his obedience and as the keenest among the youth to learn and practise the techniques of war (1.9.5), qualities that Socrates believed inclined a soul to excellence (*Memorabilia* 4.1.2). Cyrus is furthermore said to have been the most kingly and worthiest to rule of all the Persians since Cyrus the Great (*Anabasis* 1.9.1). So, there is a unique opportunity to get close to a veritable model of kingship, a chance which both Xenophon and Proxenos, given their backgrounds and interest in the problem of how to rule, will not want

---

55 The material such as it is permits a range of readings. For example, taking as a backdrop Rop's thesis that the Persians used *xenia* as a means of imperialism and that Greek states and politicians sought out foreign patronage (2019: 86–7), we might suggest that Xenophon saw service with Cyrus as a means of winning influence for himself at home. Powell and Richer (2020: ix) set the journey in the context of state relations, drawing a comparison between Xenophon and Sparta and T. E. Lawrence and the British Empire.

to have missed out on.⁵⁶ And as Socrates is to say: 'Need we be ashamed of imitating the king of the Persians?' (*Oikonomikos* 4.4).

The matter of their association with Cyrus is, however, problematised on several counts, first and foremost by the true objective of the campaign. Xenophon's claim in the introductory passage that he and Proxenos had been deceived (ἐξαπατηθείς) about the expedition's aim looks as if it is intended to exonerate them from involvement in an unjust conspiracy, one, moreover, whose target his own city at subsequent junctures was on working terms with.⁵⁷ For the fact is that Cyrus seems to have had no just cause to make an attempt on the Persian throne, being driven only by his own ambition. This is the later judgement of Plutarch (*Artaxerxes* 3.5, 6.3) and, notably, Xenophon does not seek to provide a political or moral justification for the rebellion. Having offered a brief summary of the court turmoil that attended the death of the father and which nearly cost Cyrus his life, he writes that the young prince, 'dishonoured and having been put in great danger, ... set about planning how to avoid ever again being at his brother's mercy, and how instead to become King in his place if he could' (1.1.4). Not shying away from the very personal nature of the enterprise, Xenophon adds that in this aim he was supported by his mother: '[Parysatis] was on Cyrus's side, for she loved him rather than Artaxerxes, even though it was Artaxerxes who was the King' (Παρύσατις μὲν δὴ ἡ μήτηρ ὑπῆρχε τῷ Κύρῳ, φιλοῦσα αὐτὸν μᾶλλον ἢ τὸν βασιλεύοντα Ἀρταξέρξην, 1.1.4).⁵⁸

A second difficulty with the association for the young philosophers is the less virtuous side of Cyrus's character. We get a hint of this already in the first meeting he has with Xenophon at Sardis. Cyrus tells him that 'as soon as the campaign was over' (τάχιστα ἡ στρατεία λήξῃ, 3.1.9) he would send him home. In the next line we are informed that 'it was said' (ἐλέγετο) the expedition was against the Pisidians, so implying that someone else communicated the objective. In any event, even if he did not lie to them, Cyrus has not been open with Xenophon and Proxenos,

---

56 See H-R 11, who also cite Mary Renault in *The Last of the Wine*, and Brennan 2011: 213–14. But as I go on to point out, the fact that Cyrus's leadership does not turn out to be stellar calls into question Proxenos' judgement and, behind that, his training with Gorgias.

57 Young men deceived: 3.1.9–10. The pair had set out from Sardis believing Cyrus intended to subdue a troublesome tribe within his satrapy, and only when it was apparently too late realised that he was in fact marching against the King. Cyrus's stated plan: 1.2.1; Xenophon writes that only Klearchos knew of Cyrus's true plan (3.1.10). Diodoros, however, suggests that the commanders had been informed (14.19.9).

58 Lee (2016a: 105) contests the view held by many Achaemenid historians that Cyrus faced wide resistance to his enterprise from the imperial elites, so perhaps there was some justifiable basis for the coup even if such evidence is not apparent in *Anabasis*.

his guest-friend. With the duplicity of Tissaphernes fresh in our minds, we may be inclined to see Cyrus as sharing this trait and wonder if Xenophon should not have made further enquiry then about the expedition (on Tissaphernes' own suspicion see below).[59] The same of course applies to Proxenos, whose letter to Xenophon, in which he asserted that he valued the prince above his own country, assumes a different complexion in light of the subsequent leadership failings of Cyrus on the expedition.

Germane to this discussion is the fact that, beyond the carefully guarded interactions in *Anabasis*, Xenophon does provide enough to warrant real concern about the virtue of the prince. One incident from *Hellenika* where Cyrus executed two royals who had failed to show him a mark of respect which he felt was owed (2.1.8) was referred to in Chapter 3; I highlight another here touching on the prime virtues of obedience and self-discipline. Shortly after his arrival in the west to take up the role he had been appointed to by his father, Cyrus informed a party of Spartan envoys who had requested an increase in pay for their sailors that, while he would do everything to aid their cause, 'it was not possible for him to do anything beyond what the King had ordered' (1.5.5). Yet this admirable obedience seems to falter shortly afterward when the leaders are drinking to each other's health and, on a further request about the sailor's pay, he raises this from three to four obols a day, in addition paying their back pay and advancing them one month's wages (1.5.6–7).

The deception claim at 3.1.9–10 (note 57) also serves to draw attention to Xenophon's and his similarly youthful guest-friend's naivety, both in their believing in the unassailable virtue of Cyrus and in their lack of geopolitical nous (and recall the response of Phalinos to the young philosopher: 2.1.13). The scale of the force, and Cyrus's ambition – apparent from his support for Sparta in the Peloponnesian War – was not unknown to them, but unlike the experienced satrap Tissaphernes, they did not see that the expedition's declared purpose was suspect (1.2.4). Even when they learn of Cyrus's true aim, it seems not to strike them that they are part of a coup against a legitimate ruler:

> by the time that they reached Kilikia, it seemed clear to everyone that the expedition was against the King. Unwilling though they were, and fearful of the journey, the majority still followed along from a sense of shame toward Cyrus and toward each other; and among these was Xenophon. (3.1.10)

The same defensive tack is discernible in Xenophon's overlooking of Socrates' advice and his posing a leading question to the oracle at Delphi

---

59 On designing/plotting (ἐπίβουλος) as a desirable quality in a general, see *Mem.* 3.1.6. But it is open to question whether this should apply to allies as well as enemies.

(3.1.5–6). The gradual maturing of Xenophon's character through the expedition is an important part of the text's Socratic nature, demonstrating as it does how wisdom grows through the interplay of right learning and experience.

Proxenos

Turning to look more closely at Proxenos, we know from his obituary (2.6.16–20) that he was a student of Gorgias the Sophist and that from his youth 'he wanted to become a man capable of achieving great things' (2.6.16). Joining Cyrus was a way to develop his abilities and advance his ambitions, and indeed he envisaged that the guest-friend exchange would yield 'a great name, great power, and much wealth' (2.6.17). While Xenophon is, we sense, critical of his expectation, he remarks that Proxenos' ambition was moderated by a moral compass:

> But though he very much desired these things, he also made it quite clear that he would not wish to obtain any of them with the aid of wrongdoing (μετὰ ἀδικίας): he thought that it was necessary to achieve them in company with justice and honour, and not otherwise. (2.6.18)

With this picture of Proxenos, and Xenophon's own association with Socrates, a journey facilitating development and enterprise is framed for the young men.[60] Travelling to learn was a long-established way of broadening the mind, and capacity to reason was considered to grow in tandem with increasing experience. Exemplary wise men were often interminable travellers: Solon, Thales, Hekataios and Pythagoras for example. For young men, moreover, the journey cycle was akin to a rite of passage, a returning home in a state of maturity following a testing experience. The *Anabasis* story maps that life journey almost exactly and itself reaffirms its transformative power. We can measure the distance Xenophon's character has come on his journey between its furthest points: from the high-spirited commander of the rearguard chasing shadows beyond the Zapatas River (3.3.8) to the controlled and thoughtful leader at Byzantium, the first Greek city (7.1.18–24).

From another perspective, there is the unequivocal impression from his writings that Xenophon for one preferred to be putting his learning into practice and learning from practice rather than sharing in the types of activities that at one point had earned Socrates the (literary) reputation of being 'a mere chatterer with my head in the air' (*Oikonomikos* 11.3).

---

60 On potential prior evidence for the youthful pair being involved in philosophical activity, see Chapter 1 p. 33. See note 65 for a hint of sophistry in Xenophon.

For both himself and Proxenos, then, we can readily imagine that travel – seeing places, meeting people, discovering new *nomoi* – in the company of an outstanding prince offered a highly attractive path to self-improvement.[61]

It is apt to remark that the demise of Proxenos and the success of Xenophon on the retreat emphasises the greater desirability of the Socratic education over that of Gorgias and the other sophists (see *Kynegetikos* 13.1–9, *Memorabilia* 1.6.13 for negative attitude towards sophists).[62] The obituary of Proxenos in one respect is a judgement on Gorgias and his brand of teaching:

> [17] Since he [Proxenos] had kept company with Gorgias, he thought that he was already capable of acting as a commander … [19] He was capable of commanding good and honourable people, but by contrast he was not capable of instilling respect or fear toward himself in the ordinary soldiers: on the contrary, he stood in awe of his soldiers rather more than those under his command did of him, and it was clear he was more afraid of being disliked by his soldiers than his soldiers were of disobeying him. [20] He thought that in order to be and to appear to be fit for command, it was sufficient to praise those who acted well and to abstain from praising those who did wrong. (2.6.17, 19–20)

Socrates

The third assertion in the passage under examination is that Xenophon consulted Socrates about whether he should join Cyrus. He goes on to tell us how he acted and how in turn the philosopher responded to his action:

> [6] Xenophon went there [to Delphi] and asked Apollo to which of the gods should he perform sacrifices and offer prayers in order to make the journey which he had in mind in accordance with the best and most honourable course of action and then, his mission honourably accomplished, to reach safety again. Apollo in response

---

61 Howland (2000: 878) remarks that the ascent – the journey from death to life, darkness to light, confusion to clarity – is by this time a well-established paradigm of education. He envisages Xenophon's journey of discovery in terms similar to those described here but with a different emphasis on the Socratic relationship: 'The *Anabasis* is also … the story of Xenophon's intellectual and moral growth. It traces the path of his personal appropriation of the wisdom of Socrates, whom Xenophon leaves behind in Athens' (876).

62 However, Dorion (2017: 41–5), evaluating Xenophon's numerous criticisms of the sophists in *Kynegetikos* and highlighting the contradiction with the positive representation of Prodikos in *Memorabilia*, concludes that the *Kynegetikos* material is not representative of his general attitude to the sophists. Thomas 2018 gives a possible explanation of the precise target (Plato) Xenophon had in mind in the hunting handbook.

told him the names of the gods to whom he should perform sacrifice. [7] After he had come back again, he recounted the oracle to Socrates, and when Socrates heard it, he strongly criticised Xenophon because he had not first asked whether it would be more fitting for him to make his way abroad or to remain at home, instead making his own judgement that he ought to go and enquiring only how he might make his way with the greatest honour. But since that was the question he had asked, he had to act, Socrates said, as the god had ordered him to do. (3.1.6–7)

The meeting with Socrates has long attracted the attention of readers and is, without doubt, a key episode in the work (there are in fact two meetings, one when Xenophon takes the letter from Proxenos to Socrates, the second when he returns from his trip to Delphi). We can note that only on one other occasion do the two appear together.[63] The episode has been used to support the view that Xenophon was a prominent pupil of Socrates and has been summoned as evidence for supporting separate claims that associations with Cyrus and Socrates respectively constituted the cause of his banishment from Athens. The meeting furthermore bolsters the reading of *Anabasis* as personal apologia: in consulting the philosopher, Xenophon shows prudence with regards to his plans, while his response reveals his immaturity at that juncture. And perhaps as well it furnishes some grounds for arguing that the author attempted to enhance the legacy of the expedition through a Socratic connection, or even that Socrates' concern about his joining Cyrus was used to obscure the circumstances behind his departure from the city in 401.[64] I suggest that at 3.1.5, and especially 3.1.7, the author expects us to appreciate that underlying the given summaries are dialogues between teacher and pupil such as the sort we read in *Memorabilia*. Their exclusion is one signal that this work is of a different type to conventional Socratic *logoi*.

With his taste for paradigm, we cannot be sure about the details of Xenophon's encounters with Socrates, but even if they did not happen in the ways reported, their literary value is not reduced, their prime function in the narrative being to situate Socrates at the heart of Xenophon's decision to join Cyrus. At once the philosophical aspect of the enterprise is underscored, and Socrates, by his concern, becomes a presence that will

---

63 Xenophon and Socrates: *Mem.* 1.3.8–13. In light of the following argument about Xenophon's state of maturity, it may be relevant that during this colourful exchange Socrates addresses him as Ὦ μῶρε (idiot/simpleton).
64 This last possibility was mooted in Chapter 1 pp. 39–40. On the concern of Socrates, Baragwanath (2016: 127) observes that his advice appears to arise from his 'own subjective experience: the future troubles he envisages for Xenophon parallel his own in relation to the Athenians'.

be linked to the trials his pupil is fated to undergo in the months ahead. Xenophon's failure to follow the advice given by Socrates emphasises his youthful character and at the same time serves to exonerate his teacher from any suspicion that it was under his influence that Xenophon left to join Cyrus.[65] The establishment of Xenophon's state of immaturity further adds to the dramatic tension in the story by casting into doubt his ability to undertake the daunting challenge of leadership: an early tactical mistake which draws the ire of Cheirisophos confirms the scale of the challenge facing the young Athenian (3.3.8–11). This also serves as a baseline against which cumulative successes in leading the men to safety can be measured; it is, indeed, the process of growth through the journey and its implicit link to the Socratic education which I believe Xenophon wishes to draw his readers' attention to.[66]

While, as we see in the final part of the chapter, it is chiefly through Xenophon's character's exemplifying of Socratic principles that the philosopher's image is held in the reader's mind, the author brings into play other means, too, to achieve this aim. Arguing that Socrates' presence has already been marked in the very opening lines of Book 3 through the use of *aporia*, Howland points out that the word is 'the hallmark of a philosophical encounter with Socrates'.[67] David Thomas shows we have multiple

---

65 The failure to do what he is told in itself allows for multiple readings. Wencis (1977: 47) thinks that it offers a glimpse of 'Xenophon's ability to make his own decisions, a foreshadowing of his potential for leadership'; Wood (1964: 35) sees a show of youthful carefreeness. Dorion (2018c) remarks that the question asked was sophistic, designed to extract a favourable answer. As such it is tempting to imagine the influence of Proxenos, who is integral to the question and with whom Xenophon may have had more involvement than is ordinarily assumed: as younger men they may have had an interest in Prodikos the Sophist (see Chapter 1 p. 33). Consequently, the frustration of Socrates is seen in potentially new light. I remark that Xenophon did not completely disregard Socrates: it is only after their second consultation, and in accordance with his explicit instruction, that he makes the sacrifice prescribed at Delphi.

66 Development of Xenophon's character: commits basic tactical error but responds with successful solution (3.3.8–20); early in *parabasis* fails to keep control of his men, twice suffering breakdowns of discipline (5.2.4, 16), but by the end he exerts complete influence over the men (7.1.22–3); the chance to earn greater honour and to enhance his reputation tempts him to accept the leadership at Sinope (6.1.20), in contrast to later at Byzantium, where he shows a keen grasp of geopolitics (7.1.25–31); at Kotyora sacrifices performed privately lead to public unrest (5.6.16), while later, at Kalpe Harbour, Xenophon has it announced that whoever wishes can be present at them (6.4.15, 20); by the close of the journey he has attained a high state of *autarkeia* (7.8).

67 Howland 2000: 880, and see Gray, note 13 above. For a discussion of the usage of *aporia* through the text, see Rood 2014. H-R (71) write that the aporia motif 'structures the account of the retreat, which is marked by an alternation between obstacles overcome and the emergence of new difficulties'. I suggested in the previous section that in one of his first appearances in the story, *aporia* was the outcome of 'Xenophon's' intervention (in the episode involving Greeks and barbarians at 2.5.35–42).

occasions where this term is used and where it is Xenophon who finds a way out of the *aporia*: 3.1.11, 3.1.12, 3.1.26, 4.3.8, 6.3.9, 6.6.11.[68] Its use and its dispelling by Xenophon lends the later narrative a Socratic texture and, in some sense, makes the book a story about solving problems.

Other ways of recalling are identifiable. At Kotyora, when Xenophon (along with the other generals) stands trial before the army (5.8.1), the body he has struggled to benefit, the fate of Socrates is implicitly recalled. While Xenophon overturns the charge by virtue of his defence speech, the episode does foreshadow the author's exile, also a form of physical exclusion from the *polis*. Then Xenophon's loyalty to the army, his repeated and selfless commitment to its safety (4.5.7–21, 7.6.11, 7.7.57–7.8.1), echoes Socrates' care for those around him (for example at *Anabasis* 3.1.5; Plutarch, *Alkibiades* 7.2–3).

Buzzetti discerns the presence of Socrates in *Anabasis* long before Xenophon's introduction into the story. The telling of the myth of Marsyas at Kelainai in Book 1 is said to be intended to evoke the philosopher and his own struggle with Apollo. A later interesting connection is drawn with the Mossynoikoi in Book 5, who are supposed to be stand-ins for the Socratics, and the end of Book 7 is argued to be 'a parody of the parody of the *Clouds*', which serves to confirm that Xenophon thinks of himself as a Socratic.[69] On the historical side, Marincola sees in the trial of Orontas in Book 1 a Socratic question-and-answer format;[70] on the same episode, it bears remarking that Cyrus's earlier forgiveness of Orontas is the sort of action often seen in Socratic contexts, where the intention is to strengthen a relationship. On Buzzetti's general treatment, while his emphasising of the Socratic connection is undoubtedly right, I am less persuaded by his concluding argument that *Anabasis* is above all an introduction to philosophy intended to encourage Xenophon's readers to study his four Socratic writings. Granted the text itself invites reflection on the presence and absence of the virtues and could therefore be said to lead to sources where these are considered as a matter of philosophy, I think a main intention of the author's is for readers to witness the practical benefit of the Socratic education and to see at close hand what it comprises.

A question worth considering before moving on is what Socrates' attitude would have been to Proxenos' letter had Cyrus not happened to be regarded as an enemy of Athens. On the surface, the answer seems plain enough; indeed, a passage in *Oikonomikos* (4.18, discussed below with caveat) implies he certainly would have approved of the initiative. Yet, with Alkibiades and Kritias in his mind, it would not be surprising if Socrates were circumspect about an ambitious associate becoming involved in the

---

68 Thomas, in press. My thanks to David Thomas for letting me have a copy of this piece prior to publication.
69 Buzzetti 2014: Marsyas (55–6), Mossynoikoi (201–4), *Clouds* (292–3).
70 Marincola 2017: 107.

high end of the political sphere, and one is inclined to think that the actions of Cyrus during his satrapal reign furnished grounds for anticipating what was to come (see for example *Hellenika* 1.5.1-7, 2.1.8-9, 2.1.13-14). While we can readily believe that the young men, Xenophon and Proxenos, had not yet the foresight to do so, Cyrus's form would not have escaped Socrates' notice. Even if we disregard the dark side of the prince's character and consider the ostensible purpose of the expedition (while the detail was not in the letter, it was probably known that the purported object was the Pisidians), it may be that that would have resulted in resistance from Socrates. In *Memorabilia* (3.5.26) he comments in seemingly favourable terms on renegade tribes in the King's territory who are able to do damage to it and preserve their own freedom (αὐτοὶ δὲ ζῆν ἐλεύθεροι). Xenophon joining an expedition whose purpose was to limit political freedom (*Anabasis* 1.2.1) may not in this light have earned Socrates' unqualified approval.

Still, as described in Xenophon's obituary of him, Cyrus displays several qualities one would see in a Socratic leader, among them, as remarked, φιλομαθής (love of learning) and μελετηρός (diligent in practice). More specifically, at *Oikonomikos* 4.18 Socrates declares that, 'if Cyrus had only lived, it seems that he would have proved an excellent ruler' (and see *Memorabilia* 4.1.2). The qualities which he has in mind include the loyalty shown to Cyrus at the time of greatest danger (*Oikonomikos* 4.19) and his own productive way of being in the world: a vignette is recalled whereby the prince meets Lysander in his garden and, to the stupefaction of the Spartan, explains that he has planted all the trees himself and that when in good health he never sits down to dinner 'without first working hard at some task of war or agriculture, or exerting myself somehow' (4.24). On the other hand, *Oikonomikos* is not primarily a historiographical text, and there are questions about its dramatic dating. If this is 399, as many consider, the overambitious and indeed morally suspect nature of Cyrus's expedition would by then have been known to Socrates, as would the reports of his earlier questionable conduct as satrap. This may be another case of the author's agenda and historical reality being in tension. On balance, in consideration of Cyrus's personal history and Socrates seeing that his enterprise was one based on ambition, I think he would not have offered encouragement to his pupil.

One final matter to ponder is Xenophon's persistent representing of Socrates in an oblique way – his refusal to admit him to a text that I argue is in notable measure about him. If he is indeed such an important influence in *Anabasis*, why doesn't the author situate him in the heart of the action? 'As Xenophon discussed the dilemma with the other commanders, he recalled Socrates once saying . . .'? One part of the answer is a wish not to press a link with the rebellion of Cyrus. As a parallel, I noted earlier Dorion's highlighting of places where Xenophon steps in to defend Socrates over what might be seen as undesirable links. Another reason resides in Xenophon's innovative literary approach. While all his Socratic works are closely linked, the product of a single agenda rather than offerings with a distinctive genesis, each adopts a different approach to the subject, employing diverse settings and characters. *Anabasis* as a novel treatment is consistent with this reading and is a marker of the author's innovative instinct. I think as well that the absence enables Xenophon's growth as a character and a leader to be seen as more organic. His association with Socrates has stirred his desire for wisdom and provided him with the intellectual capacity to learn to learn. Socrates cannot be everywhere at all times, but his teaching and its benefits can endure.

The Philosopher Armed

The elements compressed into 3.1.4–7 and discussed in terms of Socrates, Cyrus and his attempt on the throne and Proxenos' philosophical interest, together form the background against which the account is to be read. The young Athenian, a student of Socrates ambitious to learn from a prince of the Persian court, proceeds to set off across the Aegean on his personal *anabasis*: 'Xenophon, for his part, accordingly offered sacrifices to the gods whom Apollo had ordained, and set sail; he caught up with Proxenos and Cyrus in Sardis when they were about to depart along the road to the interior, and was introduced to Cyrus' (3.1.8).

Then, we are suddenly back in real narrative time, where Xenophon's world has changed dramatically. With the Greek high command decapitated, he finds himself in mortal peril in a land far from Greece. Awakening from a dream, he articulates his new reality, his linear analysis and persistent questioning of himself emphasising already his Socratic training:

> [13] ... Why am I lying down? The night is far advanced, and it is likely that along with the day will come the enemy. If we fall into the hands of the King, what is to stop us from having to behold all the most grievous sights imaginable, from suffering all the most terrible torments, and from dying in the course of humiliating maltreatment? [14] Nobody is making preparations or concerning themselves with how we may defend ourselves, but instead we are lying around as if it was possible to live in peace and quiet. Take me, for example: from what city am I expecting the general to come to take action here? What age am I waiting to reach? For I shall not grow any older if I hand myself over to the enemy today! (3.1.13–14)

So the student is impelled into action. Rising, he calls together the captains of his slain companion, Proxenos, and urges them to take their fate into their own hands. 'Let us not wait for other people to approach us and summon us to perform noble deeds – let us ourselves take the lead in rousing the others to reveal their worth' (3.1.24). Xenophon is appointed as the leader of this contingent and, following a conclave of generals, an assembly of the entire army is called. The young Athenian accoutres himself in his finest armour and prepares to address the soldiers. His character and learning are now to be tested in the crucible of war. Socrates is on trial again: success will be a testimony to the worth of his teaching, failure, another proof of his pernicious influence on the youth of Athens.

The Socratic Commander Again

In this final part of the chapter, the correlation between the performance of Xenophon's character on the retreat and key tenets of the Socratic education as elucidated in Xenophon's own works, principally *Memorabilia*, is further established. In Chapter 3, it was shown how 'Xenophon' on the retreat appears to closely follow Socrates' teaching on military leadership as recorded in *Memorabilia* 3.1–5, and it was argued that this guidance was a notable factor in his success. In what follows, I seek to show how both ethical aspects of Socrates' teaching and adoption of his intellectual rigour were still more valuable elements of Xenophon's leadership, which we can in turn see as paradigmatic for military leaders universally, but perhaps especially so for *strategoi* and *rhetores* in the particular social and political environment at Athens. In this sense, 'Xenophon' might serve as the embodiment of the Socratic education, *Anabasis* a one-stop reference site for the complete leader in the field.

But the work is not merely descriptive, offering a static model wherein the careful reader can delineate the attributes of the ideal leader. Analogous to *Memorabilia*, where we witness the process of learning through Socrates' questioning of aspiring leaders, who are revealed to lack the knowledge they require to rule effectively, in *Anabasis* the author presents us with an individual journey towards wisdom based on the interplay of Socratic virtue and intellectual acuity with lived experience (rather, say, than on the self-knowledge produced by concentrated reflection and articulated in set-piece conversations).[71] As I go on to show, the virtues on display are predominantly those which Xenophon associates with

---

71 In Chapter 3, in a discussion of the relationship between *Memorabilia* and *Anabasis*, I drew attention to Kaldellis' suggestion for reading *logoi–erga* in Eunapios' tribute to Xenophon as discourses about virtue versus accounts of virtuous actions (2015: 24). We can note too T-H's (11) statement that virtue in Xenophon's Socratic writings 'is not an abstract moral aspiration but a practical skill for succeeding in any and all spheres of life, from household management to the *polis*'.

Socrates, and although naturally those are not uniquely Socratic, together with features such as *elenchus* and argumentation from analogy they characterise a distinctively Socratic education.[72] Starting with the immature youth who disregards the advice of his teacher and embarks on his *anabasis* in a state of excess (as a reminder, he has with him an attendant, possibly several horses and, in addition to his regular panoply, splendid armaments), we arrive at the end in the company of a self-aware and highly capable leader. A further dimension in this philosophical model is the reader, for whom the narrative itself prompts consideration about the nature of the virtues and the consequences of their presence and absence (for example, 4.7.13–14: see Chapter 2 pp. 68–9). This is similar to what I argued for in the discussion of leadership didaxis in Chapter 3 p. 91: Xenophon, having presented a case where a leader is confronted with a problem/opportunity, leaves the reader to reflect for themselves on the decision taken.

In the homogeneous moral universe of Xenophon's writings, almost all of the virtues and concepts related to the Socratic *kaloskagathos* are identifiable. If the thesis that Xenophon's character in *Anabasis* is represented as an exemplary product of the Socratic education is to hold, then we should readily see on display the cardinal virtues of self-sufficiency (αὐτάρκεια), self-control (ἐγκράτεια), endurance (καρτερία) and piety (εὐσέβεια).[73] Apart from their role in a productive life, the importance of these is that they are the basis for the hard work of gaining true insight and wisdom, Xenophon's personal goal at the outset of the journey as I argue for it. There are, furthermore, elements of Socrates' dialectic – *elenchus*, analytical thinking, speech-making, use of analogy – which we would expect to see evidence of in Xenophon's activities. Then there are impediments to the just leader, such as *hubris* and excessive *philotimia*, which a Socratic

---

72 On the question of whether Xenophon distinguished between inherited and acquired qualities, see Due 1989: 147–52. Plato's *Meno* opens with a question about the origin of virtue. Pownall 2004: 29–37 offers an overview of the most important moral virtues for the educated elite of the fourth century, including, where they overlap, comparison of these in the hands of Plato (wisdom, courage, self-control, justice) and Xenophon.

73 It might be possible to form these virtues into a hierarchy. Dorion (2006: 97) regards self-control, endurance and self-sufficiency as paramount: 'this triad forms the core of Socratic ethics in Xenophon's writings'. Surprisingly, he does not include *Anabasis* in his list of other Xenophontic works – *Kyroupaideia, Hiero, Agesilaos, Lakedaimonion Politeia* – in which the author attributes to the lead protagonists (Cyrus, Simonides, Agesilaos and Lykourgos respectively) 'the same characteristics, virtues, and doctrines which Socrates incarnates in the four logoi Sokratikoi' (105). That said, it is true that *Anabasis* does not explicitly mention the prime virtues, a fact which understandably tempts writers to reject the text as having Socratic relevance; see also more recently Hobden (2020: 85–94), who does not include *Anabasis* in a treatment of 'Philosophy in action' in Xenophon's works.

should strive to avoid, and again we would expect to see evidence of this from 'Xenophon': the more so as other pupils of the master let him down in this regard and fuelled claims that he was guilty of corrupting the youth of Athens. While many of the episodes and instances looked at have already been examined or touched on in the book, I bring them together in this final part of the chapter in order to produce a substantive case for Xenophon's character conforming to that of an exemplary Socratic leader.

Self-Control

In *Memorabilia* (1.5.1) Xenophon posits self-control (ἐγκράτεια) as a virtue and invites his readers to judge for themselves whether Socrates helped men to attain this quality. He concludes his presentation with Socrates asking:

> [4] 'Should every man not hold self-control to be the foundation of all virtue, and first lay this foundation firmly in his soul? [5] For who without this can learn any good or practise it worthily? Or what man that is the slave of his pleasures is not in an evil plight body and soul alike?' ... [6] Such were his words; but his own self-control was shown yet more clearly by his deeds than by his words. (1.5.4–6)[74]

As I show, Xenophon, in *erga* more than *logoi*, displays this virtue throughout the retreat, enabling us to see up close its value for his character and leadership while underscoring how he has benefited from his association with Socrates. The pointed absence of this quality in others at critical junctures underlines the self-evident but easy to underappreciate fact that it is difficult both to master and to maintain. One of its characteristics is that we often only become aware of it when our expectation for the outcome from a given set of circumstances is not met.

Despite the adverse circumstances, and the responsibilities which he carries as a leader of the retreating army, Xenophon rarely if ever displays loss of self-control in tense or upsetting situations (for his predecessors' doing so, see 1.8.26, Cyrus, and 1.5.14, Klearchos). In several situations we see that he is angry but that he checks his temper so that he is not led into taking an action or decision that may subsequently prove to be detrimental to his own or the army's interests. We have an early example in the Kardouchian mountains, when the army comes under attack and the rear is left exposed, with the result that two of Xenophon's best men are killed:

---

74 For Socrates emphasising *enkrateia*, see further *Mem.* 2.1, 3.14, 4.5; *Apol.* 15–16. Due (1989: 197) sees it as an important theme in *Agesilaos* and *Kyroupaideia*. Bringing out the contrast with Plato, Dorion in a study of *sophia* in *Memorabilia* (2012) argues that *enkrateia* takes precedence over *sophia* in the moral thinking of Xenophon's Socrates.

> When they reached the end of the day's march, Xenophon, just as he was, went straight up to Cheirisophos and began to blame him because he had not waited and they had been forced to fight while fleeing. 'And now,' he said, 'two good and honourable men (δύο καλώ τε καὶ ἀγαθὼ ἄνδρε) are dead and we were unable either to recover their bodies or to bury them.' (4.1.19)

It is notable that he waits until they have arrived at their stopping place, when the temptation must have been to break off from the rear during the march to confront the Spartan. Despite his evident distress, he does not allow this episode to cloud his judgement, and immediately turns his attention to the challenge of moving forward through the enemy's territory (4.1.22).

On bodily appetites and desires, sex is not absent in *Anabasis*, but it is not notably coloured as a moral issue, and it does not touch Xenophon's character at all. Food and drink receive more coverage, though not as much as one might expect in a story where the acquisition of these is a constant factor. Taking an example late in the narrative, the Thracian warlord Seuthes invites the Greek generals and captains to a dinner, and much food and wine is available. Xenophon describes how one of the Greeks, an Arcadian by the name of Arystas, heaped bread and meat on his knees and did not interrupt his eating even when wine was served. Xenophon designs the scene so as to represent himself as being in a binary relation to Arystas. 'Give it to [Xenophon],' he has Arystas tell the wine-bearer, 'for he is already past the serious business and I am not yet' (7.3.24). In highlighting the gluttony of Arystas, he draws attention to his own moderation, and perhaps too alludes to the self-centredness of the Arcadians, who earlier in the march had left the army en masse to pursue their own interests.

Yet he subsequently reveals that he has allowed the wine to trump his control of his appetites. Climbing to his feet when the drinking horn (τὸ κέρας) came to him again ('already somewhat drunk', 7.3.29), he pledged himself and his companions to the service of Seuthes, boasting that they would bring great benefit to him:

> 'With their assistance, if the gods so will it, you shall obtain a great deal of land, some of it your ancestral domain recovered once more and some of it new land now acquired by you; and you shall also acquire many horses, and many men and beautiful women.' (7.3.31)

The moment seems benign enough, but in the later context of the strained relations between Xenophon and the army over suspicions about his dealings with Seuthes it assumes distinct significance. As argued in the previous chapter, the pledge may have angered some in the army and been a factor behind the serious accusation of corruption that was subsequently made against him (7.6.9–10). Using an instance of his own weakness at this penultimate juncture, Xenophon embeds a Socratic warning about the dangers of *akrasia* (incontinence) and underscores the fact that the practice of virtue requires constant attention.[75]

The consequences of poor self-control is a theme which runs through the work. Xenophon regularly underlines the indispensability of *enkrateia* by including incidents where its absence can carry serious implications for individuals and sometimes for the army as a whole: I examined the case of Cheirisophos losing control and striking the guide, who then fled, in Chapter 3 pp. 110–12.[76]

Self-Sufficiency

In *Apologia*, when Socrates is explaining to the gobsmacked jury at his trial why Apollo regarded him as by far the best of all human beings, the philosopher emphasises his self-sufficiency (αὐτάρκεια). *Autarkeia* might be described as a virtue which resides in a person's ability to know their own needs and to meet those needs by themselves.[77] As Socrates teaches, the resources each individual consumes vary, but it is incumbent on the aspiring *kaloskagathos* to reduce his dependence on material goods until such point as his requirements are minimal. This is put more eloquently by the philosopher in *Memorabilia*:

> 'You seem, Antiphon, to imagine that happiness consists in luxury and extravagance. But my belief is that to have no wants is divine; to

---

75 There may be an implied contrast between Xenophon's weakness in holding alcohol and Socrates' famous strength (Plato, *Symp.* 220a), a measure of the distance between master and pupil even at this advanced stage of the journey. Xenophon's inability to hold drink properly also invites a contrast to Cyrus the Younger. 'He [Cyrus] said he carried a sturdier heart than his brother, was more of a philosopher, and better versed in the wisdom of the Magi, and could drink and carry more wine than he' (Plutarch, *Artax.* 6). This apparent weakness is, though, consistent with the tenor of Book 7, which may have as its purpose a complicating of the leadership model Xenophon represents. I consider this further in the Conclusions.

76 The unguarded guide flees: 4.6.2–3. The negative consequences of weak self-control are highlighted throughout the author's works, and we see Spartans featuring regularly, for example in the *Hellenika* story of Alketas, whose infatuation with a boy led to a prisoner escape and the revolting of Oreos from Sparta (5.4.56–7).

77 In this discussion the focus is on the material world, but the concept is relevant in relation to knowledge as well, as I touch on below in the case of the army's governance. We can note that Socrates in *Memorabilia* is said to have 'relied on himself for his knowledge' of what was the better and the worse (4.8.11). Dorion (2006: 105) maintains that the Socrates of Plato had no concern with *autarkeia*, and see Edmunds 2018: 258.

have as few as possible comes next to the divine; and as that which is divine is supreme, so that which approaches nearest to its nature is nearest to the supreme.' (1.6.10)

Aside from references to Socrates' own self-sufficiency (1.2.1, 1.2.14, 4.8.11), the idea arises at other places in *Memorabilia*, for example through Socrates' conviction that a person should do all they can for themselves before turning to the gods for help (1.1.9). The virtue not surprisingly features in other of Xenophon's Socratic works. In *Oikonomikos*, Cyrus the Younger's agricultural activity earns him praise for his implicit meeting of his own needs (4.18–24); in the *Symposion*, Antisthenes explains that, thanks to Socrates, his wealth consists of his having no needs:

'I have enough so that I can eat until I reach a point where I no longer feel hungry and drink until I do not feel thirsty and have enough clothing so that when out of doors I do not feel the cold any more than my superlatively wealthy friend Kallias here.' (4.37)

With reference to the trial defence, in the later report by Diogenes Laertios (2.40–1) Socrates declined a speech prepared for him by Lysias in preference to his own as its fineness did not suit him, but the rejection also underscores his enduring *autarkeia*.

In *Anabasis* we witness how Xenophon's character progresses towards *autarkeia*. We have a convenient benchmark for this, in that we know he comes on the expedition well prepared for a military campaign, on the face of it a sign of *autarkeia*: he has money (inferred from the fact that Cyrus's first payment only comes four months after the start, 1.2.12), several horses (3.3.19), a shield-bearer (4.2.20) and perhaps two panoplies (3.2.7). But by the same token there is an undeniable hint of excess, a sense pressed when we learn that for an address to the army he adorns himself in splendid arms. His surplus at the beginning symbolises how far he is from being developed philosophically; the depletion of his resources over the journey, so that near the end he has hardly any money (7.8.2), no shield-bearer (4.2.20) and only one horse (7.8.2), nicely corresponds with the maturing of his character which has taken place on the retreat and marks his arrival at a state, in Socratic terms, closer to the divine.

Once he crosses back into Asia, an encounter with a soothsayer leads to a dramatic change in his material fortunes. Having made the sacrifices recommended by the soothsayer, on the way to Pergamum he comes to lead a plundering raid against a Persian noble and his family. At first look it seems we have a startling turn from virtue to banditry, but the successful action demonstrates Xenophon's ability to supply his own needs and those of his most trusted friends (7.8.11) when it is not opposed by the gods.

Moving to the level of the community, with the army in some sense functioning as a democratic polity, we encounter a question about the competence of its governance. Under Xenophon's guidance matters on the retreat are often decided by vote in an assembly of all the men, an indication of a degree of self-sufficiency in terms of knowledge. Although the question of Socrates' attitude to democracy is not straightforward, our picture of him from Xenophon suggests he would not have eagerly endorsed this, his view in principle being that those most knowledgeable of the issues in question should take the decisions, here the army's leadership of seven generals. Are we, then, looking at an area where 'Xenophon' is not behaving in exemplary Socratic fashion, whether through lack of wisdom or choice? Is he acting contrary to the spirit of *Memorabilia* 3.9.10 (see Chapter 3, opening quote) by marginalising the high command in favour of the *demos*? I do not think so, not least as the soldiers' lack of expertise is mitigated by astute management of the decision-making process. An instance at Trapezous, looked at in Chapter 3 (p. 118), illustrates this and imparts an underlying sense that the leadership is leading. As a reminder, the army has come together to discuss the remainder of the journey, and Xenophon is putting forward proposals about what they should do. Each is passed, up until he presents the one to have the roads repaired in case they need to proceed by land:

> At this the soldiers cried out that there was no need to go by road. As Xenophon perceived that they were being gripped by folly, he did not put anything to a vote on this topic but instead persuaded the cities to mend the roads voluntarily, saying that they would more quickly be rid of the army if the roads were made passable. (5.1.14)

We should take account as well of the fact that the soldiers did know about warfare and so in principle themselves had some competency in the field. I recall my earlier view that neither Xenophon nor Socrates was opposed to the idea of democracy in its original Hellenic form (Chapter 3 pp. 119–20), but to its evolved shape, which was disconnected from these roots and vulnerable to manipulation by political actors.

As he does with other virtues, Xenophon demonstrates the importance of *autarkeia* by showing what happens when it is not present or is put aside. Through Books 5–6 he carefully charts the negative impact of the army's moving away from the ideal of self-sufficiency which it had begun to cultivate on the march upcountry (see for example 1.5.1–3) and almost fully realised on the march down to the sea (3.2.27–8). At Harmene, a port in the vicinity of Sinope, he writes: 'As they seemed to be getting near to Greece, the question of how they might arrive home with something in hand now began to press on them even more than it had previously' (6.1.17). At Herakleia, further along the Black Sea coast, dissatisfied with the gifts of hospitality provided by that city, the men gather and decide themselves to demand more, a mark of their lacking in *sophia*. This ploy being unsuccessful, the Arcadians and Achaeans split away, believing they will fare better on their own (6.2.4–12). But in pursuing booty – the excess which has now become their goal – they lose coherence as a force and eventually are encircled and ground down by barbarians (6.3.2–9). It is only Xenophon's willingness and ability to relieve them that averts a disastrous fate.

The army's movement away on the geographical *parabasis* from the high state of *autarkeia* it had attained on the *katabasis* (see 2.1.6, 3.2.34–8, 3.4.17, 4.1.12–14) is thus shown to chart its disintegration as a successful community. Although it was to be reconstituted, dogged in Thrace by its singular concern for booty, the army never recovered the spirit that had enabled it to surmount the enormous challenges it faced on the retreat to the sea. Starting from the same condition of material excess as the main body (3.2.27–8), Xenophon's personal journey, as we have seen, has had a different trajectory. The lavishly equipped, somewhat naive young man whom we are introduced to on the banks of the Zapatas arrives at Lampsakos a wiser, leaner and more capable human being. As much as any other measure, this outcome brings into relief the value of his education.

Endurance

A close relationship between endurance (καρτερία) and self-control is apparent, both denoting forms of resistance.[78] One way of distinguishing them has *enkrateia* associated with the realm of desires and *karteria* with physical circumstances.[79] As endurance is a prominent feature of Socrates' representation both in terms of his lifestyle (*Memorabilia* 1.2.1, 1.6.2; Plato, *Symposion* 220a–d) and philosophy (*Memorabilia* 2.1.6), and given our backdrop is an arduous journey, we should be able to demonstrate remarkable instances of it in Xenophon's character's performance.

Sustained Physical Effort (3.4.46–9)

Xenophon leads a Greek contingent in a contest with the Persians to secure a height above their route. Responding to a charge by one of the soldiers in the midst of the operation that he has an unfair advantage over the others,

---

78 See Edmunds 2018: 253, who notes that the bases of the two words (κρατ- and καρτ-) are the same.
79 Due contends that Xenophon is not precise in his use of terms and that in *Kyroupaideia* 'he does not discern between ἐγκράτεια and καρτερία' (1989: 174). I suggest that the circumstances of the story in *Anabasis* serve to bring more into relief a distinction between the two terms.

Xenophon dismounts from his horse and, still with his cavalry breastplate on, takes the shield of his accuser and continues apace uphill.[80] The hostile reaction of the others compels the man to take back his shield, and Xenophon remounts; because of the steep terrain near the top, he again has to go on foot with his equipment, but in the race against the enemy he and his men get there first. This success shows the importance of physical fitness in any worldly enterprise, bearing out one of the arguments which Xenophon made in a speech at the Zapatas River for the likelihood of the Greeks prevailing over the Persians. 'What's more, our bodies are better able than theirs to bear cold and heat and hard work (πόνους φέρειν)' (3.1.23).[81]

Braving the Elements (4.4.11–12)

The harsh conditions of the Armenian winter made progress for the army slow and difficult. A heavy fall of snow one night covered the men where they slept; where it did not fall off it kept them warm, and there was a great reluctance to rise in the morning. Xenophon, however, got up lightly clad (γυμνός) and began to chop wood for fire. This action in turn encouraged others, who got to their feet and began to build fires. Tuplin tentatively suggests a link between this episode and Socrates' famed endurance in winter; in Plato's *Symposion* (220a–b) we hear how on campaign in freezing conditions he went about with just his cloak (ἱμάτιον).[82] We find a further potential allusion to the philosopher and his minimal attire shortly on in the march, where the dreadful effect of leather shoes freezing on the feet is described: 4.5.13. That fate would never come to Socrates, who was always barefoot (ἀνυπόδητος) as part of his conviction that by exposing himself continuously to the environment he would endure everything more easily (*Memorabilia* 1.6.6–7; and see *Symposion* 220b, where he made his way barefoot over ice more easily than the rest did in shoes). It bears notice that in the episode in the snow we have 'Xenophon' doing what Socrates does: inspiring others by his own example.

Not Ceasing from Labours (5.1.2)

We would expect the absence of endurance to be a regular motif in a laborious journey. We saw it in the case of the man whose struggle to carry his

---

80 Cavalrymen may have had heavier armour than hoplites: see H-R 176, and generally Lee 2007: 111–17.
81 On Xenophon's emphasising of the virtues of hard work in *Oikonomikos*, see Christ 2020: 85–97.
82 Tuplin 2003: 133 n.64. Diogenes (2.56) writes that Xenophon made Socrates his exact model (Σωκράτην ζηλώσας ἀκριβῶς), though in the present case 'Xenophon' outdoes his mentor by not having any cloak on him at all.

shield led him to cast about and blame Xenophon for his own comparative physical weakness, and again with the two soldiers in the snow, one of whom was unable to go on, while the other sought to avoid carrying him. In this case, where one man buries the other alive, lack of endurance equates with moral weakness (5.8.8–11). At the collective level we have several examples too. When supplies run out at Kalpe Harbour, the men become desperate to leave their shelter to raid the countryside despite the risks, but Xenophon himself tolerates the oppressive circumstances. Prior to this, at the end of the march down to the sea, the desire to avoid hardship manifests itself in an imagined state of physical inertia. In a sentiment strongly shared by the other soldiers, Leon of Thurii declares that he has had enough of toil and wishes to complete the journey home by sea, 'stretched out at my ease, like Odysseus' (ἐκταθεὶς ὥσπερ Ὀδυσσεὺς, 5.1.2). Only Xenophon, implicitly willing to go by land, has the foresight to appreciate the danger that might materialise by ruling this option out and, this time surreptitiously (by arranging for the cities along the coast to repair the roads: cf. above 4.4.11–12), ensures that the army (eventually) moves on.

Piety

In the genesis of the story, when Xenophon asked him for advice on whether he should go to meet Cyrus the Younger, Socrates, aware of the political sensitivities, referred his pupil to the oracle at Delphi. The importance of the matter induced him to defer to the gods, and his action in turn was an acknowledgement of the limits of his own wisdom. This may be at the heart of Xenophon's notion of piety (εὐσέβεια) as a virtue: human knowledge is limited – a fact symbolised by the gods – and recognition of this is critical in any form of endeavour. Socrates' later reaction to Xenophon's failure to ask the right question underlines his conventional piety: 'But since that was the question he had asked, he had to act, Socrates said, as the god had ordered him to' (3.1.7; see *Memorabilia* 1.1.2).[83]

Reflecting this conservative outlook, on the retreat Xenophon's character regularly consults the gods. In fact, hardly any course of action is undertaken without there first being an attempt to discern divine will, which is duly obeyed, with gratitude offered for successful outcomes. Throughout the march he sacrifices only to traditional deities.[84] The examples of piety I give in this section range across the retreat and beyond, so showing the constancy of Xenophon's reverence for the gods and the degree to which they are an

---

83 As Gray (1998: 99) puts it, Xenophon 'characterises Socrates as supremely wise and supremely pious, obeying the oracle in spite of his forebodings'.
84 Zeus Meilichios, whom he sacrifices to at the end, had been honoured by his family for at least a generation: 7.8.4. By strange deities (ἕτερα δὲ καινὰ δαιμόνια) Socrates' accusers meant non-Olympians (see *Apologia* 24). The sacrifice Xenophon makes to Zeus Meilichios at Ophryneion may be relevant to the Spartan campaign, but I am not sure.

enduring part of his everyday life. These examples emphasise the performance of ritual: there are many more occasions in which the lead character invokes or swears by a deity, or speaks of the consequences of impiety for others, for example of oath-breaking, 3.2.10, and arrogance, 6.3.18.

Seemingly complicating Xenophon's piety is the degree to which he uses religion to leverage his directing of the army. In the first two examples, I look at the intertwining of piety and leadership, but it should be said that attitudes towards the utility of religion in his time were less circumscribed than they became in successor cultures and societies. By his use of piety I mean that, much in the same way as democracy, Xenophon regarded religion as an effective way of influencing and maintaining control over a constituency. This is not to say he was not pious, but simply recognises that he saw religion could be beneficial in the exercise of leadership.

One further observation before turning to the examples is that none of the other principal leaders pays anything like the same amount of attention to the conduct of religious matters as Xenophon does. There are numerous occasions from Tarsus to the Zapatas River on which Klearchos might have sought divine guidance, yet in the narrative he does so only once (2.1.9). In contrast to Xenophon at Sinope, Cheirisophos apparently does not sacrifice to find out if it is in the soldiers' and his own interests to accept the sole command (6.1.32; cf. 6.1.31); nor does he sacrifice in the wake of his success (see *Hipparchikos* 1.1). It may not be coincidental that shortly afterwards we learn abruptly that his leadership was short-lived: '[Cheirisophos'] overall command was dissolved then and there on the sixth or seventh day from when he was elected' (6.2.12). I remark that unlike for the other Greek leaders, Xenophon does not supply an obituary for Cheirisophos. Cyrus does sacrifice before the crucial battle (1.8.15), but is not conspicuously pious through the march upcountry; Buzzetti indeed argues that he is impious.[85]

Xenophon's piety leads us therefore to think that it is a distinct ingredient of his success as well as being relevant to his defence of Socrates. In this latter regard there is surely an implied contrast between Xenophon's godliness and the alleged scandalous impiety of another pupil of Socrates, Alkibiades, who was said to have defaced the Hermes statues in Athens and profaned the Eleusinian Mysteries (Thucydides 6.27–8). One peculiarity concerning Xenophon's relationship with the gods raises itself at the end of the story, although, as I indicated in note 84, it may be explained by or bound up with the sacrifice at Ophryneion. This is Xenophon's apparent failure to consult the gods on the matter of his joining the Spartan campaign. I think in every other preceding case where a major decision involving his role was taken,

---

85 Buzzetti 2014: 10–13.

he did so. It may reflect the fact that within the *Anabasis* storyline he has not told us he made the decision to join Thibron.

Pledges by the Zapatas River (3.2.9) (and see also 4.3.8–13, Centrites River)

As Xenophon begins his momentous address to the army on the dawn following the seizure of their generals, somebody in the assembly sneezes, and at once the soldiers prostrate themselves to the god.[86] Xenophon acts to complement this devoutness by recommending that they 'should vow to this god [Zeus the Saviour] to perform a sacrifice for our safe delivery whenever we first arrive in friendly territory; and we should make a further vow to perform sacrifices to the other gods as well, to the best of our ability' (3.2.9). The army pledged this by a show of hands, and the solemn vows were made and the paean sung. Only 'when they had properly attended to the business of the gods' did Xenophon continue his address (for fulfilment of these vows, see 4.8.25).

Right at the beginning we see how Xenophon's piety is foregrounded and how it is set to be a dual-faceted feature of his leadership. Seizing on the moment of the sneeze, he declares it an omen from Zeus the Saviour, delivered at the point when the talk was of salvation. Before launching into his speech proper, he has thus skilfully framed his rhetoric against the backdrop of divine approval. (I note that this configuring of his leadership profile reflects that of Cyrus the Great in *Kyroupaideia*: see 1.5.6.)

Waiting for a Positive Sign from the Gods at Kalpe Harbour (6.4.12–22, 25)

The army has reunited at Kalpe Harbour on the Black Sea after a brief and unsuccessful period of division into three units. Xenophon recommends that they continue their onward journey on foot, which is urgent, as they have exhausted the supplies in their current location. He and the other generals offer sacrifice on this subject, but the signs are not propitious for the journey (6.4.13); the next day Xenophon offers sacrifice again, three times, but still the signs are not in their favour, and the soldiers become agitated, as their provisions have now run out (6.4.16). Xenophon therefore decides to sacrifice on the question of going out for provisions instead of the journey, but again the outcome is negative (6.4.17–19). Following this, the men, going hungry, keep coming to his tent, but 'he refused to lead them out unless appropriate sacred signs were forthcoming' (6.4.19).

---

86 A sneeze, as an involuntary action, was considered to be a divine signal. See also Plutarch, *Them.* 13.2, and Homer, *Od.* 17.541–8.

The next day he offers sacrifice and huge numbers press around, but once again there is disappointment. The victims having been exhausted, an ox is bought and sacrificed, yet there is no respite (6.4.22). At this stage, seeking to enhance his own standing if not to undermine Xenophon's, another of the generals arranges a foray from the harbour. However, the enemy rout the men who go out, with as many as 500 killed (6.4.23–4). Receiving news of the desperate situation, Xenophon takes an ox and after sacrificing, leads out to give aid (6.4.25). In this case he does not report the outcome of the sacrifice, from which we can infer it was probably a blood-sacrifice (*sphagia*), a different type to the one he had been performing and one likely to produce the desired result.[87]

The events at Kalpe Harbour emphasise 'Xenophon's' piety and underscore the power of religious ritual to determine a course of (in)action. Overall, he has insisted on waiting for the sign on five separate occasions, despite the increasingly fraught circumstances. The wider background to the events is worth noting. The soldiers are anxious to continue on the journey, as they fear there is a plan to found a colony at this site; Xenophon, though he may indeed be minded to found a city, is agreeable to going along with this desire to move on, subject to favourable sacrifices. As we just saw, over several days these persistently fail to be propitious, with the result that even with their provisions dangerously low the men will not venture out on their own for supplies. With one exception (6.4.22), Xenophon performs the sacrifices himself, and even though anyone who wishes can attend, his role provides a degree of control over the ritual: when and where it is performed, the question asked (his approach at 6.4.17 calls to mind the deftness he shows in putting his question about the expedition to the oracle at Delphi, 3.1.5–6) and reading the signs where others present do not have the ability to do so. This last encompasses a key Socratic lesson, namely that commanders should acquire a knowledge of all branches relevant to their profession, as we know Xenophon has done with divination (*Memorabilia* 4.1.2; see *Anabasis* 5.6.29).

Through the Troad and Aeolis (7.8)

At the end of the long journey, Xenophon's concern shifts from the army's welfare to his own. After two years campaigning, he is penniless and is now

---

[87] It is probable that the earlier sacrifices involved inspecting the entrails (*hiera*), whereas on this last occasion he inspected the flow of blood from the animal's neck (*sphagia*). The two types were typically used in different situations, the latter reserved as a pre-battle ritual. Although it must have been possible for blood-sacrifice to fail (see 6.5.8, where a 'first attempt' is mentioned), this form of divination was more likely than inspection of entrails to produce a positive outcome. On the subject of divination in *Anabasis*, see further Flower 2021.

even forced to sell his horse to fund his passage home (7.8.2, 6). While this unhappy outcome might seem to indicate some divine disapproval, for all the attention he has paid to the gods, the situation does fulfil the prediction made by a soothsayer at the outset of his adventure. As he left Ephesos, Xenophon saw an eagle perched on his right, screeching. The soothsayer who was escorting him interpreted this to mean that the journey he was setting out on would bring him into great danger, for the eagle when sitting is vulnerable: small birds can swarm it, or a snake can strike. Neither would there be much reward, as the eagle gets its food on the wing, not hunting by foot. But the journey would bring him glory and fame, the eagle being the bird of Zeus the King (6.1.23). Xenophon's sale of his horse – moreover his means of transport – out of need in Lampsakos can thus be read symbolically, ending his participation in the expedition and with that the period whereby there would be little reward. The fact that the Spartans, who he will join in a new campaign (7.8.6), promptly buy back the horse for him marks the extraordinary nature of the sale. As already described, shortly afterward, and after having made the sacrifices prescribed by Eukleides the soothsayer, he wins booty for himself and his close friends.

After the Expedition

Xenophon shows that his piety is of an enduring sort by relating in a flashforward how he later used his share from the sale of captives to honour pledges made by the army to both Apollo and Artemis. The offering he makes to Apollo at Delphi does not take place until his return to Greece (5.3.5; but see Diogenes 2.51), which was probably not until several years after the conclusion of the expedition, while he fulfils his pledge to Artemis (building a temple and altar) only after the Spartans have settled him in an estate in the Peloponnese. He literally inscribes evidence of his faithfulness at the Artemis temple in Skillous (5.4.13). These substantial gaps in time highlight the lasting quality of his piety. Noteworthy as well is the report in Diogenes (2.54) that later, when he received the news of the death of one of his sons in battle, Xenophon happened to be sacrificing. From the evidence of *Anabasis*, we can reasonably well say that the religious element is as significant as any other in the make-up of the Socratic leader.

Benefiting Others

In a certain sense, selflessness defines Xenophon's character on the retreat. While such a disposition might be said to be the instinct of any good commander, or exemplary citizen, his close alignment with the ideal nonetheless draws our attention. I underline that this quality (which, like a number of the others discussed, we could label in different ways)[88] is a vital ingredient in Xenophon's success as a leader, building as it does the willingness of the men to follow him and to work with each other to overcome their enemies. I highlight three occasions where his actions to benefit others seem deserving of mention.

Helping the Hungry and Exhausted (4.5.7–21)

While Cheirisophos and those in the front part of the army stay the night in villages they have reached, Xenophon and the rearguard remain out in the freezing cold. Some of the men perish, others suffer from frostbite, snow blindness and exhaustion, with a number unable to go on. When Xenophon cannot persuade these men to move, he and those who are able attack and scatter bandits who are preying on the tail. Earlier, learning that men were fainting from hunger, he himself sought out anything edible and drinkable from the baggage train and had that distributed.

Breaks Off to Rescue Arcadians Surrounded by Enemy (6.3.10–23)

Having taken the decision to leave the army and pursue booty on its own, the Arcadian contingent gets into serious trouble and is surrounded on a hill by Thracians. Xenophon learns of their predicament through intelligence-gathering and, halting the journey of his part of the army, sets out with the force to effect a rescue. The night-time tactics he deploys result in the Thracians breaking off their siege, leaving the way open for the Arcadians to make their way back to the coast, where the army reunites again.

Turns Back to Help the Soldiers in Thrace after Having Left the Army (7.6.11)

Xenophon has made clear that once the army has reached safety, his plan is to return to Athens. However, after he has left for home, he learns that the men are in difficulty, and he returns to Thrace to help (on this see further Chapter 4 n.17). This, and indeed the previous examples, furnish evidence for Seuthes' disapproving description of Xenophon as 'the

---

88 Touching briefly on other expressions, Due writes that Xenophon's Cyrus the Great's *philanthropy* is the key to his success, 'which consists in his ability to make people obey him willingly' (1989: 167). Sandridge (2012: 155) identifies 'paying attention' as a pervasive element in Xenophon's theory of leadership, a view registered by H-R (124), who talk of 'attentiveness', a quality that encompasses attention to one's own safety and also to the well-being of subordinates. Examples of this in *Anabasis* include 3.2.34 (implies Xenophon has enquired about provisions) and 7.3.12 (Xenophon is thinking of risk and future safety).

soldiers' friend' (φιλοστρατιώτης, 7.6.4). They also serve to reinforce the idea of Xenophon as a stand-in for Socrates. With the military context in mind, we remember the reports of how Socrates acted to save others in battle: at Potidaea he stood over Alkibiades and 'with the most conspicuous bravery saved him, armour and all' (Plutarch, *Alkibiades* 7.3); at Delium in one tradition he is said to have saved Xenophon when he had fallen off of his horse and the enemy were pressing the Athenians (Diogenes, *Socrates* 2.22).

Love of Learning

Thus [Socrates] would often say he was 'in love'; but clearly his heart was set not on those who were fair to outward view, but on those whose souls excelled in goodness. These excellent beings he recognised by their quickness to learn whatever subject they studied, ability to remember what they learned, and desire for every kind of knowledge on which depend good management of a household and estate and tactful dealing with men and affairs of men. (*Memorabilia* 4.1.2)

As an exemplary Socratic, we should be able to identify in 'Xenophon's' performance the qualities that constitute this character type. I take them in the order laid down in the passage.

Quickness to Learn

Almost immediately after they have crossed the Zapatas River, the army is pursued by the Persians. The Greek rear comes under severe pressure, and Xenophon, without consultation with Timasion or the other generals, leads out a contingent in response. The force is unable to overtake the enemy and is rendered more vulnerable for having detached from the main body (3.3.9–10). The action furthermore retarded the progress of the army at a critical phase of the retreat. Upon halting the march, Cheirisophos and the oldest of the generals blamed Xenophon, 'because he had gone away from the phalanx in pursuit and put himself in danger without being able to harm the enemy to any greater extent at all' (3.3.11). Xenophon acknowledges his error ('When [he] heard this, he freely said that the criticisms were correct', ἀκούσας δὲ Ξενοφῶν ἔλεγεν ὅτι ὀρθῶς αἰτιῷντο, 3.3.12), but goes on to point out that the episode has exposed their paramount need for cavalry and slingers. The measures he proposes to remedy this are adopted and, as a result, the army can fend off a sustained attack the following day.

On first reading, Xenophon's hastening off to pursue the enemy on foot could be taken as youthful rashness, and while there is an element of this, it may be more accurate to characterise it as tactical naivety, evidence of his inexperience in military matters. At the same time, his willingness to acknowledge the error and learn from the episode evidences a mind operating in a critical fashion. This capacity to learn quickly (ταχύ τε μανθάνειν) from mistakes, whether innate or acquired through education, is no less valuable than any set of learned tactics a commander might take away from a course in generalship and is a key trait of successful leadership (see also 3.2.38). The lesson is emphasised throughout the retreat by contrasting Xenophon's thoughtful responses to challenges with the unreflective and typically less effective actions of other leaders.

Ability to Remember What Was Learned

In giving us the backstory to his involvement in the expedition, Xenophon reveals how he was reprimanded by Socrates for not asking the oracle the question in the way he was supposed to (3.1.7). In the later course of the march, Xenophon's character makes further divine consultations about his participation, and on these occasions (6.2.15, 7.6.44) he formulates his questions as meaningful 'either/or' ones, just as Socrates had wanted when he sent him to Delphi.

In the context of leadership practice, we see recall when, out in Thrace on a raid, Xenophon dismounts his horse in order to lead the men on foot. 'The hoplites will run more quickly, and willingly, if I too am on foot when I lead them' (7.3.45). This action pointedly remembers the episode in the early phase of the retreat (detailed above) when Xenophon is chastised by one of the men for being on horseback while they were on foot (3.4.47).

Desire for the Knowledge on Which Good Management Depends

At a general level, this is evinced by Xenophon's motivation (as I have argued for it) for undertaking the journey with Cyrus the Younger. Within the expedition there are numerous examples where Xenophon is at the heart of episodes in which knowledge of subjects relevant to his command is sought and acquired. There is the cause of soldiers fainting on the march in Armenia (Xenophon 'did not recognize the condition they were suffering from', but discovers it from someone who was familiar with it, 4.5.7–8), and in the same book the village chief who provided instruction on managing horses in the snow ('[He] then explained to [Xenophon] that they should tie bags around the feet of the horses and draft animals when they were leading them through the snow, as without these bags they would sink down in it up to the belly', 4.5.36). This may be a particularly good example, as Xenophon knows about horses, and this demonstrates his recognition that even on a familiar subject his knowledge is limited.

Two further subjects of relevance worth noting are augury, a branch of knowledge not strongly associated with other leaders in *Anabasis*, and foreign language proficiency, a feature generally absent among the Greek leadership. Augury, as we saw in the previous section, was an important element within the operational sphere. For soldiers and officers alike, the sacred rituals tended to be experienced passively, though they were often in attendance at their performance. For his part, Xenophon engages actively, observing the process so that he himself continues to build his knowledge of it. Telling us once that their soothsayer interpreted a favourable outcome from a sacrifice that Xenophon himself had made, he remarks that Silenos 'knew that I am not ignorant on these matters, because I'm always present at the sacred rites' (5.6.29; see Diogenes 2.56). I highlighted above the benefit of this knowledge to his leadership; the fact that other leaders do not often sacrifice suggests that it may not have been a field they were competent in.

In Chapter 1, I wondered about Xenophon's knowledge of foreign languages and inferred from *Anabasis* that he was probably not proficient in any of the Near Eastern ones. However, he went on to spend five years more in Anatolia, so he might have acquired some capacity then. We should set this against the fact that there are barbarians in the story who know Greek; there is the Makronian peltast who is one of the Ten Thousand (4.8.4) and, notably, the Thracian warlord Seuthes (7.6.8). It may be curious in the Socratic context, and indeed the wider Hellenic one, that the subject receives little attention in Xenophon's works and is not prominent in historiography generally.

Tactful Dealing with Men

At Sinope, the men decide to choose a single ruler to lead them, and they approach Xenophon. Although their interest flatters him and he considers that the role would enhance his reputation and might enable him to be the cause of some good to the army, he pauses to reflect:

> [21] Thoughts of this type strengthened him in his desire to become commander-in-chief. But on the other hand whenever he reflected that for every human being it is unclear what the future will bring, and that for this reason there would be a danger of throwing away even the reputation he had already achieved, he was unclear which way to go. [22] And being at a loss, it seemed to him that it was best to consult the gods. (6.1.21–2)

The moment of introspection, the check on his desire and acknowledgement of the limits of his own wisdom, is classically Socratic. Xenophon now, as he had done before embarking on the journey, sacrificed to Zeus the King; the result being unfavourable, he duly decided not to accept the leadership, should he be elected.

In the meantime, the men had proposed him, but before they could vote he spoke out and declared that taking the role could be a source of serious trouble for all with the Spartans (6.1.26-8). When they still insisted, he then referred to the sacrifices he undertook, in light of which revelation the men decided to choose Cheirisophos (6.1.31-2). His handling of this episode – notably his evasion of a dangerous role and maintenance of honour in the eyes of the men – demonstrates his 'tactful dealing with men and affairs of men'. There are a couple of points on the leadership development theme to draw as well from the affair, firstly the observation that Xenophon deploys piety as instrument of last resort in a difficult situation. Secondly, his emergence as a mature leader is marked by his foreseeing that the motivation of the men – maximising their booty – meant that the role of sole commander would be based on a highly unstable platform. We also witness his resistance, by way of reflection on the human experience, to the natural temptation to accrue honour for himself.

Speech, **Elenchus,** *Analytical Thinking, Analogy*

As well as being morally good, Socrates was intellectually and verbally sharp, qualities that help to explain the fascination which he exerted over contemporaries. From the conversations recorded in the writings of the Socratics, certain modes of expression of his cerebral power stand out. While all of his students might not have the innate ability to develop these on their own, through cultivation of self-discipline and study of his method they could hope to grow their own capacity. Indeed, it is what we would expect to see in those who 'loved to learn'. Xenophon's own example in *Anabasis* serves again to guide and inspire learners.

Speech

In *Memorabilia, Oikonomikos* and *Symposion*, Xenophon perpetuates Socratic values by way of conversations initiated by or involving the philosopher. While Xenophon's character in *Anabasis* does do a lot of talking, it is not typically in the same way. Instead, we have much more speech-making than conversation. Nonetheless, the speeches can equally function as exemplary material, mostly but not always on the subject of leadership, and a commander's ability to speak effectively is a skill singled out for its importance by Socrates (*Memorabilia* 3.3.11). We can consider persuasive speeches by Xenophon, which play a key role in his success as a leader, as analogous to Socrates' conversations and appreciate this engagement as another way in which his character does the same sorts of things Socrates does in the course of his work.

Elenchus

Early in the retreat we get our first taste of Xenophon's dialectical skills through his engagement with Apollonides. A captain who spoke in the Boiotian dialect but who turned out to be Lydian, Apollonides asserted that the Greeks stood no chance of survival other than through entreating with the King. Xenophon proceeds to undermine his rationality through a series of questions that call to mind their prior experience with the King (3.1.26–9). On the Black Sea coast, again after a figure in the army challenges Xenophon personally, he defends himself by way of the question-and-answer format (5.8.9–11). We also have the method deployed in self-reflection, as at the crucial juncture in Mesopotamia after the generals are seized (3.1.13–14).

Analytical Thinking

Mirroring the approach of his teacher when improving a subject, 'Xenophon' engages with professional and personal challenges in a methodical way so that he can devise an optimal outcome. Time and again when a crisis envelops the retreating army and *aporia* descends, it is Xenophon who produces the solution. Rather than simply supplying this in the narrative, as we see, he builds it up so that the stages of resolution are transparent. This process draws attention to the disciplined cognitive action as much as to the solution itself.

A Problem Well Defined is Half Solved (4.6.5–13)

On the *katabasis*, the army finds that local tribes arrayed along a high ridge block its way forward. Cheirisophos, leading the army, is indecisive and waits until the rear has come up so that a discussion can take place. One of the generals, Kleanor, recommends they attack as soon as they have eaten, for delay, he argues wisely, will embolden the enemy. Xenophon then has his say, beginning by defining carefully what their objective is:

> 'If we really have to fight (εἰ μὲν ἀνάγκη ἐστὶ μάχεσθαι),[89] our preparations must be directed to fighting as effectively as possible. But if our objective is to get over the pass as easily as we can, it seems to me that what we have to consider is how to sustain the minimum number of wounds, and how to squander the minimum number of our men's lives.' (4.6.10)

He then proceeds to outline his proposed solution (including as part of it a lesson on how to use terrain to advantage, 4.6.11–13), which is successful.

---

89 H-R (158–9) remark on the use of *ananke* (necessity) with the present tense as marking the problem observed as universal. H-R 167 for motif of *anagke* as teacher.

The Sun Sets in the West and Rises in the East (5.7.5–11)

At Kotyora on the Black Sea coast, becoming aware of rising discord among the men on foot of a rumour that he was intending to deceive them and lead the army back east to the Phasis River, Xenophon quickly convenes an assembly and addresses the matter in a conspicuously logical way:

> 'You know, of course,' he said, 'where the sun rises and where it sets, and that if anyone intends to go to Greece, he must make his way toward the evening sun, but if anyone wants to go to the barbarians, he must make his way in the opposite direction, toward the dawn. So is there anyone who could possibly deceive you into believing that where the sun rises, it is there that it sets, and that where it sets, it is from there that it rises?' (5.7.6)

This is followed by references to north and south winds, so that by allusion to the cardinal compass points he exposes the fraudulent nature of the charge against him.

Argument from Analogy

This is another stock in trade of Socrates'. In a narrative marked by lengthy persuasive speeches and argued to have a Socratic texture, we should expect to come across instances of argumentation from analogy. One occurs when Xenophon is justifying his physical beating of a man who had sought to bury an exhausted soldier alive rather than continue to carry him as he had been ordered:

> [19] 'Nevertheless I don't hit anyone, [20] for I see that you are in fair weather. But when there is a storm and a great sea is getting up, don't you know that for a mere nod the boatswain gets angry with those in the bows and the helmsman gets angry with those in the stern? For in such circumstances even small mistakes are enough to bring the whole ship to ruin.' (5.8.19–20)

Impediments to Just Leadership: Ambition, Hubris, *Excessive* Philotimia

In looking for the model Socratic commander, it is not enough to find unequivocal evidence of the virtues and of physical and intellectual capability. Vices such as *hubris* and excessive love of honour go against the ethos of the *kaloskagathos* and endanger good leadership, so being able to resist them is as important as the positive embrace of the cardinal virtues.

This is illustrated in the wider Socratic world by the cases of Alkibiades and Kritias, whose personal failings on these counts undermine their successes. Before looking at Xenophon's character in *Anabasis*, it is worth considering how other commanders in the story measure up Socratically. I look at two individuals in the work marked as inclined towards philosophy (one internally, the other outside the text), but not among those regularly studied as leadership figures. The seizure of these men, Menon the Thessalian and Proxenos of Boiotian, at the Zapatas River results in obituaries that are strongly didactic in character.

Menon

In his obituary at 2.6 Xenophon figures Menon as about the worst individual ever born. He steals from friends, feels affection for no one and generally conducts himself through lies, injustice and slander. We get a flavour on the march when we see him persuade his men to cross the Euphrates before the rest of the army so that, 'without any danger to yourselves or any hard work' (οὔτε κινδυνεύσαντες οὔτε πονήσαντες, 1.4.14), they may secure honour and favour from Cyrus. This is in striking contrast to an earlier appearance which he makes in the literature – in a Platonic dialogue named after him, no less. In this, the dramatic date of which is around 402, Menon, a pupil of Gorgias the Sophist, is depicted in conversation with Socrates about the nature of virtue. 'Can you tell me, Socrates,' he asks in the opening of the dialogue, 'whether virtue can be taught, or is acquired by practice, not teaching? Or if neither by practice nor by learning, whether it comes to mankind by nature or in some other way?' (70a). In Xenophon's account, that putative contact proves not to have had any positive effect whatsoever. I am not sure what to make of this. It could certainly be an instance of Xenophon correcting Plato, although Plato does expose the influence of Gorgianic sophistry. Perhaps Menon's discrediting as an 'anti-Socrates' hints at someone who may actually have had the stature to be featured by another author in a central role in a rival Socratic (or Gorgianic) history of the march. I mean, it would not take too much imagination to invert the lens and see Menon as an outstanding young leader whose life was cut short by Persian treachery.

Proxenos

A pupil of Gorgias too, Proxenos is another figure in philosophical clothing whose performance on the retreat is of interest. More subtly painted than the irredeemable Menon, his qualities are nonetheless eclipsed by his overarching ambition. We learn that his training with Gorgias left him thinking he was already capable of acting as a commander, and that, by joining Cyrus, 'he would obtain a great name, great power and much wealth' (2.6.17). That desire for great things, which one thinks would almost certainly have been checked through association with Socrates, marks the different quality of his training and, ultimately, undermines his leadership effectiveness. Worth noting is the way Proxenos is introduced in his obituary, this (without the fees) being typical of how an interlocutor comes into contact with Socrates. 'From his earliest youth, Proxenos the Boiotian wanted to become a man capable of achieving great things, and because of this desire he paid fees to Gorgias the Leontine' (2.6.16).

'Xenophon'

Xenophon in *Anabasis* is shown to be resistant to, if not completely untouched by, the weaknesses which others in leadership roles display. We saw in the last chapter an incident on the Black Sea coast where his character is accused of *hubris*, and how he persuasively defended himself against this serious charge. Earlier in this one, we witnessed an instance whereby he checks the instinct for personal honour by declining to seek the army's leadership at Sinope. As a final mini case study, I look at a similar situation when the army is in Byzantium.

The extraordinary affair where the men seize the city but relent and hand it back to the Spartans as a result of Xenophon's intervention is one that has been looked at several times in this study. In Chapter 4, I suggested that Xenophon's actions here may have seriously piqued his fellow Athenians, who could have seen the seizure as a chance to benefit them. This time I look at it from his own perspective and highlight how it demonstrates his resistance to the temptation for power and glory.

Especially after the way they had been treated by the Spartans, one could understand the determination of the soldiers to take over the city, and on the face of it their belief that they would be successful seemed realistic. No longer a disparate collection of mercenaries as they had been at the beginning, the Ten Thousand had formed into a formidable force for all the trials they had undergone. One of the men, in terms we might suppose would have appealed to the late Proxenos, articulates the situation at the moment of taking the city: 'Now you can become a big man, Xenophon. You have a city, you have triremes, you have money, and you have all these men. Now, if you wanted, you would help us and we would make you great' (7.1.21).

Xenophon too must have felt tempted by the prospect of becoming a great man, yet he not only resists this but, in a rhetorical tour de force, persuades the men to put aside their own ambitions. This exemplary speech, underpinned by reason and moral righteousness, shows Xenophon the character in his finest hour. With no mention of the splendid panoply in which he addressed the men at the Zapatas, and now the commander of choice for the men because of his leadership on the retreat, the reader

Figure 5.1 View towards the sea from spur of Polut Dağı in the Black Sea Mountains. (Author)

cannot fail to be impressed as the soldiers ground their weapons in obedience, and then, following the speech, agree to substitute their arms for virtue. Xenophon's proposed dispatch to the Spartans, which emphasises the obedience of the men (7.1.31), calls to mind his earlier description of them as a community of *kaloikagathoi* (6.4.8), a potential that through his agency now seems to be in reach.

Conclusions
The Philosopher Unarmed

An enduring challenge for scholars of Xenophon's *Anabasis* has been to provide an explanation for the work. The difficulty stems from the multifaceted nature of the text, from uncertainty about the author's motivation for writing and from his binary orientation as historian–philosopher. The combined effect, as one writer put it, is that the work has resisted a commonly agreed-upon modern classification.[1] A central argument of this study is that, by way of his focus on leadership and apologia, Xenophon in *Anabasis* gives us his version of Socrates and demonstrates his worth through Xenophon the character's success. Viewed from another angle, the *Anabasis* project presents Socrates in an unfamiliar way and philosophical setting: the larger-than-life figure of the man himself, vocabulary, inward gaze and Athenian background that distinguish conventional Socratica are all virtually absent. Yet, as I have tried to show, the work is imbued with a philosophical tenor, mainly through 'Xenophon' in the story acting in a manner like Socrates and putting into action principles of Socrates' teaching. We are implicitly invited to compare the Socrates of Xenophon to other versions of the philosopher, and to other philosophers such as Gorgias, the teacher of Proxenos and Menon, and to judge for ourselves which is most beneficial to us, our friends and country.

As remarked in the Introduction, the philosophical aspect of the text does not rely only on the Socratic connection. The beginning of the work, which has attracted much interest for its absence of any indication of intent, casts it in a quite traditional philosophical frame: a young prince, treated unjustly by his older brother, and driven by his own ambition and sense of rectitude, seeks to unseat the new king and to rule instead of him. At the outset we are prompted to think about right and wrong and the nature of justice and power. The bare outline of the story provided furthermore makes

---

1 LaForse (2005: 2), who cites as well Tuplin's comment that the work is 'generically-speaking eccentric' (2003: 140). Tuplin elsewhere writes: 'it [*Anabasis*] is generally supposed to have had purposes less naive than its external appearance might suggest, even if descriptions of that purpose certainly differ' (1993: 13).

us want to learn more about the Persian actors, who we are already familiar with as historical figures. The journey ahead, grounded spatially and chronologically through the march record, holds out the promise of revealing insights into their world. That *Anabasis* is set in a historiographical form is undoubtedly one of the reasons why for modern readers it has remained separated from the author's other philosophical writings, yet in light of their prominence in the oeuvre, perhaps what we should have been looking for is evidence that the work is positively disconnected from the world of Socrates. By way of an answer to the question 'What is it?', I suggested *Anabasis* is primarily a 'Socratic history', with the philosopher's values perpetuated through the character of his student on the long retreat homeward of the Greeks who went upcountry with Cyrus the Younger.

The core themes of *Anabasis* are leadership and apologia. It is widely accepted that the oeuvre, too, is marked by interest in leadership and a strong apologetic *Tendenz*. On the latter, Xenophon's four Socratic works are concerned with defending and promoting the memory of the philosopher; *Agesilaos* and *Kynegetikos* are, at an important level, defences of their respective subjects, while in *Hellenika* the author devotes substantial space to the rule of the Thirty at Athens, subtly distancing himself in this from the harsher side of the regime. It is this subtlety, or low-intensity treatment of a pervasive theme, that defines Xenophon's writings and is a factor contributing to the generic elusiveness of some.

A further distinctive feature is a taste for didacticism, one which may well be attributable to the influence of Socrates. In some works, such as the technical treatises, the didactic element is explicit; in others it is less apparent but no less a force in the text. In *Anabasis*, for example, the subject of military leadership is pervasive, yet integrated into the storyline to such a degree that its presence might go unnoticed to those not interested in the topic; those who are interested benefit from a range of situational lessons and a thoughtful if implicit critique of leadership styles as well as occasional first-hand interjections by Xenophon as author and character. In addition, there is insight into the problem of how to manage mercenary soldiers, an issue topical in the early and middle parts of the fourth century. It is worth noting how the didactic aspect of the work interrelates with apologia. By having his own character embody a form of leadership predicated on the practical teaching and moral qualities found in his Socratic writings, Xenophon promotes the value of his training with the philosopher and implicitly defends him; at the same time, the exemplary words and deeds of his character reflect on the author and historical figure behind the book. We could also look at this inversely: apologetic episodes serve to highlight key qualities in Xenophon's leadership.

Besides these core ones, a number of the other themes and concerns that feature regularly in the author's works are present in *Anabasis*. These include, in varying degrees of force, horsemanship and the benefits of cavalry, panhellenism, identity, friendship, memorialisation of individuals and peoples, commentary on Spartan hegemony of Greece, moral and political philosophy, and the relations between men and gods. While the story of Cyrus's attempt on the Persian throne and its aftermath proved to be an ideal vehicle for Xenophon to express his wide-ranging interests, we should not doubt that the event itself matters. If it did not and we were uncoupled from history, what we would have is a second instalment, or a prototype, of *Kyroupaideia*, the experiences of the younger Cyrus now furnishing suitable material for the author. Instead, his interweaving of thematic strands with events on the ground enriches the text and makes it, as Wencis put it, 'pleasing and profitable to the reader'.[2]

* * *

Turning to key elements and arguments of the monograph, I started with an overview of modern scholarship on Xenophon, noting that recent decades have witnessed a major revival of interest in the author and his work. As a benchmark, Neal Wood in a paper in the 1960s summarised the prevailing view:

> Xenophon's reputation has suffered a very obvious decline since the last century. Although by the time Milton was guiding his nephews through the pages of the *Anabasis* and *Cyropaedia*, Xenophon was becoming staple English schoolboy fare, today few Americans, except for students of Greek, trouble to read him. Even the *Anabasis* seems to have lost much of its literary appeal.[3]

In Chapter 1, in establishing a personal context, I highlighted the fact that Xenophon grew up in a privileged milieu. His social class was defined by comparative wealth, connections at home and abroad, educational background and, arguably, by a conviction of superiority, of a right to lead and to take part in governing the state.[4] As I argued in Chapter 3, in part doubtless because of his experience on the retreat of the Ten Thousand, Xenophon came to hold a relatively positive view of democracy, even if his partiality towards it was rooted in pragmatism (cf. note 5, proto-democracy).

---

2 Wencis 1977: 44.
3 Wood 1964: 37.
4 The right to power: Thucydides 6.16; Xenophon, *PH* 2.1. Christ puts forward a thesis that a major concern of Xenophon's was to challenge elite assumptions about their right to power by virtue of wealth and birth, and to educate this class in such a way as to make them effective public leaders. This written advice is said to be analogous to the role of his Socrates, who converses with elite interlocutors (2020: 38–9).

He was connected in a meaningful way, probably as a student, with Socrates. His revelation that he consulted him on Proxenos' letter about Cyrus the Younger is indicative of a confidential relationship by 401 (see *Memorabilia* 1.1.6). Though the association of country 'gentleman' and city-bound thinker might seem a little incongruous, underlying the relationship were common pro-Spartan and anti-democracy instincts (I argue that because of his experiences on the long march, Xenophon's attitudes on both counts were certainly modified). This orientation was ultimately to place the men on the wrong side of the authorities. The outcome for both was, in a sense, the same, in that they were to be deprived of the homeland for which each demonstrated deep patriotism.[5]

Xenophon does not mention the decree of exile against him at Athens in any of his works except *Anabasis*. In so doing he prompts the reader to consider the text at some level with the decree in mind. Although the references to it appear late, in Book 7, the exile has been subtly alluded to earlier. In Book 3, Xenophon has a dream in which his father's house is set ablaze, thought by some to be an allusion to his exile, while before this in an analepsis Socrates expresses concern that were he to become linked to Cyrus the Younger, Xenophon would land himself in trouble with the Athenians, as Cyrus was reputed to have assisted the Lakedaimonians in their war against Athens. In terms of the decree itself, I suggested that the formal charge against him proceeded from the outcome Socrates had feared: Socrates is a paragon of wisdom in Xenophon's writings and was possessed with foresight, so it would be surprising if the author had him get this wrong. I suppose, then, that hearing of the philosopher's concern, the reader, for whom the event was fairly recent history, would quite naturally have called to mind the author's exile.

As to why Xenophon makes no overt comment on, let alone defence against, the charge(s), one reason could be that the circumstances at the time of writing made it awkward or unwise for him to do so. I suggested too that his silence reflects his attitude in some important way. It may be contempt for the charge, which I argue he answers obliquely through his depiction of his character's relations with others on the retreat, or it could be that his pointed detachment from the issue of his exile is meant to mark his obedience to the laws. Throughout his writings, Xenophon is at pains to

---

5 It is apparent from the excerpt in *Anabasis* (3.1.5) that neither Xenophon nor Socrates were seriously concerned about Cyrus the Younger's role in their city's defeat; that might be thought to put a question mark over their patriotism, but in my view it rather speaks to their attitude towards the current democracy (see *Mem.* 3.7.5–8, and e.g. Plato *Resp.* 558c, 488a–489d). In Chapter 3, I suggested that for both men 'proto-Hellenic democracy' wherein the weight of decisions was felt profoundly by those making them was an ideal.

CONCLUSIONS: THE PHILOSOPHER UNARMED   249

underline this Socratic precept: see, for instance, *Memorabilia* 4.4.1–4 for the conduct of the philosopher himself, then *Agesilaos* 1.36 and 7.2, where the king is praised for being obedient to Sparta's laws, and *Kynegetikos* 12.14, where a good education is said to teach 'a man to observe laws'.

I argued that the real or underlying cause of the exile was different to the formal one, being rather a desire by the democracy to uproot the opposition to it. In Chapter 4, I mooted a new reason for which the democracy could have identified Xenophon as unpatriotic, namely his failure to convert the storming of Byzantium by the Ten Thousand into political benefit for Athens. The words of the men themselves clearly indicate the potential of the event to serve as a dress-down for Sparta and maybe to be the beginning of better times for the democracy: 'Now you can become a big man, Xenophon. You have a city, you have triremes, you have money, and you have all these men. Now, if you wanted, you would help us and we would make you great' (7.1.21). With regards to the date of the decree, I argued that it was passed 'early', in 399, quite possibly while Xenophon was leading the Cyreans down the Asia Minor coast to join Thibron.

* * *

The second chapter of the book, focusing on historiographical and literary elements, posed several questions. For whom was *Anabasis* written? What are its precedents and influences? And what is it? As remarked, a generic description has proven to be elusive, notwithstanding the considerable attention in modern times. I have suggested a form of 'Socratic history': a narrative based on, and to a notable extent driven by, a historical event or period and in which the author embeds a reflection of the philosopher and promotes his values. The Socratic commander described in Chapters 3 and 5 evinces this idea, as the (mostly) chronologically ordered events of the retreat are relayed in significant part through his performance. In seeking to come to a more complete description of the term, I looked at the cases of *Hellenika* and *Kyroupaideia*, noting that each is successively further removed than *Anabasis* from the historical record. As a variant on the idea, we could as well assign the work to 'Socratic biography', Xenophon's character being a model Socratic officer.

I explored the author's use of exemplars and the extent of his apologetic agenda. Although not unique by any means in his paradigmatic expression, perhaps the degree to which he brought this to bear in *Anabasis* is unique. Likewise, his attention to apologetic matters is remarkable. I highlighted two particular features of this, the concept of literary apologia and the strategies the author uses to support it, and his defences respectively of the *hippeis* at Athens and of the mercenaries on the campaign. With regards to the Ten Thousand, I showed that Xenophon's representation of the men is subtle, and that in order to bring his own stance into full relief we need to put aside the filter of heroic retreat and consider afresh the detailed reports he provides. Noting that the subject of his personal apologia is considered in Chapter 4, I remarked that the preponderance of exempla in the text is an indicator that instruction is one of its defining features.

* * *

Leadership is a major interest throughout the Xenophontic corpus. In different works the author engages with the subject in contexts ranging from empires (*Kyroupaideia*) to the household (*Oikonomikos*). In *Anabasis* he summons his substantial experience of war to present a detailed picture of different military leaders and leadership styles in a non-fictional setting. In Chapter 3, I showed that his use of exemplars and focus on successive army leaders marked his presentation as instructive and that his didacticism worked on two levels. Firstly, there are 'situational lessons', wherein the behaviour of a commander in a challenging situation is observed. These usually conform to a 'problem–action–result' formula and are given force by their being situated in a real context, even if the detail provided may not correspond at all points to a real event.[6] In this way the narrative produces vivid images of recognisable historical figures in action, and by this colouring the author ensures that the experiences of good and bad practice which he wishes to share are all the more effectively digested. Xenophon will have been known for the range of his military experiences and his connections with high-level martial figures around the eastern Mediterranean, and many readers therefore will have approached *Anabasis* expecting to learn something on the subject and by the same token will have been alive to the nuances of his narrative. The instruction so provided, while not to be characterised as systematic, covers most of the key areas – discipline, motivation, divination, tactics, strategy, diplomacy, provisioning, financial management – that a military commander must aspire to be master of on campaign.

The second level of instruction is embedded in the structure of the narrative and revolves around an exposition of leadership styles. Three different ones are treated – Persian, Spartan and Athenian. Through successive focus on exponents of each, their distinctive features are brought out, as are their

---

[6] An assumption of the monograph is that in *Anabasis* Xenophon roots his exemplars in a real historical and geographical context. It bears remarking that that is a way in which the work does differ from his conventional Socratic writings. On the latter as a literary genre, Tuplin (2018: 606) writes: 'Socratic literature represents a special category inasmuch as, whatever the philosophical agenda (variable from author to author), the entire enterprise is founded upon fictive historical narrative.'

respective strengths and weaknesses, with the implied conclusion that the optimal is that which Xenophon himself represents. The death of all the preceding leaders furthermore symbolises the limits of their approaches. Notably, through his exposure of the weakness of Spartan rule beyond their own borders, Xenophon is commenting on Spartan hegemony of Greece and providing a lucid historical backdrop for its ultimate end. His own style, with its emphasis on key democratic elements such as voting and speech, was not just typically Athenian but had a decided Socratic flavour too. In the chapter, I demonstrated a close link between the philosopher's advice on generalship in *Memorabilia* (3.1–5) and Xenophon's character's leadership in *Anabasis*, while in Chapter 5, distinctively ethical aspects of the 'Socratic commander' were highlighted.

Although on occasion he offers direct instruction, either as narrator or character, in the main Xenophon's didacticism is realised indirectly, through example. A noteworthy feature of his teaching approach is his deft interrelating of events and leaders. For example, when Klearchos descends into muddy canals early on the retreat to help with the task of moving on, we recall Cyrus's reliance on orders alone when his wagons had become stuck in mud along the Euphrates; similarly, Klearchos' tight marshalling of the first days of the retreat, even with a truce in force, draws a sharp contrast with Cyrus's laxity on the final stage into Babylonia. Other leaders in the story, principally Tissaphernes, Proxenos and Menon, partially function to bring out qualities, and the lack thereof, in the main subjects (Cyrus, Klearchos, Cheirisophos and Xenophon).

* * *

The undeclared but unambiguous conclusion of Xenophon's exposition on leadership styles points to a further element of his agenda: personal apologia. In representing his character in the story as a successful leader in the Athenian mould, he is supplying a background for his fellow citizens to consider should they have had historic concerns about his activities at home and abroad. The particular emphasis on delineating his relations with Cyrus and Sparta respectively highlighted in Chapter 4 suggests a certain shaping of the narrative with these matters in mind. I argued, however, that Xenophon signals that the work is not intended to be read autobiographically by representing himself as an exemplar and, in *Hellenika*, attributing the work to another. The pseudonym functions as an advertisement by the author to his readers that he is in the story an ideal version of himself, a model Socratic officer. Nevertheless, any exemplary narrative about someone who also exists in the outside world (and in this case that someone is also the author) has a potentially apologetic effect, and Xenophon did not really stand in the way of this. Even if the presentation of the narrative/narrator produced some initial perplexity, few must have doubted that he was in fact the author, and the later *Hellenika* intervention is best seen as a corrective aimed at those who may have been a little too ready to take the exemplary performance of 'Xenophon' as his own.

His exile was not the only matter calling out for a defence. On the march a number of charges were levelled against him, several of these – deceiving the soldiers, *hubris*, corruption – especially damaging to a man whose writings promote virtuous conduct. That he should go to lengths to refute these and other character stains, such as mercenary service, is a reflection of the depth of his concern for his personal reputation. The discreditable actions of the mercenaries on the retreat were a further dimension that called for attention: Xenophon as a leader carried a degree of responsibility for their behaviour, and he was also personally implicated in suspect actions.

A caveat concerning Xenophon's personal apologia is that in the context of an ideal representation, what we might have is the impression of apologia rather than consciously designed apologetic episodes; a further one is the likely presence of literary apologia. I examined in Chapter 4 the possibility that some episodes betrayed a literary aspect, so that in effect Xenophon went beyond responding to an accusation by adapting his defence in order that personal qualities were brought out or reinforced. A potential example of this occurs in Book 5, where he defends himself against striking a soldier in the snow. I do not believe episodes featuring in the narrative are fictitious, but rather that, as with his leadership exempla, the author has selected events and adapted them so as to fit better with his writing aims. The putative presence of literary apologia reorientates us away from veiled personal defence and towards the themes of leadership didaxis and Socratic defence.

There are several other grounds for questioning personal apologia as a defining element of the work. One is less of a belief today in the existence of another account of the march to which Xenophon was supposed to be responding. A second, as Michael Flower points out, is the significant gap in time between the march and publication of the work.[7] Taking this up with the example mentioned above, it seems unlikely that, on foot of a dispute with a baggage carrier in the snow some thirty years before, Xenophon was prompted to justify in writing his action in striking the man (5.8). What I suggested we have in this case and others is, as outlined, the use of an apologetic situation to further the author's agenda. By using the accusation of *hubris*, Xenophon is showing that his character does not behave in this way, something he might wish to do to underline his Socratic credentials at the time of writing, or alternatively, as Tim Rood has argued, the

---

7 Flower 2012: 33.

CONCLUSIONS: THE PHILOSOPHER UNARMED 253

episode could speak to leadership didaxis by spotlighting the importance of discipline in command.[8]

* * *

Chapter 5 was mainly concerned with revealing ways in which Xenophon's character in *Anabasis* is Socratic. The Socratic stamp of his leadership was brought out in Chapter 3, where I related specific passages on military leadership in the *Memorabilia* with Xenophon's character's actions in *Anabasis*. Highlighting another level of linkage between the philosopher and his student, in this last chapter I showed that Xenophon's stature as a commander is undergirded by his embracing of key Socratic virtues. Examples from *Anabasis* illustrate how these ethical qualities drive his leadership and serve to enhance its effectiveness. That the value of Socrates seems self-evident to a modern audience is to overlook the fact that in contemporary writings he was sometimes a marginal, lampooned figure, and that he was just one of many practising philosophers at Athens. As Xenophon hints in his obituary of his friend Proxenos, who paid to study under the famous sophist Gorgias, there was no shortage of teachers offering ways to attain high ends. I suggest that we should see Socrates as a part of this competitive field and that a major part of Xenophon's mission in *Anabasis* is to advertise the value of his own teacher's education.[9]

In the chapter, in an approach similar to Gera's in her study of *Kyroupaideia*, I made the case for a pervasive Socratic presence in *Anabasis* by identifying traces of the philosopher in the narrative outside of his single appearance at 3.1.5–7.[10] Evidence for his presence was identified in two

---

8 Rood 2006: 55–6.
9 Socrates never took money, although as Xenophon hints disapprovingly at *Mem.* 1.2.60, some of the Socratics did: 'Some indeed, after getting from him [Socrates] a few trifles for nothing, became vendors of them for a great price to others, and showed none of his sympathy with the people, refusing to talk with those who had no money to give them.' Dorion (2017: 49) believes he has Aristippos in mind here. On the contemporary view of Socrates, it is worth stressing that the Socratics are giving us their story of the man – one whom the majority on a jury of 500 sentenced to death. This was a sophisticated citizenry schooled in democratic culture and steeled by the impact of war and civil war. For all the well-founded enthusiasm of Socrates' followers, clearly by no means everyone thought he was a suitable role model to emulate.
10 'Socrates in Persia': Gera 1993: 26–131. If with different approaches to the one I offer, Straussians have argued for a key Socratic presence in *Anabasis*. A prominent exponent of this view, Eric Buzzetti, argued in his monograph that the work is 'above all an introduction to philosophy' (2014: 296). See also Burns 2015, and Stauffer (2015: 306), who articulates a different dynamic to the one I have identified: 'But Strauss' interest, or at least his emphasis, proves to be focused not so much on the *influence* of Socrates on Xenophon as on the *difference* between the two men.'

interlinked aspects: the performance of Xenophon's character, and the enterprise of Xenophon the author. For the first, 'Xenophon' exemplifies Socratic principles throughout the retreat, so we are regularly reminded of the teacher's influence as the army negotiates its way through hostile terrains and tribal territories. I suggested too that Xenophon's character in the story could be seen as a stand-in for the philosopher, given that he often does the sorts of things which Socrates does in the traditional cycle of four. Even if, then, positive outcomes in the search for Socrates in *Anabasis* do not demonstrate that it is certainly a Socratic work, they do show that it is consistent with the philosopher's methods and principles.

The second aspect comprised the leadership and apologia themes. Leadership didaxis is a signature of Xenophon's Socrates, and the prominence of the theme in *Anabasis* lends the work a Socratic flavour. It bears mention that Xenophon as author is himself teaching, technically (primarily on the subject of military leadership) and on ethics, so becoming and being the continuation of Socrates. On the historic charges against him, we could and perhaps should consider that their foregrounding in *Memorabilia* is not so much a statement that the work is fundamentally an apologetic one as a signal that it is concerned with the question of the value of the philosopher and his teaching. I think this is equally true of *Anabasis*, and we should therefore consider it in this light. The configuration of the narrative, with Socrates and his pupil placed at its heart (3.1.4–7), prompts us to summon for ourselves the charge of corrupting the youth, while the same key consultation scene serves to put us in mind of the impiety charge: Socrates' decision to send his pupil to Delphi, and his acceptance of the oracle notwithstanding Xenophon had not asked the question he was supposed to, impinges directly on his attitude towards the gods. So, in contrast to their open advertisement in *Memorabilia*, in *Anabasis* the charges are encoded in the set piece which formally introduces both men into the narrative. I add that the high intensity of the events which form the backdrop to their meeting obliges the reader to pay special attention to the circumstances: by involving Proxenos, the pupil of Gorgias, and then Socrates, Xenophon frames his joining of Cyrus the Younger in philosophical terms. The meeting with Socrates marks their close relationship and reminds us too of relationships in *Memorabilia* whereby the philosopher counsels unwise young men.

The events which subsequently unfold on the march, now seen on one level against the backdrop of the charges, see Xenophon take on an unenviable leadership role, transforming his journey of self-development into a searching test of character. His performance from this juncture reflects on his training with Socrates, revealing how it is underpinned by the cardinal virtues of self-control, endurance and self-sufficiency. His outstanding success on the retreat amounts to a powerful testimony to the worth of his education and stands in counterpoint to the performances of others, such as Proxenos and Menon, who among other failings did not display restraint in personal ambition.[11] Xenophon's character's embracing of the full range of Socratic precepts and his resistance to excessive 'love of honour' and ambition complete a rounded image of a Socratic figure. Although for various reasons not particularly strong as evidence, Diogenes Laertios' summary in his biography of Xenophon is worth noting:

> He was a worthy man in general, particularly fond of horses and hunting, an able tactician as is clear from his writings, pious, fond of sacrificing, and an expert in augury from the victims; and he made Socrates his exact model (καὶ Σωκράτην ζηλώσας ἀκριβῶς). (*Lives* 2.56)

One of the obstacles to the Socratic reading may be the fact that the story is situated outside the physical world of Athens, the setting for *Apologia*, *Memorabilia*, *Symposion* and *Oikonomikos*, or, as Tuplin describes it, 'the Athenian decor – topographical, material, institutional, cultural – that defines the environment within which Socrates operates'.[12] Inside the text there are other ways to explain Xenophon's exemplary character and alternative ways to interpret the author's intentions in the book. There is the enduring personal apologia view, alluded to by Sarah Ferrario, who considers that Xenophon's self-representation may be connected with the construction of historiographic memory in the text ('the *character* Xenophon still behaves in ways that show him planning specifically for his own historical legacy');[13] so we could see the author substituting a picture of 'Xenophon', the redoubtable leader of a Greek army in distress, for the picture of Xenophon, the rash and some chose to say traitorous associate of Cyrus. Others see him critically reflecting on his youthful self, with the work pointing up the fact that 'he was, no less than many other young men who associated with Socrates, unmindful of his master's teachings'.[14] Then it could be said that what we have in terms of the Socratic element are merely markers intended to keep us in mind of Xenophon's connection as a younger man with the philosopher. Neither does one have to take Xenophon's character to be a literary exemplar. On the basis that leading Spartans such as Agesilaos would have known what

---

11 Elsewhere Xenophon is at pains to emphasise that it was only when they left Socrates' circle that some of his students became immoderate: see *Mem.* 1.2.24–5 on Kritias and Alkibiades. *Anabasis* is a published statement of his own lifelong fidelity.
12 Tuplin 2017: 345. See also Gera 1993: 26.
13 Ferrario 2014b: 281.
14 Humble 2018: 591; McCloskey 2021 follows a somewhat similar line.

Xenophon did on the retreat, and on the assumption that he was in some way invested with them, Powell envisages this audience as an external control: 'If the writer wished to be persuasive to Spartans ... his non-eulogistic picture of his own, and Spartan, leadership in 401–399 had to be largely correct.'[15]

* * *

That *Anabasis* continues to attract diverse responses from its readers is a measure of its richness, a case in point for Calvino's maxim that a classic is a book that never finishes saying what it has to say.[16] The interpretation offered here is incomplete, and another reader might take up one or more of its loose strands, or upend the whole by presenting a case for something entirely different. If the argument that *Anabasis* is a type of Socratic work is entertained, then a natural next step would be to explore in greater detail what the implications of this are for our understanding of Xenophon's oeuvre, for his standing as a literary figure and for our understanding of Socrates.

A peculiarity, one of the loose strands in the monograph, that I would like to finish with, is the apparent stumbling of Xenophon's character in Book 7. In saying this I do not mean to argue for a discontinuity between this book and the preceding ones as, in terms of Xenophon's leadership and the apologia theme (in 7, defending against corruption charges), that is not really the case. As remarked in Chapter 3, and highlighted in the closing of the final chapter, his extraordinary success at Byzantium for one speaks against it. The circumstances, too, if less dramatic, are in many ways more challenging.

Being a sort of sequel that follows the natural conclusion of the march at Byzantium, the first Greek city which the army came to, and entailing a rambling set of marches aimed at survival and securing booty, in Book 7 we see Xenophon depicted against these less flattering tones: carrying the sole burden of leadership from early on, he is also a more vulnerable individual.[17] As if aware of what lies ahead, he even signals a reluctance to enter the bleak Thracian landscape by his own declared wish at Chrysopolis

---

15 Powell 2020: 55.
16 Calvino 1999: 5. In the *ABC of Reading*, Ezra Pound (1961: 13–14) wrote: 'A classic is classic not because it conforms to certain structural rules, or fits certain definitions (of which its author had quite probably never heard). It is classic because of a certain eternal and irrepressible freshness.'
17 Though we had not discussed the topic during our long collaboration on LXA, David Thomas arrived at a similar view, laid out in his forthcoming book chapter, 'Xenophon's Woes in Thrace: The Very Model of a Modern Mercenary Commander?'.

(opposite Byzantium) to leave the army and return home. In the course of the winter, when, arguably even more so than in Book 4, we are never quite sure of where we are, we see that he has not after all attained the ideal of self-control. In one episode where he has taken too much wine, he vainly boasts that as his gift he will place the army in the service of his host, the Thracian paradynast Seuthes. This slip may have been a cause of provoking unrest among the men, mercenaries desperate for their pay, and they ultimately charge him with defrauding them and seek to have him stoned to death. As a fate reserved for bad commanders, stoning by the men is an upending of the stature Xenophon's character has acquired through the march. There is in addition a sense, present from the first appearance of Seuthes' messenger at the Bosphoros and reinforced through exchanges over the winter, that Xenophon has somehow given in to temptation and allowed himself to be a beneficiary of the barbarian's largesse, even if this did not turn out to be substantial. I do not take the lesson here to be a negative one – that the ideal state of *enkrateia* is unattainable, or that Xenophon failed to attain it – but that it is a continual struggle and requires continuous attention (*Memorabilia* 1.2.19–23). In this regard, the enigmatic final book seeks to cool the aura surrounding the figure whom we saw at its very beginning at the height of his power, saving the men, himself and the city through an exemplary speech on the Thracian Square in Byzantium. By his subsequent recording of his personal failings and the undignified atmosphere in which he is effectively forced to plead for his life, I suppose he wishes to underline the truth that virtue is hard earned and can only ever be maintained by constant attention.

Appendix A
Xenophon's Life and Times

Date	Xenophon	Events
431		Outbreak of war between Athenian Empire and Peloponnesian League led by Sparta
c.430	Xenophon born in Attica (but some put his birth earlier)	
410s	Becomes a follower of Socrates	Treaties between Sparta and Persia
410–405	Participates in later campaigns of Peloponnesian War	Cyrus the Younger sent to Asia Minor by the King; supports Sparta in war against Athens
404		Peloponnesian War ends; Spartan hegemony over Greece begins
404–403	Involved with anti-democratic side in civil war at Athens	Rule of the Thirty at Athens; restoration of democracy
401	Xenophon leaves Athens and joins Cyrus the Younger in Asia Minor	Democracy force marches against Eleusis

Expedition of Cyrus the Younger; the prince killed at Battle of Cunaxa

Retreat of the Ten Thousand begins; Tissaphernes seizes Greek generals at the Zapatas River |
| 400 | Defends himself against accusations of hubris and of secretly looking to found a colony

Forestalls seizure of Byzantium by the army

Leads the Greeks into service with the paradynast Seuthes in Thrace | The retreating mercenaries plunder and disrupt communities in eastern Anatolia and along the southern Black Sea coast |

XENOPHON'S LIFE AND TIMES

Date	Xenophon	Events
399	Xenophon accused of corruption in Thrace Enriched by raids on wealthy Persian nobleman Joins Spartan campaign against Persia in Asia Minor *Terminus post quem* for his exile from Athens	Sparta sends Thibron to Asia Minor to campaign against Persia; remnants of the Ten Thousand recruited Trial and death of Socrates at Athens
396		Expedition of Agesilaos against Persians in Asia Minor
395		Tissaphernes executed
395–387		Corinthian War: Athens and other Greek states, supported by Persia, attack Sparta
394	Returns to Greece with Agesilaos Present at Battle of Koroneia on victorious Spartan side; sometime thereafter given an estate near Olympia in the Peloponnese	Agesilaos recalled by Sparta to fight enemies
387/6	Xenophon at Skillous	Persia regains sovereignty over Greek cities of Asia Minor by way of Peace of Antalkidas; treaty re-establishes Spartan hegemony in Greece in weaker form
c.380	Xenophon at Skillous	Isokrates publishes *Panegyrikos*, his treatise on panhellenism
370s	Xenophon at Skillous Major writing phase begins (see Appendix B for works)	
371/0	Forced to leave estate	Battle of Leuktra: Sparta defeated by Thebes
360s	Finishes writing *Anabasis* and completes several other works, including *Memorabilia*	Theban hegemony of Greece
362	One of his sons, Gryllos, killed in skirmish prior to Battle of Mantineia	
c.350	Xenophon dies, location uncertain	

Appendix B
Xenophon's Writings

Name (abbreviation used in this book)	Estimated date of composition	OCT pages	Main subjects	Genre indication
Agesilaos (*Ages.*)	after 360	31	King Agesilaos, Sparta, leadership	Encomium, biography
Apologia (*Apol.*)	late 370s (but possibly much earlier)	9	Defence of Socrates: account of his defence speech at his trial in 399	Socratic work
Hellenika (*Hell.*)	Books 1–2.3.10: 380s? 2.3.11–7.5.27: early 350s	270	A history of Xenophon's times; relations between Sparta and Athens; empire and imperialist methods	(Socratic) history
Hiero (*Hie.*)	after 360	25	Political philosophy, statesmanship	Quasi-Socratic work
Hipparchikos (Cavalry Commander) (*Hipp.*)	mid-360s?	25	Cavalry, leadership	Handbook
Kynegetikos (On Hunting) (*Kyn.*)	390s	40	Instruction on hunting	Handbook
Kyrou Anabasis (*An.*)	late 370s–early 360s	250	Expedition of Cyrus the Younger, military leadership, apologia (principally for Xenophon and Socrates), Sparta	Socratic history
Kyroupaideia (Education of Cyrus) (*Kyr.*)	360–358	363	Cyrus the Great, Persia, leadership	Biography, political treatise, historical fiction, Socratic historiography

Name (abbreviation used in this book)	Estimated date of composition	OCT pages	Main subjects	Genre indication
Lakedaimonion Politeia (Spartan Constitution) (*Lak.*)	378–377?	23	Sparta	Politeia literature
Memorabilia (*Mem.*)	late 370s–early 360s	140	Defence of Socrates against trial charges, recollections of his teachings and personal virtue	Socratic work
Oikonomikos (*Oik.*)	mid-360s	68	Farming and household management advice involving Socrates	Socratic work
Peri Hippikes (On the Art of Horsemanship) (*PH*)	late 360s?	30	Instruction on horsemanship	Handbook
Poroi (Ways and Means) (*Por.*)	mid-350s	18	Political economy of Athens	Economic treatise
Symposion (*Symp.*)	mid-360s?	37	An evening with Socrates and his friends	Socratic work
Athenaion Politeia (Athenian Constitution) (*Ath. Pol.*) (This work was included amongst Xenophon's in antiquity but modern scholars do not think it is his)	424–423?	14	Athens, democracy	Political treatise

Bibliography

Aalders, G. 1953. 'Date and Intention of Xenophon's *Hiero*'. *Mnemosyne* 6: 208–15.
Adams, C. 2007. 'Introduction'. Pages 1–4 in *Travel, Geography and Culture in Ancient Greece, Egypt and the Near East*. Edited by C. Adams and J. Roy. Oxford.
Ahbel-Rappe, S. 2009. *Socrates: A Guide for the Perplexed*. London.
Ahbel-Rappe, S., and R. Kamtekar, eds. 2006. *A Companion to Socrates*. Oxford.
Aldrete, G. 2008. Review of K. Yellin, *Battle Exhortation: The Rhetoric of Combat Leadership*. *Bryn Mawr Classical Review* 2008.11.32.
Allan, R., I. de Jong and C. de Jonge. 2017. 'From *Enargeia* to Immersion: The Ancient Roots of a Modern Concept'. *Style* 51: 34–51.
Almagor, E. 2012. 'Ctesias and the Importance of His Writings Revisited'. *Electrum* 19: 9–40.
—— 2018. *Plutarch and the Persica*. Edinburgh.
Ambler, W., trans., preface. 2008. *Xenophon: The Anabasis of Cyrus*. Ithaca, NY.
Anderson, J. 1974. *Xenophon*. New York.
—— 1986. 'Xenophon at Corinth'. Pages 36–9 in *Corinthiaca: Studies in Honor of Darrell A. Amyx*. Edited by M. Del Chiaro. Colombia, MO.
Anson, E. 2010. 'The General's Pre-Battle Exhortation in Graeco-Roman Warfare'. *Greece and Rome* 57: 304–18.
Aslan, E. 2014. 'Bithynia Bölgesi Kalpe Limanı'. *Olba* 22: 129–53.
Aupperle, K. 1996. 'Crossroads – Spontaneous Organizational Reconfiguration: A Historical Example Based on Xenophon's Anabasis'. *Organization Science* 7: 445–60.
Azoulay, V. 2004. 'Exchange as Entrapment: Mercenary Xenophon?'. Pages 289–304 in *The Long March: Xenophon and the Ten Thousand*. Edited by R. Lane Fox. New Haven, CT.
Bacon, F. 1605. *The Advancement of Learning*. London.
Badian, E. 2004. 'Xenophon the Athenian'. Pages 33–53 in *Xenophon and His World*. Edited by C. Tuplin. Stuttgart.
Bandini, M., and L.-A. Dorion. 2000. *Xénophon: Mémorables. Tome I: Introduction générale. Livre 1*. Paris.
Baragwanath, E. 2008. *Motivation and Narrative in Herodotus*. Oxford.
—— 2016. 'Knowing Future Time in Xenophon's *Anabasis*'. Pages 119–39 in *Knowing Future Time in and through Greek Historiography*. Edited by A. Lianeri. Berlin.

Barber, G. 1935. *The Historian Ephorus*. Cambridge.
Bassett, S. 1999. 'The Death of Cyrus the Younger'. *Classical Quarterly* 49: 473–83.
—— 2001. 'The Enigma of Clearchus the Spartan'. *Ancient History Bulletin* 15: 1–13.
Bell, G. 1911. *Amurath to Amurath*. London.
Bigwood, J. 1978. 'Ctesias as Historian of the Persian Wars'. *Phoenix* 32: 19–41.
—— 1983. 'The Ancient Accounts of the Battle of Cunaxa'. *American Journal of Philology* 104: 340–57.
Blok, V. 2019. 'Xenophon's Philosophy of Management'. Pages 1–19 in *Handbook of Philosophy of Management. Handbooks in Philosophy Series*. Edited by C. Neesham and S. Segal. Cham.
Bonner, R. 1910. 'The Name "Ten Thousand"'. *Classical Philology* 5: 97–9.
Boucher, A. 1913. *L'Anabase de Xénophon (Retraite des dix mille), avec un commentaire historique et militaire*. Paris.
Bradley, P. 2010. 'Irony and the Narrator in Xenophon's *Anabasis*'. Pages 520–52 in *Xenophon*. Oxford Readings in Classical Studies. Edited by V. Gray. Oxford. (Originally published 2001. Pages 59–84 in *Essays in Honor of Gordon Williams: Twenty-Five Years at Yale*. Edited by E. Tylawsky and C. Weiss. New Haven, CT.)
—— 2011. 'Xenophon's *Anabasis*: Reading the End with Zeus the Merciful'. *Arethusa* 44: 279–310.
Breitenbach, H. 1950. *Historiographische Anschauungsformen Xenophons* (Diss., University of Basel). Freiburg.
—— 1967. 'Xenophon (6): Xenophon von Athen'. *Paulys Real-Encyclopädie* IX.A.2: 1567–1928, 1981/2–2051, 2502.
—— 1970. 'Hellenica Oxyrhynchia'. *Paulys Real-Encyclopädie* Supplement 12: 383–426.
Brennan, S. 2008. 'Chronological pointers in Xenophon's *Anabasis*'. *Bulletin of the Institute of Classical Studies* 51: 51–61.
—— 2011. *Apologia in Xenophon's Anabasis* (Diss., University of Exeter). Exeter.
—— 2012. 'Mind the Gap: A Snow Lacuna in Xenophon's *Anabasis*?'. Pages 307–39 in *Xenophon: Ethical Principles and Historical Enquiry*. Edited by F. Hobden and C. Tuplin. Leiden.
—— 2021a. 'Introduction'. Pages xiii–xlix in *The Landmark Xenophon's Anabasis*. Translated by D. Thomas. Edited by S. Brennan and D. Thomas. New York.
—— 2021b. 'The Chronology of the March'. Appendix Q in *The Landmark Xenophon's Anabasis*. Translated by D. Thomas. Edited by S. Brennan and D. Thomas. New York.
—— forthcoming. 'The March Record in Xenophon's *Anabasis*: Sources, Accuracy, Function'.
Briant, P., ed. 1995. *Dans les pas des Dix-Mille: Peuples et pays du Proche-Orient vus par un Grec*. Toulouse.
Brickhouse, T., and N. Smith, eds. 2000. *The Philosophy of Socrates*. Boulder, CO.
—— 2001. *The Trial and Execution of Socrates: Sources and Controversies*. Oxford.
Brock, R. 2004. 'Xenophon's Political Imagery'. Pages 247–57 in *Xenophon and His World*. Edited by C. Tuplin. Stuttgart.
Brunt, P. 1980. 'On Historical Fragments and Epitomes'. *Classical Quarterly* 30: 477–94.

Bugh, G. 1988. *The Horsemen of Athens*. Princeton.
Burgess, J. 2010. 'Travel Literature in Antiquity'. *The Literary Encyclopaedia*. http://www.litencyc.com/php/stopics.php?rec=true&UID=7224
Burnet, J. 1914. *Greek Philosophy. Part I: Thales to Plato*. London.
Burns, T., ed. 2015. *Brill's Companion to Leo Strauss' Writings on Classical Political Thought*. Leiden.
Buxton, R., ed. 2016. *Aspects of Leadership in Xenophon. Histos* Supplement 5.
—— 2017. 'Xenophon on Leadership: Commanders as Friends'. Pages 323–37 in *The Cambridge Companion to Xenophon*. Edited by M. Flower. Cambridge.
Buzzetti, E. 2008. 'Introduction'. Pages 1–35 in *Xenophon: The Anabasis of Cyrus*. Translated with preface by W. Ambler. Ithaca, NY.
—— 2014. *Xenophon the Socratic Prince: The Argument of the Anabasis of Cyrus*. New York.
Calvino, I. 1999. 'Xenophon's *Anabasis*'. Pages 19–23 in *Why Read the Classics?* Translated by M. McLaughlin (Italian original 1991). New York.
Cartledge, P. 1987. *Agesilaos and the Crisis of Sparta*. London.
—— 2002. *The Greeks: A Portrait of Self and Others*. 2nd ed. Oxford.
—— 2016. *Democracy: A Life*. New York.
—— 2021. 'Xenophon and Sparta'. Appendix B in *The Landmark Xenophon's Anabasis*. Translated by D. Thomas. Edited by S. Brennan and D. Thomas. New York.
Casson, L. 1974. *Travel in the Ancient World*. Toronto.
Cawkwell, G. 1972. 'Introduction'. Pages 9–48 in *Xenophon: The Persian Expedition*. Translated (1949) by R. Warner. London.
—— 1979. 'Introduction'. Pages 7–46 in *Xenophon: A History of My Times (Hellenica)*. Translated (1966) by R. Warner. London.
—— 2004. 'When, How and Why Did Xenophon Write the *Anabasis*?'. Pages 47–67 in *The Long March: Xenophon and the Ten Thousand*. Edited by R. Lane Fox. New Haven, CT.
Christ, M. 2020. *Xenophon and the Athenian Democracy: The Education of an Elite Citizenry*. Cambridge.
Cizek, A. 1975. 'From the Historical Truth to the Literary Convention: The Life of Cyrus the Great Viewed by Herodotus, Ctesias and Xenophon'. *L'Antiquité Classique* 44: 531–52.
Cook, J. 1983. *The Persian Empire*. London.
Cuniberti, G. 2011. 'The Direct Participation of Xenophon in the Narrated Events and His Historiographic Evaluation. *Hellenica* III-IV, 1: The Continued and Overturned *Anabasis*'. *Historiká* 1: 61–80.
Dalby, A. 1992. 'Greeks Abroad: Social Organisation and Food among the Ten Thousand'. *Journal of Hellenic Studies* 112: 16–30.
Dan, A. 2014. 'Xenophon's *Anabasis* and the Common Greek Mental Modelling of Spaces'. Pages 157–98 in *Features of Common Sense Geography: Implicit Knowledge Structures in Ancient Geographical Texts*. Edited by K. Geus and M. Thiering. Berlin.
Danzig, G. 2007. 'Xenophon's Wicked Persian, or What's Wrong with Tissaphernes? Xenophon's Views on Lying and Breaking Oaths'. Pages 27–50 in *Persian*

Responses: Political and Cultural Interaction with(in) the Achaemenid Empire. Edited by C. Tuplin. Swansea.

—— 2018. 'Introduction to the Comparative Study of Plato and Xenophon'. Pages 1–30 in *Plato and Xenophon: Comparative Studies.* Edited by G. Danzig, D. Johnson and D. Morrison. Leiden.

Danzig, G., D. Johnson and D. Morrison, eds. 2018. *Plato and Xenophon: Comparative Studies.* Leiden.

Defosse, P. 1968. 'À propos du début insolite des *Helléniques*'. *Revue belge de philologie et d'histoire* 46: 5–24.

Delebecque, É. 1947. 'Notes sur L'*Anabase*'. *Lettres d'humanité* 6: 41–101.

—— 1957. *Essai sur la vie de Xénophon.* Paris.

Denyer, N., ed., comm. 2019. *Plato and Xenophon: Apologies of Socrates.* Cambridge.

Diels, H., and W. Kranz, eds. 1960–1. *Die Fragmente der Vorsokratiker.* 10th ed. Berlin.

Diken, B. 2021. *The New Despotism: The Revival of an Old Monster.* London.

Dillery, J. 1995. *Xenophon and the History of His Times.* London.

—— 1998. 'Introduction'. Pages 1–40 in *Xenophon: Anabasis.* Translated by C. Brownson 1922, revised by J. Dillery, corrected reprint 2001. Cambridge, MA.

—— 2009. Review of J. Lee, *A Greek Army on the March: Soldiers and Survival in Xenophon's Anabasis. Polis* 26: 403–7.

—— 2017. 'Xenophon: The Small Works'. Pages 195–219 in *The Cambridge Companion to Xenophon.* Edited by M. Flower. Cambridge.

Dobski, B. 2009. 'Athenian Democracy Refounded: Xenophon's Political History in the *Hellenika*'. *Polis* 26: 316–38.

Dorion, L.-A. 2006. 'Xenophon's Socrates'. Pages 93–109 in *A Companion to Socrates.* Edited by S. Ahbel-Rappe and R. Kamtekar. Oxford.

—— 2012. 'The Nature and Status of *sophia* in the *Memorabilia*'. Pages 455–75 in *Xenophon: Ethical Principles and Historical Enquiry.* Edited by F. Hobden and C. Tuplin. Leiden.

—— 2017. 'Xenophon and Greek Philosophy'. Pages 37–56 in *The Cambridge Companion to Xenophon.* Edited by M. Flower. Cambridge.

—— 2018a. 'Comparative Exegesis and the Socratic Problem'. Pages 55–70 in *Plato and Xenophon: Comparative Studies.* Edited by G. Danzig, D. Johnson and D. Morrison. Leiden.

—— 2018b. 'Plato and Xenophon on the Different Reasons that Socrates Always Obeys the Law'. Pages 487–509 in *Plato and Xenophon: Comparative Studies.* Edited by G. Danzig, D. Johnson and D. Morrison. Leiden.

—— 2018c. 'The Reception of Xenophon's Meeting with Socrates'. *Conference on Anabases in Antiquity and Beyond.* Heraklion. 19–21 October.

Dover, K., ed., comm. 1968. *Aristophanes: Clouds.* Oxford.

—— 1974. *Greek Popular Morality in the Time of Plato and Aristotle.* Oxford.

Drucker, P. 1954. *The Practice of Management.* New York.

Due, B. 1989. *The Cyropaedia: Xenophon's Aims and Methods.* Aarhus.

Dunn, F., and T. Cole, eds. 1992. *Beginnings in Classical Literature.* Yale Classical Studies 29. Cambridge.

Dürrbach, F. 1893. 'L'Apologie de Xénophon dans l'*Anabase*'. *Revue des Études Grecques* 6: 343–86.

Edmunds, L. 2018. 'Xenophon's Triad of Socratic Virtues and the Poverty of Socrates'. Pages 252–76 in *Plato and Xenophon: Comparative Studies*. Edited by G. Danzig, D. Johnson and D. Morrison. Leiden.

Ehrhardt, C. 1994. 'Two Notes on Xenophon, Anabasis'. *Ancient History Bulletin* 8: 1–4.

Ellis, A. 2016. 'A Socratic History: Theology in Xenophon's Rewriting of Herodotus' Croesus *Logos*'. *Journal of Hellenic Studies* 136: 73–91.

Erbse, H. 2010. 'Xenophon's *Anabasis*'. Pages 476–501 in *Xenophon*. Oxford Readings in Classical Studies. Edited by V. Gray. Oxford (Translated from 1966 German original in *Gymnasium* 73: 485–505).

Fallis, L. 2015. 'Six Portraits of Political Ambition in Xenophon's *Memorabilia*'. *American Political Science Review* 109: 79–92.

Farrell, C. 2012. *Xenophon in Context: Advising Athens and Democracy* (Diss., King's College London). London.

Ferrario, S. 2012. 'Historical Agency and Self-Awareness in Xenophon's *Hellenica* and *Anabasis*'. Pages 341–76 in *Xenophon: Ethical Principles and Historical Enquiry*. Edited by F. Hobden and C. Tuplin. Leiden.

—— 2014a. *Historical Agency and the 'Great Man' in Classical Greece*. Cambridge.

—— 2014b. 'The Tools of Memory: Crafting Historical Legacy in Fourth-Century Greece'. Pages 263–88 in *Between Thucydides and Polybius: The Golden Age of Greek Historiography*. Edited by G. Parmeggiani. Cambridge, MA.

Finley, M. 2004. 'Athenian Demagogues'. Pages 163–84 in *Athenian Democracy*. Edited by P. Rhodes. Oxford. (Originally published in *Past and Present* 21: 3–24 [1962].)

Flower, M. 1994. *Theopompus of Chios: History and Rhetoric in the Fourth Century B.C.* Oxford.

—— 2000. 'From Simonides to Isocrates: The Fifth-Century Origins of Fourth-Century Panhellenism'. *Classical Antiquity* 19: 65–101.

—— 2012. *Xenophon's Anabasis or the Expedition of Cyrus*. Oxford.

—— 2017a. 'Introduction'. Pages 1–12 in *The Cambridge Companion to Xenophon*. Edited by M. Flower. Cambridge.

—— 2017b. 'Xenophon as a Historian'. Pages 301–22 in *The Cambridge Companion to Xenophon*. Edited by M. Flower. Cambridge.

—— 2021. *Divinity and Divining*. Appendix G in *The Landmark Xenophon's Anabasis*. Translated by D. Thomas. Edited by S. Brennan and D. Thomas. New York.

Gera, D. 1993. *Xenophon's Cyropaedia: Style, Genre, and Literary Technique*. Oxford.

—— 2007. 'Xenophon's Socrateses'. Pages 33–50 in *Socrates from Antiquity to the Enlightenment*. Edited by M. Trapp. Aldershot.

Gill, C. 1973. 'The Death of Socrates'. *Classical Quarterly* 23: 25–8.

Gish, D. 2009. 'Spartan Justice: The Conspiracy of Kinadon in Xenophon's *Hellenika*'. *Polis* 26: 339–69.

—— 2012. 'Defending *dēmokratia*: Athenian Justice and the Trial of the Arginusae Generals in Xenophon's *Hellenica*'. Pages 161–212 in *Xenophon: Ethical Principles and Historical Enquiry*. Edited by F. Hobden and C. Tuplin. Leiden.

—— 2016. Review of E. Buzzetti, *Xenophon the Socratic Prince: The Argument of the Anabasis of Cyrus*. *Polis* 33: 408–13.

Gish, D., and W. Ambler. 2009. 'The Political Thought of Xenophon'. *Polis* 26: 181–4.
Golden, M. 2015. *Children and Childhood in Classical Athens*. 2nd ed. Baltimore, MD.
Goldhill, S. 1998. 'The Seductions of the Gaze: Socrates and His Girlfriends'. Pages 105–24 in *Kosmos: Essays in Order, Conflict and Community in Classical Athens*. Edited by P. Cartledge, P. Millett and S. von Reden. Cambridge.
Grant, M. 1989. *The Classical Greeks*. London.
Gray, V. 1980. 'The Years 375 to 371 BC: A Case Study in the Reliability of Diodorus Siculus and Xenophon'. *Classical Quarterly* 30: 306–26.
—— 1986. 'Xenophon's *Hiero* and the Meeting of the Wise Man and Tyrant in Greek Literature'. *Classical Quarterly* 36: 115–23.
—— 1987. 'The Value of Diodorus Siculus for the Years 411–386 BC'. *Hermes* 115: 72–89.
—— 1989. 'Xenophon's Defence of Socrates: The Rhetorical Background to the Socratic Problem'. *Classical Quarterly* 39: 136–40.
—— 1991. 'Continuous History and Xenophon, *Hellenika* 1–2.3.10'. *American Journal of Philology* 112: 201–28.
—— 1998. *The Framing of Socrates: The Literary Interpretation of Xenophon's Memorabilia*. Stuttgart.
—— ed. 2007. *Xenophon on Government*. Cambridge.
—— 2010. 'Introduction'. Pages 1–28 in *Xenophon*. Oxford Readings in Classical Studies. Edited by V. Gray. Oxford.
—— 2011a. *Xenophon's Mirror of Princes: Reading the Reflections*. Oxford.
—— 2011b. 'Classical Greece'. Pages 1–36 in *Political Autobiographies and Memoirs in Antiquity*. Edited by G. Marasco. Leiden.
—— 2021. 'Panhellenism'. Appendix E in *The Landmark Xenophon's Anabasis*. Translated by D. Thomas. Edited by S. Brennan and D. Thomas. New York.
Grayson, C. 1975. 'Did Xenophon Intend to Write History?'. Pages 31–43 in *The Ancient Historian and His Materials: Essays in Honour of C. E. Stevens on His Seventieth Birthday*. Edited by B. Levick. Farnborough.
Green, P. 1994. 'Text and Context in the Matter of Xenophon's Exile'. Pages 215–27 in *Ventures into Greek History*. Edited by I. Worthington. Oxford.
Grethlein, J. 2012. 'Xenophon's *Anabasis* from Character to Narrator'. *Journal of Hellenic Studies* 132: 23–40.
—— 2013. *Experience and Teleology in Ancient Historiography: 'Futures Past' from Herodotus to Augustine*. Cambridge.
Griffith, G. 1935. *The Mercenaries of the Hellenistic World*. Cambridge.
Grote, G. 1850. *History of Greece*. Vol. 8 (of 12). London.
Günther, S. 2015. Review of E. Buzzetti, *Xenophon the Socratic Prince: The Argument of the Anabasis of Cyrus*. *Bryn Mawr Classical Review* 2015.04.19.
Guthrie, W. 1971. *Socrates*. Cambridge.
Gwynn, A. 1929. 'Xenophon and Sophaenetus'. *Classical Quarterly* 23: 39–40.
Hägg, T. 2012. *The Art of Biography in Antiquity*. Cambridge.
Hansen, M. 1983. 'The Athenian "Politicians", 403–322 B.C.'. *Greek, Roman, and Byzantine Studies* 24: 33–55.
Hanson, V. 1999. *The Other Greeks: The Family Farm and the Agrarian Roots of Western Civilization*. 2nd ed. Berkeley.

Harris, W. 1989. *Ancient Literacy*. Cambridge, MA.

Harman, R. 2016. 'Colonisation, *Nostos*, and the Foreign Environment in Xenophon's *Anabasis*'. Pages 133–50 in *The Routledge Handbook of Identity and Environment in the Classical and Medieval Worlds*. Edited by R. Kennedy and M. Jones-Lewis. New York.

Hayek, M., et al. 2014. 'In-Extremis Leadership of Sartrean Authenticity: Examples from Xenophon's *Anabasis*'. *Journal of Management History* 20: 292–310.

Haywood, J. 2016. 'Divine Narratives in Xenophon's *Anabasis*'. *Histos* 10: 85–110.

Henry, W. 1966. *Greek Historical Writing: A Historiographical Essay Based on Xenophon's Hellenica*. Chicago.

Herman, G. 1987. *Ritualised Friendship and the Greek City*. Cambridge.

Higgins, W. 1977. *Xenophon the Athenian: The Problem of the Individual and the Society of the Polis*. Albany, NY.

Hindley, C. 1994. 'Eros and Military Command in Xenophon'. *Classical Quarterly* 44: 347–66.

Hirsch, S. 1985. *The Friendship of the Barbarians: Xenophon and the Persian Empire*. Hanover, NH.

Hobden, F. 2005. 'Reading Xenophon's *Symposium*'. *Ramus* 34: 93–111.

—— 2017. 'Xenophon's Oeconomicus'. Pages 152–73 in *The Cambridge Companion to Xenophon*. Edited by M. Flower. Cambridge.

—— 2020. *Xenophon*. London.

—— 2021. 'Xenophon War Criminal? Or, Reading Anabasis Otherwise'. *Conference on Xenophon*. Liverpool. July.

Høeg, C. 1950. 'Χενοφῶντος Κύρου ἀνάβασις: Oeuvre anonyme ou pseudonyme ou orthonyme?'. *Classica et Mediaevalia* 11: 151–79.

Horn, R. 1935. 'The Last Three Books of Xenophon's *Anabasis*'. *Classical Weekly* 28: 156–9.

Hornblower, S. 1987. *Thucydides*. Baltimore, MD.

—— 2000. 'Sticks, Stones, and Spartans: The Sociology of Spartan Violence'. Pages 57–82 in *War and Violence in Ancient Greece*. Edited by H. van Wees. London.

—— 2004. '"This was Decided" (*edoxe tauta*): The Army as *polis* in Xenophon's *Anabasis* – and Elsewhere'. Pages 243–63 in *The Long March: Xenophon and the Ten Thousand*. Edited by R. Lane Fox. New Haven, CT.

—— 2011. *The Greek World 479–323 BC*. 4th ed. New York.

Hornblower, S., and A. Spawforth, eds. 2012. *Oxford Classical Dictionary*. 4th ed. Oxford.

Howland, J. 2000. 'Xenophon's Philosophic Odyssey: On the *Anabasis* and Plato's *Republic*'. *The American Political Science Review* 94: 875–89.

Huitink, L. 2019. '"There Was a River on Their Left-Hand Side": Xenophon's *Anabasis*, Arrival Scenes, Reflector Narrative and the Evolving Language of Greek Historiography'. Pages 185–226 in *Formes et fonctions des langues littéraires en Grèce ancienne. Entretiens sur l'Antiquité Classique* 65. Edited by A. Willi. Geneva.

Huitink, L., and T. Rood, eds., comm. 2019. *Xenophon Anabasis Book III*. Cambridge.

Humble, N. 1997. *Xenophon's View of Sparta: A Study of the Anabasis, Hellenica and Respublica Lacedaemoniorum* (Diss., McMaster University). Hamilton, ON.

—— 2002. 'The Limits of Biography: The Case of Xenophon'. Pages 66–87 in *Pleiades Setting: Essays for Pat Cronin on his 65th birthday*. Edited by K. Sidwell. Cork.

—— 2006. Review of R. Lane Fox (ed.), *The Long March: Xenophon and the Ten Thousand*. *The Classical Review* 56: 41–3.

—— 2011. 'Xenophon's *Anabasis*: Self and Other in Fourth-Century Greece'. Pages 14–31 in *Mediterranean Travels: Writing Self and Other from the Ancient World to Contemporary Society*. Edited by P. Crowley, N. Humble and S. Ross. Oxford.

—— 2018. 'Xenophon's Philosophical Approach to Writing: Socratic Elements in the Non-Socratic Works'. Pages 577–97 in *Socrates and the Socratic Dialogue*. Edited by A. Stavru and C. Moore. Leiden.

—— 2020. 'True History: Xenophon's *Agesilaos* and the Encomiastic Genre'. Pages 291–317 in *Xenophon and Sparta*. Edited by A. Powell and N. Richer. Swansea.

Humphreys, J., *et al.* 2011. 'Towards the Augmenting Role of Authenticity: Xenophon as Leadership Theorist'. *Management and Organizational History* 6: 183–207.

Huss, B. 1999. 'The Dancing Sokrates and the Laughing Xenophon, or the Other "Symposium"'. *American Journal of Philology* 120: 381–409.

Hyland, J. 2018. *Persian Interventions: The Achaemenid Empire, Athens, and Sparta, 450–386 BCE*. Baltimore, MD.

Jacoby, F., ed. 1923–58. *Die Fragmente der griechischen Historiker*. 15 vols. Berlin and Leiden.

Jansen, J. 2007. *After Empire: Xenophon's* Poroi *and the Reorientation of Athens' Political Economy* (Diss., University of Texas at Austin). Austin.

—— 2014. 'Greek Oath Breakers? The Arrest of the Generals in Xenophon's *Anabasis* Reexamined'. *Mnemosyne* 67: 122–30.

Johnson, D. 2005. 'Xenophon at His Most Socratic (*Memorabilia* 4.2)'. *Oxford Studies in Ancient Philosophy* 29: 39–73.

—— 2018. 'From Generals to Gluttony: *Memorabilia* Book 3'. Pages 481–99 in *Socrates and the Socratic Dialogue*. Edited by A. Stavru and C. Moore. Leiden.

—— 2021. *Xenophon's Socratic Works*. New York.

Kahn, C. 1996. *Plato and the Socratic Dialogue: The Philosophical Use of a Literary Form*. Cambridge.

Kaldellis, A. 2015. *Byzantine Readings of Ancient Historians: Texts in Translation, with Introductions and Notes*. New York.

Kassel, R., and C. Austin, eds. 1983–2001. *Poetae Comici Graeci*. Berlin.

Keaveney, A. 2012. 'The Trial of Orontas: Xenophon, Anabasis I, 6'. *L'Antiquité Classique* 81: 31–41.

Kelly, D. 1996. 'Oral Xenophon'. Pages 149–63 in *Voice into Text: Orality and Literacy in Ancient Greece*. Edited by I. Worthington. Leiden.

Kelly, G. 2008. *Ammianus Marcellinus: The Allusive Historian*. Cambridge.

Khansa, E. 2020. 'Conceptions of Justice in the 1001 Nights' [Webinar]. NYU Abu Dhabi Institute. 7 December.

King, D. 2013. 'Managing Uncertainty: Lessons from Xenophon's Retreat'. *Journal of Management History* 19: 377–93.

King, H. 2012. 'Anabasis'. *Scholarship, Research, and Creative Work at Bryn Mawr College*. October 142: 121–43.

Kingsbury, A. 1956. 'The Dramatic Techniques of Xenophon's "Anabasis"'. *Classical Weekly* 49: 161–4.

Knox, B. 1985. 'Books and Readers in the Greek World: From the Beginnings to Alexandria'. Pages 1–16 in *The Cambridge History of Classical Literature*. Vol. 1. Edited by P. Easterling and B. Knox. Cambridge.

Konstan, D. 2011. 'Socrates in Aristophanes' *Clouds*'. Pages 75–90 in *The Cambridge Companion to Socrates*. Edited by D. Morrison. Cambridge.

Körte, A. 1922. 'Die Tendenz von Xenophons Anabasis'. *Neue Jahrbücher für das klassische Altertum und für Pädagogik* 49: 15–24.

Krentz, P., ed., trans., comm. 1989. *Xenophon: Hellenika I–II.3.10*. Warminster.

—— 1995. *Xenophon: Hellenika II.3.11–IV.2.8*. Warminster.

Kroeker, R. 2009. 'Xenophon as a Critic of the Athenian Democracy'. *History of Political Thought* 30: 197–228.

Kuhrt, A. 2007. *The Persian Empire: A Corpus of Sources from the Achaemenid Period*. 2 vols. London.

—— 2010. 'Achaemenid Sources'. *Workshop on Communication, Language and Power in the Achaemenid Empire: The Correspondence of the Satrap Arshama*. Oxford. 20 November.

Lachance, G. 2018. 'Xenophon and the *Elenchos*: A Formal and Comparative Analysis'. Pages 165–83 in *Plato and Xenophon: Comparative Studies*. Edited by G. Danzig, D. Johnson and D. Morrison. Leiden.

LaForse, B. 2005. 'Xenophon's *Anabasis*: The First War Memoir'. *Syllecta Classica* 16: 1–30.

—— 2013. 'Praising Agesilaus: The Limits of Panhellenic Rhetoric'. *Ancient History Bulletin* 27: 29–48.

Lee, J. 2005. 'Xenophon's *Anabasis* and the Origins of Military Autobiography'. Pages 41–60 in *Arms and the Self: War, the Military, and Autobiographical Writing*. Edited by A. Vernon. Kent, OH.

—— 2007. *A Greek Army on the March: Soldiers and Survival in Xenophon's Anabasis*. Cambridge.

—— 2016a. 'Cyrus the Younger and Artaxerxes II, 401 BC: An Achaemenid Civil War Reconsidered'. Pages 103–21 in *Revolt and Resistance in the Ancient Classical World and the Near East*. Edited by J. Collins and J. Manning. Leiden.

—— 2016b. 'Tissaphernes and the Achaemenid Defense of Western Anatolia, 412–395 BC'. Pages 262–81 in *Circum Mare: Themes in Ancient Warfare*. Edited by J. Armstrong. Leiden.

—— 2017. 'Xenophon and His Times'. Pages 15–36 in *The Cambridge Companion to Xenophon*. Edited by M. Flower. Cambridge.

Lendle, O. 1995. *Kommentar zu Xenophons Anabasis*. Darmstadt.

Lenfant, D. 2004. *Ctésias de Cnide: La Perse. L'Inde. Autres fragments*. Paris.

—— 2014. 'Greek Monographs on the Persian World: The Fourth Century BCE and Its Innovations'. Pages 197–210 in *Between Thucydides and Polybius: The Golden Age of Greek Historiography*. Edited by G. Parmeggiani. Cambridge, MA.

Lesky, A. 1963. *Geschichte der griechischen Literatur*. 2nd ed. Bern.

Lipka, M. 2002. *Xenophon's Spartan Constitution: Introduction, Text, Commentary*. Berlin.

Llewellyn-Jones, L., and J. Robson. 2010. *Ctesias' History of Persia: Tales of the Orient*. London.
Long, A. 1988. 'Socrates in Hellenistic Philosophy'. *Classical Quarterly* 38: 150–71.
Luccioni, J. 1947. *Les idées politiques et sociales de Xénophon*. Paris.
Luce, T. 1997. *The Greek Historians*. London.
Ludwig, P. 2017. 'Xenophon as a Socratic Reader of Thucydides'. Pages 515–30 in *The Oxford Handbook of Thucydides*. Edited by R. Balot, S. Forsdyke and E. Foster. Oxford.
Luraghi, N. 2017. 'Xenophon's Place in Fourth-Century Greek Historiography'. Pages 84–100 in *The Cambridge Companion to Xenophon*. Edited by M. Flower. Cambridge.
McCloskey, B. 2017. 'Xenophon the Philosopher: *E Pluribus Plura*'. *American Journal of Philology* 138: 605–40.
—— 2021. 'Xenophon the Great and the Dialectic of the *Anabasis*'. *Conference on Xenophon*. Liverpool. July.
MacDowell, D. 2009. *Demosthenes the Orator*. Oxford.
McKechnie, P. 1989. *Outsiders in the Greek Cities in the Fourth Century BC*. London.
MacLaren, M. 1934. 'Xenophon and Themistogenes'. *Transactions and Proceedings of the American Philological Association* 65: 240–7.
—— 1979. 'A Supposed Lacuna at the Beginning of Xenophon's Hellenica'. *American Journal of Philology* 100: 228–38.
Macleod, M., ed., trans. 2008. *Xenophon: Apology and Memorabilia I*. Oxford.
Mahaffy, J. 1895. *A History of Classical Greek Literature*. Vol. 2, Part 2. London.
Manfredi, V. 1986. *La Strada dei Diecimila: Topografia e geografia dell'Oriente di Senofonte*. Milan.
Manning, S. 2018. 'A Prosopography of the Followers of Cyrus the Younger'. *Ancient History Bulletin* 32: 1–24.
Marasco, G., ed. 2011. *Political Autobiographies and Memoirs in Antiquity*. Leiden.
Marincola, J. 1999. 'Genre, Convention, and Innovation in Greco-Roman Historiography'. Pages 281–324 in *The Limits of Historiography: Genre and Narrative in Ancient Historical Texts*. Edited by C. Kraus. Leiden.
—— 2007. 'Introduction'. Pages 1–9 in *A Companion to Greek and Roman Historiography*. 2 vols. Edited by J. Marincola. Oxford.
—— 2014. 'Rethinking Isocrates and Historiography'. Pages 39–61 in *Between Thucydides and Polybius: The Golden Age of Greek Historiography*. Edited by G. Parmeggiani. Cambridge, MA.
—— 2017. 'Xenophon's *Anabasis* and *Hellenica*'. Pages 103–18 in *The Cambridge Companion to Xenophon*. Edited by M. Flower. Cambridge.
Marr, J., and P. Rhodes, eds., trans., comm. 2008. *The 'Old Oligarch': The Constitution of the Athenians Attributed to Xenophon*. Oxford.
Mesk, J. 1922/3. 'Die Tendenz der Xenophontischen Anabasis'. *Wiener Studien* 43: 136–46.
Meyer, J. 2008. 'Typology and Acoustic Strategies of Whistled Languages: Phonetic Comparison and Perceptual Cues of Whistled Vowels'. *Journal of the International Phonetic Association* 38: 69–94.

Millender, E. 2012. 'Spartan "Friendship" and Xenophon's Crafting of the *Anabasis*'. Pages 377–425 in *Xenophon: Ethical Principles and Historical Enquiry*. Edited by F. Hobden and C. Tuplin. Leiden.

—— 2020. 'Foxes at Home, Lions Abroad: Spartan Commanders in Xenophon's *Anabasis*.' Pages 223–59 in *Xenophon and Sparta*. Edited by A. Powell and N. Richer. Swansea.

Miller, H. 1984. 'The Practical and Economic Background to the Greek Mercenary Explosion'. *Greece and Rome* 31: 153–60.

Mitchell, L. 2008. 'Thucydides and the Monarch in Democracy'. *Polis* 25: 1–30.

Momigliano, A. 1990. *The Classical Foundations of Modern Historiography*. Berkeley.

—— 1993. *The Development of Greek Biography*. Expanded edition. Cambridge, MA.

Morrison, D. 2010. 'Xenophon's Socrates as Teacher'. Pages 195–227 in *Xenophon*. Oxford Readings in Classical Studies. Edited by V. Gray. Oxford. (Originally published 1994. Pages 181–208 in *The Socratic Movement*. Edited by P. Vander Waerdt. Ithaca, NY.)

—— ed. 2011. *The Cambridge Companion to Socrates*. Cambridge.

Most, G. 1989. 'The Stranger's Stratagem: Self-Disclosure and Self-Sufficiency in Greek Culture'. *Journal of Hellenic Studies* 109: 114–33.

Munn, M. 2000. *The School of History: Athens in the Age of Socrates*. Berkeley.

Muntz, C. 2017. *Diodorus Siculus and the World of the Late Roman Republic*. New York.

Nadon, C. 2001. *Xenophon's Prince: Republic and Empire in the Cyropaedia*. Berkeley.

Nails, D. 1995. *Agora, Academy, and the Conduct of Philosophy*. Dordrecht.

—— 2006. 'The Trial and Death of Socrates'. Pages 5–20 in *A Companion to Socrates*. Edited by S. Ahbel-Rappe and R. Kamtekar. Oxford.

Nee, L. 2009. 'The City on Trial: Socrates' Indictment of the Gentleman in Xenophon's *Oeconomicus*'. *Polis* 26: 246–70.

Nicolai, R. 2014. 'At the Boundary of Historiography: Xenophon and His Corpus'. Pages 63–87 in *Between Thucydides and Polybius: The Golden Age of Greek Historiography*. Edited by G. Parmeggiani. Cambridge, MA.

—— 2018. 'Genre, Models and Functions of Xenophon's *Anabasis* in Comparison with Isocrates' λόγοι'. *Trends in Classics* 10: 197–217.

Niebuhr, B. 1827. 'Über Xenophons Hellenika'. *Rheinisches Museum* 1: 194–8 (reprinted with postscript in 1828).

Ní-Mheallaigh, K. 2010. 'The Game of the Name: Onymity and the Contract of Reading in Lucian'. Pages 121–32 in *Lucian of Samosata: Greek Writer and Roman Citizen*. Edited by F. Mestre and P. Gómez. Barcelona.

Nussbaum, G. 1967. *The Ten Thousand: A Study in Social Organisation and Action in Xenophon's Anabasis*. Leiden.

Ober, J. 2011. 'Socrates and Democratic Athens'. Pages 138–78 in *The Cambridge Companion to Socrates*. Edited by D. Morrison. Cambridge.

Occhipinti, E. 2016. *The Hellenica Oxyrhynchia and Historiography: New Research Perspectives*. Leiden.

Ogden, D. 2002. *Magic, Witchcraft, and Ghosts in the Greek and Roman Worlds: A Sourcebook*. Oxford.

Pangle, T. 2018. *The Socratic Way of Life: Xenophon's Memorabilia*. Chicago.

—— 2020. *Socrates Founding Political Philosophy in Xenophon's Economist, Symposium, and Apology*. Chicago.
Parke, H. 1933. *Greek Mercenary Soldiers: From the Earliest Times to the Battle of Ipsus*. Oxford.
Parmeggiani, G. 2011. *Eforo di Cuma: Studi di storiografia greca*. Bologna.
—— ed. 2014. *Between Thucydides and Polybius: The Golden Age of Greek Historiography*. Cambridge, MA.
Pelling, C. 2013. 'Xenophon's and Caesar's Third-Person Narratives – or Are They?'. Pages 39–73 in *The Author's Voice in Classical and Late Antiquity*. Edited by A. Marmodoro and J. Hill. Oxford.
Pernot, L. 2008. *A l'école des anciens: Professeurs, élèves et étudiants*. Paris.
Pitcher, L. 2012. 'Themistogenes of Syracuse (108)'. *Brill's New Jacoby (online)*. Edited by I. Worthington. http://dx.doi.org/10.1163/1873-5363_bnj_a108
Pomeroy, S. 1994. *Xenophon: Oeconomicus. A Social and Historical Commentary*. Oxford.
Pound, E. 1961. *ABC of Reading*. London.
Powell, A. 2020. '"One Little *skytale*": Xenophon, Truth-Telling in His Major Works, and Spartan Imperialism'. Pages 1–63 in *Xenophon and Sparta*. Edited by A. Powell and N. Richer. Swansea.
Powell, A., and N. Richer. 2020. 'Introductions and Acknowledgements'. Pages ix–xv in *Xenophon and Sparta*. Edited by A. Powell and N. Richer. Swansea.
Pownall, F. 2004. *Lessons from the Past: The Moral Use of History in Fourth-Century Prose*. Ann Arbor, MI.
Prentice, W. 1947. 'Themistogenes of Syracuse an Error of a Copyist'. *American Journal of Philology* 68: 73–7.
Pritchard, D. 2018. 'The Horsemen of Classical Athens: Some Considerations on Their Recruitment and Social Background'. *Athenaeum* 106: 439–53.
Purves, A. 2010. *Space and Time in Ancient Greek Narrative*. New York.
Rahn, P. 1971. 'Xenophon's Developing Historiography'. *Transactions and Proceedings of the American Philological Association* 102: 497–508.
—— 1981. 'The Date of Xenophon's Exile'. Pages 103–19 in *Classical Contributions: Studies in Honour of Michael Francis McGregor*. Edited by G. Shrimpton and D. McCargar. New York.
Redfield, J. 1995. 'Homo Domesticus'. Pages 153–83 in *The Greeks*. Edited by J.-P. Vernant. Translated by C. Lambert and T. Fagan. Chicago.
—— 2018a. 'The Origins of the Socratic Dialogue: Plato, Xenophon, and the Others'. Pages 125–38 in *Socrates and the Socratic Dialogue*. Edited by A. Stavru and C. Moore. Leiden.
—— 2018b. 'Xenophon and the Socratics'. Pages 115–27 in *Plato and Xenophon: Comparative Studies*. Edited by G. Danzig, D. Johnson and D. Morrison. Leiden.
Reichel, M. 2007. 'Xenophon als Biograph'. Pages 25–44 in *Die griechische Biographie in hellenistischer Zeit*. Edited by M. Erler and S. Schorn. Berlin.
Rhodes, P. 1981. *A Commentary on the Aristotelian Athenaion Politeia*. Oxford.
—— ed. 2004. *Athenian Democracy*. Oxford.
Roisman, J. 1985–8. 'Klearchos in Xenophon's *Anabasis*'. *Scripta Classica* 8–9: 30–52.

—— 1988. 'Anaxibios and Xenophon's *Anabasis*'. *Ancient History Bulletin* 2: 80–7.
Rood, T. 2004a. 'Panhellenism and Self-Presentation: Xenophon's Speeches'. Pages 305–29 in *The Long March: Xenophon and the Ten Thousand*. Edited by R. Lane Fox. New Haven, CT.
—— 2004b. 'Xenophon and Diodorus: Continuing Thucydides'. Pages 341–95 in *Xenophon and His World*. Edited by C. Tuplin. Stuttgart.
—— 2005. 'Introduction'. Pages vii–xxxiv in *Xenophon: The Expedition of Cyrus*. Translated by R. Waterfield. Oxford.
—— 2006. 'Advice and Advisers in Xenophon's *Anabasis*'. Pages 47–61 in *Advice and Its Rhetoric in Greece and Rome*. Edited by D. Spencer and E. Theodorakopoulos. Bari.
—— 2010. 'Xenophon's Parasangs'. *Journal of Hellenic Studies* 130: 51–66.
—— 2012. 'A Delightful Retreat: Xenophon and the Picturesque'. Pages 89–121 in *Xenophon: Ethical Principles and Historical Enquiry*. Edited by F. Hobden and C. Tuplin. Leiden.
—— 2013. 'Redeeming Xenophon: Historiographical Reception and the Transhistorical'. *Classical Receptions Journal* 5: 199–211.
—— 2014. 'Space and Landscape in Xenophon's *Anabasis*'. Pages 63–93 in *Space, Place, and Landscape in Ancient Greek Literature and Culture*. Edited by K. Gilhuly and N. Worman. Cambridge.
—— 2015. 'Political Thought in Xenophon: Straussian Readings of the *Anabasis*'. *Polis* 32: 143–65.
—— 2017. 'Xenophon's Narrative Style'. Pages 263–78 in *The Cambridge Companion to Xenophon*. Edited by M. Flower. Cambridge.
Rood, T., and M. Tamiolaki, eds. In press. *Xenophon's Anabasis and Its Reception*. Berlin.
Rop, J. 2019. *Greek Military Service in the Ancient East, 401–330 BCE*. Cambridge.
Rossetti, L. 2011. *Le dialogue Socratique*. Paris
Rowe, C., and G. Boys-Stones, eds. 2013. *The Circle of Socrates: Readings in the First-Generation Socratics*. Indianapolis.
Roy, J. 1967. 'The Mercenaries of Cyrus'. *Historia* 16: 287–323.
—— 2004. 'The Ambitions of a Mercenary'. Pages 264–88 in *The Long March: Xenophon and the Ten Thousand*. Edited by R. Lane Fox. New Haven, CT.
—— 2007. 'Xenophon's *Anabasis* as a Traveller's Memoir'. Pages 66–77 in *Travel, Geography and Culture in Ancient Greece, Egypt and the Near East*. Edited by C. Adams and J. Roy. Oxford.
Russell, B. 1946. *History of Western Philosophy*. London.
Sabbah, G. 2003. 'Ammianus Marcellinus'. Pages 43–84 in *Greek and Roman Historiography in Late Antiquity: Fourth to Sixth century A.D.* Edited by G. Marasco. Leiden.
Sandbach, F. 1985. 'Plato and the Socratic Work of Xenophon'. Pages 478–97 in *The Cambridge History of Classical Literature*. Vol. 1. Edited by P. Easterling and B. Knox. Cambridge.
Sandridge, N. 2012. *Loving Humanity, Learning, and Being Honored: The Foundations of Leadership in Xenophon's Education of Cyrus*. Cambridge, MA.
Sato, N. 2008. 'A Religious and Political Trial: Another Aspect of Anytos' Prosecution of Socrates'. *KODAI: Journal of Ancient History* 15: 25–40.

Schachner, A., and H. Sağlamtimur. 2008. 'Xenophons Überquerung des Kentrites: ein archäologischer Nachtrag'. *Istanbuler Mitteilungen* 58: 411–17.
Schwartz, E. 1889. 'Quellenuntersuchungen zur griechischen Geschichte'. *Rheinisches Museum* 44: 104–26, 161–93. (Republished in *Gesammelte Schriften* 2 (1956): 136–74.)
Scott, M. 2010. *Delphi and Olympia: The Spatial Politics of Panhellenism in the Archaic and Classical Periods*. Cambridge.
Seager, R. 2001. 'Xenophon and the Athenian Democratic Ideology'. *Classical Quarterly* 51: 385–97.
Sebell, D. 2021. *Xenophon's Socratic Education: Reason, Religion, and the Limits of Politics*. Philadelphia, PA.
Smith, N. 2018. 'Aristotle on Socrates'. Pages 601–22 in *Socrates and the Socratic Dialogue*. Edited by A. Stavru and C. Moore. Leiden.
Spaulding, O. 1937. *Pen and Sword in Greece and Rome*. Princeton.
Spence, I. 1993. *The Cavalry of Classical Greece: A Social and Military History with Particular Reference to Athens*. Oxford.
Stadter, P. 2007. 'Biography and History'. Pages 528–40 in *A Companion to Greek and Roman Historiography*. Vol. 2. Edited by J. Marincola. Oxford.
Stauffer, D. 2015. 'The Difference between Socrates and Xenophon in Leo Strauss' Account of Xenophon's *Anabasis*'. Pages 305–13 in *Brill's Companion to Leo Strauss' Writings on Classical Political Thought*. Edited by T. Burns. Leiden.
Stavru, A. 2018. 'Socrates' Physiognomy: Plato and Xenophon in Comparison'. Pages 208–51 in *Plato and Xenophon: Comparative Studies*. Edited by G. Danzig, D. Johnson and D. Morrison. Leiden.
Stokes, M. 2012. 'Three Defences of Socrates: Relative Chronology, Politics and Religion'. Pages 243–67 in *Xenophon: Ethical Principles and Historical Enquiry*. Edited by F. Hobden and C. Tuplin. Leiden.
Strauss, B. 1986. *Athens after the Peloponnesian War: Class, Faction and Policy 403–386 B.C.* Ithaca, NY.
—— 1993. *Fathers and Sons in Athens: Ideology and Society in the Era of the Peloponnesian War*. London.
Strauss, L. 1970. *Xenophon's Socratic Discourse: An Interpretation of the Oeconomicus*. Ithaca, NY.
—— 1972. *Xenophon's Socrates*. Ithaca, NY.
—— 1975. 'Xenophon's *Anabasis*'. *A Journal of Political Philosophy* 4: 117–47.
Stronk, J. 1995. *The Ten Thousand in Thrace: An Archaeological and Historical Commentary on Xenophon's Anabasis, Books VI.iii–vi – VII*. Amsterdam.
—— 2007. 'Ctesias of Cnidus, a Reappraisal'. *Mnemosyne* 60: 25–58.
—— 2010. *Ctesias' Persian History. Part 1: Introduction, Text, and Translation*. Düsseldorf.
Stylianou, P. 2004. 'One *Anabasis* or Two?'. Pages 68–96 in *The Long March: Xenophon and the Ten Thousand*. Edited by R. Lane Fox. New Haven, CT.
Swaddling, J. 1980. *The Ancient Olympic Games*. London.
Talbert, R., ed. 2000. *Barrington Atlas of the Greek and Roman World*. Princeton.
Tamiolaki, M. 2008. 'Les *Helléniques* entre tradition et innovation: Aspects de la relation intertextuelle de Xénophon avec Hérodote et Thucydide'. *Cahiers des études anciennes* 45: 15–52.

—— 2012. 'Virtue and Leadership in Xenophon: Ideal Leaders or Ideal Losers?'. Pages 563–89 in *Xenophon: Ethical Principles and Historical Enquiry*. Edited by F. Hobden and C. Tuplin. Leiden.

—— 2015. Review of E. Buzzetti, *Xenophon the Socratic Prince: The Argument of the Anabasis of Cyrus*. *Classics Journal Online* 2015.10.07.

—— 2017. 'Xenophon's *Cyropaedia*: Tentative Answers to an Enigma'. Pages 174–94 in *The Cambridge Companion to Xenophon*. Edited by M. Flower. Cambridge.

—— 2018. 'Introduction'. *Conference on Anabases in Antiquity and Beyond*. Heraklion. 19–21 October.

Tarn, W. 1927. 'Persia, from Xerxes to Alexander'. Pages 1–24 in *The Cambridge Ancient History VI: Macedon: 401–301 BC*. Edited by J. Bury, S. Cook and F. Adcock. Cambridge.

Thomas, D. 2009. 'Introduction'. Pages ix–lxvi in *The Landmark Xenophon's Hellenika*. Translated by J. Marincola. Edited by B. Strassler. New York.

—— 2018. 'The Enemies of Hunting in Xenophon's *Cynegeticus*'. Pages 612–39 in *Plato and Xenophon: Comparative Studies*. Edited by G. Danzig, D. Johnson and D. Morrison. Leiden.

—— 2021a. 'Translator's Notes'. Pages 487–506 in *The Landmark Xenophon's Anabasis*. Translated by D. Thomas. Edited by S. Brennan and D. Thomas. New York.

—— 2021b. 'The Size and Makeup of the Ten Thousand'. Appendix I in *The Landmark Xenophon's Anabasis*. Translated by D. Thomas. Edited by S. Brennan and D. Thomas. New York.

—— 2021c. 'The Battle of Cunaxa'. Appendix L in *The Landmark Xenophon's Anabasis*. Translated by D. Thomas. Edited by S. Brennan and D. Thomas. New York.

—— 2021d. 'Other Ancient Sources on the Ten Thousand'. Appendix M in *The Landmark Xenophon's Anabasis*. Translated by D. Thomas. Edited by S. Brennan and D. Thomas. New York.

—— in press. 'Xenophon's Woes in Thrace: The Very Model of a Modern Mercenary Commander?'. *Xenophon's Anabasis and Its Reception*. Edited by T. Rood and M. Tamiolaki. Berlin.

Trundle, M. 2004. *Greek Mercenaries: From the Late Archaic Period to Alexander*. London.

Tsagalis, C. 2009. 'Names and Narrative Techniques in Xenophon's *Anabasis*'. Pages 451–79 in *Narratology and Interpretation: The Content of Narrative Form in Ancient Literature*. Edited by J. Grethlein and A. Rengakos. New York.

Tuplin, C. 1987. 'Xenophon's Exile Again'. Pages 59–68 in *Homo Viator: Classical Essays for John Bramble*. Edited by Michael Whitby, P. Hardie and Mary Whitby. Bristol.

—— 1991. 'Modern and Ancient Travellers in the Achaemenid Empire: Byron's *Road to Oxiana* and Xenophon's *Anabasis*'. Pages 37–57 in *Achaemenid History VII. Through Travellers' Eyes: European Travellers on the Iranian Monuments*. Edited by H. Sancisi-Weerdenburg and J. Drijvers. Leiden.

—— 1993. *The Failings of Empire: A Reading of Xenophon Hellenica 2.3.11–7.5.27*. Stuttgart.

—— 1999. 'On the Track of the Ten Thousand'. *Revue des Études Anciennes* 101: 331–66.

―― 2003. 'Heroes in Xenophon's *Anabasis*'. Pages 115-56 in *Modelli eroici dall'antichita alla cultura europea*. Edited by A. Barzanò et al. Rome.
―― 2004. 'Xenophon, Artemis and Scillus'. Pages 251-81 in *Spartan Society*. Edited by T. Figueira. Swansea.
―― 2007. 'Xenophon in Anatolia'. Pages 7-31 in *The Achaemenid Impact on Local Populations and Cultures in Anatolia*. Edited by İ. Delemen. Istanbul.
―― 2012. 'Xenophon (1)'. *The Oxford Classical Dictionary*. 4th ed. Oxford.
―― 2017. 'Xenophon and Athens'. Pages 338-59 in *The Cambridge Companion to Xenophon*. Edited by M. Flower. Cambridge.
―― 2018. 'Plato, Xenophon and Persia'. Pages 576-611 in *Plato and Xenophon: Comparative Studies*. Edited by G. Danzig, D. Johnson and D. Morrison. Leiden.
―― 2021. Discussion and commentary. *Conference on Xenophon*. Liverpool. July.
Tuplin C., and F. Hobden. 2012. 'Introduction'. Pages 1-41 in *Xenophon: Ethical Principles and Historical Enquiry*. Edited by F. Hobden and C. Tuplin. Leiden.
Turner, E. 1952. 'Athenian Books in the Fifth and Fourth Centuries BC'. Inaugural lecture given at University College London, 22 May 1951. London.
Vanderpool, E. 1965. 'The Location of the Attic Deme Erchia'. *Bulletin de correspondance hellénique* 89: 21-6.
Van Soesbergen, P. 1982/3. 'Colonisation as a Solution to Social-Economic Problems in Fourth-Century Greece: A Confrontation of Isocrates with Xenophon'. *Ancient Society* 13/14: 131-45.
Vlastos, G. 1983. 'The Historical Socrates and Athenian Democracy'. *Political Theory* 11: 495-516.
―― 1991. *Socrates: Ironist and Moral Philosopher*. Cambridge.
―― ed. 1971. *The Philosophy of Socrates: A Collection of Critical Essays*. New York.
Waterfield, R. 2004. 'Xenophon's Socratic Mission'. Pages 79-113 in *Xenophon and His World*. Edited by C. Tuplin. Stuttgart.
―― 2006. *Xenophon's Retreat: Greece, Persia and the End of The Golden Age*. London.
―― 2009. *Why Socrates Died: Dispelling the Myths*. London.
―― 2011. 'Greed and the Mixed Constitution in Xenophon's *Anabasis*'. *Ariadne* 17: 127-56.
―― 2013. 'Quest for the Historical Socrates'. Pages 1-19 in *The Bloomsbury Companion to Socrates*. Edited by J. Bussanich and N. Smith. London.
―― 2021. 'Xenophon and Socrates'. Appendix A in *The Landmark Xenophon's Anabasis*. Translated by D. Thomas. Edited by S. Brennan and D. Thomas. New York.
Wencis, L. 1977. '*Hypopsia* and the Structure of Xenophon's *Anabasis*'. *Classical Journal* 73: 44-9.
Westlake, H. 1987. 'Diodorus and the Expedition of Cyrus'. *Phoenix* 41: 241-54.
Whidden, C. 2008. 'Cyrus's Imperial Household: An Aristotelian Reading of Xenophon's *Cyropaedia*'. *Polis* 25: 31-62.
Whitehead, D., trans., intro., comm. 2019. *Xenophon: Poroi*. Oxford.
Wilson, S. 2016. *Thinking Differently about Leadership: A Critical History of Leadership Studies*. Cheltenham.
Wood, N. 1964. 'Xenophon's Theory of Leadership'. *Classica et Mediaevalia* 25: 33-66.

Woodhead, A. 1981. *The Study of Greek Inscriptions*. 2nd ed. Cambridge.
Wolpert, A. 2002. *Remembering Defeat: Civil War and Civic Memory in Ancient Athens*. Baltimore, MD.
Wright, W., trans. 1922. *Philostratos and Eunapios, Lives of the Sophists*. Cambridge, MA.
Wylie, G. 1992. 'Cunaxa and Xenophon'. *L'Antiquité Classique* 61: 119–34.

Editions of *Anabasis*

Brownson, C., ed., trans. 1922. *Xenophon Anabasis*. Loeb: Cambridge, MA. Revised, with Introduction, by J. Dillery 1998 (corrected reprint 2001).
Hude, C., ed. 1931. *Xenophontis Expeditio Cyri*. Teubner: Leipzig. Revised by J. Peters 1972.
Marchant, E., ed. 1904. *Expeditio Cyri. Xenophontis Opera Omnia*. Vol. 3. Oxford Classical Texts: Oxford.
Masqueray, P., ed., trans. 1930/1. *Xénophon, Anabase*. Budé: Paris.

Translations of Ancient Works

Aischines

Against Timarchos (In Tim.). C. Adams. Loeb: Cambridge, MA. 1919.

Aristotle

Athenian Constitution (Ath. Pol.). H. Rackham. Loeb: Cambridge, MA. 1935.
Nicomachean Ethics (Eth. Nic.). H. Rackham. Loeb: Cambridge, MA. 1926.

Arrian

The Campaigns of Alexander (Anab.). P. Mensch. Pantheon Books: New York. 2010.

Cicero

Tusculan Disputations (Tusc.). J. King. Loeb: Cambridge, MA. 1927.
Letters to Quintus (QFr.). D. Shackleton Bailey. Loeb: Cambridge, MA. 2002.

Diodoros

Universal History. Books 1–15.19 (Diod. Sic.). C. Oldfather. Loeb: Cambridge, MA. 1933–54.

Dio Chrysostom

Discourse (Or.) 18: On Training for Public Speaking. J. Cohoon. Loeb: Cambridge, MA. 1939.

Diogenes Laertios

Lives of Eminent Philosophers (Diog. Laert.). R. Hicks. 2 vols. Loeb: Cambridge, MA. 1925.

Herodotus

The Histories (Hdt.). A. Purvis. Pantheon Books: New York. 2007.

Isokrates

Antidosis (Antid.). G. Norlin. Loeb: Cambridge, MA. 1929.
Panegyricus (Paneg.). G. Norlin. Loeb: Cambridge, MA. 1928.

Lysias

Against Eratosthenes (12). W. Lamb. Loeb: Cambridge, MA. 1930.
On the Scrutiny of Evandros (26). W. Lamb. Loeb: Cambridge, MA. 1930.

Plato

Laws (Leg.). R. Bury. 2 vols. Loeb: Cambridge, MA. 1968.
Meno. W. Lamb. Loeb: Cambridge, MA. 1924.
Seventh Letter (Ep.). (Ascribed to Plato). R. Bury. Loeb: Cambridge, MA. 1966.

Plutarch

Alcibiades (Alc.). B. Perrin. Loeb: Cambridge, MA. 1916.
Aristides (Arist.). B. Perrin. Loeb: Cambridge, MA. 1914.
Artaxerxes (Artax.). B. Perrin. Loeb: Cambridge, MA. 1926.

Thucydides

A Comprehensive Guide to the Peloponnesian War (Thuc.). R. Crawley (1874, updated for the Landmark edition by R. Strassler). Free Press: New York. 1996.

Xenophon

Agesilaos. E. Marchant. Loeb: Cambridge, MA. 1925.
Anabasis. D. Thomas. Pantheon Books: New York. 2021.
Apologia. O. Todd. Loeb: Cambridge, MA. 1923.
Hellenika. J. Marincola. Pantheon Books: New York. 2009.
Hiero. E. Marchant. Loeb: Cambridge, MA. 1925.
Hipparchikos (The Cavalry Commander). E. Marchant. Loeb: Cambridge, MA. 1925.
Kynegetikos (On Hunting). E. Marchant. Loeb: Cambridge, MA. 1925.
Kyroupaideia (Cyropaedia). W. Miller. 2 vols. Loeb: Cambridge, MA. 1914.

Lakedaimonion Politeia (Constitution of the Lacedaemonians). E. Marchant. Loeb: Cambridge, MA. 1925.
Memorabilia. E. Marchant. Loeb: Cambridge, MA. 1923.
Oikonomikos. E. Marchant. Loeb: Cambridge, MA. 1923.
Peri Hippikes (On the Art of Horsemanship). E. Marchant. Loeb: Cambridge, MA. 1925.
Poroi (Ways and Means). E. Marchant. Loeb: Cambridge, MA. 1925.
Symposion. O. Todd. Loeb: Cambridge, MA. 1923.

Index

Note: Page numbers in italics refer to the illustrations and appendices

Achaemenids, 59, 88, 101; *see also* Artaxerxes; Cyrus; Parysatis; Xerxes
Agasias of Stymphalos, 103
Agesilaos, 18–19, 26, 43, 49, 69, 172, 180, 182
Agesilaos, 24, 48, 93, 94, 246
agonistic culture, 17, 119n, 197n
Aineias of Stymphalos, 68–9
Aischines (Athenian orator), 194, 195, 204
Aischines (Socratic), 32n, 196
akrasia (incontinence, opp. *enkrateia*), 224
Alexander of Macedonia, 47, 53
Alkibiades, 118–19, 140, 192–3, 195, 217, 230, 235
Ammianus (historian), 52
Anabasis
  apologia, strands, 72
  charges against Socrates encoded in, 186, 254
  dating, 25
  didactic aspect, 56, 63, 78, 80, 83, 87, 92, 144, 149, 241
  expedition accounts, other, 150–64, 252
  genre question, 6, 51–7, 245–6
  historiography, 51–2, 55, 84–5, 187
  intertextuality, 25, 132, 133, 135, 138, 156
  literary features, 62–81, 144, 249–50
  manuscript history, 47n, 206
  march record, 51, 55, 64, 162n, 246
  narrator, 52–3, 156, 158, 251–2
  readership, 48–51
  reception, 52n, 187n, 247, 256
  themes and concerns, 3–6, 17, 21, 48–50, 63, 83–4, 88, 107, 137, 150, 157, 173, 201n, 224
  see also panhellenism; pseudonym; Xenophon
anachronism, 23n, 28n, 64
Anaxibios (Spartan *nauarchos*), 107, 112, 168, 171, 173, 179, 184
Anbar (province, Iraq), 85n, 86
Antisthenes (Socratic), 23, 31n, 62, 196, 225
Anytos (accuser of Socrates), 193, 194–5
Apollo, 6, 142, 217, 224, 233
Apollonides of Lydia, 123, 143, 239
apologia *see Anabasis*, themes and concerns; Socrates; Xenophon
Apologia, 23, 48, 199n, 200, 224
aporia, 186, 202, 208, 216–17, 239
Arginousai
  battle (406), 33, 34
  trial of generals, 34, 46, 120, 130, 191, 192n, 200
Ariaios (Persian general), 108, 208

INDEX

Aristarchos (Spartan harmost), 107, 112, 179
Aristippos of Thessaly, 96, 167n
Aristippos (Socratic), 31n, 196
Aristophanes, 188, 190n, 191, 198
Aristotle, 39n, 101n, 188–9, 197
Armenia, 105, 236
Arrian (historian), 52n, 152
Artagerses (commander of King's guard), 72, 77n
Artaxerxes (referred to many times as 'the King'), 1, 42, 72, 162n, 166, 211
Artemis, 19, 171n, 233
Arystas of Arcadia, 223
Asidates (wealthy Persian), 127
Athenaion Politeia, 10n, 21
Athens, 13, 16, 49–50, 58, 120, 133, 165, 168, 182–3, 192, 220, 230
   cavalry (*hippeis*), 13, 33, 36, 37–8, 39, 40, 44, 75–7, 129
   civil war, 26, 33–4, 57, 171, 193
   Delphi, treasury, 43
   education, 16–17, 116
   euthuna (public audit of officials), 121
   laws, 14, 33, 34–5, 121–2
   restoration of the democracy, 36–8, 44
   Thirty, 33–4, 36–7, 39, 194
   see also Peloponnesian War; Socrates; Xenophon (historian)
augury, 237, 255
autarkeia see self-sufficiency
autobiography, 6, 11, 77–8, 115n, 187

Babylonia, 1, 65, 85, 87, 94, 101, 105, 106
Brasidas (Spartan general), 112
Buzzetti, E., 54, 56, 201, 217, 230
Byzantium, 154, 168, 169–70, 178
   first Greek city, 155, 213
   Ten Thousand and, 44, 119, 134, 146, 179, 182–3, 249
   Xenophon's speech, 130, 173–4, 242
   see also Xenophon (historical), exile

cavalry, 145, 199
   apologia, 75–7
   Persian, 77n, 101, 110
   retreat, on, 40n, 76–7, 80, 125, 235
   see also *Anabasis*, themes and concerns; Athens
Centrites River, 89, 116n
Charmande, 97, 99
Cheirisophos of Sparta, 88, 90, 91, 109, 113, 129, 142, 209
   death, 89, 94
   elected leader at Sinope, 90n, 103
   exchanges with Xenophon, 120, 126, 174–7
   guide, assaults, 110–11, 224
   leadership, 102–3, 108–12
   speeches, 108
Chrysopolis, 180, 256
Cicero, 21, 60, 115n
Corinth, 20
corruption, 120, 164, 168, 175; see also Xenophon (character); Spartans
Cunaxa, battle (401), 65–6, 100, 105
   accounts, 65n, 162
   Cyrus the Younger, 71–2, 97, 118
   see also panhellenism
Cyreans see Ten Thousand
Cyrus the Great, 59, 60, 62, 71, 94, 196, 200, 210, 231
Cyrus the Younger
   army, 1, 84, 160, 174
   Athens and, 41, 45, 248n
   death, 28, 71–2
   duplicity, 211–12
   Greek influences, 50–1, 98–9, 101
   leadership, 85–7, 87–8, 91, 94–102
   Lysander and, 41n, 167n, 218
   obituary, 92–4, 101, 210, 218
   rebellion, 41, 52, 165–7, 211
   Sparta and, 45, 55, 103n, 212
   speeches, 98
   Xenophon and, 17n, 75, 94, 165–7, 208–9, 210–12, 219

Delphi, 6, 21, 35, 43, 142, 202, 233
democracy, 119n, 121–3, 133n, 134, 226; *see also* Xenophon (historical)
Dexippos (Lakonian *perioikos*), 178
Dio Chrysostom (orator), 115n, 203
Diodoros Siculus (historian), 65n, 151, 153–5
Diogenes Laertios (biographer), 12–13, 15, 29, 42, 193, 203, 233, 255
divination, 232; *see also* augury
Drilai, 134

elenchus, 198, 208–9, 221, 239
Eleusis, 36, 38–41
enargeia (vividness), 62
endurance (*karteria*), 31, 221, 227–9
enkrateia see self-discipline
Ephesos, 19, 170, 180, 233
Ephoros, 65n, 151–5
ephors, 36, 75, 100
Epyaxa (Kilikian queen), 96
Erchia (Attica), 10, 13
Eukleides (soothsayer), 170, 233
Eunapios (historian), 29n, 128
Euphrates River, 85, 86, 88, 97, 101, 110, 121, 241
exile, 109, 165, 180n, 217; *see also* Xenophon (historical)

Flower, M., 21, 55, 139
friendship *see Anabasis*, themes and concerns; guest-friendship

Gorgias of Leontini, 94, 210, 213, 214, 241–2, 245, 253
Grote, G., viii–ix, 18n
guest-friendship, 14, 147, 148n, 168, 210

Hellenika
 apologia, 34–5, 138
 dating, 24
 historiography, 56, 91n
 Socratic history as, 58–9
 see also Socrates

Herakleia, 119, 226–7
Herodotos, 51, 55, 56n, 60, 71, 135
Hiero, 24, 201
Hipparchikos, 13, 17, 20, 21–2, 24
hippeis see cavalry
historiography *see Anabasis*; *Hellenika*
hoplites, 128, 164, 228n
hubris, 140, 143, 221, 240; *see also* Xenophon (character)

identity, 20, 76, 94n
Isokrates, 16, 57n, 74–5, 78, 151, 159–61

kaloskagathos (beautiful and good), 187, 192, 210, 221, 224, 240
Kalpe Harbour, 66–8, 70, 149, 229, 231–2
Kardouchoi, 1, 74, 177, 222
karteria see endurance
Kaÿstros Plain, 95, 125
Kleandros (Spartan harmost), 113, 167–8, 173, 179, 184
Klearchos of Sparta, 66, 97–8, 111, 121n, 162, 209, 230
 age, 16, 102
 ambition, 107
 Cyrus and, 65, 88, 99–100
 leadership, 87, 102–8, 112
 obituary, 93, 95–6, 100, 122
 speeches, 104, 130
Koroneia, battle (394), 18, 42, 182
Kotyora, 67, 74, 121, 123, 141–2, 217, 240
Kritias, 140, 192, 193, 195, 241
Ktesias, 60, 64, 71n, 151, 153, 161–3
Kynegetikos, 24–5, 46, 48, 214n
Kyroupaideia, 51, 63, 71, 94, 115n, 196, 247
 dating, 24
 genre, 4, 52n, 54n
 Socratic history as, 59–62
 see also Socrates

Lakedaimonion Politeia, 25, 48, 102, 201
Lampsakos, 227, 233
languages, 17, 50, 122, 237

leadership *see Anabasis*, themes and concerns; Cheirisophos; Cyrus the Younger; Klearchos; Socrates; Xenophon (character)
Leon of Thurii, 229
Leuktra, battle (371), 18, 20, 23, 25
literary apologia, 6, 62, 77–81, 139, 144, 196; *see also Memorabilia*
literary culture, 23n, 139, 208
Lucian (writer), 15–16, 53, 187
Lykios the Athenian, 40n, 76
Lysander, 33, 38n, 99, 167n, 172, 218
Lysias (Athenian orator), 37–8, 194, 225

Mantineia, battle (362), 21, 76
march record *see Anabasis*
Memorabilia, 28, 118–19, 124, 131, 192, 199, 215, 238
  charges against Socrates, 48, 79, 186, 196, 200
  dating, 22–3
  intertextuality, 25, 128, 132–3, 196, 202, 220
  literary apologia as, 78n, 79
  see also Socrates
memorialisation, 94; *see also Anabasis*, themes and concerns
Meno (Plato), 221n, 241
Menon of Thessaly, 71, 94, 97–8, 101, 102, 241
mercenaries
  ancient world, 40n, 43n, 72, 101n, 164, 166n
  dangers of relying on, 62n, 96, 101
  management of, 95, 99, 134, 160–1, 242–4
  motivation, 161, 238
military treatises, 83, 95
moderation (*sophrosune*), 223
Mossynoikoi, 129–30, 217

Nikomachides (Socratic interlocutor), 130
nostos, 21, 52, 181; *see also* Xenophon (character), Athens

obituaries, 68, 85, 92–4, 100, 241
Oikonomikos, 19, 22–3, 28, 48, 158, 200, 217, 218, 238
Olympia, 19, 43n, 204
Orontas (Persian noble), 87–8, 217
Oxyrhynchos Historian, 151, 163–4

panhellenism, 20, 50, 51, 64–8, 159, 164; *see also Anabasis*, themes and concerns
parasangs, 51, 85
Parysatis, 88, 94
Pasion the Megarian, 88, 104
Pausanias (Spartan king), 36–7, 38, 40, 172
Peloponnesian War, 16, 32, 50, 103, 114, 171, 212
peltasts, 175, 176
Pericles, 114, 117, 120, 131, 140, 171, 189
Peri Hippikes, 13, 24
Persia *see* Achaemenids
Persika, 64, 153, 161–3
Phalinos (advisor to the Persians), 205–8, 212
Pharnabazos (satrap), 172, 179
philotimia (love of honour), 221, 240
Pisidians, 166, 167, 211, 218
Plato, 23, 26, 27, 29–31, 51, 62, 72, 241; *see also* Socratics
Plutarch, 53, 66, 100n, 114, 136, 152, 156, 157, 163, 211
Polykrates (sophist), 194, 195
Poroi, 20, 21, 24, 48, 76, 201
Prodikos (sophist), 26, 33, 191
proskunesis (Persian practice of showing deference), 97
Proxenos of Boiotia, 14, 33, 35, 45, 167, 208, 209–12, 213–14, 219
  ambition, 49, 213
  Gorgias, student of, 94, 213, 241–2, 245
  leadership, 98, 214, 218
  obituary, 185–6, 214, 241
  speech, 98

pseudonym, 136, 156, 157–9, 187n, 206–7; *see also* Themistogenes

sacrifices *see* Xenophon (character), piety
Sardis, 2, 167, 211, 219
satraps *see* Pharnabazos, Tissaphernes
self-control (*enkrateia*), 31, 97, 101, 135, 221, 222–4, 227, 238
self-sufficiency (*autarkeia*), 31, 135, 161, 181, 194n, 221, 224–7
Seuthes, 15, 91, 134, 145, 146, 147–9, 170, 179, 184, 234–5
   Athens and, 147, 168
   hosts dinner, 149, 223
   knowledge of Greek, 237
   see also Xenophon (character)
Silenos (soothsayer), 141, 142, 237
Sinope, 67, 103, 119, 142, 144, 170n, 184, 226, 237
Skillous, 2, 19, 20, 22, 23, 25, 69–70, 171n, 204, 233
slaves, 13, 171n
Socrates
   charges against and trial, 5, 191, 193–6, 224
   Clouds in, 190n, 191
   contemporary view of, 48, 193, 195, 188, 204–5, 213, 253
   Cyrus the Younger and, 158, 217–18
   democracy and, 119–20, 226
   Hellenika in, 34–5, 58–9, 200–1
   Kyroupaideia in, 59–62, 200
   laws, obedience to, 46, 191–2
   leadership on, 81, 118, 124–31
   Oikonomikos in, 158, 198, 200, 211, 213, 218
   poverty on, 169
   Pythagorean as, 188
   teaching method, 63, 190–1, 192, 208, 220, 240
   Xenophon and, 6, 12–13, 26–32, 39–40, 41, 45, 49–50, 142, 214–19, 235
   see also Anabasis, themes and concerns; self-sufficiency
Socrates literary-philosophical industry, 4, 7, 25, 58, 79, 186, 196
Socratic commander *see* Xenophon (character)
Socratic history, 6, 47, 57–62, 94, 101, 187, 204; *see also Hellenika*; *Kyroupaideia*
Socratic question, the, 131–2, 189n, 197–8
Socratics, 4, 5, 25, 62, 186, 188–91, 196–9, 200–5, 238
Sophainetos of Stymphalos, 90, 123, 150, 151–4, 162
sophia see wisdom
sophists, 116, 190n, 214; *see also* Gorgias
sophrosune (moderation), 223
Soteridas the Sicyonian, 80–1
Souda, 12, 156, 157, 163
Sparta
   Athens and, 32–9, 44–5, 165, 171, 174, 182
   Cyrus and, 55, 103, 212
   hegemony of Greek world, 20, 50, 112–13, 173
   Persia and, 105, 168, 172, 179
   see also Anabasis, themes and concerns; Peloponnesian War
Spartans
   anger, prone to, 95, 97–8, 110–12
   competitive, 173–6
   corruption, 179, 180n
   leadership, 102–13
   self-interested, 104, 107
   supporting Xenophon, 69, 146, 172, 233
   see also Cheirisophos; Klearchos
speeches, 109, 114, 117, 120, 140; *see also* Klearchos; Xenophon (character)
Strauss, L., 30
Symposion, 15, 23, 28, 48, 200, 225, 238

Tacticus, Aineias, 83, 152
Taochoi, 51, 68–9, 74, 188
Tarsus, 44, 100, 103, 108, 130, 160, 166, 230
Ten Thousand,
  Achaeans, 141, 227
  apologia, 73–5
  Arcadians, 223, 227, 234
  Athenians, 40n, 43–4, 114, 131, 183
  crimes, 74–5, 144, 160n
  demanding money, 166, 227
  kaloikagathoi as, 68, 161, 244
  know warfare, 226
  leadership, 75, 90, 142, 148n, 155, 172, 178–9, 237–8
  numbers, 1, 84, 155
  quasi-democracy as, 119, 121, 133
  Rhodians, 125
  split up, 223, 227
  see also mercenaries
Teleutias (Spartan commander), 111–12
Thapsakos, 121, 166
Themistocles, 114, 131
Themistogenes of Syracuse, 12, 53, 136, 150, 156–9; *see also* pseudonym
Theopompos of Athens, 157n, 159, 206–7
Theopompos of Chios (historian), 151, 163
Thibron (Spartan commander), 37, 40, 75, 165, 168–9, 180, 183
Thucydides, 24, 51, 55, 58, 91n, 114, 117n, 140, 163
Tigris River, 89, 91, 106, 129, 208
Timasion the Dardanian, 14, 90, 123, 141, 142, 178, 235
Tissaphernes (satrap), 1–2, 90–1, 168, 180, 212
  Cunaxa, 65–6
  Cyrus's intentions, suspects, 88, 212
  duplicity, 88, 99, 107, 212
  Greek commanders, captures, 102, 106–8, 113, 155, 162, 209
  standing, 107–8, 181

toil (*ponos*), 19, 228, 229, 241
Trapezous, 67, 118, 123, 134, 144, 153
trials *see* Arginousai; Orontas; Socrates; Xenophon (character)
Tzetzes (Byzantine grammarian), 157

willing obedience, 81, 101, 107, 110, 127, 133, 135, 143, 149
wine, 67, 223, 224n
wisdom (*sophia*), 5, 32, 88, 192, 199, 213, 219, 220, 221, 226, 227
  limits, 134, 229, 237
  literature, 124

Xenias of Parrasia, 88, 104
Xenophon, author
  apologia, 7, 10, 56, 72, 78–9, 139, 160, 246
  chronology of writings, 21–5, *260–1*
  influence of Socrates, 22–5, 26–32, 57–62, 185–8, 246
  literary innovation, 62–4, 83, 158, 204, 205, 219
  literary project, 19, 21, 22
  Plato and, 23n, 132, 196–9, 241
  reticence, 136–7, 172, 187
  Socratica, 23, 132, 188, 197–205
  wordplay, 157n, 206
  see also Anabasis themes and concerns
Xenophon, character in *Anabasis*
  approachability, 122
  Athens, plans return to, 18, 20–1, 42n, 146, 169–70, 180, 183–4, 234
  cavalry, forms, 74, 80, 125, 235
  corruption, accused, 72, 137, 144–50, 168, 224
  deceiving the soldiers, accused, 141–3, 240
  dreams, 14, 21, 45
  exemplar as, 2, 11, 63, 82, 115, 122–3, 133, 137, 158, 185, 205
  fitness, 16–17, 227–8
  foreshadowed, 75–6, 207–8, 216n
  helps soldiers and army, 145–6, 170, 233–5

hubris, accused, 105, 121–2, 139, 143–4, 242
leadership, 113–31, 134, 220–44
piety, 19, 32, 72, 142, 145, 221, 229–33, 237–8
Seuthes and, 15, 81, 90–1, 127, 134, 146n, 147–9, 168, 170–1, 179, 223
Socrates, stand in for, 3, 185, 228, 235, 238
Socratic commander as, 124–31, 220–40
speeches, 4–5, 49, 89, 108, 113–14, 115–17, 130, 139, 171, 203, 238, 240
transparency, 123, 146–7
trial at Kotyora, 121–2, 217, 242
see also Anabasis, themes and concerns; Cyrus the Younger; Spartans
Xenophon, historical figure
age, 14–16
democracy and, 114, 115–20, 134, 230, 247
departure from Athens, 16n, 35–41, 171, 215
education, 16–18, 31, 63, 116, 192, 193n, 214, 217
exile from Athens, 5, 35, 42–6, 171–2, 180–4: repeal of, 20
hippeus (horseman) at Athens, 13, 40, 76, 138, 172
knowledge of augury, 237, 255
knowledge of horses, 13, 17, 84, 236
knowledge of languages, 17, 237
mercenary service, 40n, 150, 160–1, 164–71
Peloponnesian War, 16, 18n, 32–3, *258*
philosopher as, 3–4, 29–32, 53, 128, 197–9
sons, 12n, 13, 19, 20, 76, 136n, 172, 233
Sparta and, 18–19, 26, 50, 113n, 168, 171–3, 180–4, 195
Thirty and, 33–4, 40–1, 138
see also Socrates
Xerxes, 95, 114

Zapatas River (Greater Zab), 1, 6, 76, 89, 121, 125, 175, 207, 231
Zeus, 156, 229n, 231, 233, 237–8